Books in the Security Series

Computer Security Fundamentals
ISBN: 0-13-171129-6

Information Security: Principles and Practices
ISBN: 0-13-154729-1

Firewalls and VPNs: Principles and Practices
ISBN: 0-13-154731-3

Security Policies and Procedures: Principles and Practices
ISBN: 0-13-186691-5

Network Defense and Countermeasures: Principles and Practices
ISBN: 0-13-171126-1

Intrusion Detection: Principles and Practices
ISBN: 0-13-154730-5

Disaster Recovery: Principles and Practices
ISBN: 0-13-171127-X

Computer Forensics: Principles and Practices
ISBN: 0-13-154727-5

Firewalls and VPNs
Principles and Practices

RICHARD W. TIBBS
Radford University

EDWARD B. OAKES
Radford University

PEARSON

Prentice
Hall

Upper Saddle River, New Jersey 07458

Library of Congress Cataloging-in-Publication Data

Tibbs, Richard W.
  Firewalls and VPNs : principles and practices / Richard W. Tibbs, Edward B.
Oakes.-- 1st ed.
     p. cm.
  Includes bibliographical references and index.
  ISBN 0-13-154731-3
  1. Computer security. 2. Computer networks--Security measures. 3.
Firewalls (Computer security) 4. Extranets (Computer networks) I. Oakes,
Edward B. II. Title.
  QA76.9.A25T525 2005
  005.8--dc22

                          2005012530

Vice President and Publisher: Natalie E. Anderson
Executive Acquisitions Editor, Print: Stephanie Wall
Executive Acquisitions Editor, Media: Richard Keaveny
Editorial Project Manager: Emilie Herman
Editorial Assistants: Brian Hoehl, Bambi Dawn Marchigano, Alana Meyers, Sandra Bernales
Senior Media Project Managers: Cathi Profitko, Steve Gagliostro
Marketing Manager: Sarah Davis
Marketing Assistant: Lisa Taylor
Managing Editor: Lynda Castillo
Production Project Manager: Vanessa Nuttry
Manufacturing Buyer: Natacha Moore
Design Manager: Maria Lange
Art Director/Interior Design/Cover Design: Blair Brown
Cover Illustration/Photo: Gettyimages/Photodisc Blue
Composition/Full-Service Project Management: Custom Editorial Productions Inc.
Cover Printer: Courier/Stoughton
Printer/Binder: Courier/Stoughton

Credits and acknowledgments borrowed from other sources and reproduced, with permission, in this book appear on appropriate page in text.

Microsoft® and Windows® are registered trademarks of the Microsoft Corporation in the U.S.A. and other countries. Screen shots and icons reprinted with permission from the Microsoft Corporation. This book is not sponsored or endorsed by or affiliated with the Microsoft Corporation.

Pearson Education LTD.
Pearson Education Singapore, Pte. Ltd
Pearson Education, Canada, Ltd
Pearson Education–Japan

Pearson Education Australia PTY, Limited
Pearson Education North Asia Ltd
Pearson Educación de Mexico, S.A. de C.V.
Pearson Education Malaysia, Pte. Ltd

10 9 8 7 6 5 4 3 2
ISBN 0-13-154731-3

Contents in Brief

Table of Contents

To Debbie and Jess.

-Rick

To my wife, Missy, whom I love dearly.

-Ed

Security Series Walk-Through

The Prentice Hall Security Series prepares students for careers in IT security by providing practical advice and hands-on training from industry experts. All of the books in this series are filled with real-world examples to help readers apply what they learn to the workplace. This walk-through highlights the key elements in this book created to help students along the way.

Chapter Objectives. These short-term, attainable goals outline what will be covered in the chapter text.

Chapter Introduction. Each chapter begins with an explanation of why these topics are important and how the chapter fits into the overall organization of the book.

In Practice. Takes concepts from the book and shows how they are applied in the workplace.

FYI. Additional information on topics that go beyond the scope of the book.

Caution. Critical, not-to-be forgotten information that is directly relevant to the surrounding text.

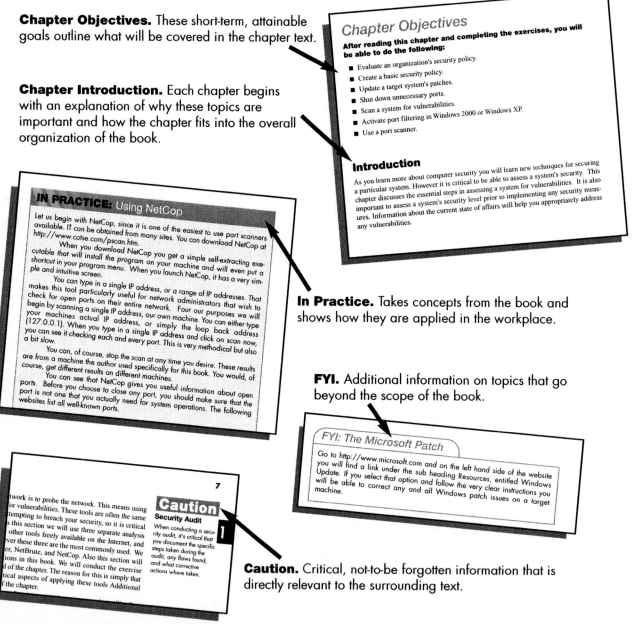

Chapter Objectives

After reading this chapter and completing the exercises, you will be able to do the following:

- Evaluate an organization's security policy.
- Create a basic security policy.
- Update a target system's patches.
- Shut down unnecessary ports.
- Scan a system for vulnerabilities.
- Activate port filtering in Windows 2000 or Windows XP.
- Use a port scanner.

Introduction

As you learn more about computer security you will learn new techniques for securing a particular system. However it is critical to be able to assess a system's security. This chapter discusses the essential steps in assessing a system for vulnerabilities. It is also important to assess a system's security level prior to implementing any security measures. Information about the current state of affairs will help you appropriately address any vulnerabilities.

IN PRACTICE: Using NetCop

Let us begin with NetCop, since it is one of the easiest to use port scanners available. IT can be obtained from many sites. You can download NetCop at http://www.cotse.com/pscan.htm.

When you download NetCop you get a simple self-extracting executable that will install the program on your machine and will even put a shortcut in your program menu. When you launch NetCop, it has a very simple and intuitive screen.

You can type in a single IP address, or a range of IP addresses. That makes this tool particularly useful for network administrators that wish to check for open ports on their entire network. Four our purposes we will begin by scanning a single IP address, our own machine. You can either type your machines actual IP address, or simply the loop back address (127.0.0.1). When you type in a single IP address and click on scan now, you can see it checking each and every port. This is very methodical but also a bit slow.

You can, of course, stop the scan at any time you desire. These results are from a machine the author used specifically for this book. You would, of course, get different results on different machines.

You can see that NetCop gives you useful information about open ports. Before you choose to close any port, you should make sure that the port is not one that you actually need for system operations. The following websites list all well-known ports.

FYI: The Microsoft Patch

Go to http://www.microsoft.com and on the left hand side of the website you will find a link under the sub heading Resources, entitled Windows Update. If you select that option and follow the very clear instructions you will be able to correct any and all Windows patch issues on a target machine.

7

twork is to probe the network. This means using or vulnerabilities. These tools are often the same tempting to breach your security, so it is critical n this section we will use three separate analysis other tools freely available on the Internet, and ver these three are the most commonly used. We er, NetBrute, and NetCop. Also this section will ions in this book. We will conduct the exercise d of the chapter. The reason for this is simply that tical aspects of applying these tools Additional f the chapter.

Caution

Security Audit

When conducting a security audit, it's critical that you document the specific steps taken during the audit, any flaws found, and what corrective actions where taken.

1

Test Your Skills

Each chapter ends with exercises designed to reinforce the chapter objectives. Four types of evaluation follow each chapter.

Multiple Choice Questions. Test the reader's understanding of the text.

Exercises. Brief, guided projects designed around individual concepts found in the chapter.

Projects. Longer, guided projects that combine lessons from the chapter.

Case Study. A real-world scenario to resolve using lessons learned in the chapter.

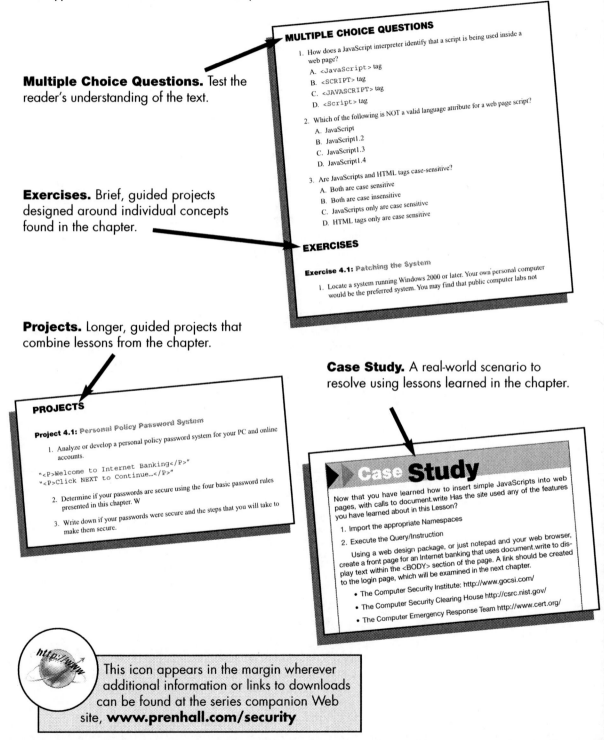

MULTIPLE CHOICE QUESTIONS

1. How does a JavaScript interpreter identify that a script is being used inside a web page?
   A. `<JavaScript>` tag
   B. `<SCRIPT>` tag
   C. `<JAVASCRIPT>` tag
   D. `<Script>` tag

2. Which of the following is NOT a valid language attribute for a web page script?
   A. JavaScript
   B. JavaScript1.2
   C. JavaScript1.3
   D. JavaScript1.4

3. Are JavaScripts and HTML tags case-sensitive?
   A. Both are case sensitive
   B. Both are case insensitive
   C. JavaScripts only are case sensitive
   D. HTML tags only are case sensitive

EXERCISES

Exercise 4.1: *Patching the System*

1. Locate a system running Windows 2000 or later. Your own personal computer would be the preferred system. You may find that public computer labs not

PROJECTS

Project 4.1: *Personal Policy Password System*

1. Analyze or develop a personal policy password system for your PC and online accounts.

```
"<P>Welcome to Internet Banking</P>"
"<P>Click NEXT to Continue...</P>"
```

2. Determine if your passwords are secure using the four basic password rules presented in this chapter. W

3. Write down if your passwords were secure and the steps that you will take to make them secure.

Case Study

Now that you have learned how to insert simple JavaScripts into web pages, with calls to document.write Has the site used any of the features you have learned about in this Lesson?

1. Import the appropriate Namespaces
2. Execute the Query/Instruction

Using a web design package, or just notepad and your web browser, create a front page for an Internet banking that uses document.write to display text within the `<BODY>` section of the page. A link should be created to the login page, which will be examined in the next chapter.

- The Computer Security Institute: http://www.gocsi.com/
- The Computer Security Clearing House http://csrc.nist.gov/
- The Computer Emergency Response Team http://www.cert.org/

This icon appears in the margin wherever additional information or links to downloads can be found at the series companion Web site, **www.prenhall.com/security**

About the Authors

Dr. Richard W. Tibbs

Dr. Tibbs earned a Ph.D. from George Mason University's College of System and Information Technology Engineering, specializing in operations research. He holds an M.S. in Computer Science and a B.S. in Applied Mathematics from the University of Colorado, Boulder.

His research interests are network security, network and computer capacity planning, queueing theory and simulation, traffic monitoring and analysis, and adaptive routing in telecommunications networks. He is a member of ACM, IEEE, and INFORMS.

Dr. Tibbs worked in industry, government, and academia for more than 20 years before joining Radford University as a full-time faculty member. His industry background includes aerospace, telecommunications, and software development. His government background includes the U.S. Geological Survey and the MITRE Corporation, a federally funded research and development center where he worked on Department of Transportation projects.

Mr. Edward B. Oakes

Mr. Oakes earned a B.S. in Computer Science from Radford University and is currently completing an M.S. in Education with concentration in Technology. In 2004 he was awarded the Anna Lee Stewart Award for Contributions to Faculty Development.

He is currently the Director of Academic Computing at Radford University and has more than 14 years of experience in networking and security. In addition to other roles, he has served as the Information Security Officer for Radford University for more than five years. His interests include network security, wireless computing, and incorporating technology into the classroom.

Preface

Network security has become an increasingly important subject as more and more people depend on connected offices, homes, and remote workspaces. The Federal Bureau of Investigation (FBI) reports an increasing number of compromised security attacks each year. With the proliferation of cyber attacks and the increasing reliance on networks and remote access to them comes a growing demand for systems like firewalls and virtual private networks (VPNs) to protect organizations and individuals from threats. Likewise, organizations are calling for properly equipped professionals who can oversee security software and hardware. The goal of *Firewalls and VPNs: Principles and Practices* is to prepare students (future professionals) for installing, using, and managing firewalls and virtual private networks (VPNs).

The book begins with a refresher course on basic network and computer security concepts, focusing specifically on Network and Data Link Layer Protocols and the transport protocols TCP and UDP. Once the groundwork is laid out, the text turns to the need for network protection and the specifics of installing and operating firewalls. Students will read about threats to computer networks, with clear explanations about what each threat intends to do to a system and how it intends to accomplish its mission. Readers will learn to protect systems against these dangers by reading about and using specific firewall technology, tools, and techniques, with one chapter devoted entirely to hands-on installation and configuration of a firewall. Then the book turns to the topic of VPNs, illustrating how VPN technologies provide secure communications across the Internet—currently the least costly solution to secure communications between corporate locations. Finally, students will get an idea about day-to-day firewall maintenance with an introduction to logging.

The examples, exercises, and projects throughout the text use low-cost, easily available hardware to create a small network and help students understand and learn about firewalls and VPNs. All of the required software will run from either a CD-ROM or floppy disk without installation on the hard drive; therefore, a computer can be used for exercises and then immediately be rebooted and used for another purpose. The book uses four open-source projects: one specializing in firewalls, two in VPNs, and one integrating all the others. While there is documentation for these projects on open-source Web sites, such sites assume the reader is quite well grounded in networking and highly experienced with Linux. In our opinion, this assumption leaves students or small business owners with little to no experience in those areas at a loss. The tools and technologies used throughout this book seek to address the needs of these less experienced users.

Despite our partiality for open-source projects and Linux-oriented applications, we also provide a number of exercises using commercial operating systems and software firewalls. Furthermore, we provide extensive references reviewing commercial and open-source VPN solutions. It is inevitable that Windows-Linux integration will be the prevalent trend for many years. So throughout the book, we point out Windows applications that can be used to access the open-source, primarily Linux, firewall and VPN technologies.

Colleges and universities have been strapped by budget limitations due to many factors in the economy, and the value of free open-source solutions for students is hindered by only one thing: the lack of an appropriate textbook that illustrates the principles underlying security technology, as well as complete hands-on exercises for the laboratory. We hope this book fills that need.

Audience

Firewalls and VPNs: Principles and Practices is suitable for community and four-year college students with a basic understanding of TCP/IP networks. The book heavily references a Linux-based firewall and several Linux-based tools, but the student does not need prior knowledge of Linux to complete the exercises and projects. The book can be used in its entirety for a single course on firewalls and VPNs, or Parts Two and Three can be used in conjunction with an introductory text on networking for courses that will provide a more thorough understanding of network concepts. To fully utilize the book, the course should include a laboratory where students can take advantage of the extensive hands-on exercises, projects, and case studies.

Overview of the Book

Part One *Networking Concepts and the TCP/IP Protocol Suite* (Chapters 1 and 2)

The chapters in Part One review security and introductory networking coverage of the TCP/IP Protocol suite. This section is designed to be a refresher on TCP/IP and an introduction to basic security concepts. This part can be used as augmentation or skipped altogether when the book is used in conjunction with an elementary text on networking.

Chapter 1 *Introduction to Network and Data Link Layer Protocols* gives students a common understanding of the TCP/IP stack. Coverage includes a description of MAC addresses and filtering and details IP Protocol and the IP header. Hands-on projects have students using subnetting and supernetting to allocate and aggregate IP address blocks and using sniffers and other tools to monitor/capture network traffic. Chapter 2 *Transport Control Protocol (TCP) and User Datagram Protocol (UDP) in Detail* introduces TCP protocol and the TCP finite state machine. Since state filtering on TCP protocol headers is an important concept in firewalls, students will learn to trace the flow of packaets during a TCP session. Because VPNs frequently embed their packets in UDP, Chapter 2 closely examines the UDP header and the primary applications that use UDP. To reinforce the concepts in Chapter 2, students will perform some basic network diagnoses using the ping and traceroute utilities.

Part Two *Firewall Basics* (Chapters 3, 4, 5, 6, and 7)

Part Two introduces several types of firewalls and takes an extensive look at installing the firewall, creating a firewall policy, and understanding how firewall rules and policies affect network traffic.

Chapter 3 *Software, Small Office, and Enterprise Firewalls* covers a variety of free and commercial firewalls, including the Windows XP firewall and the Mac OS X firewall. This chapter also introduces the reader to router Access Control Lists and the ipables facility in Linux Kernels. The Nmap tool is used to introduce port scanners and a tool to determine open ports on the network.

Chapter 4 *Threats, Packet Filtering, and Stateful Firewalls* begins an overview of the many threats that networks face from the Internet, as well as internal networks. Packet filtering is the main job of a firewall, and there are main methods—stateless and stateful—to determine whether to allow or deny packets. Chapter 4 also includes a thorough overview of IP routing and how it affects decisions that a router or firewall should make. Nessus is introduced in this chapter as a tool for advanced network scanning.

Chapter 5 *Illustrated Exercises in Basic Firewall Installation* is intended as the first firewall experience for readers, including installation projects. Chapter 5 explains the individual configuration files and an overview of the Linux Embedded Appliance Firewall (LEAF) features.

Firewalls protect the internal network from external attack and control access of the internal machines to the Internet. Chapter 6 *Determining Requirements for the Firewall* provides information on the services and applications allowed through the firewall. This chapter helps guide the network administrator through the steps of building a firewall policy. This chapter explores services that can be provided by the firewall or must be allowed to pass through the firewall, for example by port forwarding. This chapter also continues the discussion of router Access Control Lists begun in Chapter 3.

Chapter 7 *Introduction to Advanced Firewall Concepts and Terminology* continues the discussion of iptables begun in Chapter 3, comparing iptables to the Shorewall facility of LEAF. It also continues the discussion of threats begun in Chapter 4. Chapter 7 explores in more depth how the firewall can provide services to the internal network with several configuration examples.

Part Three *VPNs and Logging* (Chapters 8 and 9)

Part Three *VPNs and Logging* covers virtual private networks and instruction for using log files to perform post-analysis of network events. The concepts in this part do depend to some extent on understanding the topics in Part Two, but you may choose to cover certain sections from Part Three even if Part Two isn't covered in the classroom.

Chapter 8 *Exploring and Using Virtual Private Networks* covers IPSec, Transport Layer Security (TLS, aka Secure Socket Layer), and VPNs in detail, with several projects devoted to each. This chapter also includes an overview of Point-to-Point Tunneling Protocol. It discusses how to secure wireless and wired network connections in a medical setting, congruent with the Health Information Privacy and Portability Act (HIPPA). Chapter 8 continues further the discussion of threats in the context of key exchange for VPNs. It also includes a description of setting up an individual certificate authority using open-source software to facilitate student laboratory projects.

Chapter 9 *Integrating Firewall and System Logs* takes up several topics including log servers and the "data fusion" issues that can occur when system, firewall, and router logs are drawn together. The purpose of this chapter is to ease the burden of network and system administrators when a security breach is discovered. Assessment of damages and of perpetrators is particularly important in this setting. Chapter topics include an introduction to the syslog daemon in Linux, Microsoft Windows logging, and coverage of the daemon tools (daemontl) package and other logging configurations available in LEAF.

End-of-chapter exercises, projects, and case studies progressively increase in difficulty over the course of the book. Case studies are drawn from real-world situations.

Conventions Used in This Book

To help you get the most from the text, we've used a few conventions throughout the book.

IN PRACTICE: About In Practice

These show readers how to take concepts from the book and apply them in the workplace.

FYI: About FYIs

These boxes offer additional information on topics that go beyond the scope of the book.

Caution

About Cautions

Cautions appear in the margins of the text. They flag critical, not-to-be for-gotten information that is directly relevant to the surrounding text.

Snippets and blocks of code are boxed and numbered, and can be downloaded from the companion Web site (**www.prenhall.com/security**).

New key terms appear in ***bold italics***.

 This icon appears in the margin wherever more information can be found at the series companion Web site, **www.prenhall.com/security**.

Instructor and Student Resources

Instructor's Resource Center on CD-ROM

The Instructor's Resource Center on CD-ROM (IRC on CD) is distributed to instructors only and is an interactive library of assets and links. It includes:

- Instructor's Manual. Provides instructional tips, an introduction to each chapter, teaching objectives, teaching suggestions, and answers to end-of-chapter questions and problems.

- PowerPoint Slide Presentations. Provides a chapter-by-chapter review of the book content for use in the classroom.

- Test Bank. This TestGen-compatible test bank file can be used with Prentice Hall's TestGen software (available as a free download at **www.prenhall.com/testgen**). TestGen is a test generator that lets you view and easily edit test bank questions, transfer them to tests, and print in a variety of formats suitable to your teaching situation. The program also offers many options for organizing and displaying test banks and tests. A built-in random number and text generator makes it ideal for creating multiple versions of tests that involve calculations and provides more possible test items than test bank questions. Powerful search and sort functions let you easily locate questions and arrange them in the order you prefer.

Companion Web Site

The Companion Web site (**www.prenhall.com/security**) is a Pearson learning tool that provides students and instructors with online support. Here you will find:

- Interactive Study Guide, a Web-based interactive quiz designed to provide students with a convenient online mechanism for self-testing their comprehension of the book material.

- Additional Web projects and resources to put into practice the concepts taught in each chapter.

- ISO CD-ROM images for the firewall and SLAX to provide the foundation for many of the projects and exercises.

Quality Assurance

We would like to extend our thanks to the Quality Assurance team for their attention to detail and their efforts to make sure that we got it right.

Technical Editors
Erich Titl

Charles Steinkuehler

Reviewers
Charles R. Esparza
Glendale Community College

Jeff Dorsz
Saddleback College

Acknowledgments

I would like to acknowledge the people on the following open-source user listserves: leaf-user, shorewall-user, openvpn-user. I would especially like to thank Tom Eastep, Charles Steinkuehler, Erich Titl, and James Yonan for their help. I would also like to acknowledge my co-author, Ed Oakes, without whom this book would not be possible.
                                                                                    -Richard Tibbs

I would like to acknowledge Tomas Matejicek for his creation and continued work on the SLAX Linux Live distribution and everyone else who has contributed to the SLAX project. I would also like to acknowledge my co-author, Rick Tibbs, who has worked extremely hard to make this book a success. A special thanks to Nicole Sulgit and Megan Smith-Creed for their patience during the editing of this book. Finally, I would like to thank Janie Hensdell, Kathy Harris, and my parents for supporting me and helping me make it through the past several months.
                                                                                    -Edward Oakes

Part One

Networking Concepts and the TCP/IP Suite

The chapters in Part One review security and introductory networking coverage of the TCP/IP Protocol suite. This section is designed to be a refresher on TCP/IP and an introduction to basic security concepts. This part can be used as augmentation or skipped altogether when the book is used in conjunction with an elementary text on networking.

- **Chapter 1:** Introduction to Network and Data Link Layer Protocols
- **Chapter 2:** Transmission Control Protocol (TCP) and User Datagram Protocol (UDP) In Detail

Chapter 1

Introduction to Network and Data Link Layer Protocols

Chapter Objectives

After reading this chapter and completing the exercises, you will be able to do the following:

- Define security in basic terms.
- Describe the TCP/IP stack.
- Explain Ethernet Media Access Control (MAC) addresses, how they are assigned, how they are used, and the difference between unicast, broadcast, and multicast addresses. Understand promiscuous mode operation of network interface cards (NICs).
- Explain how MAC address filtering works and where it is useful.
- Briefly summarize the history and the important points of the IP Protocol, and describe the IP header in detail. Explain the classes of IP addresses, subnets, and subnet masks. Use subnetting and supernetting to allocate and aggregate IP address blocks.
- Monitor or capture network traffic via a sniffer or other tool. Explain what a firewall does with a packet to prevent unwanted traffic.

Introduction

Much like the American Wild West, the Internet is a dangerous place. Train robbers have been replaced with Denial of Service (DoS) attacks, and masked bandits have been replaced by hackers. However, millions of people have valid reasons to use the Internet, and a majority of legitimate enterprises, including e-commerce, have an Internet presence. This rugged landscape can make it difficult, however, to discern the good guys from the bad guys.

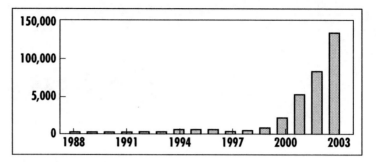

FIGURE 1.1 CERT incident reports.

A measure of the threat present in the Internet is the number of reported incidents, which has been rising dramatically in the past several years, as shown in Figure 1.1.

FYI: CERT

Established in 1988, the CERT® Coordination Center (CERT/CC) is a center of Internet security expertise, located at the Software Engineering Institute (**www.sei.cmu.edu/**), a federally funded research and development center operated by Carnegie Mellon University. This center provides an excellent resource for updated security information. Visit **www.cert.org** to learn more about CERT.

Despite these dangers, connecting your internal network to the Internet is virtually mandatory for business, government, and educational organizations. Protecting the organization from unwanted activities such as hackers and DoS, has become a substantial and important task.

This book will cover two major topics in the effort to protect systems from the dangers of connectivity:

- *Firewalls*—methods to protect systems in enterprise networks from the Internet

- *Virtual private networks* (VPNs)—technology using encryption to allow confidential, authenticated transmission across the Internet

To configure effective firewalls and VPNs, you must understand how these tools fit into the overall aim of network security and how TCP/IP protocols, particularly Network and Data Link Layer Protocols, work. This chapter begins with a brief description of network security and evolves into a detailed description of the Ethernet Data Link and IP Layers (Layers 2 and 3) of the Internet protocols.

A Concise Definition of Security

The subject of security involves a wide range of topics, spanning network security, host and server "hardening," and file system security, to name a few. This definition is necessarily brief, and most of the topics below, especially firewalls and VPNs, are expanded greatly in subsequent chapters.

In principle, security amounts to four fundamental functions:

- *Authentication*—Nearly everyone who uses a computer is familiar with authentication. Whenever you log into a computer or a network using a user ID and a password, you are being authenticated.

- *Confidentiality*—Confidentiality is the art and science of keeping documents confidential, revealing the contents only to authorized individuals. Various forms of encryption allow us to keep the contents of documents and files secret.

- *Integrity*—Integrity is a method to ensure that a document has not been altered by a third party. Two tools that can tell if a document has been altered are encryption and hash codes.

- *Nonrepudiation*—Nonrepudiation has to do with being able to verify with absolute certainty that a document came from the originating person. If, for example, the originator sends an inflammatory document, perhaps causing a war to break out, but denies he sent the document, he is said to have repudiated the document. The principal tools supporting nonrepudiation are digital signatures and digital certificates.

- *Availability*—Availability means the service or function of the network is useful.

These four functions underlie all of the principles and techniques in VPNs described throughout this book. In later chapters you will study IP Security (IPSec) Protocol, Transport Layer Security (TLS) and Point-to-Point Tunneling Protocol (PPTP). Each of these protocols deals with each of these four functions in a different way.

Protocols

A large number of protocols are associated with security. Security protocol suites use different combinations of authentication, confidentiality, integrity, and nonrepudiation protocols. We can loosely group them as follows:

- Authentication Protocols
  Examples: CHAP, MS-CHAP, EAP, Authentication Header (AH)

- Encryption Protocols for Confidentiality

  Examples: Encapsulation Security Header (ESP), Transport Layer Security (TLS) Record Protocol

- Key Management Protocols

  Example: Internet Key Management (IKE) Protocol

- Integrity Methods

  Example: MD5 and SHA hash functions

Often, authentication and key management protocols work together. For example, in IPSec, both AH and ESP Protocols employ the IKE Protocols to negotiate keys during the setup of a secure connection.

Architecture and Policy for Security

The architecture and policy for a university will be very different from the National Security Agency. The architecture and policy for security is the overall plan to protect an organization's systems or network. The architecture refers to the arrangement of physical components of the plan—hardware and software. The security policy is part of the architecture and will include not only the methods and procedures for protecting a system, but also steps to recover information or assess damage after a breach in security. Organizations that require open public access will effectively take greater risks. The architecture for a university could be as simple as follows:

- Internet Service Provider (ISP)

- Firewall

- Internal Network: routers, switches, and local area networks (LANs)

Applications

The applications associated with security can be grouped as Kerberos, firewalls, and VPNs.

Kerberos Kerberos is an open-source, and quite elaborate, authentication system. The elements of Kerberos go beyond password authentication in several dimensions. For the purposes of this discussion, we will define normal authentication as the process of logging into a computer that is not connected to a network. The only option to the computer is to authenticate you based on a password and user ID. Normally, a computer keeps an encrypted version of each user's password in a protected file that is only accessible by a system administrator. When you type your password, a one-way encryption process is applied. This encrypted value is then compared with the stored password in the password file. If it matches, you are allowed to logon. This is the process typical of authentication protocols like PAP or CHAP.

To understand Kerberos, you must be familiar with the terminology used to describe different aspects of the system. The components of a Kerberos environment are called domains, principals, and resources. These terms are unique to Kerberos. A Kerberos domain is the scope, or network, for which Kerberos is the authentication method. A principal is a user, also called the supplicant, who wishes to access the domain. The resource is an object on the server, such as a file or database, that the principal would like to use. A domain is also called a *realm* and resources are sometimes called *principals.*

Three services are internal to the Kerberos system: the authentication service that ensures the principal is authorized to access the domain, a ticket-granting service that allows secured access to the domain for a certain time span, and the service, such as viewing a database, that the principal seeks to access.

Although Kerberos goes beyond a normal authentication protocol such as CHAP, it does employ user IDs and passwords. But the most unusual aspect of Kerberos is the ticket-granting service. As the name implies, a ticket with a short lifetime is given to the principal. This ticket is then used to contact the service that the principal seeks. The reason for the ticket lifetime is an attack called the replay attack.

FYI: The Replay Attack

The idea of a replay attack is to obtain a copy of a secure transaction and issue the transaction again. Different security technologies present different risks in this regard. One way to guard against replay attacks is to have a small lifetime (e.g., 5 seconds) for any object in a security system, such as a Kerberos ticket.

Firewalls In past centuries, houses for common people were built primarily of wood. When wood houses were located close to one another, a fire in a single house could rapidly engulf an entire neighborhood. In modern years, building codes have required a brick or cinderblock wall—a firewall—to be put between houses in close proximity, such as row-houses, condominiums, and townhouses. These non-flammable walls are designed to protect fire from spreading from one house to another.

Networking has adapted the term firewall to mean a device that protects a network from imminent threats present on the Internet. Firewalls have become particularly important as broadband technology, such as cable and digital subscriber line (DSL) modems, have become common in residences. Broadband services leave home systems open to many threats including viruses, worms, and other attacks. Firewalls can be hardware "appliances" or software that runs on a PC to protect the network connections.

VPNs Since the early 1990s, virtually every modern corporation, and the majority of households, has had access to the Internet. Prior to the Internet era, however, data communications was very costly and less efficient. Data communications methods that became popular in the early 1970s began with the availability of private-line networks based on the Plesiosynchronous Digital Hierarchy (PDH)—for example, T1 and T3 service. These private line networks were used to link diverse geographical offices, forming a unified digital data communication network, built around packet switching technology. These private line networks were expensive, since a large company would have a monthly lease for a digital line whose cost was proportional to speed and distance, and many links were required.

In the 1980s, packet-switched data networks (PSDNs) became popular and are still used today. The most popular version is Frame Relay (FR). Several major carriers, such as AT&T and Sprint, offer PSDN service. The advantage of PSDNs is that several companies can share a single network since data traffic comes in bursts, with long silence periods between packets. The problem with PSDNs is that, while they can be secured, they are not interconnected; that is, Sprint's FR network is not connected to AT&T's FR network.

VPNs provide an economical alternative that can be used to provide several benefits to any organization. First, VPNs use the Internet. Second, VPNs are secure, using all of the aspects of encryption technologies. Since virtually every organization has access to the Internet, this ensures global access. Additional benefits of VPNs are:

■ Remote access for traveling employees

■ Telecommuting from home

■ Extranets: building partnerships with other corporations, suppliers, and customers

The last item has become a major reason larger corporations are pursuing VPNs. VPNs reduce delays and paperwork. For instance, in a manufacturing company, an extranet with a supplier allows the company to access ordering software and place orders for supplies. Similarly, a customer extranet allows customers to place orders for equipment and products. Furthermore, many different companies can collaborate on a common project through an extranet.

Firewalls and VPNs are the main topics of this book, and you will learn much more about them in the subsequent chapters.

Encryption Technologies

An encryption technology must have a cipher algorithm (called "cipher" for short) and one or more keys. The cipher uses the keys to encrypt and decrypt the messages. The unencrypted text is called *cleartext,* while the encrypted text is called the *ciphertext.*

Encryption methods have a long and interesting history. The earliest known method was called the Caesar Cipher and was used by Roman armies as they conquered the ancient world. This cipher was a simple alphabetic shift, and the key was the number of characters to be shifted.

Encryption technologies can be sorted into the following categories:

- One-way encryption, suitable for password-based authentication

- Two-way encryption where the data must be encrypted and decrypted, with two sub-categories:
  - Secret-key, also called Symmetric or Pre-Shared Key encryption
  - Public Key Infrastructure (PKI)

The PKI technology, invented in the 1970s, has been the most beneficial to society as a whole. In PKI, an individual holds a private key that is kept secure. In addition, a public key is available to anyone. Only the combination of public and private keys can be used to accomplish the encryption/decryption process. This public/private key pair is the basis for digital signatures and digital certificates.

Encryption, whether symmetric or PKI, produces a ciphertext document roughly the length of the original. Another part of encryption technology, called *digital signatures,* requires a small, constant-length item that is independent of the length of the original document, but is unique to that document. A solution to this problem is an algorithm called a hash code. *Hash codes* provide a unique, fixed-length representation that can be used as a digital signature.

The final cornerstone in encryption technology is the *digital certificate.* This object is a method to assure that a digital signature truly belongs to the person sending it. Digital certificates are produced by independent, unregulated companies that are highly trustworthy.

Related Technologies

There are several technologies related to the focus of this book. One is called *intrusion detection* (Sans 2005). The idea behind intrusion detection is to scan all traffic entering a network and try to determine if the traffic represents an attack of some sort. There are two basic forms of intrusion detection:

- Host-based Intrusion Detection Systems (HIDS)

- Network Intrusion Detection Systems (NIDS)

Recently a new marketing terminology has arisen, calling the two basic intrusion detection systems Intrusion Prevention Systems (IPS).

Another technology related to security is SecurID. This is a small metal object the size of a credit card. Inside, a chip generates random numbers unique to the card. All persons allowed to access a certain network have the same random number streams being generated at a central authentication server. Upon login, the number on a person's card must be typed into a dialup or Internet connection to authenticate the user.

A third, exotic technology is biometric security. This technology involves retinal scans, fingerprint scans, or other methods to uniquely identify each individual.

Testing, Analysis, and Incident Response

Every security system must be tested to be trusted. Several tools are available for this purpose, some combining testing and analysis functions. The simplest testing tool is called Nmap, and its method is to attempt to find available services in a network. Nmap is freely available on the Internet. Once Nmap has identified services that are open, the next step is turning these services off, if they are not needed.

Services such as file sharing or other network access utilities are occasionally left running on important servers unintentionally. Ideally, internal network administrators find these services first and remove them from the system. This is part of a process called *server hardening.*

A testing tool that includes analysis is called Nessus (**www.nessus. org/**). This free, widely-used product includes Nmap and other tools. Another commercial tool for thorough testing and analysis is Saint (**www. saintcorporation.com**).

Finally, no matter how well tested the system is, attacks still succeed. Incident response is the art and science of determining what happened and how to proceed thereafter. This is frequently called *cyber forensics.*

The 2003 CSI/FBI Survey (Robertson 2003) is a survey of companies, educational organizations, and government bodies conducted to assess whether computer and network security is increasing. In 2003, 98 percent of the organizations sampled were using firewalls. This should motivate the study of the topic in this book: as the implementation of security systems rise so does the need for professionals who understand firewalls and VPNs. To better understand firewalls and VPNs, we present a review of the TCP/IP protocol suite in this and in-depth coverage of TCP in the next chapter.

The TCP/IP Protocol Suite

All computers on the Internet use the TCP/IP Protocol to communicate. The development of the TCP/IP Protocol suite grew out of the U.S. Defense Department's Defense Advanced Research Project Agency (DARPA). As computing emerged in the late 1960s, a need grew to connect incompatible operating systems and exchange information between host computers. In 1969, a network that connected four universities—Stanford Research Institute (SRI), UCLA, University of California (UC) Santa Barbara, and the University of Utah—was developed, establishing the Advanced Research Project Agency Network (ARPANET). Initially, Network Control Protocol (NCP) was used as a basis of communication on ARPANET.

In 1974, Vint Cerf and Bob Kahn published a paper entitled "A Protocol for Packet Network Intercommunication," which described transmission-control protocol (TCP) and an improvement over NCP for host-to-host communication. Future refinements of TCP led to the separation of routing information into the Internet Protocol (IP) in 1978 and, thus, the protocol suite became known as TCP/IP.

In 1982, TCP/IP replaced NCP on ARPANET and quickly grew in popularity as more and more universities were connected to the network. Since the ARPANET was a government funded project, it was limited to research, education, and governmental uses; therefore, commercial vendors developed their own protocols that were not based on TCP/IP. In 1986, the first meeting of the Internet Engineering Task Force (IETF) convened, beginning the process of standards definition for the Internet.

Further developments included the introduction of the World Wide Web in 1991, the graphical Mosaic Web browser in 1993, and the end of sponsorship of the Internet backbone by the National Science Foundation in 1995. These developments led to a vast amount of commercial interest and the development of the Internet as we know it today. Because all computers connected to the Internet must use TCP/IP to communicate, commercial organizations abandoned their own proprietary protocols so they could take advantage of the opportunities provided by the Internet. Now, TCP/IP has become the dominant networking protocol throughout the world.

TCP/IP is comprised of two main components:

- ***Transmission Control Protocol (TCP)*** manages the flow of packets between systems, ensuring that network data is broken into manageable chunks and that delivery of all packets is reliable.

- ***Internet Protocol (IP)*** handles the addressing and routing of packets between hosts.

The TCP/IP protocol suite is called a protocol stack because in a diagram it looks like a stack of pancakes. TCP/IP is a "layered" concept as are most protocol suites. ***Protocol layering*** is a method of dividing a piece of work that is too big for a single monolithic program into smaller tasks (Stevens 1993). The TCP/IP stack is displayed in Figure 1.2.

The Application Layer is, as the name implies, a computer program performing a valuable function, such as a Web browser or a Web server. The Transport Layer is responsible for host-to-host management of either connection-oriented (TCP) or connectionless (UDP) service. The Inter-Network Layer, also called simply the Network Layer, is responsible for packet routing and path determination. The Data Link Layer is responsible for hop-by-hop, or network-by-network management of the data, including low-level error checking.

FYI: TCP/IP and OSI

Was there a protocol stack that preceded TCP/IP? Yes, the Open Systems Interconnect (OSI) stack existed many years earlier. We compare the layers below.

TCP/IP	OSI
Application	Application
Application	Presentation
Application	Session
Transport	Transport
Inter-Network	Inter-Network (Network)
Data Link	Data Link
Physical	Physical

Note that the Application Layer of the TCP/IP Protocol stack applies to three of the layers of the OSI stack. This correspondence is not always consistent. The TCP Transport Layer has elements of the Session Layer in its operation. File Transfer Protocol (FTP) is an "application protocol" that incorporates both Session and Presentation Layers. The way FTP absorbs the Presentation Layer can be seen through the use of FTP's bin and ascii directives. When the ascii directive is active, the character set of the source operating system is translated to that of the destination operating system. The bin directive is intended for executables, so no character translation is performed.

The TCP/IP Protocol suite has kept correspondence between the bottom four layers of the OSI stack.

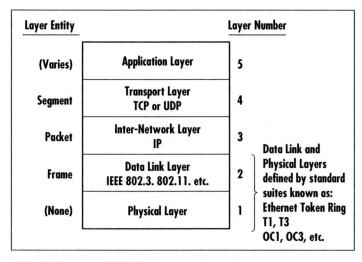

FIGURE 1.2 TCP/IP Protocol stack.

Data Link Layer Frame Acceptance Modes and Addressing

Our discussion of the TCP/IP Protocol stack begins with the Data Link Layer. The Data Link Layer is one of the most important layers in the TCP/IP protocol stack. It is responsible for ensuring the successful transmission of objects called frames, which are individual groups of binary bits. Among the other duties of the Data Link Layer are error detection and, in some protocols, flow control.

There are several types of data link protocols, and we focus here on the Ethernet technology common in local area networks (NATs). Ethernet is actually a specification of both the Physical and Data Link Layers. The Data Link Layer in Ethernet is composed of sublayers. The first is called Logical Link Control and the second sublayer is called *Media Access Control (MAC).* Ethernet frames have addresses called *MAC addresses.*

Ethernet's protocols are implemented by a Network Interface Card (NIC) inside a computer. These NICs implement three acceptance modes for Ethernet frames:

- Unicast and Broadcast Addresses

- Multicast Addresses

- Network Interface *Promiscuous Mode,* wherein all packets are accepted

There are two main types of Ethernet connectivity devices:

■ Ethernet switches

■ Broadcast hubs, sometimes called "dumb hubs"

An Ethernet switch implements a table associating MAC addresses with physical ports on the switch. As traffic passes through the switch, the switch inspects the header of the Ethernet frame to determine what the source MAC address is, and enters a row in the table for each device and its physical port number. This allows the switch to direct traffic to each machine on the basis of MAC destination addresses appearing in future frames.

By contrast, a broadcast hub sends any incoming traffic out all physical ports on the hub. This is somewhat inefficient. Hubs predated Etherenet switches by many years, and Etherenet has always had a special protocol to deal with the following issue.

Ethernet is an asynchronous protocol; that is, any NIC on any machine can send a frame whenever it wants to. As a result, there is the possibility that two NICs may transmit a frame at nearly the same time. Electronically, these frames will produce a collision. When this happens, data in both frames becomes corrupted. To deal with this, a special protocol of the 802.3 sub layer is implemented called Carrier Sense Multple Access/Collision Avoidance (CSMA/CD). This protocol is implemented by NICs, not by switches or hubs.

Broadcast hubs are frequently used for traffic monitoring applications, since any machine on one port can see all the traffic on the local network. Broadcast hubs are somewhat hard to find, and are usually only capable of 10 Mbps data rate.

Ethernet switches can also be used for traffic monitoring. Most Ethernet switches, except for inexpensive "zero-configuration" switches, include a capability called a monitor port. This port can be used to monitor any other port, or an entire virtual LAN (VLAN). (See FYI: Virtual LANs.)
The Ethernet standard defines sub-layers for the Data Link layer (see Figure 1.3). These layers include *Institute for Electrical and Electronics Engineers (IEEE) standards* 802.3 and 802.2 (IEEE Computer Society 2002; IEEE Computer Society 1998). IEEE 802.3 defines the basic Media Access Control (MAC) Layer, while IEEE 802.2 includes two protocols, as follows:

■ IEEE 802.3 – MAC

■ IIEEE 802.2

• Logical Link Control (LLC)

• Sub-Network Attachment Point (SNAP)

One of the most important fields of the 802.3 MAC header is the type field. Figure 1.3 displays a few type fields (also called "ether-types"). The

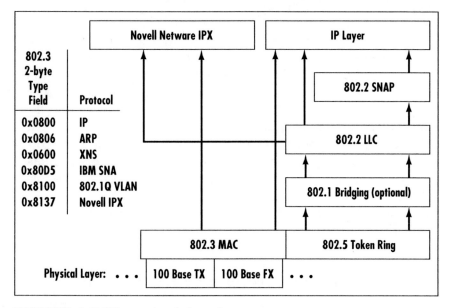

FIGURE 1.3 Ethernet sub-layering.

designers of 802.3 intended for the standard to be widely implemented with different network layers, and it was not clear that IP would become the dominant network layer protocol (IEEE Computer Society 2002). Other network layers such as Xerox's XNS, Novell NetWare's IPX/SPX, Microsoft's NetBEUI, and IBM's SNA were available and still are today.

The type field can also be used as a length field for the case of so-called "raw" Ethernet frames. This works because the maximum length of the payload portion of the 802.3 frame is 1,500 bytes for an "untagged frame"—by definition, any Ethernet frame without IEEE 802.1Q VLANs (IEEE Computer Society 2003).

FYI: Virtual LANs

What are virtual LANs? VLANs arose in situations where multiple functional groups of employees used a common LAN. An example would be a small company with a single internal LAN where Marketing, Human Resources, and Engineering mingled their traffic on a single Ethernet LAN. Suppose each of those groups had a separate server. It would be a security concern if the other groups could capture traffic from Human Resources and obtain employee salary information.

CONTINUED ON NEXT PAGE

> **CONTINUED**
>
> VLANs allow properly configured switches to separate the traffic, keeping Human Resources traffic away from certain paths. This is done by identifying specific hardware switch ports as part of a specific VLAN. This is by no means a complete security solution, of course. The main benefit of VLANs is a reduction in the amount of broadcast traffic propagated throughout the LAN. Broadcasts are often a significant portion of traffic, and are contained on a switch port-by-port basis within the appropriate VLAN, whereas without VLANs, the broadcasts would propagate throughout the entire LAN.
>
> When an IEEE 802.1Q VLAN is indicated, the frame length is 1522. Type codes can include IEEE 802.1Q virtual LANs (VLANs), or another upper layer protocol. Any type code will be greater than or equal to 1536 (0600 hexadecimal—for some reason we lose the several values between 1522 and 1536).

Figure 1.3 also shows the 802.2 LLC as a possible payload of 802.3 or other LAN technologies. The Ethernet type code for IP is 0800 hexadecimal, which is 2048 decimal. As a consequence, a mixture of any of the frame formats shown in Figure 1.3 (and in Figure 1.4) can co-exist on a single Ethernet LAN, while any 802.3 frame with a length value less than or equal to 1500 is assumed to have an 802.2 LLC payload.

Figure 1.3 shows the flexibility of LLC with respect to the MAC layer in use. LLC can be a "clearing house" for many different LAN technologies, including Ethernet and 802.5 Token Ring, as well as several different network layers. SNAP reverts to the use of type codes, in fact adopting the same codes as the 802.3 MAC frames.

The Ethernet Data Link frame is diagrammed in Figure 1.4, showing several frame formats. The figure also shows the possibility of encapsulating SNAP inside LLC. The LLC protocol works with Service Access Points (SAPs) rather than a type code in order to identify an upper layer protocol to which the payload belongs.

With LLC, there is both a source and destination SAP (see Figure 1.4); therefore, the receiving layer can determine the sending service type.

Figure 1.4 also shows a short list of SAP codes. The IP or Novell IPX Protocols can be reached by a simple 802.3 frame or with an additional 802.2 header. Another feature of the 802.2 protocol is the ability to work with International Standards Organization (ISO) protocols. Such protocols are not in wide use today, as the IETF standards have become dominant.

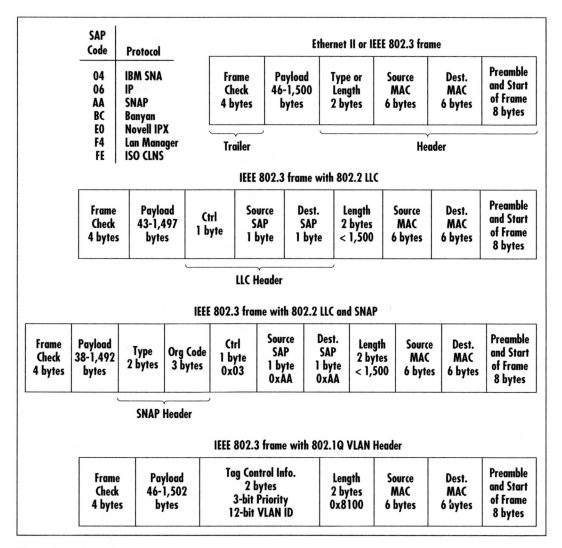

FIGURE 1.4 Ethernet frame formats.

Note in Figure 1.4 that the total frame length of an untagged frame is 1,518 bytes (this figure excludes the preamble and start of frame bytes), whereas the tagged frames are allowed to be 1,522 bytes total, per the current 802.3 specification.

Ethernet Media Access Control (MAC)

MAC addresses are 6-byte (48-bit) numbers, typically expressed as 12 hexadecimal digits, and used to uniquely identify a NIC. Throughout the world, every NIC is manufactured with a unique MAC address providing a

Vendor	First 3 bytes of HW Address (hexadecimal)
3Com	00:01:01, 00:01:02, 00:01:03 ...
Cisco	00:00:00, 00:01:42, 00:01:43 ...
Sun	00:03:BA, 00:20:F2, 00:00:7D, 08:00:20
Linksys	00:04:5A, 00:06:25, 00:0C:41, 00:0F:66
HP/Compaq	00:0B:CD

FIGURE 1.5 Sample vendor-specific MAC ranges from **www.standards.ieee.org/ regauth/oui/index.shtml**.

unique network identifier. MAC addresses are typically written or displayed in hexadecimal format using colons or hyphens to separate the bytes (a1:b2:c3:d4:e5:f6 or a1-b2-c3-d4-e5-f6).

The first three bytes of a MAC address indicate the vendor or manufacturer of the NIC. Each manufacturer is assigned one or several ranges of MAC addresses they can use. This provides an easy way for network analyzers and other network monitoring tools to easily determine the manufacturer of a device to help narrow down the search when looking for a problem device. Figure 1.5 illustrates a few.

The MAC is part of the Data Link Layer and provides an interface to the Physical Layer. Each computer listens for packets with its unique MAC address and only accepts packets with its MAC address in the destination MAC address portion of the MAC frame (except for the broadcast address and promiscuous mode, which are addressed below).

MAC address filtering has become very popular as a low level approach to preventing network access. (See Figure 1.6.) MAC address filtering allows a switch, router, or firewall to communicate only with a specified list of hosts based on their MAC address. This provides a basic layer of security by allowing only a predefined set of hosts to access the network. This is acceptable for small networks, but can be quite time consuming if a large number of hosts will be connecting to the network, since the administrator is often required to enter the MAC address of each host individually. This is quite common in wireless LAN environments.

Unicast and Broadcast Addresses

Unicast addresses are the individual hardware addresses configured by the vendor on each NIC at the time of manufacture. Without additional configuration, the NIC will respond to two destination hardware (MAC) addresses in the header of a data link frame. The 48-bit unicast address is one and the other is the hardware broadcast address (in hexadecimal notation, FF:FF:FF:FF:FF:FF).

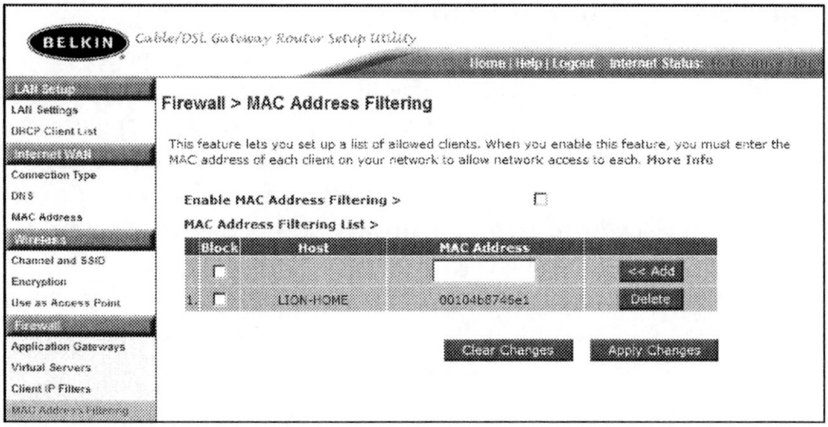

FIGURE 1.6 Sample MAC address filter configuration—Belkin Corporation WLAN Access Point.

NICs are available for common PC equipment for a variety of technologies: Ethernet, Token Ring, wireless LAN (WLAN), and even wide area network (WAN) technology like ANSI T1. Most firewall applications will use two Ethernet interfaces. One interface will normally be assigned to the internal network, while the other interface will face the outside world.

Without additional configuration, most operating systems will auto-detect new hardware. This includes recent versions of Linux and Microsoft Windows. In this nominal mode upon auto-detection by an existing operating system installed on the PC, or upon installation of a new operating system, the PC user will have the opportunity to configure an IP address and other information for the NIC.

Multicast Addresses

With additional configuration, the NIC can also respond to hardware-level multicast addresses. With these additional addresses, the NIC will respond to the Unicast, Broadcast, and Multicast addresses by computing a checksum of the frame payload and comparing it with the checksum contained in the trailer. If the two checksums match, the payload data will be extracted and delivered to the proper upper-layer application based on the type field in the frames header. Otherwise, the frame will be silently discarded. Multicast addresses are rarely necessary in a host PC. In a firewall, multicast addresses should not be allowed to cross the firewall at all, unless an application like Microsoft's Netmeeting or CUSeeMe/WhitePine (**www.fvc.com/**) is in use on the internal network.

Promiscuous Mode—When Is It Appropriate?

Another mode of frame acceptance is called promiscuous mode. In this mode, all packets will be accepted, regardless of destination MAC address. Promiscuous mode is frequently used by traffic monitoring applications (so-called sniffer software like the popular open-source package Ethereal) on Ethernet LAN interfaces. As with multicast mode, it is a sign that something is wrong when found on a firewall interface. It is perfectly normal for traffic monitoring or intrusion detection applications.

Occasionally, firewall applications include traffic monitoring and/or intrusion detection functions. In this case, promiscuous mode is expected. Otherwise, it may be the sign of a break-in.

Introduction to Internet Protocol (IP)

The IP Protocol involves IP packets that comprise a header and a payload. The *IP header* is shown in Figure 1.7. The primary items in the IP header that are used for filtering by firewalls are the source and destination IP addresses. In addition, the protocol (or type) field is important. The Time to Live (TTL) field, the Flags field, and occasionally certain options (for example, source routing) may be useful for filtering purposes.

IP Header Contents

The version field indicates what version of IP Protocol is contained in the packet. Currently IP version 4 (IPV4) is the dominant standard, but IP version 6 (IPV6) is also defined. IPV4 uses 32-bit addresses, while IPV6 uses

FIGURE 1.7 IP header detail.

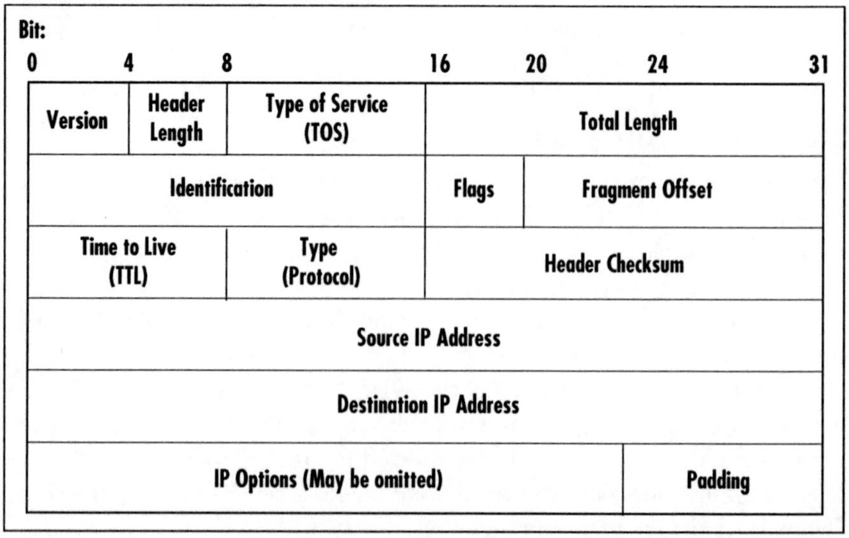

128-bit addresses. The header length field in IPV4 is a length in 32-bit words. The Type of Service (TOS) field is used for several purposes. The first was envisioned in the original IP Request for Comments (RFC), RFC 0791 (Information Sciences Institute 1981). RFC 0791 defined the TOS field, and it was detailed further in RFC 0795 (Postel 1981) to allow a packet to be routed differently based on the preference set in the TOS bits for several criteria:

1. Precedence (3 bits)
2. Delay (1 bit)
3. Reliability (1 bit)
4. Throughput (1 bit)
5. Reserved (2 bits)

Several levels of precedence, defined in RFC 0791, indicate the importance of the IP datagram (Information Sciences Institute 1981). The value of 000 indicates a routine packet, whereas 110 and 111 indicate network control, the highest priority, usually associated with routing protocol traffic. Each of the delay, reliability, and throughput bits has a meaning of "normal" with a bit value of 0 and "low" if the bit is set to 1.

FYI: Differentiated Services (DiffServ)

Currently, the Differentiated Services suite of RFCs, including RFC 2474 (Nichols et al. 1998), use the first six bits of the TOS field to determine how packets are serviced in terms of priority queueing mechanisms and buffer capacity. These six bits are re-titled the Diff-Serv Code Point (DSCP) bits. This is a redefinition of the use of the bits comprising the IP Precedence field, and the Delay, Reliability and Throughput bits. There is complete backward compatibility with previous uses of those six bits, depending on configuration and DSCP mapping methods.

Each value of the DSCP bits is called a Per-Hop Behavior (PHB). Generally, the authors of the DiffServ RFCs maintained backward compatibility with the several values of the IP Precedence field, namely 111, 110, and 000. The precedence value 000 has always meant "routine" traffic, e.g., best effort, and the default PHB 000000 retains that designation. Half of the 64 possible DSCPs are intended for standardization, and half are reserved for experimental or local use.

As a consequence of services offered by a network such as DiffServ, and the defined PHBs, some values of the TOS field may be suspicious. If the internal network does not support differentiated services, then perhaps the packets are an attempt to cause a program error and gain some inappropriate control.

The total length field indicates the complete length of the packet including payload and header in bytes. The maximum length is 65,535 octets, but normally packet size is determined by the minimum of the maximum transmission unit (MTU) along the path that the packet traverses. Usually this will be determined by an Ethernet network at the origination point (i.e., a total length of about 1,500 bytes plus the 20-byte IP header), but some WAN links may have smaller MTUs (occasionally 512 bytes or 536 bytes). Such an MTU somewhere in the middle of the packet's path may cause fragmentation of the IP packet into several smaller IP packets.

The flags field of the IP header contains three bits:

1. Bit 0 is always 0 and is reserved;
2. Bit 1 indicates whether the IP packet can be fragmented, i.e., broken apart into separate packets; and
3. Bit 2 indicates to the receiving unit if this is the last fragment in a series.

Clearly some combinations of bits in the flags field might be invalid, offering an opportunity to filter and discard them in a firewall.

The Identification field is a unique number assigned to a datagram fragment to allow the fragments to be reassembled into the original IP packet at the destination host.

The TTL field is an integer that is decremented by every router (literally by every IP layer) through which the packet passes. If the TTL becomes zero, the packet is discarded.

The Protocol Type field indicates what upper layer is to receive the IP payload. For example, *Transport Control Protocol (TCP)* is protocol type 6, *User Datagram Protocol (UDP)* is 17, *Internet Control Message Protocol (ICMP,* aka "ping") is type 1, and the routing protocols *Interior Gateway Routing Protocol (IGRP)* and *Open Shortest Path First (OSPF)* are 88 and 89 respectively. The Header Checksum is used to control errors in the header only.

The IP Options field breaks down into several sub-fields:

1. Option type octet
   Copy Flag (1 bit)
   Class (2 bits)
   Number (5 bits)
2. Option length
3. Option data

Unsupported options may provide a further opportunity to filter and discard unwanted packets. A list of the option type codes can be found at **www.iana.org/assignments/ip-parameters**.

IP Addresses IP addresses, as introduced above, are 32-bit binary numbers. The conventional representation of these numbers is in dotted-decimal form, where each of the four bytes of the binary IP address is converted to decimal, with periods between the decimal numbers. Figure 1.8 illustrates this with a few examples.

Binary IP address	Dotted-Decimal IP address
10001001001011010110100010101100	137.45.104.172
11000000101010000000000100000000	192.168.1.0

FIGURE 1.8 Binary-to-dotted decimal conversion of IP addresses.

The IP addressing scheme for the internet was first introduced in RFC 943 (Reynolds and Postel 1985). A network ID is always represented using zeroes in the place of the bits representing the hosts (see the section on subnetting). For example, the IP address 192.168.1.0 is a Class C network ID representing 254 hosts. The IP address 137.45.104.172 represents a specific host in the Class B network whose network ID is 137.45.0.0. IP addresses at an early point in the development of the IP protocol were divided into two portions:

- The network portion

- The host portion

Figure 1.9 illustrates this for a Class C IP address from the network with ID 192.168.1.0.

A central issue is how to obtain a mapping between IP addresses and any hardware address such as an Ethernet MAC address. This must be done, because until the entire Ethernet frame can be completed, no

FIGURE 1.9 IP address network and host portion.

Network Portion	Host Portion
110000001010100000000001	00000000

communication can take place. A necessary piece of information to complete the Ethernet frame is the destination MAC address, whereas the sending machine knows its own source MAC address. The scenario we present is the following: the IP Layer has a destination IP address and has passed this address to the Data Link Layer, in this case Ethernet. How does Ethernet determine the destination MAC address associated with the IP address? The answer is another protocol called *Address Resolution Protocol (ARP)*. Every machine must have an ARP Protocol to resolve IP addresses into hardware addresses.

ARP is a protocol that has two simple messages: a request and a reply. The request is often called "WHO-HAS" and indicates a request for the machine having a certain IP address. The WHO-HAS message is sent to the hardware broadcast address which is 12 hexadecimal "F" digits in the case of Ethernet. This ensures that any machine on the local network will receive the message. The reply message takes the form of a Data Link Layer unicast message from the owner of the IP address to the machine making the request. The ARP Protocol maintains a cache of all such exchanges containing the MAC address and the associated IP address. This prevents the necessity of future ARP exchanges to obtain the same address.

IP Address Subnetting To complete the coverage of IP addresses, the subject of subnets must be examined. Originally, the IETF defined several classes of Unicast IP addresses called network addresses or network IDs. These classes are illustrated in Table 1.1. The table shows IP addresses for each of several classes in dotted-decimal notation where the items marked "xxx" represent values between 001 and 254. Any contiguous values of xxx = 255 would represent a broadcast address for the particular network (for example, the broadcast address for the Class A private network known as 10.0.0.0 would be 10.255.255.255) and IP packets with broadcast addresses reach all hosts on that network. This text concentrates on Classes A, B, and C. For more information on multicast Class D, and Class E see RFC 1112 (Deering 1989)

Every IP address or Network ID is associated with a mask. The mask is simply another 32-bit binary number indicating where the bits representing the network lie in the IP addresses for the network. Binary ones are placed in all bit positions in the mask where a constant network ID may be extracted by performing a binary AND operation between the mask and any destination IP address in an IP header. This provides a rapid method of extracting the network portion of the destination IP address for purposes of routing. For example, any host on a Class A network always has exactly 8 bits in the left-hand portion of the IP address that are fixed, or constant. The network ID 1.0.0.0 will only have host IP addresses ranging from 1.0.0.1 through 1.255.255.254—about 16 million hosts. What if an ISP had a single Class A but several subscribers? It would be convenient to subnet the Class A into several Class B networks.

TABLE 1.1 Classes of IP addresses (RFC 1700).

	Public	Private	Network Mask (/n)	Unicast/ Multicast
Reserved	000.xxx.xxx.xxx		255.0.0.0 (/8)	Unicast
Class A	001.xxx.xxx.xxx – 126.xxx.xxx.xxx	10.xxx.xxx.xxx	255.0.0.0 (/8)	Unicast
Class B	128.000.xxx.xxx – 191.254.xxx.xxx	172.016.xxx.xxx – 172.031.xxx.xxx	255.255.0.0 (/16)	Unicast
Class C	192.000.000.xxx – 223.254.254.xxx	192.168.001.xxx –192.254.254.xxx	255.255.255.0 (/24)	Unicast
Class D	224.000.000.001 – 232.255.255.255		255.255.255.0 (/24)	Multicast – Link Local
Class D	233.000.000.000 – 238.255.255.255		255.255.255.0 (/24)	Multicast – Global Scope
Class D	239.255.000.000 – 239.255.255.255		255.255.0.0 (/16)	Multicast – P V4I Local Scope
Class D	239.000.000.000 – 239.255.255.255		255.0.0.0 (/8)	Multicast – Administrative Scope RFC 2365 (See Meyer 1998.)
Class D	239.192.000.000 – 239.192.255.255		255.252.0.0 (/14)	Multicast – Organization Local Scope
Class E	240.xxx.xxx.xxx – 255.255.255.254 255.255.255.255			Future Use Local Net Broadcast
Loopback	127.x.x.x			Unicast

Notice that the host addresses cannot include 1.0.0.0, since that is the network ID, nor can a host address be equal to the network broadcast address 1.255.255.255. Two addresses are lost from the 24 bits representing the host addresses. Therefore, the following formula calculates the number of host addresses given h host bits:

$$\#hosts = 2^h = 2$$

For a Class A network, this formula yields 16,777,214 possible host IP addresses.

RFC 950 acknowledges that few organizations would need 16 million host computers. Many large companies and ISPs obtained Class A licenses, but never used all of their addresses. So, to alleviate the wasted space, subnetting (literally, subdividing a network into multiple separate subnets) was

FIGURE 1.10 IP address network, subnet, and host portion.

defined in RFC 950 (Mogul and Postel 1985). The process of subnetting re-quires defining a new portion of the IP address called the subnet portion. Figure 1.10 illustrates this new subnet portion for a Class B network that is being subdivided into Class C-size subnetworks.

With this new portion, an ISP or other organization could put different subnets on different transmission technologies, and different geographic loca-tions. There are some restrictions in RFC 950, however, that are collectively called "classful subnetting" (Mogul and Postel 1985). It is still necessary to preserve the original overall network ID (137.45.0.0) and broadcast address (137.45.255.255) for the network. In the Class B case displayed in Figure 1.10, no matter where the individual subnets are located, packets arriving from the Internet can still use the original Class B broadcast address, 137.45.255.255. Similarly, the original Class B network ID must not be assigned as a subnet ID. As a consequence, the subnetting procedure could not use 137.45.0.0 as a sub-net ID, and the first available subnet ID is 137.45.1.0.

Each subnet has its own subnet ID and subnet broadcast address, so the formula used earlier for the number of hosts still applies. In addition, we have a new formula for the number of subnets in classful subnetting, given s subnet bits.

$$\#subnets = 2^s - 2$$

Therefore, in the case described in Figure 1.10, subnetting a Class B network into subnetworks that are the size of Class C yields 254 subnets since $s = 8$ bits. The subnet mask is now 255.255.255.0, as it would be for an ordinary Class C network.

The reader will find, upon examining the details of classful subnetting, that two blocks of IP host addresses are lost—hence the subtraction of 2 in the subnet formula. In the preceding example two entire subnets are lost:

■ 137.45.0.0—the first subnet

■ 137.45.255.0—the last subnet

This is because in the case of subnet 137.45.0.0 it is ambiguous whether we are talking about the entire Class B or just one Class C "carve-out." To resolve the ambiguity, we must include the mask length to distin-guish the two networks:

- 137.45.0.0/16 refers to the entire Class B

- 137.45.0.0/24 refers to a Class C "carve-out"

Another ambiguity arises with the subnet 137.45.255.0. In the case of 137.45.255.0, that subnet would have the broadcast address 137.45.255.255, again causing an ambiguity: Are we sending a broadcast to the entire Class B or just the last subnet?

Imagine if the number of subnet bits was $s=3$ in the above problem. Then there would be six massive subnets, each containing 8,190 hosts. To rectify this problem and regain vast quantities of IP addresses, *Classless Inter-Domain Routing (CIDR)* was introduced by RFC 1518 (Rekhter and Li 1993) and RFC 1519 (Fuller et al. 1993) to remove the artificial class structure of IP addresses introduced in RFC 0791. RFC 1519 also introduced the concept of *Variable Length Subnet Masks (VLSM)* so that an organization could subnet each to suit larger or smaller groups of computers.

Before RFCs 950 and 1519, the assumed mask size was based on the class of IP address found in the destination field of any IP packet. A router could simply put a destination IP address in the correct range (Class A, B, C) to identify its network portion. Now, there was flexibility in defining the mask length to be any number, not just 8, 16, or 24. As a consequence of RFC 950, which introduced subnets, a mask must be associated with each interface (Mogul and Postel 1985, p.6). However RFC 950 still relied on the class structure of RFC 0791, while allowing a variable length subnet mask to be used for each interface, RFC 950 forbids the use of any subnet that would conflict with the original network's network ID or network broadcast. In the case of figure 1.10, RFC 950 would disallow the use of a Class C-sized subnet called 137.45.0.0 or similar subnet numbered 137.45.255.0.

One reason that RFC 950 stopped short of allowing the flexibility of CIDR, is that certain routing protocols were not capable of transmitting masks associated with subnetworks. This situation was not remedied for most routing protocols until 1998, 13 years after RFC 950 was published. To illustrate the issue here, suppose you have a computer located on a network halfway around the world from the 137.45.0.0 network. This network has decided to define a Class C-sized subnet called 137.45.0.0. When you send packets to a machine on this subnet, the routers on the internal networks at 137.45.0.0 cannot distinguish between the overall Class B network 137.45.0.0 and the Class C subnet 137.45.0.0, until the packet arrives at the router connected to Class C subnet 137.45.0.0. In other words, there is no routing intelligence that can get your packet onto the correct path.

When RFC 1519 introduced CIDR in 1993, it became necessary to associate an explicit mask with each network or subnetwork for IP routing to work. This is a small price to pay for reclaiming large amounts of IP addresses—including the first and last subnets mentioned above. As a result, work began on redesigning routing protocols to transmit mask lengths for each distant subnetwork. One of those routing protocols was Routing Information Protocol (RIP). The first version of RIP did not transmit masks associated with each subnetwork. RIP Version 2 (RIPV2) resolved this problem (Malkin 1998).

Note that many organizations still retain classful subnetting today even though their equipment is capable of supporting CIDR. An additional benefit of CIDR is sometimes called super-netting, or address aggregation. This is important for ISPs, because the size of the default-free Internet routing table that ISPs must implement is approaching 200,000 rows, each representing a network or subnet. CIDR allows the ISPs to collapse any number of subnets into a single row wherever IP routing would take the packets for those subnets to the same next-hop. Reducing the size of a table that must be searched for every packet can significantly reduce router processing requirements.

IN PRACTICE: IP Subnet Calculators

There are several ways to obtain an IP subnet calculator and other useful tools. An elegant online calculator is available at **www.jafar.com/java/jipcalc/jipdemo.html**. This java applet with a very nice GUI allows you to dial the number of subnet bits. Note that this calculator assumes a CIDR-ized network.

A second option is a free download from **www.wildpackets. com**. A general purpose network calculator is available that contains a subnet calculator. This product is suitable for Windows 95 through XP. This product may be blocked by software firewalls, however.

How would a large organization ever configure thousands of computers with unique IP addresses? The answer is ***Dynamic Host Configuration Protocol (DHCP),*** which requires a DHCP server to be available to all computers that are to use this facility. As with most client-server applications, the PC host that wants to obtain an IP address (and other configuration items) must have a DHCP client program. Virtually all operating systems supply such DHCP clients by default. In Windows, the way to specify use of DHCP is depicted in Figure 1.11. First, from the Start menu, select Settings and then Network Connections. Then, right click an Ethernet connection and select Properties. In the Properties dialog box, scroll down and select the item labeled "Internet Protocol (TCP/IP)." Then click the Properties button. When the radio button "Obtain IP address automatically" is checked, this means use DHCP.

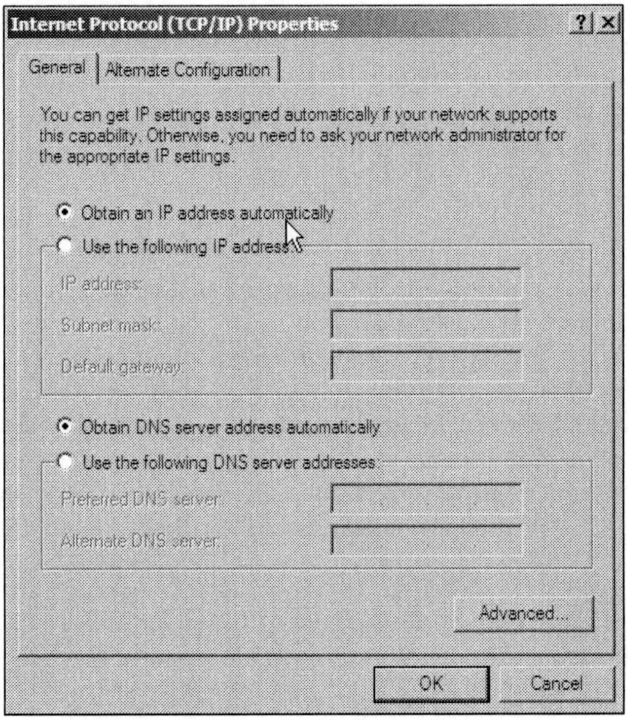

FIGURE 1.11 Windows DHCP configuration.

In addition to an IP address, several other configuration items are usually provided by DHCP:

- IP address
- Default Gateway—the router that can be used for traffic to other subnets
- Domain Name Servers (DNS)
- (Optional) Windows Internet Name Servers (WINS)
- (Optional) Print servers

Filtering Parameters

As indicated in the Ethernet Media Access Control section, MAC address filtering is the lowest level of filtering available. The second level of filtering is *IP packet filtering* based on the IP header content. This can be considered an entry level firewall. (A third level of filtering based on TCP header content is discussed later.) Packet filters provide a high performance tool for blocking unwanted network traffic but do not examine the packet payload and, therefore, can easily allow hazardous packets to enter a network.

Caution

Windows TCP/ IP Properties

You will need to specify a static IP address, Default Gateway and DNS server(s) if you unclick the radio button for "Obtain IP address automatically." To make sure you do not change your configuration, make sure to click Cancel.

Packet filtering can be implemented by a router. The source and destination IP address determine whether to permit or deny the packet. (A router can also filter based on TCP or UDP port numbers. See Chapter 2.) In addition, the IP addressing scheme defines categories of addresses similar to hardware addresses discussed above:

- Network IDs (network addresses)

- Unicast IP addresses (specific individual hosts)

- Multicast IP addresses (a specific collection of hosts)

- Broadcast IP addresses (all hosts on a network)

The detailed contents of the IP packet and Ethernet MAC frame headers have been described. Determination of what parameters can be useful for filtering is the objective of this section. The most fundamental idea about packet filtering from a security standpoint is to filter and drop or reject all packets from the following categories including but not limited to:

- Protocols that are not supported on the internal network

- Services that are not supported (based on TCP/UDP port numbers—see Chapter 2)

- Suspicious or malformed packets or frames that contain invalid header information

- Packets or frames that contain suspicious content

- A sequence of packets or frames that does not fit the pattern of a normal transaction or connection, i.e., a sequence of packets destined for each IP address in an entire subnet in increasing order of the addresses

- Other possible situations

Protocol   Each of the headers described above has a protocol type field. The type field for the Ethernet 802.3 frames was originally defined in RFC 1700 (Reynolds and Postel 1994), but has been superceded by the Internet Assigned Numbers Authority (IANA). For the most up-to-date list of number assignments, see **www.iana.org/assignments/ethernet-numbers**. You will find an enormous number of assignments, even for companies that no longer exist. The equipment that those companies manufactured may be still in use, so the numbers must be kept. The official list of LLC SAP codes is kept by the IEEE, but a short list of the LLC SAP codes is available at **www.iana.org/assignments/ieee-802-numbers**.

The IP protocol type field was first defined by RFC 1700 (Reynolds and Postel 1994). This has also been superceded by an online list at **www.iana.org**. RFC 1700 still provides a substantial identification of most of the payloads that IP datagrams will carry.

IP Datagram Content We have briefly discussed MAC address filtering and packet filtering as methods of basic security. Both of these methods rely on examining the MAC frame header or the IP content header information but do not go deeper into the packet to analyze the payload. ***Stateful packet inspection*** is the third method of packet analysis to consider. Stateful inspection looks not only at the header contents but analyzes the payload data to determine if it is indeed valid.

Typical Filtering Applications

This section describes typical filtering applications. We can distinguish two different general classes of filtering applications:

- Passive, where no action is taken in the operational network

- Active, where some kind of decision is made whether the packet can enter the operational network

Traffic Monitoring Understanding and monitoring network traffic is a key component of successful implementation of any type of network firewall, and monitoring is often performed for reasons aside from network security (capacity planning, debugging network problems, and estimating traffic statistical properties for quality of service). Traffic monitoring is in the passive category of filtering applications, since it provides copies of network packets for subsequent analysis.

It is often difficult to create a rule or network policy without additional details about the flow of data on the network. Sniffers make use of promiscuous mode to listen to all of the traffic on a network and capture the full detail of every packet. It is frequently desirable to exclude certain kinds of packets from a full trace. This is the kind of filtering that traffic monitors perform.

The tcpdump program is one utility that performs general purpose traffic monitoring. It was written for the Unix operating system. This program is still available today for most operating systems, including Linux and Windows. It is available from **www.tcpdump.org/**. The tcpdump program supports command line options to select certain Link Layer Protocol types (for example, the Address Resolution Protocol (ARP)) or IP Protocol types like ICMP.

There are many commercial sniffers on the market, including a few free tools that can provide an overwhelming amount of data and information. Basic packet capture can be provided via the Microsoft Network Monitor or tcpdump (Linux/Unix/Windows). These tools can capture the packet details based on a suite of command line or configurable options and can capture all packets in a file for later analysis. Ethereal is a more advanced package that can be used as a complete tool to capture and analyze the network, or it can be used to analyze a network dump from other software packages such as tcpdump, Microsoft Network Monitor, and many commercial packages. Ethereal can be downloaded from **www.ethereal.com/**. Other open-source network monitoring packages include IPtraf and ntop. A good Web site for such applications is **www.topology.org**.

Several commercial network monitoring capabilities are available. One is McAfee corporation's Sniffer line of products. The price for these products can range from $1,000 to more than $5,000, depending on choice of transmission interface. Lower costs exist for 10/100 Ethernet applications, higher for WAN and Gigabit and 10 Gigabit Ethernet capability. (See **www.networkassociates.com.**)

Another line of commercial products that goes beyond sniffing is available through NetScout (**www.netscout.com**). These products are generally more expensive and offer a mix of passive and active methods. Active methods, called performance probes, send test packets across a network to evaluate delay and packet loss.

All traffic monitoring products use one or both of two technologies:

- Packet capture libraries

- Simple Network Management Protocol (SNMP) features

Packet capture libraries are, in simplest terms, a collection of programs that interface with the Data Link Layer to obtain copies of frames. The libpcap libraries are available for Unix varieties of operating systems, while winpcap libraries are available for Windows operating systems. You must download and install these libraries for sniffers to work. See the Web site www.tcpdump.org for links to libpcap and winpcap.

SNMP is a protocol that is supported by virtually every device, including hosts, routers, and switches. SNMP can be used to remotely obtain counts of packets, frames, or other objects at various layers of the TCP/IP stack.

Intrusion Detection—A Brief Introduction *Intrusion detection tools* detect malicious or potentially dangerous network traffic or hacking attempts. Detection of inappropriate activities, however, does not necessarily prevent them. With the use of intrusion detection systems (IDS), someone needs to constantly monitor the events and follow a plan developed for responding to vulnerabilities or dangerous hosts. The goal of an IDS is to detect port scans, unauthorized access to services, telnet, ssh, internal Web servers, and other common services. The actions that IDS can take in response include a wide range:

- Accept the packet
- Drop the packet
- Reject the packet

1

- Use a variety of transport layer methods (see Chapter 2)

- Logging

IDS typically record detailed log information including a timestamp and the IP address of the attacker. There are two types of IDS: so-called Network Intrusion Detection Systems (NIDS), such as the open-source package Snort (**www.snort.org**) or Host Intrusion Detection Systems (HIDS or simply IDS) typified by Tripwire (**www.tripwire.org**, **www.tripwire.com**). NIDS focus on network packets while IDS focus on processes on the host.

Firewalls—Another Filtering Application This brings us to the subject of firewalls. Firewalls provide a number of opportunities to classify packets based on the parameters of data link and IP header contents. In addition, firewalls provide the benefit of direct, immediate actions. The basic actions available are:

- Accept the packet (forward to the internal network)

- Drop the packet

- Reject the packet, sending an appropriate ICMP code to the sender

- Logging

These actions go beyond simple packet filter and traffic monitoring programs like tcpdump or Ethereal, which copy packet traffic to a file or a console screen. Firewalls provide an immediate action based on each packet. Stateful firewalls can also keep track of sequences of packets, differentiating between legitimate TCP connections and other sequences of packets.

FYI: Software Firewalls

Software firewalls abound for Windows and Linux. A good clearing house can be found at **www.free-firewall.org/**. Many free firewalls have diluted features, as described at this Web site.

As discussed above, there are more powerful firewalls that keep state on connections—stateful firewalls. A Cisco VPN client that includes a stateful firewall is available for Linux and Windows through XP. This is a commercial product. Right-click the VPN icon (a yellow lock symbol) in the system tray after initiating the VPN connection, and the stateful firewall can be enabled or disabled via a checkbox.

A modestly priced stateful firewall for Windows is also available from **www.tinysoftware.com/home/tiny**. Finally, in Linux Kernel 2.4 and beyond, a stateful firewall system called iptables is usually included.

Summary

Connecting to the Internet is almost essential in the modern world. But the increased convenience of connectivity brings with it an increased risk. Because the Internet is so open and accessible, it leaves legitimate users vulnerable unscrupulous individuals. To protect property and information from attack through the Internet, organizations turn to security professionals. Two of the tools these professionals use to protect their organizations are firewalls and VPNs. In this chapter, you learned how TCP/IP Protocols, particularly Network and Data Link Layer Protocols, work and you were introduced to filtering parameters and filtering applications, such as simple packet monitoring and firewalls. Now you are ready to explore TCP and UDP in more depth. Learning more about these two layers in the TCP/IP stack and how traffic moves on the Internet will prepare you to manage that traffic with a firewall.

Test Your Skills

MULTIPLE CHOICE QUESTIONS

1. Security can be defined as:

   A. Authentication

   B. Confidentiality

   C. Integrity

   D. Non-repudiation

   E. All of the above

2. One of the most important fields of the 802.3 MAC header is the _____ field.

   A. Broadcast

   B. Payload

   C. Type

   D. Data

3. TCP/IP is comprised of these two components:

   A. Transfer Communication Packets (TCP) and Internet Packets (IP)

   B. Transfer Control Packets (TCP) and Internetworking Packets (IP)

   C. True communication program (TCP) and Independent Program (IP)

   D. Transmission Control Protocol (TCP) and Internet Protocol (IP)

1

4. Which of the following is NOT an acceptance mode for data link frames?

   A. Unicast

   B. Promiscuous

   C. Multicast

   D. Netcast

5. Which of the following is NOT a valid Ethernet MAC address?

   A. 00-c1-d1-a1-80-99

   B. 00-2g-a1-67-62-88

   C. 0a:92:1a:22:33:4c

   D. 00-2a-2c-11-9a-f2

6. The first three bytes of a MAC address indicates

   A. the vendor or manufacturer of the computer.

   B. the vendor or manufacturer of the Network Interface Card.

   C. a unique serial number issued by the manufacturer.

   D. the TCP subnet to which a computer is connected.

7. _____ filtering provides a low level method of preventing network access and is typically implemented in switches.

   A. Source address

   B. Destination address

   C. MAC address

   D. IP address

8. _____ is currently the dominant version of the IP protocol and is indicated by the first field in the IP header.

   A. IPV3

   B. IPV4

   C. IPV5

   D. IPV6

9. If the TTL field in the IP header is zero, the packet is

   A. permitted.

   B. forwarded.

   C. discarded.

   D. rewritten.

10. Which of the following will NOT be found in the Protocol Type field?
    A. IP Address
    B. TCP
    C. UDP
    D. ICMP

11. IP Addresses are 32-bit binary numbers traditionally written in _____ form.
    A. hexidecimal
    B. binary
    C. dotted Decimal
    D. octal

12. IP packets with _____ addresses reach all hosts on that network.
    A. unicast
    B. broadcast
    C. IP
    D. promiscuous

13. The _____ helps provide a rapid method for extracting the network portion of the destination address to determine if the packet needs to be routed.
    A. broadcast address
    B. IP address
    C. network mask
    D. gateway

14. A Class C IP address network range allows for _____ hosts.
    A. 264
    B. 256
    C. 255
    D. 254

15. The default Network Mask for a Class C network is:
    A. 2255.0.0.0
    B. 2255.255.0.0
    C. 2255.255.255.0
    D. 2255.255.252.0

16. _____ provide a high performance tool for blocking unwanted traffic based only on header content.

    A. Firewalls

    B. Sniffers

    C. Packet filters

    D. Network analyzers

17. This mode is useful for traffic monitoring applications or sniffers:

    A. multicast

    B. promiscuous

    C. broadcast

    D. unicast

18. Traffic monitoring provides:

    A. the ability to permit or deny packets.

    B. options to prevent dangerous network traffic.

    C. a copy of network traffic for analysis.

    D. a way to filter packets based on MAC addresses.

19. _____ are important because they help detect malicious or potentially dangerous network traffic based on patterns of activity.

    A. Traffic monitors

    B. Intrusion detection systems

    C. Firewalls

    D. Routers

20. The primary items in the IP headers used by firewalls for _____ is the source and destination IP address.

    A. analysis

    B. filtering

    C. logging

    D. packet capture

EXERCISES

Exercise 1.1: IP Addresses Binary-to-Dotted-Decimal Notation

1. Translate the following 32-bit binary number to dotted-decimal notation:

   ```
   11000000 10101000 00001010 00000001
   ```

2. Translate the following IP address into binary:

   `137.45.23.19`

Exercise 1.2: Subnets and Masking

Senredna Corporation is a rapidly expanding accounting company. Back in the 1980s the company was assigned a Class C address 193.1.1.0 by the Internet Address and Naming Authority (IANA) and has a single corporate network in its headquarters. The other offices dial in to this network via modem. The president and CEO of Senredna, Jane Doe, has just realized that the company is using its corporate network as a critical resource for all of its accounting audits and wants to expand the network to tie all of its offices together. Senredna has four offices worldwide including the headquarters, with plans to open two new offices in the next five years. Each office needs a subnet from the Class C in compliance with RFC 950 (i.e., classful subnetting) and is to be connected by routers to the other offices. Each office has no more than 20 hosts and servers. You must provide the following information to Ms. Doe:

1. To provide six subnets, how many subnet bits will be needed?

2. How many hosts can be supported on each subnet?

3. Will Senredna need more IP addresses for the hosts and servers in each office?

4. What will be the new subnet mask?

5. What are the first two subnet IDs under the new subnetting scheme?

6. What are the first hosts in each of the first two subnets?

7. What are the broadcast addresses of the first two subnets?

8. What is the last subnet ID?

9. What is the first host in the last subnet?

10. What is the broadcast address in the last subnet?

Exercise 1.3: DeepFry University

DeepFry University is a rapidly expanding "virtual university" that uses online courses from its headquarters somewhere in the southern United States. Now that it has an accredited computer science program, its popularity has grown so rapidly that the university has outgrown its Class C network. It has obtained a Class B license 129.1.0.0 and is also moving into 16 new buildings across a large metropolitan area. DeepFry has decided to use classless subnetting so as to make maximum use of its Class B address space, in compliance with RFC 1519. Each of the buildings is expected to have approximately 2,500 hosts and servers. Design a subnetting of the Class B that leaves room for expansion of more than 2,500 hosts.

1. How many subnet bits are required by your solution?

2. How many hosts can be supported on each subnet?

3. How many subnets in total are provided?

4. What will be the new subnet mask?

5. What are the first two subnet IDs under the new subnetting scheme?

6. What are the first hosts in each of the first two subnets?

7. What are the broadcast addresses of the first two subnets?

8. What is the last subnet ID?

9. What is the first host in the last subnet?

10. What is the broadcast address in the last subnet?

Exercise 1.4: Identifying Classless Subnetworks

Senredna Corporation is expanding again, needing two additional offices. You are the network administrator for Senredna, and your manager has told you to download RFC 2453 (RIP version 2) and read Section 4. You researched the company's equipment and discovered that all equipment supported RFC 1519 and RFC2453 so the company could use CIDR. To avoid disrupting the existing solution to Exercise 1.2, the company decided to use classless subnetting, since it can regain two subnets: 193.1.1.0 and 193.1.1.224. Answer the following questions:

1. Is the subnet mask the same for these two new subnets?

2. How do routers internal to Senredna tell the difference between the overall Class C 193.1.1.0 and the subnet 193.1.1.0?

3. How do routers tell the difference between the overall Class C broadcast address 193.1.1.255 and the broadcast address for the subnet 193.1.1.224, which is also 193.1.1.255?

Exercise 1.5: Senredna Corporation Expands Again!

(*Note:* This advanced exercise is a sequel to Exercise 1.4.)

Senredna Corporation is expanding yet again, needing four additional small offices with at most 10 machines. You are the network administrator for Senredna. Your manager has charged you to answer the question, "Can we apply section 6 of RFC1519 to our Class C network, using VLSM?" You conclude there is no reason that Senredna cannot apply VLSM to its Class C network. (Recall from Exercise 1.4 that Senredna has adopted classless subnetting.)

You are also asked to survey the number of hosts and servers in each office and find that four of the existing offices have only ten machines. These are the subnets 193.1.1.32, 193.1.1.64, 193.1.1.96, 193.1.1.128 and 193.1.1.160. All the rest of the pre-existing 27 subnets have 16 to 20 machines.

You must now implement VLSM for the company, using one mask for the larger offices, and another mask for the other eight offices. Download RFC 1519 (CIDR) and read Section 6, then answer the following questions:

1. To provide four new subnets, how many subnet bits will be needed for the eight (four old plus four new) offices? (Include the subnet bits for the larger offices as part of your new subnetting.)

2. How many hosts can be supported on each small subnet?

3. How many smaller subnets will be provided by the new subnetting scheme? (Remember that some of the smaller subnet will overlap with existing large subnets and be unusable.) Will Senredna have additional subnets for additional small office locations beyond the four that are planned?

4. What will be the new subnet mask for the small offices?

5. What are the first two subnet IDs and their masks under the new subnetting scheme? (*Hint:* Remember that the network is now classlessly subnetted and the first subnet might have a different mask than the second.)

6. What are the first hosts in each of the first two subnets?

7. What are the broadcast addresses of the first two subnets?

8. What is the last subnet ID? (*Hint:* Remember that the network is now classlessly subnetted.)

9. What is the first host in the last subnet?

10. What is the broadcast address in the last subnet?

Exercise 1.6: Basic Network Masks

BASS.ITEC.COM has the IP address 150.131.12.100.

TROUT.ITEC.COM has the IP address 150.132.43.132.

Which of the following subnet masks indicate that BASS and TROUT are on the same major network? Select all that apply:

255.255.255.0

255.255.0.0

255.0.0.0

PROJECTS

Project 1.1: Hands-On Linking Two Linux Computers Back-to-Back

This exercise requires either two Linux computers or two Windows computers from your laboratory.

Linux

1. Obtain a cross-over cable, or fabricate one according to the instructions in Appendix A. The computers will be configured according to the following diagram:

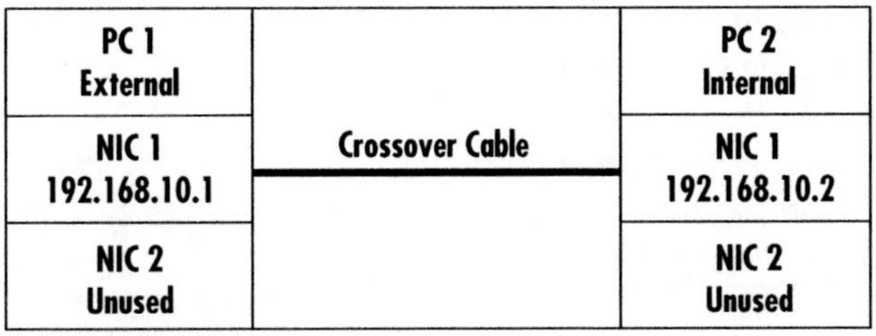

PC 1 External		PC 2 Internal
NIC 1 192.168.10.1	Crossover Cable	NIC 1 192.168.10.2
NIC 2 Unused		NIC 2 Unused

FIGURE 1.12 Connecting two PCs with a crossover cable.

2. Configure an IP address on each machine using the `ifconfig` command. (If you are unsure of the correct way to configure the IP address, refer to the `ifconfig` manual page via the `man ifconfig` command.)

3. Configure a default route on each PC using the route command.

4. When you have completed the configuration, demonstrate to your instructor connectivity between the internal and external computers using the ping command.

5. Use the `ifconfig` command to determine the MAC address of the NIC cards inside the internal and external computer.

6. Use the search tool available at IEEE.org to determine the manufacturer of the NIC card in each machine. (**standards.ieee.org/regauth/oui/index.shtml**)

Windows

1. Using two Windows computers back-to-back, use the Windows GUI to set the IP address.

2. On the Start menu, navigate to Settings. Select Network connections.

3. Find the icon for the wired Ethernet card that you have connected to the other computer and right-click it.

4. Select Properties and scroll down through the list of protocols to find Internet Protocol (TCP/IP). Select that entry and click the Properties button.

5. Click the radio button for "Use the following IP address," and select a suitable IP address and mask.

6. Do the same to the other machine, selecting a different IP address within the same subnet.

7. Start a command window and use the command ipconfig—all to determine the MAC address of the NIC cards inside the internal and external computer.

8. Use the search tool available at IEEE.org to determine the manufacturer of the NIC card in each machine. (**standards.ieee.org/regauth/oui/index.shtml**)

Project 1.2: Sniffing Network Packets Using tcpdump

Configure the back-to-back configuration as described in Project 1.1 and Figure 1.12. One method for doing this is to download the SLAX live-Linux distribution from the book Web site. Note that if you use the back-to-back configuration with a crossover cable, tcpdump will be able to see all the traffic when the NIC is put in promiscuous mode. If you find it easier to use an Ethernet switch, then you must use a montor port for this exercise. A broadcast hub is also acceptable.

Alternatively, if you have a different Linux distribution installed on a pair of computers, don't forget to install libpcap as well as tcpdump.

A final alternative is to use a pair of Windows machines. In this case, use winpcap and windump. If you have not used the SLAX distribution, you may need to install the following components:

1. Go to **www.tcpdump.org**

2. Use windump and winpcap (Windows) or tcpdump and libpcap (Unix/Linux). Read all of the instructions.

3. For Windows, download the latest winpcap installer. Close all applications and double-click to install.

4. Download the latest version of windump into a suitable directory (no installation, just an executable).

5. Open a command window and type:

   C:\<directory_of_windump>\windump.exe -i1

   -i1 means interface 1, (try -i2 or -i3 otherwise, until you see packet data scrolling through the window).

   (*Note:* If you are using a Windows machine, you may want to bump up the buffer length and screen width of your command window. To do this, right click on the blue bar at the top of the command window and click Properties, then click the Layout tab. Set the command history buffer to several hundred, and set the screen width to about 120. This will stop most lines from wrapping.)

6. If you have a Unix/Linux computer, follow the instructions for libpcap and tcpdump on **www.tcpdump.org**.

7. Use the tcpdump program on the internal machine to sniff the network traffic between the two computers. After starting tcpdumpon the internal machine, use the ping command from the external machine in this format:

   ```
   ping <ip_address_of_internal_machine>
   ```

8. Observe the tcpdump output. Use the manual page for tcpdump (man tcpdump) to determine the options necessary to log all ASCII output to the file /tmp/network.log and monitor the ping session again. View the output of /tmp/network.log and answer the following questions:

How did the output differ based on your command line arguments?

Provide a brief description of the traffic passing between the internal and external computers based on the tcpdump output you observe.

How do you think tcpdump can be useful?

Finally, save your tcpdump output if you plan to do the next project.

Project 1.3: Sniffing Network Packets Using Ethereal

Configure the back-to-back configuration as described in Project 1.1 and Figure 1.12. This project ideally requires you to complete Projects 1.1 and 1.2 first, so that you can compare tcpdump and Ethereal. If you have chosen not to do Project 1.2, simply ignore the portion of this project that compares tcpdump to Ethereal.

As with Project 1.2, this project requires an internal and external machine. One method to accomplish this project is to download the SLAX live-Linux distribution from the book Web site. Note that if you use the back-to-back configuration with a crossover cable, Ethereal will be able to see all the traffic when the NIC is put in promiscuous mode. If you find it easier to use an Ethernet switch, then you must use a monitor port for this project. If you have a broadcast hub available that is also acceptable.

1. Use the tcpdump program on the internal machine to sniff the network traffic between the two computers. After starting Ehereal on the internal machine, ping from the external machine to the internal machine and observe the Ethereal output. Answer the following questions:

   How did the output of tcpdump and Ethereal differ based on your command line arguments?

   Do you think Ethereal is more or less useful than tcpdump?

   Provide a brief description of the traffic passing between the internal and external computers based on the Ethereal output you observe.

Project 1.4: Experiment with Traffic Monitoring and Filtering in a Larger Network with a Broadcast Hub

This project is a moderately advanced project for readers who are familiar with networking. It requires a broadcast hub and several additional machines. You can use either Windows or Linux, or a combination of both machines. Depending on the size of your broadcast hub, you can support as many machines as it has ports.

The concept of this project is to obtain a trace of the ARP protocol in operation. Install any traffic monitoring software on one machine that is connected to the broadcast hub.

This project can be implemented by downloading the SLAX live-Linux distribution from the book Web site. However you will be limited to tcpdump as a traffic monitor. Otherwise, with Windows or Linux distribution installed to a hard drive, you can install Ethereal.

Filter the types of packets to obtain only ARP packets from the network. Specifically, focus on the ARP traffic and describe the step-by-step process that ARP uses to resolve an IP address to a MAC address. To do this, first begin from a client to ping to the IP address of another machine.

Use the following procedure:

1. Reboot all client machines to flush the ARP cache.

2. On a Linux machine, issue the command `arp -v -n` at a terminal. (On Windows type `arp -a` in a command window). This will display the arp cache.

3. Ping from a client machine to another machine (the sniffer must be active when you do this).

4. On a Linux machine issue the command `arp -v -n` at a terminal. (On Windows, type `arp -a`). This will display the arp cache. You should see a new entry for each machine pinged.

5. Obtain the trace of ARP packets and note the traffic.

6. Repeat the experiment pinging the IP address of the same machine.

7. Notice the difference between the first sequence of ARP messages and the second ping session. Was there any ARP traffic for the second ping session?

Write a two-page paper discussing the results of the ARP traces you obtained. Describe the step-by-step process that ARP uses to resolve an IP address of the server machine to a MAC address based on the ARP traces that you observed. If you are unsure, you can repeat the procedure above pinging a different machine to obtain another ARP trace.

Case Study

ResTech University installed a network in Tech Hall (its large 13 story residence hall) during the mid-1990s when the majority of students did not own computers. Based on wiring closet locations and the number of student rooms, four class C subnets were created to provide addresses for all students. See Figure 1.13.

Floor	Class C Range	Subnet Mask	Gateway
1-2	192.168.1.0	255.255.255.0	192.168.1.1
3-5	192.168.2.0	255.255.255.0	192.168.2.1
6-9	192.168.3.0	255.255.255.0	192.168.3.1
10-13	192.168.4.0	255.255.255.0	192.168.4.1

FIGURE 1.13 Tech Hall subnet configuration.

ResTech University uses Dynamic Host Control Protocol (DHCP) to provide IP addresses to students in all residence halls. However, the university chooses to configure DHCP with seven day leases in order to ensure students maintain the same address and can easily be located in the event of inappropriate activity from a given IP address. Due to this configuration and the fact that students occasionally bring more than one computer to campus, ResTech has run out of IP addresses for floors 1 to 2 and floors 6 to 9 during the last two semesters, while floors 3 to 5 and 10 to 13 have had several available addresses during the same semester.

ResTech is looking for a way to resolve the problem of running out of IP addresses while maintaining the seven day leases for computers. Provide a detailed description of how ResTech can resubnet the network to resolve this problem and allow for up to 900 computers in TechHall. (*Hint:* Think about supernetting. See Li et al. 1992)

What potential problems could this new configuration present for ResTech University?

Chapter 2

Transmission Control Protocol (TCP) and User Datagram Protocol (UDP) in Detail

Chapter Objectives

After reading this chapter and completing the exercises, you will be able to do the following:

- Explain the differences between TCP and UDP and the advantages of each protocol.

- Trace the flow of packets during a TCP session between two hosts defining the purpose of each field in the TCP header.

- Define the purpose of each field in the UDP header, and list the primary applications that use UDP.

- Define the difference between the source port and destination port in the TCP and UDP header.

- Explain how ICMP is useful for network testing, and use the ping and traceroute utilities for basic network diagnosis.

Introduction

To successfully design, configure, and maintain firewalls, it is important to have a thorough understanding of the flow of network packets and communication between hosts. This chapter will focus on TCP and UDP, two of the transport protocols that sit above IP in the TCP/IP stack, and how they are

FTP Data [20] FTP [21] SSH [22] Telnet [23] SMTP [25] HTTP [80] *(Service [port])*	DNS [53] bootps [67] bootpc [68] snmp [161] *(Service [port])*	
TCP *(Reliable)*	**UDP** *(Unreliable)*	**ICMP** *(Testing)*
IP *(Source IP Address s– Destination IP Address)*		
NIC – Device Drivers		

FIGURE 2.1 TCP/IP stack.

used for network communications. A thorough understanding of TCP and UDP will provide a basis for understanding how network traffic flows between hosts on the Internet, in order to prepare you for restricting traffic with a firewall.

Most applications on the Internet use the Transmission Control Protocol (TCP). TCP is a connection-oriented protocol that ensures reliable data delivery and has remarkable persistence in the face of many kinds of network and host outages. User Datagram Protocol (UDP) is a much more light-weight connectionless protocol that does not ensure reliability and, therefore, is only suited for small transmissions that are typically composed of a single IP packet. Certain important applications, such as Domain Name Service (DNS), use both TCP and UDP. Internet Control Message Protocol (ICMP) is another IP protocol and allows for control and test messages to cross the network.

Figure 2.1 illustrates how TCP, UDP, and ICMP fit into the TCP/IP stack. TCP, UDP, and ICMP are IP packets and sit on top of the IP layer. Specific applications or services use either TCP or UDP for communications.

The TCP State Machine

TCP is a connection-oriented protocol that ensures reliable data delivery and has remarkable persistence in the face of many kinds of network and host outages. RFC 793, the RFC document for the TCP protocol (Postel 1981), provides a full description of the TCP standard. It states:

The TCP is intended to provide a reliable process-to-process communication service in a multinetwork environment. The TCP is intended to be a host-to-host protocol in common use in multiple networks.

The success of the Internet is in part due to TCP and its ability to reliably communicate over the *local area network (LAN)* and the *wide area network (WAN)* using a variety of physical layers. LANs consist of high speed connections within the same building or campus environment where Ethernet, Fast Ethernet, and Gigabit Ethernet connections are typically used. WANs consist of systems in geographically different areas that are linked using connections from telephone companies including Frame Relay, T1, SMDS, ATM, and other types of telephone circuits. It doesn't matter whether network traffic is sent over a modem, ISDN, DSL, T1, or high-speed Ethernet connection; TCP guarantees the data will arrive reliably at the other end.

When a large amount of information needs to be transmitted between two hosts, TCP breaks the information into smaller, more manageable segments. The sending system then sends each packet individually, and the receiving system acknowledges each packet. If errors occur or the acknowledgments are not received, that portion of the data is retransmitted. Once the receiving system has received all of the packets, it reassembles the information into its original format. This process ensures a reliable means of communication.

TCP Session

A TCP session consists of the complete TCP conversation between two hosts, including the connection setup and disconnect. As illustrated in Figure 2.2, a TCP session can be broken down into three major areas:

- Three-Way Handshake (Establishing a connection)
- Established Mode (Transferring the data)
- Connection Teardown (Closing the connection)

A brief introduction to the components of the TCP header will be followed by a detailed description of the TCP session.

TCP Flags and Header Contents

IP allows for a variety of protocols and, therefore, the TCP header information comes after the IP header in the Internet datagram. Figure 2.3 shows the TCP header layout and all of the fields in the TCP header. A brief description and the size of each field follows:

Source Port (16 bits)
- The TCP port on the sending machine (0–65,535)

1. SYN
Three-Way Handshake
(Establish a connection)
2. SYN, ACK
3. ACK
4. ACK, DATA
ordered by sequence numbers
Established Mode
(Transfer the data)
Host
192.0.2.151
Port 2091
Web Server
192.0.2.10
Port 80
5. ACK, FIN
6. ACK
Connection Teardown
(Close the connection)
7. ACK, FIN
8. ACK

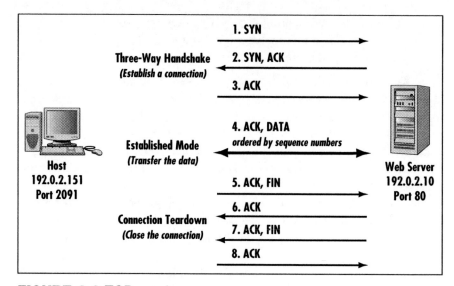

FIGURE 2.2 TCP session.

FIGURE 2.3 TCP header.

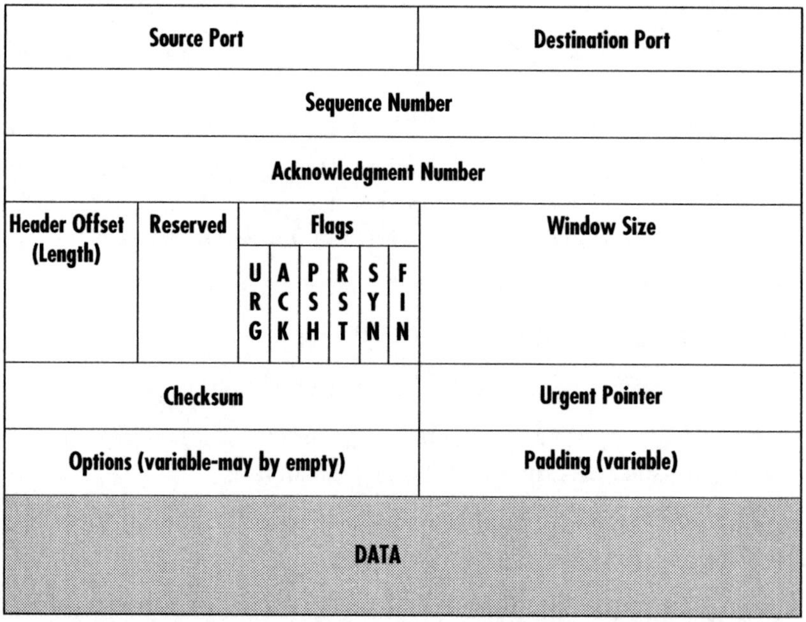

Source Port
Destination Port
Sequence Number
Acknowledgment Number
Header Offset (Length)
Reserved
Flags
URG
ACK
PSH
RST
SYN
FIN
Window Size
Checksum
Urgent Pointer
Options (variable-may by empty)
Padding (variable)
DATA

Destination Port (16 bits)

- The TCP port on the receiving machine (0–65,535)

Sequence Number (32 bits)

■ The sequence number of the first data octet in this segment. If the SYN flag is set, this field will contain the randomly chosen initial sequence number, sometimes referred to as the ISN.

Acknowledgment Number (32 bits)

■ If the ACK (Acknowledgment) flag is set, this field contains the values of the next sequence number the sender is expecting to receive. Once the initial connection is established, the ACK flag will always be set, and there will always be a value in this field.

Header Offset (4 bits)

■ The number of 32-bit words in the TCP header, thus indicating where the data begins.

Reserved (4 bits)

■ Reserved for future use. Will always be 0.

Flags (6 bits)

■ URG—Urgent Pointer field significant

■ ACK—Acknowledgment field significant

■ PSH—Push function

■ RST—Reset the connection

■ SYN—Synchronize sequence numbers

■ FIN—No more data from sender

Window Size (16 bits)

■ The number of data octets, beginning with the one indicated by the ACK field the sender is willing to accept.

Checksum (16 bits)

■ A checksum is calculated for each TCP segment and sent as part of the packet to ensure reliability. The checksum is calculated on the IP and TCP portion of the header as well as the data that is part of the segment (all 0s are used in the checksum portion of the header for checksum calculations).

Urgent Pointer (16 bits)

■ If the URG flag is set, this field contains the value of the urgent pointer as an offset from the sequence number in this segment.

Options (variable length in 8-bit increments)

■ Options are located at the end of the TCP header and can serve a variety of purposes.

Padding (variable size)

■ Because the Options field is of variable size, padding is used to ensure the TCP header is an even 32 bits in size.

The importance of the fields in the TCP header will become more apparent during the discussion of the TCP session. Before moving on to the TCP session, it is important to understand the difference between the source and destination ports.

TCP Ports

As indicated by the TCP header, each TCP packet has a source and destination port. Each TCP connection uses a specific port between 0 and 65,535. When a client/host establishes a network connection to a server, the client must know the IP address and port to use to contact the server. In most cases, the client will connect using the well-known port number for the service. Well-known ports are the standard port numbers used for specific services, such as FTP, Telnet, SMTP, DNS, and HTTP. Table 2.1 provides a list of several well-known TCP services and the standard ports they use for connections.

TABLE 2.1 Well-known ports for TCP services.

Service	Protocol	Port Number
FTP Data	TCP	20
FTP	TCP	21
SSH	TCP	22
Telnet	TCP	23
SMTP	TCP	25
DNS (Zone transfers only)	TCP	53
HTTP	TCP	80
POP3	TCP	110
Netbios-ssn	TCP	139
IMAP	TCP	143
LDAP	TCP	389
HTTPS	TCP	443
Microsoft-ds	TCP	445
Dynamically allocated ports	TCP	1024–65535

FYI: IANA

The Internet Assigned Numbers Authority (IANA) is responsible for assigning the TCP and UDP well-known ports in use on the Internet. A current list of TCP and UDP port numbers can be found at www.iana.org/assignments/port-numbers.

To help develop our understanding of the flow of packets, we will use a sample company in this example and in other examples throughout this chapter. A copy of this table is included on the book Web site if you wish to print it and refer to it as you read this chapter.

In the company layout of ABC Computers (Table 2.2), there are several departments, and each department has its own extension. If you call ABC Computers and wish to speak with someone in the marketing department, the call is directed to extension 80. If you want to speak with someone in the shipping department, the call is directed to extension 25.

The use of TCP port numbers is very similar to this idea of telephone extensions. When connecting to a Web server via an HTTP connection, the

TABLE 2.2 ABC Computers Directory.

ABC Computers Phone Number: (540) 555-1234 Fax Number: (540) 555-1235		
Contact	**Extension**	**Department**
Andrew Manufacturing	137	Manufacturing
Alex Marketing	80	Marketing
Annette Operator	53	Operator
Amy Sales	443	Sales
Amanda Service	22	Service
Anne Shipping	25	Shipping
Adam Support	23	Support
ABC Computers Customer List		
Name	**Phone**	
Connie Customer	(276) 555-6123	
Cliff Customer	(804) 555-6632	
Clarence Customer	(919) 555-6389	

Web browser connects to the IP address of the server and then specifically connects to the service running on TCP port 80. When connecting to the SMTP mail service, port 25 is used. When connecting to the secure Web service (HTTPS), port 443 is used.

IN PRACTICE: Telnet to a TCP Port

Telnet is a great application to help understand TCP connections. You can use telnet to connect to any TCP service by telnetting to the port the service is running on. To do this, add the appropriate TCP port number to the end of the telnet command.

```
telnet IP_Address PORT
```

To telnet to the SMTP mail port on a server, you would use:

```
telnet mail.example.com 25
```

Because telnet does not know what data the SMTP service is expecting to receive as part of the conversation, you will only see that the connection has been established. Once you see the connection, you know that the service is running on the server, and there are no network problems with the two computers talking with each other. If you know what data to send for the "conversation," you can enter this into the telnet window, although this is not often possible.

Caution

TCP Ports "Hiding"

Some administrators run services on nonstandard ports to enhance security and "hide" the service from potential attackers. Sophisticated attack tools will look for a variety of services on any port. You should never use security by obscurity as a means of protecting computers or information.

Unlike telephone extensions, a great deal of consistency and standardization of port numbers is on the Internet. As shown in Table 2.1, port 80 is the standard for every HTTP-based Web server on the Internet.

FYI: Typical Ports

Servers typically listen on ports lower than 1024. In the UNIX world, only "root" can launch a service running on a port number lower than 1024.

Clients usually open connections on ports 1024 to 65535.

Client-Side TCP Ports Our discussion of TCP ports up until now has focused on which port will be used on the server side. Now, we will look at which port the client will use in TCP communications.

To help understand this, take another look at the ABC Computers example. When calling ABC Computers, the person directing the call does not care what phone number the call originated from. The person will direct the call to whichever department the customer wants.

TCP communications operates in the same manner as this telephone call. The HTTP Web server on port 80 will accept the connection no matter what IP address and TCP port it originated from. The client computer uses a port in the ephemeral port range of TCP ports, which is between 1024 and 65535. The client will use a pseudorandom algorithm to pick one of the ports in this range to use for this TCP communication. Each time the client tries to establish a new connection to a server or service, it randomly selects a different TCP port.

If the client computer wishes to connect to the Web server at ABC Computers, it first chooses a pseudorandom port number from the ephemeral port range. Assume 2091 is the selected port. This will then be used as the client-side TCP port for this connection, and port 80 will be used for the server side port. After this connection takes place, if the client wishes to contact the mail server, it would generate a different pseudorandom port—assume 3102—and use this port for communications with the mail server on port 25.

The source address and port number, as well as the destination address and port number, will be key areas of focus for creating firewall rules. Therefore, you will need to become familiar with the commonly used services and their port numbers.

Three-Way Handshake (Establishing a Connection)

As indicated earlier, TCP provides a reliable means of communication between two hosts; therefore, it is imperative that the two hosts establish a logical connection or virtual circuit before data can be transmitted between the hosts. The setup of this connection is referred to as a "three-way handshake."

Figure 2.4 compares this three-way handshake to the beginning of a phone call between Connie Customer and Amy Sales. Before the conversation can begin, one party must call the other, and they will exchange a brief hello or "handshake" before beginning the "business" of the call.

The three-way handshake initializes the sequence numbers for both hosts in order to establish a reliable channel for the remainder of the TCP session. During this three-way handshake, the two systems randomly generate and exchange their ISNs. The following describes a TCP connection setup between a Web browser (client) and a Web server.

In this example, notice the client computer pseudorandomly chose to use port 2091 for the client side of the connection. This client-side port could have been any port in the ephemeral port range. Because the client is connecting to a Web server, the standard port for HTTP, port 80 is used on the server side of the connection.

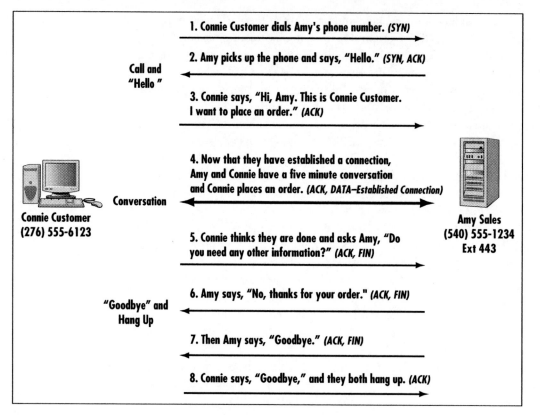

FIGURE 2.4 Telephone call compared to TCP session.

While reviewing this three-way handshake example, note the TCP header fields used and the values in each of these fields. (Refer to Figure 2.2 as you look at this connection setup.)

1. SYN (Packet from client to server)

   Source address: 192.0.2.151 Source port: 2091

   Destination address: 192.0.2.10 Destination port: 80

   • Hello Web server on port 80. I want to start a TCP session. Let's synchronize our sequence numbers. My randomly chosen ISN is 101 (SYN flag set).

2. SYN, ACK (Packet from server to client)

   Source address: 192.0.2.10 Source port: 80

   Destination address: 192.0.2.151 Destination port: 2091

   • Hello client on port 2091. I received your initial starting sequence number (ACK flag set), and the next sequence number I await from you is 102 (Acknowledgment Number). My randomly chosen ISN is 201 (SYN flag set).

3. ACK (Packet from client to server)

> Source address: 192.0.2.151 Source port: 2091

> Destination address: 192.0.2.10 Destination port: 80

- Hi again, server on port 80. I got your initial starting sequence number (ACK flag set), and the next sequence number I await from you is 202 (Acknowledgment Number). Go ahead and send me some data. The sequence number for this packet is 102.

Established Mode

Once the connection setup process has completed and the two hosts have exchanged and acknowledged ISNs, they are ready to begin sending and receiving data. At this point the two hosts have established a connection with each other and are operating in "established mode." Because this is a full duplex connection, both ends can transmit data at any time, even simultaneously.

> **FYI: Established Access Control List Entry**
>
> To allow the return traffic from the connection through a firewall, many firewalls and access control lists have a rule similar to the one below that allows return network traffic from established connections to pass through.
> PERMIT ANY 192.0.2.0 TCP ESTABLISHED

To maintain reliability and persistence, TCP relies on three main components:

- Order of segments through sequence numbers

- Checksums to maintain the internal reliability of each data segment and ensure it is free of errors.

- Flow control to regulate the data flow and keep from overwhelming slower hosts

TCP uses sequence numbers to order all segments of the TCP data transfer. The receiving system acknowledges each segment upon receipt. Due to network delays and other routing issues, TCP segments may arrive out of order. The robustness of TCP allows the receiving system to reassemble the segments into the proper sequence before they are reassembled to produce the original message.

In the following example, Steps 4a through 4c represent the data transfer during the established mode based on Figure 2.2. This indicates that three packets were transferred as part of the data transfer, but there may be many packets as part of the data transfer depending on the amount of data needing to be sent. To ensure the reliability of the TCP communication, an acknowledgment will be sent for every received packet.

4a. ACK, DATA (Packet from server to client)

Source address: 192.0.2.10 Source port: 80

Destination address: 192.0.2.151 Destination port: 2091

- I got your last packet and the next sequence number I expect from you is 103. Here is the first part of the Web page you are looking for.

4b. ACK, DATA (Packet from client to server)

Source address: 192.0.2.151 Source port: 2091

Destination address: 192.0.2.10 Destination port: 80

- I got the first part of the Web page. The next sequence number I expect from you is 203.

4c. ACK, DATA

Source address: 192.0.2.10 Source port: 80

Destination address: 192.0.2.151 Destination port: 2091

- I got your last packet and the next sequence number I expect from you is 104. Here is the rest of the Web page you are looking for.

The earlier illustration (Figure 2.4) of a telephone call between Connie Customer and Amy Sales at ABC Computers and the resulting order further illustrates how TCP sequence numbers and acknowledgments are used. As ABC Computers begins to process Connie's order, it is determined that it will require ten separate boxes to ship the complete order. Company policy dictates that all boxes weighing less than one pound are sent out via U.S. Priority Mail, and all boxes over one pound are shipped via United Postel Service (UPS). Signature confirmation is required for all shipments.

As specified in this order, eight of ten boxes need to ship via UPS, and two of the ten boxes via U.S. Priority Mail. Although the boxes are shipped via two separate carriers, they will arrive at the same physical address. This illustrates that all segments in a given TCP session are not required to take the same physical path. When the packages arrive, the carrier requires Connie to sign for the packages, acknowledging the receipt of the boxes. This makes it easy for both Connie and ABC Computers to determine if a box was lost along the way and reship any box that is missing.

TCP checksums ensure the validity of each segment as it arrives at the destination system. If any network anomalies along the way corrupt the packet, the checksum will be invalid, and the sending system will be required to resend that segment. This checksum can be compared to the packing list included with every box received from ABC Computers. The packing list ensures that the contents of each box are correct.

Flow control is accomplished in TCP through the use of window sizes and buffers. The TCP window size is slowly increased until congestion occurs. Once congestion takes place, the window size is cut in half. If further congestion occurs, the window size is adjusted appropriately. This allows hosts communicating via slow dialup connections to reliably communicate with servers on high-speed networks without overloading the dialup connection.

TCP connections remain open for long or very short periods, depending on the application. As an example, HTTP connections normally remain open for only a few seconds, while services such as telnet or ssh may remain open until the client computer closes the connection.

Connection Teardown

Once the TCP data transfer has taken place and the two hosts are ready to end the TCP session, the session must be closed. When either host determines the communication is complete, it sends a message with the Finish (FIN) flag set to 1. The other host then sends a return packet with an acknowledgment that a packet was received with the FIN flag set. It then sends its own Finish packet along with any remaining data indicating it is also ready to close the connection. Both hosts need to agree that they are ready to hang up, at which time the first host acknowledges this and they both hang up for a graceful connection teardown. (Refer back to Figure 2.2 as you look at this connection teardown.)

5. ACK, FIN (Packet from client to server)

   Source address: 192.0.2.151 Source port: 2091

   Destination address: 192.0.2.10 Destination port: 80

   • Hello, Web server on port 80. I got your last data packet (ACK) and your next sequence number is 220. I am ready to close the connection (FIN). The sequence number for this packet is 120.

6. ACK (Packet from server to client)

   Source address: 192.0.2.10 Source port: 80

   Destination address: 192.0.2.151 Destination port: 2091

   • Hello, client on port 2091. I received your FIN request (ACK).

7. FIN, ACK (Packet from server to client)

   Source address: 192.0.2.10 Source port: 80

   Destination address: 192.0.2.151 Destination port: 2091

   • Hello, client on port 2091. I received your last packet (ACK) and your next sequence number is 121. I got your request and I am ready to close the connection (FIN). The sequence number for this packet is 220.

8. ACK (Packet from client to server)

Source address: 192.0.2.151 Source port: 2091

Destination address: 192.0.2.10 Destination port: 80

- Goodbye, server on port 80. I got your last packet (ACK) and your next sequence number is 221. My sequence number for this packet is 121. I am closing the connection. (*Note:* The server closes its connection when it receives this packet and does not send back an acknowledgment.)

IN PRACTICE: Using TCPDump

As indicated in Chapter 1, tcpdump is an open source utility available on many UNIX platforms that displays the headers of packets on a network interface. The program WinDump is available for Windows computers and is a port of tcpdump to the Windows platform. This command requires privileged access to the network interface and, therefore, must be executed by the root user on UNIX systems.

Headers are captured based on an expression given when the tcpdump program is launched. The command `tcpdump src 192.0.2.151` would capture all of the packets with a source address of 192.0.2.151. The command `tcpdump dst 192.0.2.151` would capture all of the packets with a destination address of 192.0.2.151.

This utility provides an opportunity to view the header components of the TCP session. By running tcpdump during the connection discussed above, you can observe a detailed analysis of the packets that cross the network and the information from the TCP header.

```
root@slax> tcpdump host 192.0.2.151
```

This will capture all of the packets with either a source or destination address of 192.0.2.151. On the client computer, a Web browser window is opened to establish a connection to the Web server on port 80 of 192.0.2.10. The following is the output of the tcpdump program during this TCP session.

The first data we observe in the tcpdump output is the three-way handshake initiating the connection.

▶▶ CONTINUED ON NEXT PAGE

- The client 192.0.2.151 sends an initial sequence number of 3318894602.

- The server sends its initial sequence number 3138484209 and acknowledges receipt of the client's initial sequence number by adding one to this number and sending it back to the client 3318894603.

```
16:23:51.653808 IP 192.0.2.151.2091 >
192.0.2.10.http: S 3318894602:3318894602(0) win
65535 <mss 1460,nop,nop,sackOK>

16:23:51.653850 IP 192.0.2.10.http >
192.0.2.151.2091: S 3138484209:3138484209(0)
ack 3318894603 win 5840 <mss
1460,nop,nop,sackOK>

16:23:51.653985 IP 192.0.2.151.2091 >
192.0.2.10.http: . ack 1 win 65535
```

Once the initial handshake is completed, established mode begins with the actual data or conversation taking place between the two hosts.

- Each packet in established mode results in an acknowledgment.
- The acknowledgments increase as each packet is transferred.

```
16:23:51.659648 IP 192.0.2.10.http >
192.0.2.151.2091: P 1:83(82) ack 1 win 5840

16:23:51.867343 IP 192.0.2.151.2091 >
192.0.2.10.http: . ack 83 win 65453

16:23:52.732643 IP 192.0.2.151.2091 >
192.0.2.10.http: P 1:2(1) ack 83 win 65453

16:23:52.732660 IP 192.0.2.10.http >
192.0.2.151.2091: . ack 2 win 5840

16:23:52.828643 IP 192.0.2.151.2091 >
192.0.2.10.http: P 2:3(1) ack 83 win 65453

16:23:52.828651 IP 192.0.2.10.http >
192.0.2.151.2091: . ack 3 win 5840
```

CONTINUED ON NEXT PAGE

```
16:23:52.908422 IP 192.0.2.151.2091 >
192.0.2.10.http: P 3:4(1) ack 83 win 65453

16:23:52.908460 IP 192.0.2.10.http >
192.0.2.151.2091: . ack 4 win 5840

16:23:53.004501 IP 192.0.2.151.2091 >
192.0.2.10.http: P 4:5(1) ack 83 win 65453

16:23:53.004510 IP 192.0.2.10.http >
192.0.2.151.2091: . ack 5 win 5840

16:23:53.148251 IP 192.0.2.151.2091 >
192.0.2.10.http: P 5:7(2) ack 83 win 65453

16:23:53.148259 IP 192.0.2.10.http >
192.0.2.151.2091: . ack 7 win 5840

16:23:53.148369 IP 192.0.2.10.http >
192.0.2.151.2091: P 83:130(47) ack 7 win 5840
```

After the data transfer has taken place one of the hosts starts the connection teardown by sending a packet with the FIN flag set indicating the desire to close the connection.

- The server sends a FIN signal to close the connection, and both systems agree to close it.

```
16:23:53.148437 IP 192.0.2.10.http >
192.0.2.151.2091: F 130:130(0) ack 7 win 5840

16:23:53.148539 IP 192.0.2.151.2091 >
192.0.2.10.http: . ack 131 win 65406

16:23:53.148977 IP 192.0.2.151.2091 >
192.0.2.10.http: F 7:7(0) ack 131 win 65406

16:23:53.149002 IP 192.0.2.10.http >
192.0.2.151.2091: . ack 8 win 5840
```

Using tcpdump to carefully analyze the packet header information can help further develop an understanding of the components of the TCP header and the flow of network traffic.

Half Open TCP Scanning

A common practice of many port scanning utilities is to use a half open TCP connection to determine if a service is running on a given port while attempting to avoid detection. In a half open scan, the scanning host sends a SYN packet to the server to initiate the beginning of the three-way handshake. If a service is running on the specified destination port, the server responds with its own SYN packet and the ACK acknowledgment that it received the SYN packet. When the port scanning program receives the SYN+ACK return packet, it can assume a service is running on the port and there is no need to complete the remainder of the three-way handshake to establish a full connection. If no service is running on the given port, the server will send a RST (reset) packet indicating to the scanner that no service is running on that port.

Important TCP Applications

We will analyze in Chapter 6 the specific services that must be allowed to flow through the firewall. Most organizations need to allow SMTP, HTTP, and HTTPS traffic through. The following is a description of the primary TCP services that are present on most networks.

File Transfer Protocol (FTP)—Ports 20 and 21
- A protocol for transferring files both large and small across the Internet. FTP sends passwords over the network in plaintext and should be avoided if at all possible.

Secure Shell (SSH)—Port 22
- An interface and protocol to securely access the command line and files on a remote system. SSH provides the ability to securely do anything that can be done with telnet (ssh) and FTP (scp).

Telnet—Port 23
- An interface to remotely access the command line on a remote system. Telnet sends passwords over the network in plaintext and should be avoided if at all possible.

Simple Mail Transfer Protocol (SMTP)—Port 25
- Used to send and receive e-mail over the Internet. The UNIX sendmail program is the most dominant SMTP program used on the Internet.

Domain Name Service (DNS)—Port 53
- DNS looks up a given name and translates the name into an IP address. DNS primarily uses the UDP protocol for query and responses, but DNS does use TCP for transfer of zone information between master and slave DNS servers.

Hypertext Transfer Protocol (HTTP)—Port 80

- A protocol for the transfer of text, graphics, sound, video, and other multimedia files and resources over the Internet. Since the introduction of HTML in 1991 and the first graphical Web browser in 1993, HTTP has become one of the leading application protocols on the Internet.

Hypertext Transfer Protocol over Secure Socket Layer (HTTPS)—Port 443

- A secure protocol for the transfer of text, graphics, sound, video, and other multimedia files and resources over the Internet. Unlike HTTP, HTTPS packets are encrypted before being sent over the Internet to maintain confidentiality and security. Banking and Internet commerce sites should always use the HTTPS Protocol.

User Datagram Protocol (UDP)

User Datagram Protocol (UDP) is a connectionless protocol used for applications with short payloads. The most common UDP applications are BOOTP/DHCP, DNS, SNMP, and NFS. UDP is well suited for small applications that tend to ask a query and expect a small amount of information in return. Unlike TCP, UDP connections do not operate as a session, and there is no built-in reliability to guarantee the system on the other end actually received the packet. In comparison to the stateful nature of the TCP protocol, UDP is very basic and straightforward. UDP contains no flow control mechanisms; therefore, it can easily overload routers if large amounts of data are transferred.

UDP communications are similar to the way the U.S. Postal Service works. A credit card company generates a bill and mails the bill to a customer. The credit card company has no way of knowing for sure the customer received the bill, but it assumes it did. The customer then places a check in an envelope and sends a payment back to the credit card company. The customer does not get an acknowledgment that the payment was received until the next billing cycle. The U.S. Postal Service of course offers delivery confirmation and certified mail, but in its most basic form, there is no way of knowing for sure the other party received the mail.

A UDP exchange between two hosts results in only two packets crossing the network. A typical TCP exchange requires three IP packets to establish the connection, one or more packets for the actual data exchange, and four IP packets to end the connection. Therefore, UDP is well suited for applications requiring only a small amount of data transfer. Most UDP applications, including DNS, are query-and-response type of applications. With DNS, a system asks for an IP address of a given host based on a name, and the server responds with an IP address of the appropriate system. If this

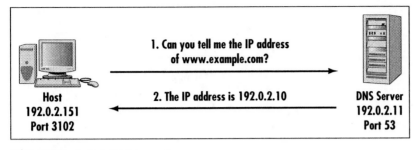

FIGURE 2.5 UDP transfer.

were done via TCP, it would take more time to establish the connection than the entire query and response takes with UDP.

Figure 2.5 is an example of a UDP connection between two computers where the client computer is making a DNS request to find the IP address of another system. The client computer pseudorandomly chooses 3102 as the port for its side of the communication and uses port 53 on the server side, since this is the well-known port used by all DNS servers.

1. Query packet from client to server

    Source address: 192.0.2.151 Source port: 3102

    Destination address: 192.0.2.11 Destination port: 53

    • DNS server on port 53, can you tell me the IP address for www.example.com?

2. Response packet from server to client

    Source address: 192.0.2.11 Source Port: 53

    Destination address: 192.0.2.151 Destination port: 3102

    • Client on port 3102, the IP address you asked for is 192.0.2.10.

UDP Header Contents

Like the TCP header, the UDP header comes after the IP header in the Internet datagram. Since UDP does not include accommodations for acknowledgments or flow control, the UPD header is short in comparison to the TCP header.

Source port (16 bits)

■ The UDP port on the sending machine (0–65,536)

Destination port (16 bits)

■ The UDP port on the receiving machine (0–65,536)

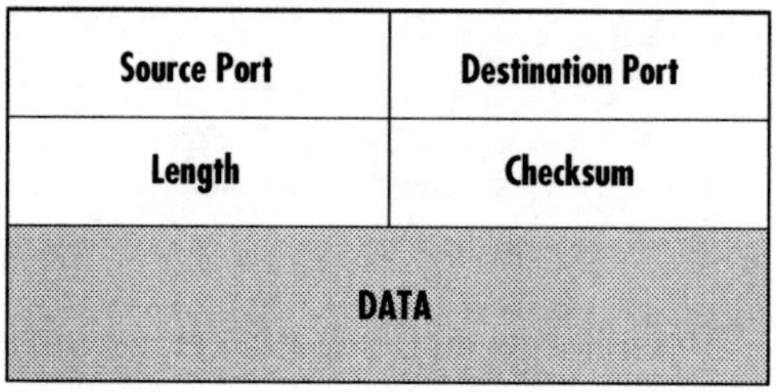

Source Port	Destination Port
Length	Checksum
DATA	

FIGURE 2.6 UDP header.

Length (16 bits)

■ The field specifies the length of the UDP datagram. The length of the UDP will always be at least 64 bits.

Checksum (16 bits)

■ Although UDP does not guarantee the packet will reach the receiving host, if the receiving host receives the packet, the checksum will ensure the data is valid. A checksum is calculated for each UDP packet and sent as part of the packet. The checksum is calculated on the IP and UDP portions of the header as well as the data that is part of the packet (all 0s are used in the checksum portion of the header for checksum calculations).

UDP Ports

As indicated by the UDP header, each UDP packet has a source and destination port. Each UDP service operates on a specific port between 0 and 65,535. Just as with TCP, when a client/host establishes a network connection to a server, the client must know the IP address and port to use to

TABLE 2.3 Well-known ports for commonly used UDP services.

Service	Protocol	Port Number
DNS	UDP & TCP	53
BOOTPS (DHCP server)	UDP	67
BOOTPC (DHCP client)	UDP	68
NTP	UDP	123
SNMP	UDP	161
SNMP-Trap	UDP	162
Syslog	UDP	514
Dynamically Allocated ports	UDP	1024–65535

contact the server. When establishing rules for a firewall, it is important to know the source and destination ports of the packets to permit or deny.

Important UDP Applications

We will analyze in Chapter 6 the specific services that must be allowed to flow through the firewall, but most organizations need to allow DNS traffic through. The following is a description of the primary UDP services that are present on almost every network.

Domain Name Service (DNS)—Port 53
- DNS looks up a given name and translates the name into an IP address. Because of DNS, users of the Internet do not need to know the IP address of every other system on the Internet. DNS uses TCP for transfer of zone information between servers.

Bootstrap Protocol (BOOTP)—Ports 67 and 68
- A protocol that automatically configures IP address information for systems.

Dynamic Host Configuration Protocol (DHCP)—Ports 67 and 68
- A more advanced version of BOOTP that allows for computers to lease an IP address for a given period of time.

Network Time Protocol (NTP)—Port 123
- NTP allows computers on the Internet to synchronize their time with a centralized time server. This ensures that all systems have the exact same time. It is crucial that all systems on a network have the exact same time. Without time synchronization, some security mechanisms such as Kerberos do not function properly. Time synchronization is also important when looking through log files for security and other problems; without proper synchronization, the time of events on different servers must be adjusted before they can be compared for anomalies.

Simple Network Management Protocol (SNMP)—Ports 161 and 162
- SNMP is a network management protocol that is used to monitor and manage any networking device, including switches, routers, and bridges.

Internet Control Message Protocol (ICMP)

Internet Control Message Protocol (ICMP) is another of the protocols in the TCP/IP stack and allows control and test messages to cross the network. ICMP messages are used to indicate when a packet is unable to reach its destination, when a gateway or router does not have the capacity to forward a packet, and when a shorter route should be used for packet

TABLE 2.4 ICMP message types.

Type	Description
0	Echo reply
3	Destination unreachable
4	Source quench
5	Redirect
8	Echo
9	Router qdvertisement
10	Router selection
11	Time exceeded
12	Parameter problem
13	Timestamp
14	Timestamp reply
15	Information request
16	Information reply
17	Address mask request
18	Address mask reply
30	Traceroute

delivery. They are also used to pass test messages between hosts (Postel, 1981). Due to the ability for test messages to create unwanted network traffic and help external users map the network, many firewalls disable portions of the ICMP functionality to enhance network security.

Table 2.4 provides a listing of the common types of ICMP messages.

ICMP Ping

The ping command is a useful troubleshooting utility that helps determine if a host is reachable or "alive." Ping makes use of the echo request and echo reply types. The following sample provides the output of a simple ping command.

```
bash-2.05b$ ping www.example.com

Pinging www.example.com(192.0.2.10) with 32 bytes
of data:

Reply from 192.0.2.10: bytes=32 time<1ms TTL=254

Reply from 192.0.2.10: bytes=32 time<1ms TTL=254

Reply from 192.0.2.10: bytes=32 time=328ms TTL=254
```

```
Reply from 192.0.2.10: bytes=32 time<1ms TTL=254
```

```
Ping statistics for 192.0.2.10:
```

```
Packets: Sent = 4, Received = 4, Lost = 0 (0%
loss),
```

```
Approximate round trip times in milli-seconds:
```

```
Minimum = 0ms, Maximum = 328ms, Average = 82ms
```

The output above indicates that the local computer has network connectivity with **www.example.com**, which is IP address 192.0.2.10. It also indicates the time it took for each of the echo-reply packets to return. The local host sends an echo-request to 192.0.2.10 and the remote system sends an echo-reply back to the local host.

ICMP TraceRoute

Traceroute is a utility that traces the network path or route a packet takes from the local system to a remote host or network. Traceroute generates packets with very small Time to Live (TTL) values. When a router or gateway receives the packet, it subtracts one from the TTL and, if it is zero, an ICMP Time Exceeded message is sent back to the originating host. Therefore, traceroute can use the TTL feature to determine each router a packet reaches by starting with a TTL of 1 and increasing the TTL by one until it reaches the target host.

```
bash-2.05b$ traceroute www.example.com
```

```
traceroute to www.example.com (192.0.2.10), 30
hops max, 40 byte packets
```

```
1 router1.example.com (192.0.2.20) 0.287 ms 0.244
ms 0.249 ms
```

```
2 inet-router.example.com (192.0.2.25) 0.648 ms
0.479 ms 0.472 ms
```

```
3 gw1-router2.example.com (192.0.2.45) 2.147 ms
1.805 ms 2.418 ms
```

```
4 www.example.com (192.0.2.10) 7.195 ms 7.929 ms
7.717 ms
```

Even though ICMP traffic is useful for troubleshooting and network testing, the potential threat of Denial of Service attacks (DoS) or Smurf attacks—where echo requests and echo replies are used to flood a network—has resulted in ICMP echo request and echo reply being disabled by many firewalls. It is important to analyze the benefits of these ICMP types with the security risks when setting up the firewall.

DNS in Details DNS has been mentioned throughout this chapter as an application that is very important to the Internet. Although DNS is a service rather than a protocol, it is important to understand how to use nslookup for several of the end-of-chapter exercises, which will further clarify TCP and UDP concepts. Therefore, this section will provide additional details on DNS and how to use nslookup to query DNS servers.

DNS provides IP address look-up services for everyone on the Internet. DNS operates on the same premise as a phone book. Computers on the Internet can only talk to each other via IP addresses. A user cannot be expected to memorize the IP address of every system on the Internet; therefore, DNS looks up a fully qualified domain name and returns the appropriate IP address for that system. The application can then pass the appropriate IP address to the TCP/IP stack, and the appropriate connection will be established.

The nslookup utility can be used to query a DNS server and determine the IP address of a given host. In the example below, the client connects to the server dnsServer.example.com and requests the IP address for www.example.com. The server responds with the IP address 192.0.2.10 for the www.example.com server.

```
Bash-2.05b$ nslookup www.example.com

Server: dnsServer.example.com

Address: 192.0.2.11

Name: www.example.com

Address: 192.0.2.10

Aliases: www.example.com
```

To guarantee network reliability, most organizations have two or more local DNS servers. DNS operates as a distributed database. Therefore, if a local DNS server does not have the requested name and IP address in its local cache, it contacts one of the root DNS servers to determine who can provide an authoritative answer to the question. Once the IP address has been found, the DNS server caches the information for future queries on the same name and returns an answer to the client.

Since computer users will try to connect to other systems on the Internet by entering a host name, DNS must operate properly for people to be able to use the Internet. Therefore, DNS is the first service to address when configuring a firewall. Systems use UDP port 53 to query the DNS server for information, so UDP traffic to port 53 must be appropriately allowed to pass through the firewall. In addition, DNS uses TCP as a reliable mechanism to transfer zone maps between master and slave servers. This zone map transfer is a server-to-server transfer among other DNS servers that have authoritative information for the same zone.

DNS Problems

DNS problems often look like a network outage to the average user. If the DNS server(s) are down or blocked by the firewall, network users may report that their computer is down and they cannot connect to anything on the network.

As a method of troubleshooting, users should be instructed to try connecting directly to the IP address of a server to help rule out the possibility of a DNS problem. If a user is unable to connect to the Web server www.example.com, she should try to connect to the same system using the IP address 192.0.2.10 to make sure there is no name resolution problem. Technicians may wish to use nslookup "nslookup www.example. com" to make sure the computer resolves the name properly.

The same is true when using applications such as netstat for troubleshooting. The –n flag should be used to prevent netstat from resolving names.

Summary

This chapter provides an introduction to TCP, UDP, and ICMP and the flow of traffic between hosts. You should now understand the TCP three-way handshake as well as the source address, destination address, source port, and destination port of packets as they travel between hosts. It is important to understand these basic networking principles before moving on to the firewall configurations in later chapters. If you are unclear on any of this information, review the figures in the chapter and make sure you understand how they represent the flow of traffic. The exercises at the end of this chapter will help you grasp these concepts.

Test Your Skills

MULTIPLE CHOICE QUESTIONS

1. Both TCP and UDP are _____ packets.
   A. IP
   B. ICMP
   C. EHP
   D. SYN

2. The success of the Internet is in part due to _____ and its ability to reliably communicate over the LAN and WAN.
   A. UDP
   B. TCP
   C. ICMP
   D. IP

3. TCP provides a(n) _____ process to handle communi-
   cation service in a multinetwork environment.
   A. efficient
   B. fast
   C. reliable
   D. secure

4. On most UNIX servers, system services run on ports
   A. below 4096.
   B. above 1024.
   C. below 1024.
   D. between 1024 and 65535.

5. Port 80 is the standard well-known port for this service:
   A. SMTP
   B. HTTP
   C. HTTPS
   D. SNMP

6. The only time the ACK flag will not be set in a TCP segment is
   A. when the first packet is transmitted.
   B. when the data packets are transmitted in established mode.
   C. when the last packet is transmitted.
   D. This flag will always be set.

7. When the SYN flag is set in the TCP header it indicates that
   A. no acknowledgment will be sent.
   B. an initial sequence number is in the sequence number field.
   C. there is data in the sequence number field.
   D. there is data in the acknowledgment number field.

8. The FIN and ACK flags are set as part of the
   A. connection setup.
   B. established mode.
   C. connection teardown.
   D. data transfer.

9. _____ is a lightweight, connectionless protocol that does not ensure reliability and, therefore, is only suited for small transmissions that are composed of a single IP packet.

   A. UDP

   B. TCP

   C. IP

   D. ICMP

10. This service operates over both TCP and UDP and provides an IP address lookup service for all computers on the Internet:

    A. SMTP

    B. SNMP

    C. DNS

    D. DHCP

11. _____ require a source port and a destination port.

    A. TCP packets

    B. UDP packets

    C. ICMP packets

    D. TCP and UDP packets

12. TCP uses _____ for flow control.

    A. acknowledgment numbers

    B. checksums

    C. sequence numbers

    D. window sizes

13. TCP uses information from the IP header and the TCP header, as well as the data to calculate the

    A. sequence number.

    B. checksum.

    C. window size.

    D. acknowledgment number.

14. The _____ indicates the next sequence number a host expects to receive.

    A. acknowledgment number

    B. sequence number

    C. header offset

    D. checksum

15. _____ provides a secure command line interface for remotely managing hosts.

    A. Telnet

    B. FTP

    C. SSH

    D. SMTP

16. ICMP is not used to provide which of the following?

    A. time exceeded

    B. echo

    C. echo reply

    D. host IP addresses

17. A UDP exchange between two hosts results in at least _____ packets crossing the network.

    A. one

    B. two

    C. seven

    D. seven or more

18. _____ is used to automatically configure IP address information.

    A. DHCP

    B. DNS

    C. BIND

    D. NTP

19. DNS uses a _____ database to get information about hosts that are not local.

    A. cached

    B. distributed

    C. local

    D. SQL

20. _____ is like a phone book, in that, when you enter a fully qualified name of a host on the Internet, it looks up the IP address of that host.

    A. NFS

    B. DNS

    C. NTP

    D. DHCP

EXERCISES

Exercise 2.1: TCP and UDP Comparison
Describe the differences between TCP and UDP, and list the advantages of each protocol.

Exercise 2.2: Listening and Established Services

1. Run the following four commands on a UNIX or Windows host:

   ```
   netstat
   ```

   ```
   netstat -n
   ```

   ```
   netstat -a
   ```

   ```
   netstat -an
   ```

2. Write a one to two paragraph description of the information provided by each command.

3. Write a summary of the differences among each of the commands; include why you would use each command.

4. Using a computer running Windows XP Service Pack 2 or later, run the command `netstat -b` and indicate how this output differs from the previous output. How might this information might be useful?

Exercise 2.3: netstat with SMTP Connections

1. Use the telnet command to telnet to the SMTP mail port on the campus mail server.

   telnet mail.university.edu 25

2. In another window on the same machine, use the `netstat -n` command to determine the source and destination ports of this connection.

3. Describe in detail the three-way handshake that took place to establish this connection.

Exercise 2.4: netstat with DNS Connections

1. Use nslookup to find the IP address of the campus mail server.

2. Immediately after running this command, execute `netstat -an`.

3. Does this connection appear in the list? Why or why not?

Exercise 2.5: DNS and nslookup

1. Use DNS to look up the IP address of two hosts on campus and two hosts off campus. What happens if you do not use the fully qualified domain name?

2. Use DNS to look up Windows update **www.windowsupdate.com** several times. Do you get the same address each time? Why or why not?

PROJECTS

Project 2.1: Network Mapping

1. Use nslookup and traceroute (UNIX) or tracert (Windows) to create a diagram of important systems and servers on the campus network. At a minimum, this map should include the following systems:

   DNS server(s)

   DHCP server

   Mail server

   Web server

   FTP server if one exists

2. For each host you place on the map, you should include:

   Fully qualified name of the host

   IP address

   Any service that runs on this host

   The port number of the service

   Whether the service is TCP or UDP

3. On a Windows host you may be able to use `ipconfig /all` from the command prompt (Start -> Run -> cmd) to gather some of this information.

Project 2.2: Use netstat to Map the SLAX System

Create a SLAX CD from the ISO image included on the book Web site. (See Appendix A for additional details.)

1. Boot a computer with the SLAX CD into server mode with the "Linux server" boot command.

2. Use the `netstat` command to create a list of all TCP services running on the machine.

Project 2.3: Understanding TCP with Tcpdump

Use two computers from your laboratory for this exercise. Before beginning, obtain a crossover cable, or fabricate one according to the instructions in Appendix A.

The computers will be configured according to Figure 2.7.

1. Use the `ifconfig` command to appropriately configure the IP addresses of the computers as indicated by Figure 2.7.

2. Use the `ping` command to ensure connectivity between the two machines.

3. Use the tcpdump program on the internal machine to sniff the network traffic between the two computers.

4. After starting tcpdump on the internal machine, telnet from the external machine to the internal machine and observe the tcpdump output.

5. Ping the internal machine from the external machine.

   ```
   ping 192.168.10.2
   ```

6. Telnet to the mail port on the internal machine.

   ```
   telnet 192.168.10.2 25
   ```

FIGURE 2.7 Connecting two PCs with a crossover cable.

PC 1 External		PC 2 Internal
NIC 1 192.168.10.1	Crossover Cable	NIC 1 192.168.10.2
NIC 2 Unused		NIC 2 Unused

7. Type quit to close the SMTP connection.

```
quit
```

8. View the output of /tmp/network.log and answer the following questions:

What traffic and protocols are present in the log file?

Provide a brief description of the traffic passing between the internal and external computers.

What part of each TCP session do you see in the log?

What information from the TCP header is shown in the log file?

List the log file entries associated with each of the following components of the TCP session:

- three-way handshake
- established connection
- connection teardown

Project 2.4: Understanding TCP and UDP Packet Headers

For this project you may use any computer connected to the Internet. Assume that you have just opened a Web browser such as Internet Explorer or Mozilla Firefox and are trying to connect to the url **leaf.sourceforge.net** to view the Leaf Web site.

1. Use ifconfig (UNIX or Linux) or ipconfig /all Windows) to determine the IP address of the local computer.

2. Use nslookup to determine the IP address of the DNS server your computer is using and the IP address of leaf.sourceforge.net.

3. List the IP header for the packet that was sent from your computer to the DNS server during the nslookup of **leaf.sourceforge.net**. Your header must contain the following fields:

Protocol

Source Address

Destination Address

Source Port

Destination Port

2

4. Use your Web browser to connect to **leaf.sourceforge.net**.

5. Create a sample IP header for the first packet that was sent from your computer to the leaf.sourceforge.net Web server. For any fields that must be present and for which the computer would use a random or arbitrary number, use a similar number.

   Protocol

   Source Address

   Destination Address

   Source Port

   Destination Port

   An example of any sequences or acknowledgment numbers that would be in this first packet

   Any flags that are set

6. Answer the following questions:

   What UDP service will be used to assist in establishing this connection?

   What port does this UDP service operate on?

   What TCP Port will be connected on the remote system?

   What TCP Port will be used on the local system?

The beginning of each school year brings a new set of problems to ResTech University. This year, a major network slowdown was detected as students returned to the residence halls. The Helpdesk has cleaned several computers infected with a new variant of the Korgo virus but knows other students still must be infected. To assist the Helpdesk in locating infected computers, the network administrator has enabled logging on the router that connects the school to the Internet.

Note: The computers at ResTech University use the IP address range 192.0.2.1–192.0.2.254.

1. What protocol and ports does the Korgo virus use?

2. What should the technicians look for in the log file that would indicate a computer is infected?

3. The network administrator knows that infected computers have an IRC server running on TCP port 113. What can the network administrator do to verify whether these computers have something running on port 113?

Assuming that Exhibit 2.1 is an excerpt of the log file, answer the following questions:

4. Which on-campus computers are infected, and what indicates this?

5. Which off-campus computers are infected, and what indicates this?

6. Which protocol and ports would the network administrator need to block to prevent further computers from being infected?

EXHIBIT 2.1

```
list 114 permitted tcp 192.0.2.1(1828) ->
137.45.126.5(25)

list 114 permitted tcp 192.0.2.2(3938) ->
137.45.62.121(445)

list 113 permitted tcp 198.82.155.45(1211) ->
192.0.2.55(445)
```

CONTINUED ON NEXT PAGE

```
list 114 permitted tcp 192.0.2.18(9587) ->
120.3.159.18(443)

list 114 permitted tcp 192.0.2.2(3939) ->
137.45.62.128(445)

list 114 permitted tcp 192.0.2.2(3940) ->
137.45.62.133(445)

list 114 permitted tcp 192.0.2.18(8912) ->
198.82.139.22(445)

list 114 permitted tcp 192.0.2.2(3941) ->
137.45.62.145(445)

list 113 permitted tcp 198.82.155.45(1212) ->
192.0.2.77(445)

list 113 permitted tcp 137.45.3.1(80) ->
192.0.2.49 (2311)

list 114 permitted tcp 192.0.2.1(1828) ->
55.186.126.5(25)

list 114 permitted tcp 192.0.2.18(8913) ->
198.82.139.32(445)

list 114 permitted tcp 192.0.2.8(6923) ->
198.8.160.129(443)

list 113 permitted tcp 137.45.126.5(6932) ->
192.0.2.1(25)

list 113 permitted tcp 198.82.155.45(1213) ->
192.0.2.93(445)

list 114 permitted tcp 192.0.2.18(8913) ->
198.82.139.32(445)

list 114 permitted tcp 192.0.2.14(7523) ->
198.8.160.129(443)
```

CONTINUED ON NEXT PAGE

2

CONTINUED

```
list 114 permitted tcp 192.0.2.18(8914) ->
137.45.3.1(80)

list 114 permitted tcp 192.0.2.2(3942) ->
137.45.62.221(445)

list 114 permitted tcp 192.0.2.18(8915) ->
198.82.139.89(445)

list 113 permitted tcp 198.82.155.45(1214) ->
192.0.2.129(445)
```

Note: The first address in the list is the source address and port, and the second address is the destination address and port.

Part Two

Firewall Basics

Part Two introduces several types of firewalls and takes an extensive look at installing the firewall, creating a firewall policy, and understanding how firewall rules and policies affect network traffic.

- **Chapter 3:** Software, Small Office, and Enterprise Firewalls
- **Chapter 4:** Threats, Packet Filtering, and Stateful Firewalls
- **Chapter 5:** Illustrated Exercises in Basic Firewall Installation
- **Chapter 6:** Determining the Requirements for the Firewall
- **Chapter 7:** Introduction to Advanced Firewall Concepts and Terminology

Chapter | 3

Software, Small Office, and Enterprise Firewalls

Chapter Objectives

After reading this chapter and completing the exercises, you will be able to do the following:

- Outline the basic types of hardware and software firewalls.
- Acknowledge the importance of personal firewalls.
- Distinguish between incoming and outgoing traffic.
- Recognize the role of IPTABLES and access control lists (ACLs).
- Test the firewall with programs and external scanners.

Introduction

The number of firewalls available on the market today makes it difficult to choose one. This chapter provides an overview of the major hardware and software firewalls to help you understand the range of products available. Although this book will focus on the open source LEAF Bering firewall, it is not appropriate for all environments. In a large corporation with many requirements, often an enterprise firewall is the only practical solution.

Access control lists (ACLs) and *IPTABLES,* which are rules that determine whether to allow or deny a network packet to pass, are the basic building blocks for many firewalls. An understanding of these concepts is necessary for the successful configuration of the firewall, so an introduction to these concepts here will prepare you for later chapters.

Before installing a firewall, it is beneficial to have a baseline report of the internal network ports that are open for attack. Several tools exist to help scan the network to determine which ports are open from the Internet. These tools can help determine if the firewall is configured correctly and performing its intended task. This chapter will provide an introduction to several online and open-source tools you can use to scan the network for open ports.

Hardware and Software Firewalls

Numerous firewalls are available on the market today, and as information security needs grow, new firewalls are introduced on a regular basis. In addition to traditional enterprise firewalls, firewall features have been incorporated into many networking devices, and personal firewalls are now offered with most operating systems. The number of available choices of firewall solutions makes it a challenge for both users and administrators to know which device will provide the needed level of protection.

The major types of firewalls are classified as follows:

- Routers as firewalls (packet filters)
- Standalone proxies, or application firewalls
- Enterprise firewalls
- Small office/home office (SOHO) firewalls
- Personal firewalls/host-based software firewalls

This section will provide a brief overview of these types of firewalls.

To choose the appropriate firewall technology, you must keep in mind the following factors:

- Budget
- Size of the organization and number of network nodes
- Level of protection needed
- Risk of intrusion and loss of data
- Level of vendor support needed
- Time required to install and manage the firewall

When setting up a security infrastructure, you will need to consider a layered approach to network security. In other words, there may be multiple devices providing some level of firewall protection between a user's computer and the Internet. This layered approach to network security is often referred to as ***defense in depth*** or security in depth (Northcutt 2003; Miles 2004). As each of the firewall categories is described, it is important to recognize how the firewall can act in conjunction with other layers of defense to provide more complete network and computer security.

Routers as Firewalls

A router is a device with two or more network interfaces that determines, for each packet arriving on an interface, what the output interface should be. Although routers are not thought of as firewalls, most routers include functionality to filter incoming and outgoing packets. Routers inspect the packet header, providing an initial layer of defense as traffic enters the network. Figure 3.1 illustrates the router as the boundary device at the edge of the corporate network connecting the company to the Internet. Although the router only provides stateless inspection, some traffic is malicious and should never pass this boundary router. Therefore, the router should be configured to deny or drop this most hazardous network traffic.

Routers use access control lists (ACLs) to look at the IP packet header information for every packet entering or leaving a given router interface. Administrators must create one list to filter incoming traffic and a separate list to filter outgoing traffic. An interface is not required to include both incoming and outgoing rules; however, if an interface has one, it will also typically

3

FIGURE 3.1 Network diagram: router and enterprise firewall.

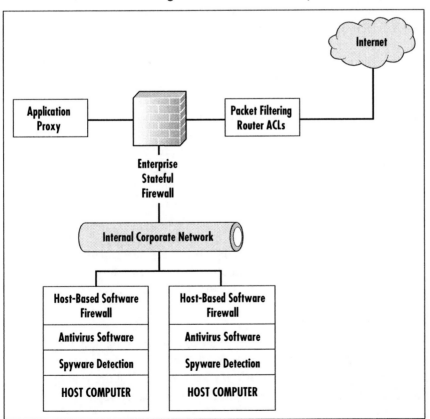

have the other. By configuring ACLs on the router, you put the first layer of defense in place. Access lists will ensure certain types of traffic are denied entrance to the network at the earliest possible point.

ACLs are useful, but since routers were not designed to serve as network firewalls, they do not usually include well-designed management interfaces to update the access lists. This makes using a router for more than an initial layer of defense cumbersome. As the number of entries in an ACL grows, the amount of time required to manage the list increases. Improper configuration of access lists can also impact the router's performance, so it is important to consider what rules are placed on the router.

Routers, therefore, should be used to provide the initial layer of defense for malicious and spoofed network traffic that should never enter the network. Another tool or product should be used for additional firewall functionality.

Standalone Proxies or Application Firewalls

The second layer of defense usually includes application firewalls, or *proxies.* Proxies are specialized firewalls that are tailored for specific protocol such as HTTP, SMTP, ARP, or FTP. Proxy servers are typically used to improve performance by caching results and to filter requests to servers that should be blocked or servers that might provide malicious content. An open-source proxy server called Squid (**www.squid-cache.org**) is available for use with the firewall used in the book.

A good example of this type of firewall is a Web server proxy. All Web service requests from clients on the internal network to well-known port 80 (Web service) are sent to the proxy. The proxy may inspect the contents of the HTTP protocol payload (usually a GET request for a Web page) to ensure the safety of the request. If the request passes various tests, it is forwarded to the actual Web server. Since the proxy server actually sent the request to the Web server rather than the client machine, the response is sent back to the proxy server. The proxy server then validates that the packet is a valid HTTP response, checks the payload for malicious data, and forwards the packet to the client on the internal network.

Many firewalls now have built-in proxy features; these are sometimes referred to as application gateways or content filtering capabilities. They go a step beyond proxy servers and look inside the payload for words, phrases, or malicious scripts to determine whether to allow or deny the traffic.

Enterprise Firewalls

Although the focus of this book is open-source firewalls, it is important to understand the significance of commercial enterprise firewalls as alternatives. Enterprise firewalls perform a wide array of functions and provide a management interface to assist with the daily task of updating and maintaining the firewall.

Enterprise firewalls have been designed from the ground up to serve as a security gateway for the network. These products provide enhanced features, management capabilities, and proprietary options that are not present in many open-source solutions. When you select an enterprise firewall, you will need to carefully evaluate the organization's needs and how the firewall meets each of those needs. This selection process should not only include technical capabilities, but the level of support and response time for problems.

Several enterprise firewalls are on the market today. They can be categorized as either software or hardware. Software firewalls allow you to purchase and install the software on hardware you purchase and maintain. Hardware firewalls are typically network appliances. The vendor provides the hardware and software in a single, integrated box. If you have extensive experience configuring hardware and feel comfortable loading your own software, a software firewall may be the best choice. If you would prefer to rely on one vendor for hardware and software support, a hardware firewall will provide a more complete solution.

The following list contains many of the enterprise-level hardware and software firewalls available today:

- Software Firewalls (run on an existing machine):

  Checkpoint Firewall 1

  Microsoft ISA Server

  Symantec Enterprise

- Hardware Firewalls (dedicated appliance):

  Cisco PIX firewall

  Nokia (Runs Checkpoint Firewall 1)

  SonicWall

  NetScreen

  Watchguard

As with any firewall solution, configuration in enterprise firewalls is key. Most enterprise firewalls rely on rules-based configurations and can be quite complex to understand without the proper training. Therefore, training is essential to maximizing the effectiveness of these firewalls.

Finally, enterprise firewalls can be quite expensive, depending on the size of the network. Therefore, it is important to analyze the features carefully.

Small Office/Home Office (SOHO) Firewalls

With the popularity of telecommuting on the rise, many people are creating offices in their homes. A small office/home office (SOHO) router can serve as a firewall and a router, providing the first layer of security for the home network. SOHO firewall devices, sometimes referred to as a Personal Firewall Appliances (Wack 2002), allow the user to protect a home network. As illustrated in Figure 3.2, the SOHO router usually serves as the home network's gateway to the Internet.

Linux Firewalls as SOHO Firewalls and Enterprise Firewalls

Open-source Linux firewalls have become popular for SOHO use. With the introduction of netfilter as a part of the Linux kernel, it is simple to add this functionality to any Linux-based system. The use of a Linux core for firewall functionality and routing has grown to the point that even companies like Linksys are using an embedded version of the Linux kernel for some of their equipment (**www.linksys.com/support/gpl.asp**). The main advantage of an open-source, Linux-based firewall is the complete configurability and number of options that can be added. If some functionality is not present, there may be a package available in the open-source community that can be added to the firewall.

Because of the low overhead and the dedicated purpose, these Linux-based firewalls can run from older computers that you may think are no longer usable—computers with slower CPUs and very little memory.

FIGURE 3.2 SOHO firewall diagram.

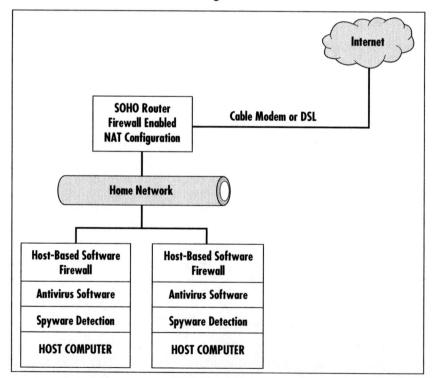

The main disadvantage of using a non-commercial (i.e., open-source) Linux firewall in the SOHO environment is the need for a technology expert who can build the necessary installation media (CD-ROMs, diskettes, etc.) and who has the detailed knowledge of networking required to configure these firewalls. Most open-source Linux firewall packages do not include a user-friendly step-by-step installation guide for the person new to networking, nor is there an intuitive GUI interface for the management of the firewall.

One of the purposes of this book is to use a Linux-based firewall as a tool to introduce you to the basic principles of network security and to help you learn strategies for configuring a firewall. The remaining chapters will serve as a guided tour of exercises in increasing difficulty, through the most popular capabilities that SOHO users want from a firewall. Chapter 7 will cover how Linux firewalls can serve as complete SOHO firewall solutions. Chapter 8 will introduce the additional capability of VPNs and show how open-source Linux firewalls can scale to the level of enterprise firewalls.

Commercial Firewalls for Small Office Environments Commercial firewalls for the SOHO environment are available from several companies that offer low-priced ($50 to $300) devices. Their main advantage is the "plug and play" nature of the devices and minimal, easy-to-understand configuration options. The main disadvantage of SOHO routers and firewalls is their lack of sophisticated features, such as content inspection. Low-priced commercial firewalls for the SOHO market may lack VPN capabilities and support for advanced applications like NetMeeting H.323 connections. However, as the popularity of these devices increases, these features are slowly being added to even relatively inexpensive devices.

Linksys, NETGEAR, and D-Link are a few of the vendors that offer equipment for the SOHO market. With the introduction and proliferation of broadband connections and 802.11 wireless networking, many of these devices have become very affordable. Often, people who purchase these devices either do not check to see if firewall functionality is included or simply do not turn on this capability. Most vendors have now resorted to enabling the firewall by default and making the user turn it off if he or she does not need the functionality.

Personal Firewalls: Host-Based Software Firewalls

Using the defense in depth (or layered security) approach, the local network may be protected from the Internet via an enterprise firewall, home office firewall, or a restrictive set of router ACL filters. This does not, however, protect hosts against internal network attacks. Employees of a corporation or students at a university may bring security threats inside the organization's security perimeter on any media, including downloaded CD-ROM images, floppy diskettes, zip disks from their homes. Another way that threats can be carried into an organization is via laptops. With the increase in portability and functionality of mobile computing and the widespread presence of broadband connectivity, a laptop computer is often used outside of the protection of the corporate firewall. Via either of these scenarios, security threats can be borne inside the security perimeter.

These threats include viruses and worms, which, in recent years, frequently install ***Trojan horses,*** or backdoor programs that continually seek out other computers to infect. Usually, the carrier of these Trojan horses is unaware that his computer is even infected. In these instances, any computer plugged into the same IP subnet as the infected machine is at risk of being attacked. Figure 3.3 illustrates the importance of a software firewall on the host machine.

The risk of internal network attacks can be demonstrated through the difficulties many university networks have had in recent years as students return to school with desktop or laptop computers that have been infected at home. Virtually all university residence halls are provided IP subnets that lead to the campus network and the Internet. These residence hall IP subnets are usually provided to an entire building. Routers separate IP subnets

FIGURE 3.3 Defense in depth in a wireless environment.

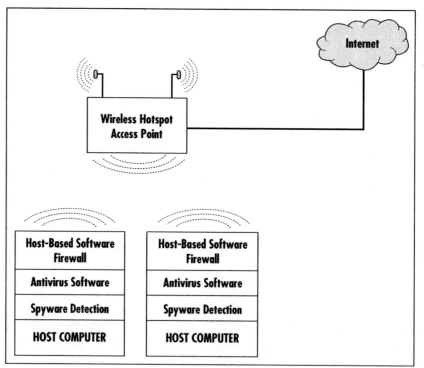

from each other. If one student brings back an infected computer, no matter how many firewalls or filters the university has in place, they do not prevent the computer from trying to attack every computer in the building, if the network is subnetted by building. The only protection from other computers on the same subnet is locally installed personal firewall software.

To prevent this type of situation, all users should have software providing sufficient protection. We suggest the following:

- Personal host-based firewall—monitors incoming connections and only allows approved packets or return traffic from established connections. Good software firewalls also inspect and prevent inappropriate outbound connections.

- Antivirus software—inspects files on the computer against a known database of virus signatures to detect and remove infected files. This software requires weekly database updates to be effective.

- Spyware software—blocks pop-up ads, browser hijacking, and other malware that might send personal information to a central server. Like antivirus software, this software must be updated regularly to detect new exploits.

- Optional intrusion detection software.

These packages are usually distinctly separate pieces of software, but many vendors have begun to bundle software suites that provide all three of these functions.

These security packages routinely provide notification messages (as in Figure 3.4) and dialog boxes when a potentially suspicious program is activated. These messages are often difficult for the end user to understand,

FIGURE 3.4 Windows XP security alert.

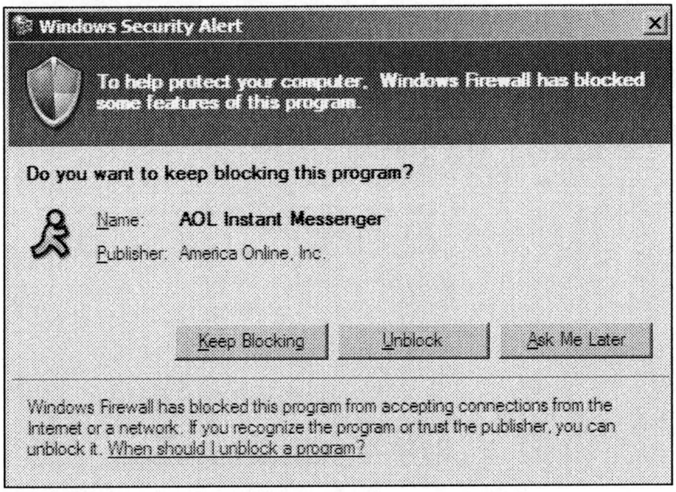

however. Most users are not security experts and may not know how to respond when a dialog box asks if a port or application should be unblocked. The user's response to a dialog box can mean the difference between being infected with, or staying safe from, a new virus or Trojan.

Unlike enterprise firewalls and router ACL filters, software firewalls directly impact the end user. The professionals responsible for network and information security in a company or organization have the key role of configuring the necessary software firewall rules and educating the user community.

Users should be trained to interpret carefully dialog box messages resulting from security software. If the message is related to an application they know should be running or a link they have clicked, it is probably safe to allow it. For example, in Figure 3.4, the user has just launched AOL Instant Messenger. The Windows firewall has detected an incoming port connection and is giving the user three choices: Keep Blocking, Unblock, or Ask Me Later. This message is easy enough for the user to understand and respond to, but if the application had not been specifically identified as "AOL Instant Messenger," the user might have found it difficult to interpret.

Another example of a message that is difficult to understand is shown in Figure 3.5. In this example, a message from Microsoft Access warns that unsafe expressions—macros, or other functions internal to an Access database are not blocked. We use this example to illustrate two issues:

FIGURE 3.5 Microsoft Access 2003 unsafe expressions alert.

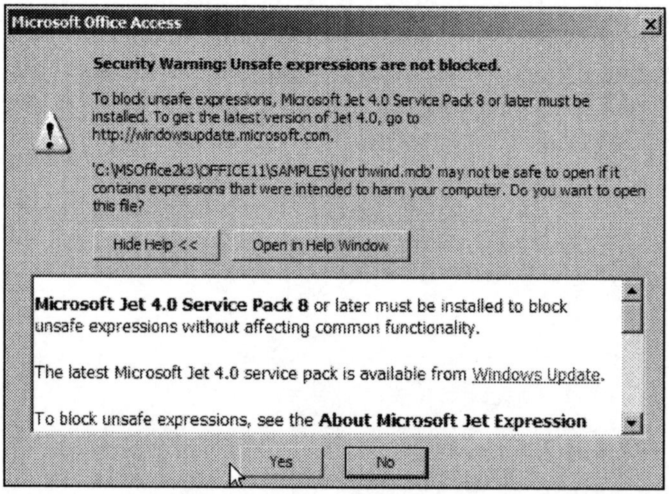

- A warning message that is difficult to understand

- A security threat that no software firewall can prevent: worms, viruses or other unsafe expressions within common Microsoft Office applications like Word or Access

This message is confusing for several reasons. First, the user is told that to block unsafe expressions, Jet Express Service Pack 8 must be installed. Second, a detailed message about the database that is causing a suspected problem appears: "C:\Program Files. . . . Do you want to open this file?" Instead of Yes or No buttons below the question, users are presented with Hide Help or Open in a Help Window. The Yes and No options are at the very bottom of the dialog box.

The repetitive appearance of the message displayed in Figure 3.5 will be annoying to any user. On the other hand, messages that announce each and every threat that was successfully blocked should be suppressed, if at all possible, so the user is not overwhelmed.

Many personal firewalls are on the market today, and the choices can be quite overwhelming. When choosing a personal firewall, it is important to consider the level of functionality it provides. At a minimum, it should include both inbound and outbound network filtering (Granger 2003). More advanced firewalls may include host-based intrusion detection capabilities to provide additional protection from sophisticated attacks.

Windows XP Firewall

Understanding the widespread need for local software firewalls on computers connected to the Internet, Microsoft has incorporated a software-based firewall as part of the Windows XP operating system. The initial release of Windows XP included the Internet Connection Firewall (ICF). With the introduction of Service Pack 2 for Windows XP, the ICF has been replaced by the Windows Firewall. The Windows Firewall (see Figure 3.6) is turned on by default on all computers when Windows XP Service Pack 2 is installed.

The Windows Firewall is a stateful software firewall that inspects all incoming traffic. The management interface enables users to specify ports and application exceptions to allow through the firewall. The Windows Firewall does not inspect or restrict outgoing traffic.

The Windows Firewall offers a first step in providing a host-based software firewall to users. If a company, organization, or individual cannot afford to purchase and support a more advanced host-based software firewall, the Windows Firewall is a good, *free* alternative. It does not provide the amount of configuration options available from other security vendors, but it does provide protection for incoming traffic.

The Windows Firewall configuration screen can be reached from the Security Center icon in the Control Panel, which is available on computers

3

Caution

Only One Software Firewall

Although multiple software firewalls can be installed on a computer, you should use only one firewall package at any given time. Determine which software firewall meets your needs, and disable or uninstall all others on the computer. This will prevent any conflicts between different software firewalls.

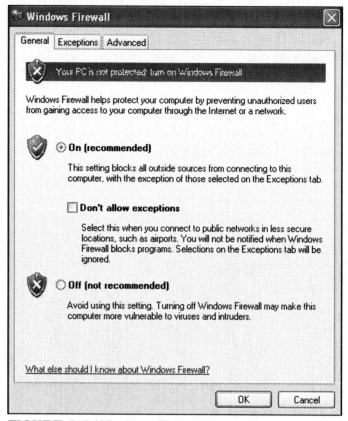

FIGURE 3.6 Windows Firewall main page.

running Windows XP Service Pack 2 and later. The Windows Firewall configuration screen can also be reached by clicking on the Change Windows Firewall settings icon on the Network Connections page.

The Exceptions tab (Figure 3.7) on the Windows Firewall configuration screen allows specific exceptions to be made for ports and applications.

- Instead of fully opening a port, if the port can be tied to a specific application, the access is more appropriately restricted.

- If an application or port does need to be opened, restrict it to only the subnet or subnets that need explicit access, if possible. Do this by selecting Edit on the program or service and then selecting Change Scope.

- If remote assistance will not be used, disable it.

- If possible, disable file and printer sharing, as this is one of the commonly misused services. If sharing is absolutely necessary, try changing the scope and only allowing access to this from "My network (subnet) only"(see Figure 3.8).

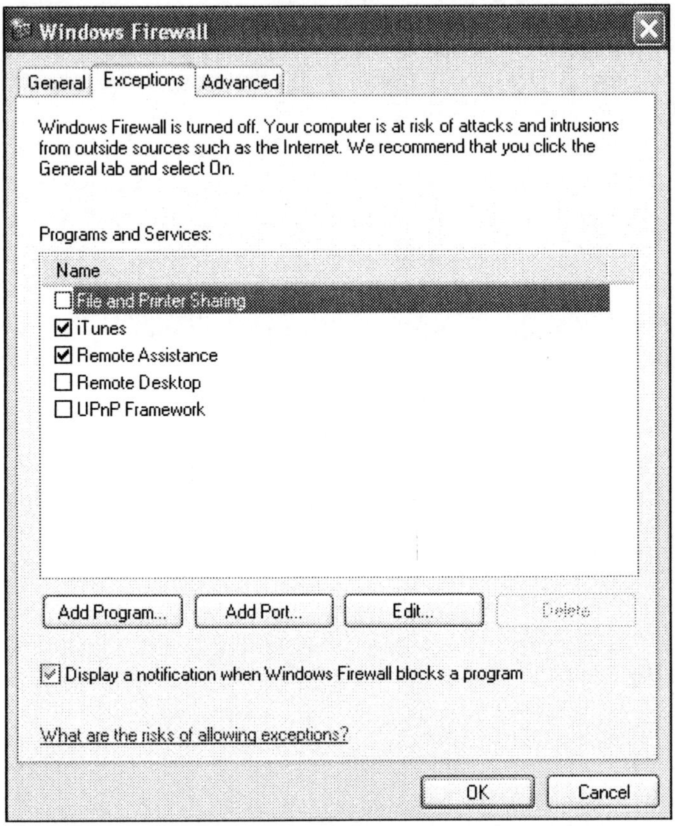

FIGURE 3.7 Windows Firewall Exceptions tab.

The Advanced tab in Figure 3.6 provides access to the details of logging and ICMP via the Settings button. By default, logging is disabled on the Windows Firewall. However, without the ability to review the log file

FIGURE 3.8 Changing scope in Windows Firewall.

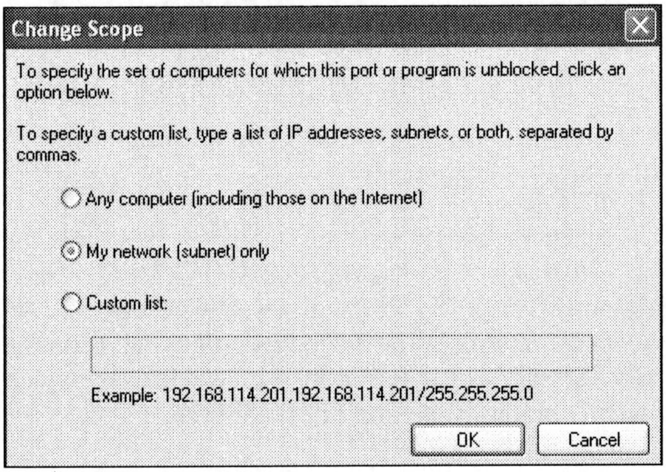

from time to time, you would find it difficult to determine if the firewall was functioning properly. Therefore, it is a good practice to, at a minimum, enable logging of Dropped Packets. Note the default location of this log file: c:\Windows\pfirewall.log.

ICMP settings are accessible from the Advanced tab shown in Figure 3.6. ICMP allows for diagnostics, testing, and reporting of error conditions. The Windows XP firewall provides a list of ICMP types you can

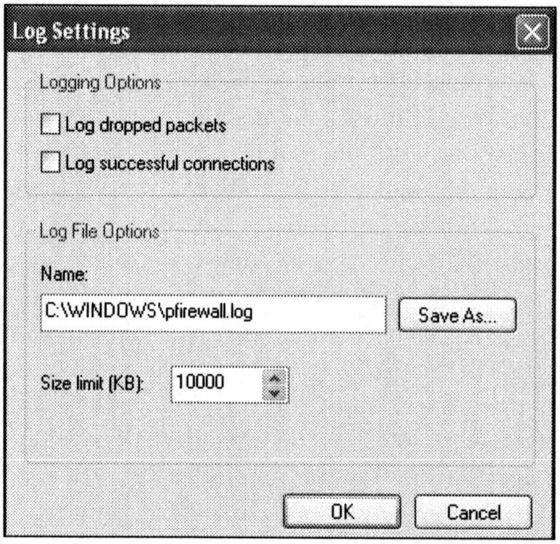

FIGURE 3.9 Logging options in Windows Firewall.

individually allow or deny. In its default mode, all of the listed ICMP types are denied by the Windows Firewall. Ping, one of the most common network troubleshooting tools, relies on echo request and echo reply ICMP messages. Therefore, if you wish to allow an external machine to ping a Windows XP host, you must place a check in the box to "Allow incoming echo request." ICMP ping floods and other ICMP Denial of Service (DoS) attacks have caused many network administrators to disable ICMP echo request and echo reply traffic at the boundary of the network.

FYI: ICMP and File Sharing

If the File and Printer Sharing services are allowed on the Exceptions tab then you cannot modify the ICMP settings for "Allow incoming echo request." The Windows Firewall requires echo requests to be allowed if TCP port 445 is enabled, which is enabled when you allow File and Printer Sharing.

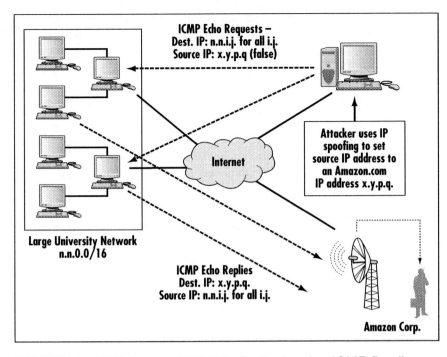

FIGURE 3.10 February 2000 DDoS attack using ICMP flooding.

A now famous ICMP Distributed Denial of Service (DDoS) attack that occurred in February 2000 involved amazon.com and is shown in Figure 3.10. This attack used the ICMP flooding technique mentioned earlier and another attack method called IP spoofing. You will learn more about these and other threats in Chapter 4.

IP spoofing is performed when a computer programmer writes a program that creates a false source IP address. In this case the programmer used a known IP address within the internal network of amazon.com. The programmer also knew the IP address range of a university (we use a class B address block for this example). The programmer then iterated through all possible IP addresses within that Class B block. Some did not exist, but others were present.

Apparently, the university allowed pings (ICMP echo requests) to enter from the Internet. Each university computer that responded sent an echo reply back to the IP address of amazon.com, resulting in degraded service.

Zone Alarm

Zone Alarm goes a step beyond the Windows Firewall by monitoring and restricting outgoing network traffic as well as incoming traffic. Zone Alarm is available at **www.zonelabs.com** and is arguably the most popular free personal firewall on the market. Zonelabs sells a professional version of the firewall with enhanced functionality, but the free version offers an extremely capable set of firewall features. Just like the Windows Firewall, Zone Alarm provides firewall protection for port connections as well as program control by monitoring and restricting applications that connect to the network.

For example, if a computer is infected with a Trojan that is establishing an outgoing connection, the Windows Firewall may never see it. However, Zone Alarm will detect this outgoing connection and provide a prompt to the user as to whether or not to allow the action.

Immediately after the installation of Zone Alarm, the user will begin getting pop-up messages for every program that tries to access the network. He will have to take a little time to read the messages and determine whether to allow the program to run and whether to "Remember the setting." Figure 3.11 provides an alert message for an outgoing SSH connection. To keep this alert from coming up every time an SSH connection is established, the "Remember the setting" checkbox must be checked. For every application known to be safe or correct, the "Remember the setting" checkbox must be clicked to prevent this alert from coming up every time the application is executed.

Zone Alarm relies heavily on the concept of zones, as do most firewalls. A *zone* is a collection of computers on a network that has a certain level of trust. Zone Alarm uses two security zones: the Internet Zone, representing insecure computers on the Internet, and the Trusted Zone to define other computers on the local network or Internet that are trusted. The connections to the Trusted Zone are less secure. This is because computers in the Trusted Zone are expected to follow a company policy or are part of a SOHO internal network. A single computer or range of computers can be added to the Trusted Zone. Figure 3.12 shows an example of the security zones in Zone Alarm.

Zone Alarm provides additional functionality beyond the incoming firewall provided by Windows Firewall, but the extra effort involved in configuring the software and knowing how to respond to the many pop-ups may confuse end users. Nevertheless, Zone Alarm is definitely a product worth considering as a personal firewall.

BlackICE

Internet Security Systems, Inc (ISS) is one of the leading vendors of intrusion-detection systems on the Internet. ISS's Web site is located at **www.iss.net**. Their BlackICE PC Protection product provides not only firewall and application protection, but integrates intrusion detection and prevention capabilities as well. This package goes a step beyond the

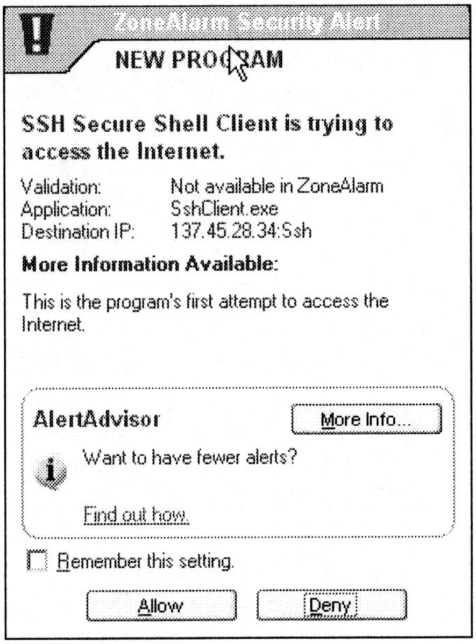

FIGURE 3.11 Outgoing SSH connection alert.

FIGURE 3.12 Firewall and zone settings.

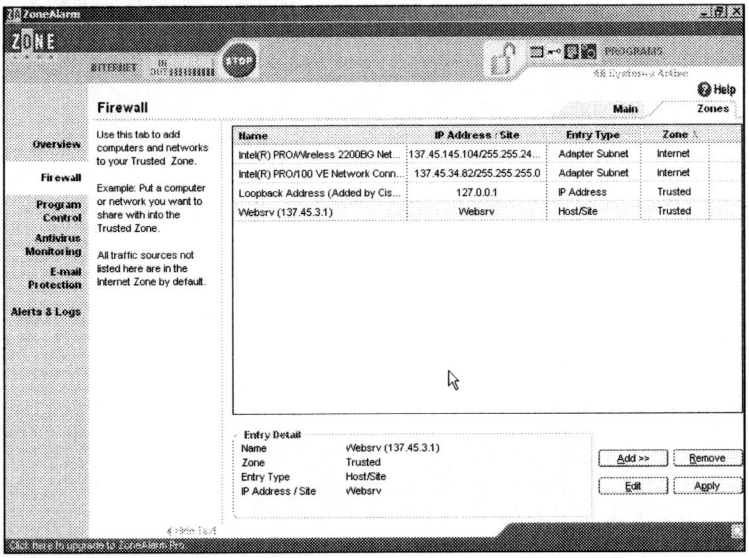

features of both Windows Firewall and Zone Alarm by detecting systems on the network trying to break in or attack and deny access to those systems.

Mac OS X Firewalls

As with most modern operating systems, the Apple Macintosh OS X includes a built-in firewall. Unfortunately, the firewall is turned off by default in the standard OS X installation. OS X is based heavily on the Berkeley Software Distribution (BSD) and therefore includes a stateful IPFirewall (ipfw) as part of the OS kernel. The ipfw is similar to iptables (see the section following introducing iptables). The OS X firewall can be enabled from the control panel by clicking the Sharing icon. Once the Sharing icon is selected, click on the Firewall tab and click the Start button. The window should then indicate that the firewall is on as shown in Figure 3.13.

Much like the Windows XP firewall, the OS X firewall blocks all incoming connections and allows all outgoing connections. The one distinction the OS X firewall has over the Windows XP firewall is that it is capable of blocking outgoing connections if it is configured using the command line options for ipfw.

The graphical interface allows limited configuration of the firewall. To add an exception to the incoming rules, click the New button on the Firewall tab and select the appropriate application from the Port Name list. As show in Figure 3.14, if you select MSN Messenger as the Port Name, the Port Range 6891-6900 is automatically entered allowing incoming connections on these ports.

The OS X graphical interface allows you to make simple changes to the firewall rules, but it does not provide access to the sophisticated features available from the ipfw package. To access the full potential of the built-in firewall, you need to use the UNIX command prompt. By opening a terminal window on the computer, you can observe the full configuration of the firewall. While logged in as root, execute `ipfw -a list` at the command prompt to view a detailed list of the firewall rules.

```
[mac-osx-client:/tmp] root# ipfw -a list

02000 1654 123904 allow ip from any to any via lo*

02010    0      0 deny ip from 127.0.0.0/8 to any in

02020    0      0 deny ip from any to 127.0.0.0/8 in

02030    0      0 deny ip from 224.0.0.0/3 to any in

02040    0      0 deny tcp from any to 224.0.0.0/3 in

02050    8    850 allow tcp from any to any out

02060    4    716 allow tcp from any to any established

02070    0      0 allow tcp from any to any 5900 in
```

```
02080    0    0 allow tcp from any to any 3283 in

02090    0    0 allow tcp from any to any 6891-6900 in

02100    0    0 allow tcp from any to any 22 in

12190    0    0 deny tcp from any to any

65535 6251737 5420061234 allow ip from any to any
```

This illustrates the basic rule set installed on the firewall. Rule 02050 allows all outgoing connections. Rule 02060 allows return traffic from established TCP sessions. Rules 02070-02100 allow incoming traffic on specific ports, and then finally Rule 12190 denies all other incoming traffic.

Advanced rules that would block or allow a specific IP address or range of IP address can be added via the command line interface.

```
ipfw add allow tcp from any to 192.0.2.10 80 in
```

FIGURE 3.13 OS X Firewall with Secure Shell Service allowed.

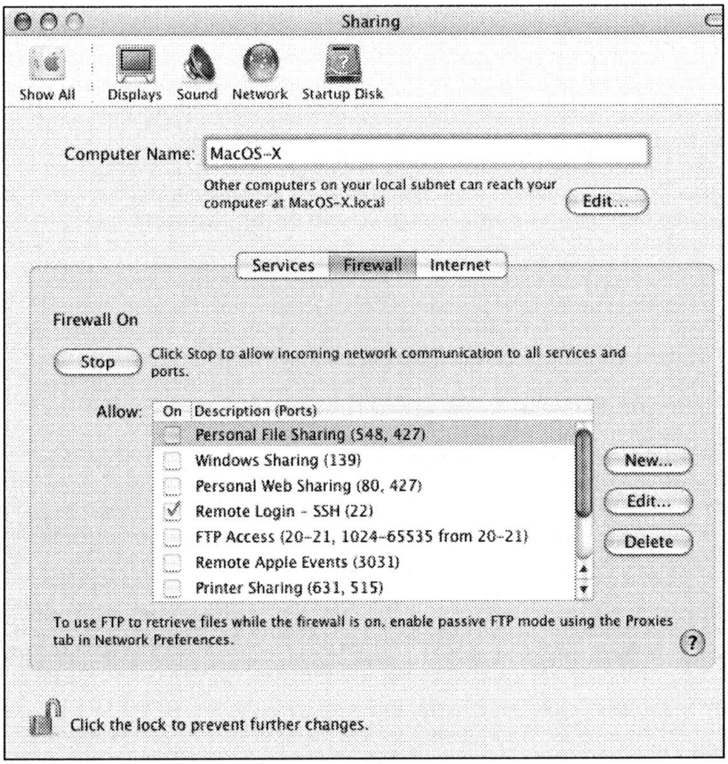

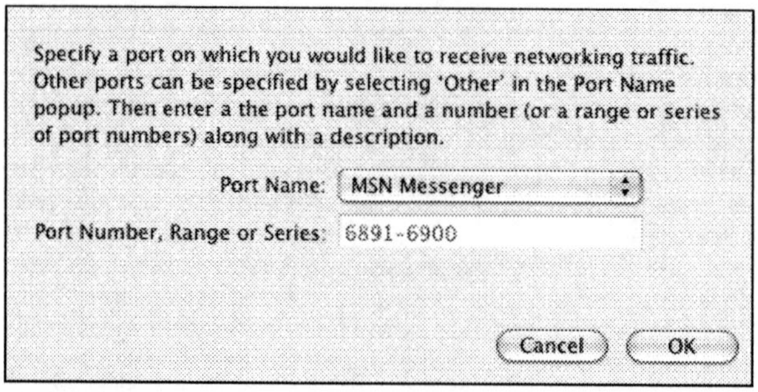

Specify a port on which you would like to receive networking traffic. Other ports can be specified by selecting 'Other' in the Port Name popup. Then enter a the port name and a number (or a range or series of port numbers) along with a description.

Port Name: MSN Messenger

Port Number, Range or Series: 6891-6900

Cancel   OK

FIGURE 3.14 OS X Firewall port exceptions.

Note here the word "in" at the end of the line can be replaced with "out" to restrict or allow outgoing connections.

Several packages have been developed to provide a more complete graphical configuration tool for configuring the ipfw rules. Brian Hill's BrickHouse (**brianhill.dyndns.org**) and Netcitadel's Firewall Builder (**www.netcitadel.com**) provide GUI-based interfaces to easily customize the ipfw rules.

Commercial OS X Firewall Packages As with Windows XP, there are numerous third-party firewall applications available that attempt to improve on the built-in OS X firewall. The built-in OS X firewall provides quite an extensive set of features and functions, therefore making it difficult for third-party products to provide a better firewall. The main advantage of third-party firewall packages for the OS X environment is that they allow the average user to configure the firewall properly. These firewall packages also include popup alerts to notify the user when an intrusion is detected. The primary OS X firewall packages include:

- NetBarrier X3 (www.intego.com)

- FireWalk X2 (www.pliris-soft.com)

- Norton Personal Firewall 3.0 (www.symantec.com)

- IPNetSentry X (www.sustworks.com)

Macworld rates the NetBarrier X3 firewall as its Editor's Choice due to its simple user interface, detection of unauthorized connections, and user alerts of external attacks (Battersby 2005).

Inside the Firewall: ACLs and IPTABLES

As previously discussed, firewalls implement rules that classify incoming or outgoing packets. By classification, we mean an attempt to inspect parts of the packet's header and, sometimes, the content. Once a packet is classified, rules determine whether the packet should be allowed to enter or leave the network. This decision is called the "action" of the rule. Cisco ACLs in Cisco routers and iptables in Linux are the software systems that implement these rules.

- ACLs rely on a list of statements entered at the command line interface.

- Iptables rely on a "chain," which is a series of rules.

Although ACL features exist in virtually every router, Cisco Systems is a market leader in data network equipment, particularly routers. Cisco equipment is widely used throughout business, government, and education. ACLs are the facility in Cisco routers that determines whether a packet should be allowed to access the network.

Cisco ACLs begin with statements, which are order-dependent, at the command line. For example:

`access-list` access-list-number {deny | permit} ….

In addition to ACLs, Network-Based Application Recognition (NBAR) is a feature of Cisco routers that alters the type of service (TOS field of the IP header) of the packet. Cisco gives a good comparison of ACLs and NBAR (Cisco Systems, September 2004), with an application to blocking the code-red threat. The MARK capability of iptables is similar to the NBAR feature in Cisco routers, as shown in Table 3.1.

In Linux, as of kernel 2.4 and beyond, a facility called iptables was implemented (see **www.netfilter.org/**). Iptables is the basis of the Linux firewalls used in this book. Similar to ACLs, Iptables use order-dependent commands. (For more information on iptables, see Chapter 6.) In Table 3.1, we compare several features of Cisco routers and the iptables facility.

Firewall Testing

As with any firewall configuration, appropriate testing is necessary to ensure that an enterprise firewall is properly configured. Misconfiguration is the key failure in most corporate and enterprise firewalls. Many security experts and consultants are available to help audit security configurations and perform penetration tests. Many users, however, do not want to hire an expert to test their security configuration, especially since configurations can change daily. In the next two sections we review several tools available to network administrators or computer users for testing firewall configurations.

Online Scanners

The first and often easiest method for a computer user is to make use of an online scanner. Several online tools and resources are available on the

Internet performing automated scans to test for common vulnerabilities and exploits against a computer.

- www.hackerwatch.org/probe
- www.pcflank.com/scanner1.htm
- www.dslreports.com/scan
- www.hackerwhacker.com/freescan.php
- www.securityspace.com

TABLE 3.1 Comparing Cisco ACLs and iptables.

Cisco ACL Parameter or Other Feature	Cisco Action	IPTABLES Rule Option	IPTABLES Action
PERMIT	Allow the packet to proceed	ACCEPT	Allow the packet to proceed
DENY	Silent discard	DROP	Silent discard
N/A	None, always continues with list	RETURN	Stop processing chain
N/A		REJECT	Non-silent discard, generates ICMP message
N/A		REDIRECT, DNAT	Changes destination IP address and/or port (port forwarding)
LOG	Generates log message	LOG	Generates log message
Cisco NAT / NPAT feature	Changes source IP address and/or port	MASQUERADE, SNAT	Changes source IP address and/or port
NBAR feature	Changes TOS bits, re-classify packets marking.	MARK, QUEUE, TOS	Changes TOS bits, re-classify packets marking. QUEUE, allows user-space program to see packet

Note that some of these utilities indicate they perform a SYN scan, which uses a half-open TCP connection to determine the existence of a service. A half-open TCP connection is one that never completes the three-way handshake described in Chapter 2. The reason for leaving the connection half-open is to avoid actually initiating the service, so that the user can locate and disable the service.

FYI: The TCP Half-Open Connection

A TCP half-open connection can occur for many reasons. If for any reason a machine at one end of the connection crashes, the other end will usually keep a connection in the half-open state for 45 to 60 seconds depending on the operating system.

A common attack using TCP half open connections is "SYN flood" attack that attempts denial of service by using all available resources on the attacked machine to keep half-open connections alive. Since it is easy for an attacker to exhaust memory resources in a short period of time, there are three main solutions: using the TCP RST flag via intrusion detection, lowering the time period of a half-open connection, and limiting the number of half-open connections to a small number less than available resources.

The TCP RST flag is used after a 45–60 second timeout to clear the connection. Lowering this time limit has the effect of clearing the half-open connections more frequently. A more sophisticated approach is using intrusion detection facilities that include active response. With intrusion detection, a pattern can be detected that an abnormal number of TCP segments with the SYN bit set have been received in a short period of time. Once again, TCP RST flags are sent to the attacker(s) to clear the connections. Another technique is to lower the number of allowed half-open connections in such a way that an attacker exhausting available memory for the TCP connections is unlikely.

Open-Source Scanners

The next option available to computer users and network administrators is to use an open-source scanner. Several open-source network scanners are available, but the two most common are Nmap and Nessus. There are advantages of open-source scanners over online scanners. One is that you can take a new machine and isolate the system from the organizations network

Caution

Network Scanning

It may be against the policy of your college, university, or organization to perform unauthorized network scans. Check with the appropriate person to make sure you are permitted to do this. Alternatively, take the approach of isolating the new system being tested from the organization's network.

while performing the scan, whereas online scanners require access to the Internet—usually through your company or university internal network.

Nmap (**www.insecure.org/nmap/**) is an open-source port scanner used to determine open ports and basic vulnerabilities on the network. Nmap attempts to determine the OS, the existence of a firewall, and open ports (services) running on a computer. Nmap quickly scans all of the hosts in a specified range and provides an output of information on these hosts. One of the main goals for Nmap is to provide a tool network administrators can use to audit their network.

Nmap is one of the utilities available on the SLAX Linux distribution that will be used with this book. A binary version of Nmap is available for Windows users from the Nmap web site.

IN PRACTICE Using Nmap

The simplest way to use Nmap is to provide Nmap with the IP address of the host you wish to scan. Executing Nmap with the IP address of a Web server will provide an output similar to that shown in Figure 3.15.

```
nmap 192.0.2.11
```

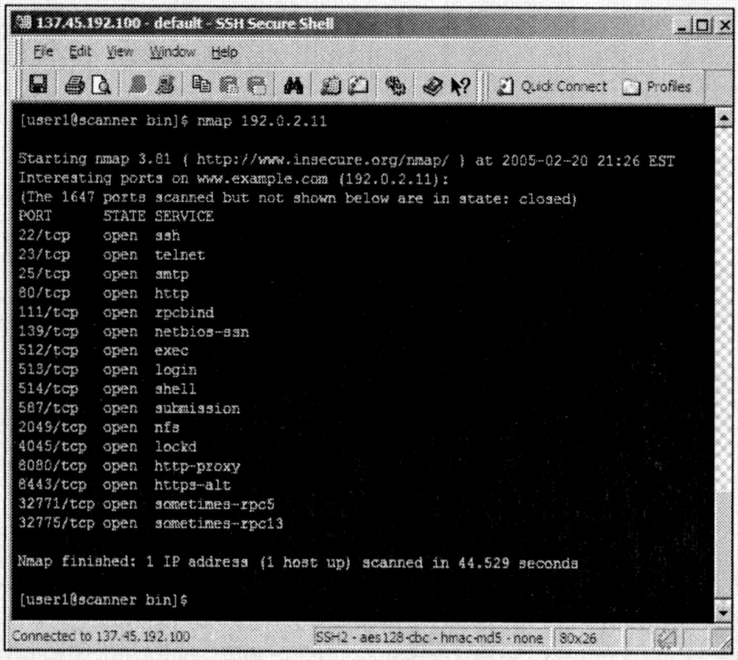

FIGURE 3.15 Nmap IP address scan.

▶ CONTINUED ON NEXT PAGE

Rather than specifying the IP address of the host to scan, the name of the host can also be specified in the Nmap command. The –v flag and the –O flag are also useful additions to the Nmap scan. The –v tells Nmap to provide verbose output while the scanning takes place. This is helpful as you begin using Nmap to make sure it is doing what you think. The –o flag tells Nmap to guess the operating system running on the remote machine. Figure 3.16 provides an example of a verbose scan of www.example.com.

```
nmap -v www.example.com

nmap -v -O www.example.com
```

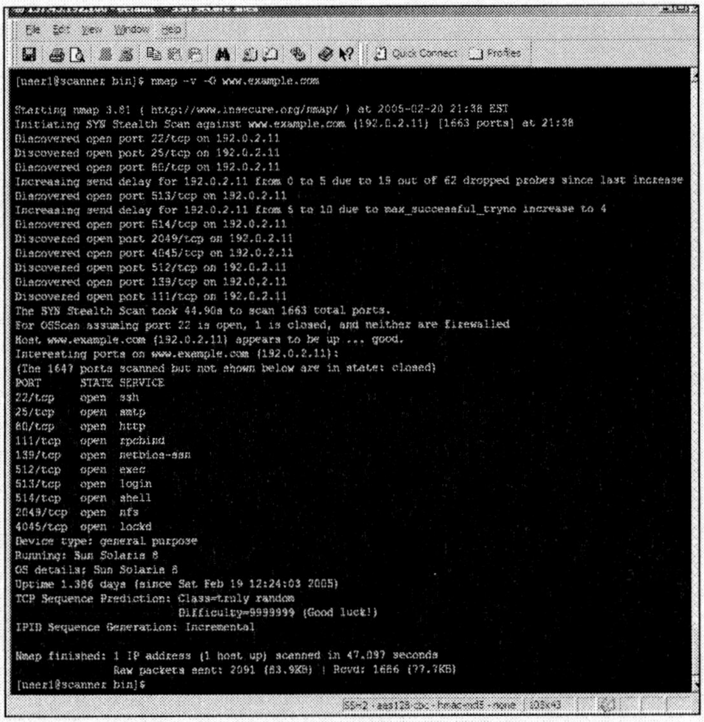

FIGURE 3.16 Nmap verbose scan.

Nmap can also be used to scan an entire subnet range for open ports. When a subnet scan is performed, a wildcard is used to replace the host range. As shown in Figure 3.17, an asterisk is used to specify all hosts in a given range should be scanned. In addition to the wildcard, a range can be specified using a hyphen

▶▶ CONTINUED ON NEXT PAGE

>> **CONTINUED**

such as 192.0.2.10-40, specifying to start by scanning 192.0.2.10, then scan 192.0.2.11 up through 192.0.2.40.

```
nmap '192.0.2.*'

nmap '192.0.2.10-40'

nmap '192.168.0.0/16'
```

Nmap is a useful tool for auditing the network to determine what ports are open on all of the servers or hosts on a given subnet.

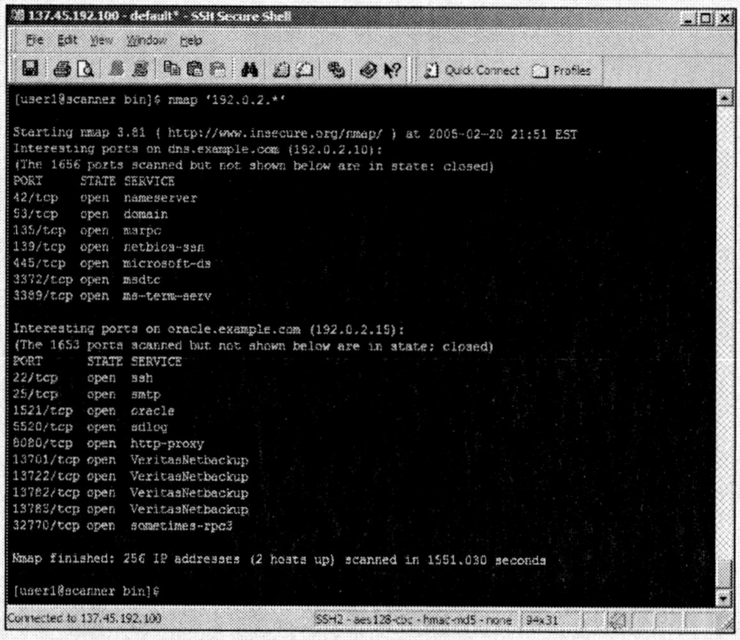

FIGURE 3.17 Nmap wildcard scan.

Nessus (**www.nessus.org/intro.html**) is a more advanced scanning tool and relies on the Nmap framework and scanning techniques. Nessus uses a modular architecture allowing plug-ins to be written to detect a plethora of vulnerabilities and missing operating system patches. Nessus provides a tool for helping network and security administrators audit the health of hosts on the network and determine the patches to install.

Nessus uses the *Network Attack Scripting Language (NASL)* as a tool to create new plug-ins. Because of the ability for anyone on the Internet to develop a scanning script based on this language, scripts to detect new vulnerabilities are published at an astounding rate. The databases of available Nessus plug-ins grow on a daily basis.

Summary

Each category of firewall has its own unique set of features and functionality, and you must perform a careful analysis to determine which firewall is needed in your environment. You should have a basic understanding of the need for a layered security approach and the potential of using several of the categories of firewalls to achieve a greater level of information security.

Personal firewalls are needed even in an environment where an enterprise firewall is installed, since they protect a computer from internal attacks. One economical personal firewall is available on any Windows XP system. It provides incoming protection and should be used if no other firewall will be installed on the host computer. Other personal firewalls, such as Zone Alarm, provide enhanced functionality that goes beyond the capabilities of the Windows Firewall.

This chapter also introduced ACLs and iptables, the fundamental software systems that implement rules in routers and Linux firewalls. We also covered an overview of the rules in ACLs, Mac OS X firewall and via the GUIs of several personal firewalls. We will look at this topic in more detail in Chapter 6.

Finally, it should be clear now that all firewalls must be tested using scanning software, if not by a professional consultant, since misconfiguration causes most failures of firewalls. In later chapters, we will scan a firewall to see its effectiveness.

Next, we'll explore in Chapter 4 more details about the threats that have become prevalent in the world of networking.

Test Your Skills

MULTIPLE CHOICE QUESTIONS

1. In a large corporate environment a(n) _____ firewall is often the only practical solution.

    A. router as a

    B. enterprise

    C. proxy

    D. SOHO

2. Defense in depth involves

    A. multiple layers of security.

    B. a single layer of security.

    C. special electronic filters on telecommunications lines.

    D. using a router as a firewall.

3. Most _____ include functionality to filter incoming and outgoing packets.

   A. switches

   B. NICs

   C. routers

   D. hubs

4. Improper configuration of access lists can impact the _____ of a router.

   A. performance

   B. scalability

   C. route tables

   D. gateway addresses

5. In a _____ , the vendor provides the hardware and software in a single integrated box.

   A. software firewall

   B. hardware firewall or appliance

   C. personal firewall

   D. Windows firewall

6. Application firewalls or _____ are specialized firewalls tailored for specific services, such as Web or mail servers.

   A. SOHO routers

   B. proxies

   C. routers

   D. host-based firewalls

7. Which of the following can act as a firewall?

   A. Cisco routers

   B. a computer with firewall software

   C. a proxy server

   D. all of the above

8. _____ is not an enterprise firewall.

   A. Checkpoint

   B. Zone Alarm

   C. PIX

   D. NetScreen

9. In general, all users should have which of the following?

    A. personal or host-based software firewall

    B. antivirus software

    C. spyware software

    D. all of the above

10. The term SOHO refers to

    A. shared online hacker organization.

    B. small office/home office.

    C. shared office housed online.

    D. standards of home offices.

11. In a corporate network, what type of firewall is needed on a host workstation if a router is set up as a firewall and an enterprise firewall exists?

    A. a proxy server

    B. a personal host-based firewall

    C. a SOHO firewall

    D. none of the above

12. The Windows Firewall does not do which of the following?

    A. filter and restrict incoming traffic

    B. filter and restrict outgoing traffic

    C. look at specific applications and connection to those applications

    D. provide exception rules for applications and ports

13. The Windows Firewall provides which of the following?

    A. stateful inspection

    L. filtering of outgoing connections

    C. content inspection

    D. all of the above

14. Zone Alarm monitors _____ , which helps to detect Trojans that might be installed on the computer.

    A. incoming connections

    B. outgoing connections

    C. proxy connections

    D. stateless connections

3

15. _____ are the basis of the Linux firewalls used in this book:

A. Iptables

B. Iptools

C. ACLs

D. Ipchains

16. _____ are the facility in Cisco routers that determines whether the packet should be allowed to access the network.

A. Iptables

B. Policies

C. ACLs

D. Netfilters

17. The Cisco ACL keyword deny is the same as _____ in iptables.

A. reject

B. drop

C. discard

D. deny

18. _____ is a necessity to ensure the proper configuration of a firewall.

A. Rebooting

B. Testing

C. Enabling logging

D. Waiting for hackers

19. _____ is an open-source port scanner used to determine open ports and basic vulnerabilities on the network.

A. Nmap

B. Netfind

C. Nslookup

D. Nbtstat

20. _____ is a network scanning tool that uses a modular architecture allowing plug-ins to be written to detect a plethora of vulnerabilities.

    A. Nmap

    B. Netfind

    C. Nslookup

    D. Nessus

EXERCISES

Exercise 3.1: Understanding the Windows Firewall Configuration

1. Find a Windows XP machine with Service Pack 2 that is connected to the network.

2. From the Start menu, navigate to the Settings option and click on Network Connections. A dialog box is presented that shows all the network connections available.

3. On the right side, you will see an entry marked "Change Windows Firewall Settings." Click that entry. Make sure Windows XP Firewall is on (that is the default).

4. Click on the Exceptions tab and view the list of Programs and Services that are allowed to connect to this computer.

5. If no programs are allowed in the Exception list, install AOL Instant Messenger and start the program. Unblock the program to allow it through the firewall.

6. Launch a Command prompt from the Accessories menu, or by using Start -> Run -> cmd.

7. At the command line, enter netsh firewall and list all of the firewall commands that are available using this command line tool.

    ```
    netsh firewall
    ```

8. At the command prompt, type:

    ```
    netsh firewall show config
    ```

    What is the output of the `netsh firewall show config` command?

9. What rule or setting in this list allows AOL Instant Messaging traffic to pass through the firewall?

10. Use this configuration information to list all of the ports that are allowed for incoming traffic.

Exercise 3.2: Windows Firewall Configurations

A user has just installed a personal Web server on her Windows XP Service Pack 2 computer and now needs to modify the Windows Firewall configuration.

1. Outline in detail which manual steps the user needs to take to reconfigure the Windows XP Firewall to allow anyone on the local subnet to connect to the personal Web server.

2. Organize what the user needs to do to allow anyone on the Internet to access the personal Web server.

Exercise 3.3: Inspect Log Records for Windows XP Firewall

1. Find a Windows XP machine with Service Pack 2 that is connected to the Internet.

2. From the Start menu, navigate to the Settings option and click on Network Connections. A dialog box is presented that shows all the network connections available.

3. On the right side, you will see an entry marked "Change Windows Firewall Settings." Click that entry. Make sure Windows XP Firewall is on (that is the default).

4. Click the Advanced tab and then click the Logging option settings button. Check the boxes for dropped packets and successful connections. (*Note:* You must uncheck the Successful Connections box once you are done with this exercise.)

5. On the Advanced tab, click the ICMP Settings button. Uncheck "Allow incoming echo request."

6. Click OK, until all your changes to Windows XP Firewall are saved.

7. Bring up a Web page to your favorite Web site.

8. Use the Start menu to navigate through programs to the Accessories menu and click the Command prompt. Type the command:

```
ipconfig -all
```

9. Make a note of the IP address of this machine, then move to another machine connected to the network, and ping the IP address of the XP machine.

10. Return to the XP machine and inspect the logs. Describe the information in the log files for successful connections (your Web page) and dropped packets (the pings).

Exercise 3.4: Windows Firewall ICMP Settings

By default ICMP echo requests along with all other ICMP traffic is disabled by the Windows XP Firewall. This exercise will help you determine the effect of the ICMP echo request settings.

1. Find a Windows XP machine with Service Pack 2 that is connected to the Internet.

2. Use ipconfig from the command line and determine the IP address of the machine.

3. From the Start menu, navigate to the Settings option and click on Network Connections. A dialog box is presented that shows all the network connections available.

4. On the right side, you will see an entry marked "Change Windows Firewall Settings." Click that entry. Make sure Windows XP Firewall is on (that is the default).

5. Click on the Advanced tab, then click on the ICMP Settings button.

6. If the Allow incoming echo request is checked, turn this off. If you were unable to turn this off, what would you need to change to turn this off?

7. Find another computer on the same subnet and ping the machine you have changed the firewall settings on. What is the response?

8. Turn the "Allow incoming echo request" setting on.

9. Find another computer on the same subnet and ping the machine you have changed the firewall settings on. What is the response?

Exercise 3.5: Mac OS X Firewall

This exercise requires a Mac running OS X with the firewall enabled.

1. Locate a Mac running OS X.3 or later.

2. Open a Terminal window and use the ipfw command to view the firewall settings.

   ```
   ipfw -a list
   ```

3. Describe the action taken by each of the firewall rules.

4. Select the new button on the Firewall tab and allow connections from two additional applications.

5. Run the ipfw –a list command again from the Terminal window. What additional lines were added? What do these lines do?

PROJECTS

Project 3.1: Magnum Corp and the TinyCorp Subsidiary

Magnum Corporation is a global corporation with 50,000 employees. Magnum has realized that its size is sometimes its worst enemy, as it cannot be as agile and responsive as smaller companies. Magnum has several small subsidiaries, including TinyCorp. TinyCorp is Magnum's "skunk works," where creative, cutting-edge projects are born. TinyCorp has only 50 employees, who use the Internet extensively for research, and who travel frequently with laptops.

Magnum has become increasingly reliant on the Internet for its work, and rough traffic estimates of its Internet traffic volume equal about 1,000,000 packets per second. Magnum has hired you to be its Chief Security Officer, a high-profile job in which you have responsibilities for Magnum and all of its subsidiaries.

What kind of firewalls will you recommend for Magnum and its subsidiaries?

Project 3.2: Install and Configure ZoneAlarm

Install Zone Alarm, and then evaluate how it compares to the Windows XP Firewall.

1. Turn off the Windows XP Firewall.

2. Download the free version of ZoneAlarm from **www.zonelabs.com**.

3. Install ZoneAlarm with the default configuration.

4. Use ping to ping another computer on the network. Does ZoneAlarm provide any information for this connection?

5. Start AOL Instant Messaging. What does ZoneAlarm do when this application is started?

6. Look at the Zones tab of the ZoneAlarm Firewall configuration page. What is the difference between the Internet and Trusted zones?

7. What advantages does ZoneAlarm provide over the Windows XP Firewall?

Project 3.3: Use Online Tools to Scan Your Machine

1. Use PC Flank's advanced port scanner to scan your machine. You can find the port scanner at **www.pcflank.com/scanner1.htm**.

2. Describe the different scan options and give some reasons for the results you receive from this scan. Include the scan results in your description. If any ports are listed as Open, include a brief description of what is running on this port.

3. If you are running Windows XP Service Pack 2, the "netstat –b" command can help you determine which programs are using each port.

Project 3.4: Install and Configure BlackICE

1. Install BlackICE on a computer.

2. Use PC Flank's advanced port scanner to scan the machine.

3. Describe your results. Include the scan results in your description.

4. What are the differences between Windows XP firewall and BlackICE in terms of the number of scan results and severity?

Project 3.5: Scan the Local Subnet with Nmap

Note: Permission to scan the subnet should be received prior to starting this project.

1. Once you have received authorization to perform a network scan, use the SLAX distribution to boot a computer in a computer lab or another subnet.

2. Use Nmap to scan the network and provide a report of the requested information.

3. Use the SLAX CD to boot a computer that is connected to the network.

4. Use the ifconfig command to determine the IP address and local subnet the SLAX machine is connected to.

5. Use Nmap to scan the local subnet.

   Example: `nmap -v -O 192.168.1.*`

6. Provide a list of all devices on this subnet, including the following information: IP address, host name, operating system.

7. Provide a list of the common ports that are open on systems on this subnet.

8. Provide a list of the computer name and the port of any systems with abnormal ports that are open.

9. Write a short summary of any corrective action you think should be taken to help secure machines on this subnet.

Case Study

The Information Technology Department at ResTech University has recently experienced an array of network problems resulting from computer viruses, unpatched computers, network scans, and various other malicious network activity. Department employees have determined that they need to implement some type of firewall to help protect faculty, staff, and students from each other, as well as from computers on the Internet. They have decided to publish a Request for Proposals (RFP) to allow vendors to propose a solution that will meet their needs.

Based on the information provided in this chapter and the current layout of their network from Figure 3.18, create a proposal for the firewall software and/or hardware they will need to secure the campus. Include updated network diagrams if appropriate. A template for the RFP submission is available on the on the book Web site.

FIGURE 3.18 Network layout.

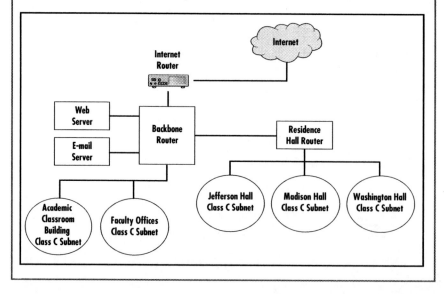

Chapter | 4

Threats, Packet Filtering, and Stateful Firewalls

Chapter Objectives

After reading this chapter and completing the exercises, you will be able to do the following:

- Explain the basics of major Internet security threats.
- Build a simple route table for a host or router.
- Recognize the need for protection at multiple levels through defense in depth and network zones.
- Detail the differences between stateless and stateful firewalls.
- Categorize the basics of proxy and content-aware firewalls.
- Use the Nessus tool for firewall and host testing.

Introduction

To understand how firewalls protect networks, you must understand threats present on the Internet. You will learn about several major security threats in this chapter and how a firewall can help mitigate these threats.

Previous chapters introduced the concept of defense in depth (DiD). We will extend this concept to map the architecture of networks into zones, which allow a firewall to identify areas with greater trust than others.

Firewalls can be organized according to their features (e.g., stateless versus stateful or proxy versus content-aware). Stateful firewalls are the primary focus of this chapter, since the iptables facility allows stateful concepts. iptables is a facility available in the LEAF firewalls used in this book.

Types of Security Threats

While threats can originate from within an internal network, these end at the organization's firewall and are often easier to track and remedy than those emanating from the Internet. This chapter will summarize Internet-borne threats in a way that illustrates basic characteristics of firewalls.

We will start by classifying attacks based on a variety of exploitable vulnerabilities. These include (but are not necessarily limited to):

- Software bugs–buffer overflow or other programming errors

- Configuration errors

- *Social engineering*–obtaining passwords, or enough information to guess passwords, asking for favors from system administrators, etc.

- *Worms* and *viruses*–self-replicating systems that require signatures to detect

- Trojan horses–an application that runs on a computer and is either hidden from the user or performs some unknown harmful action in the background

- Host and port scanning

For coverage of additional threats, see Sorensen 2004. Note that very few of these threats are actually implemented alone. For example, IP address spoofing is used frequently in conjunction with TCP connection hijacking or Denial of Service (DoS) and its distributed form DDoS.

The threats you will learn about in this chapter are:

- IP address spoofing

- Denial of Service attacks (DoS)

- TCP vulnerabilities

- Man-in-the-Middle attacks (MITM)

- Replay attacks

With the exception of the MITM and replay attacks, we will limit our discussion to what firewalls can do without resorting to authentication and encryption methods. You will learn more about authentication and encryption in Chapter 8. Some excellent resources, available on the Internet, discuss all of these threats and their mechanisms in more detail. (See Tanase 2003; Eastep 2005; Shimomura 1995; Bellovin 1989; Cisco 2004; Ferguson and Senie 1998; and Greene et al. 2001.)

As you learned earlier in reference to the Zone Alarm software firewall, the concept of zones in a network relates directly to the idea of DiD. Since a good security strategy has many layers, the zones concept can help us understand different levels of vulnerability as we proceed from the

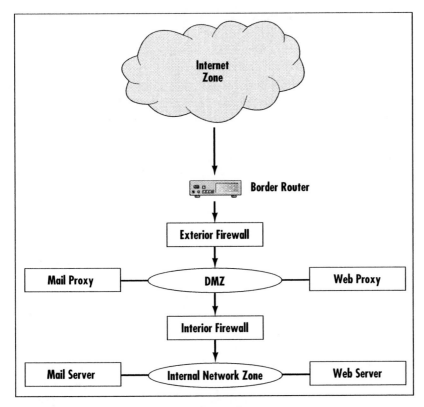

FIGURE 4.1 Illustrating the Zone Concept

exterior of an enterprise network (usually the Internet) toward the interior. Figure 4.1 illustrates this.

Figure 4.1 illustrates a layering concept that shows three zones. The first zone is the Internet, the most untrusted zone. The second is the demilitarized zone (DMZ), an area where less stringent firewall rules are applied. The third is the Internal Network, the most trusted zone. This is a typical architecture for any enterprise in business, education, or government.

The META Group is an organization that analyzes business operations. META takes the zone concept a step further than the architecture of Figure 4.1 by suggesting a four-layer zone architecture (META 2004), but rarely would an organization need that level of security. For even more protection, physical layer switches called network air gaps (NAGs) can be remotely controlled by a firewall or intrusion detection system (IDS) to physically disconnect a network from the Internet (Northcutt et al. 2003).

Now let's look at Figure 4.1 in more detail. Traffic from the Internet zone is first filtered by the border router. Routers are usually faster than firewalls for basic traffic filtering. Next an exterior firewall filters traffic further, perhaps with stateful methods before the traffic is allowed into the DMZ. The DMZ contains the services that the organization must expose to the Internet—for example, Web and mail servers—usually in the form of proxies.

An interior firewall with stronger rules then filters the traffic again before allowing it to enter the Internal Network zone. The critical resources of the enterprise are in this innermost zone, protected by as many as three devices. Any organization must make decisions on what is appropriate and necessary for its operations; some organizations do not use the optional DMZ or proxy elements. Keep in mind the zone concept as we discuss several threats below.

IP Address Spoofing

We will begin by analyzing the IP spoofing attack (Tanase 2003) (RFC 2267 1998). A spoof attack follows one of two schemes: making the attack appear as if it is coming from a trusted machine or making the attack appear as if it is coming from a different network location than the originator. Either way, the objective is to falsify or "spoof" the source IP address in the IP header.

An early form of IP address spoofing is called the LAND attack, and it results in DoS. In this simple attack, a machine forms a packet with identical source and destination IP addresses and identical source and destination port numbers. Earlier operating systems (e.g., Windows 95) would crash when such a packet was received.

To mimic a trusted machine, attackers need to know the internal address structure of the organization they are trying to attack. It would seem that the LAND attacker would need to know an IP address to which to send. However, it may be easy to guess that structure as based upon the private IP address blocks reserved by the Internet Assigned Numbers Authority (IANA), as detailed in RFC 1918 (Rekhter et al. 1996). The result could be a scenario where packets arrive from an internal machine or from the Internet, bearing a guessed IP address of another machine on the internal network.

What if no machine responds to the destination IP? There are two possibilities: either a good firewall is in place that prevents any such private source IP addresses from entering the network, or there is actually no machine at the destination IP address the attacker is using. In the latter case, the attacker simply enumerates as many IP addresses as necessary to find a machine vulnerable to attack.

Part of this problem can be solved by instructing a firewall to block private source addresses coming from the Internet. In the case of the LEAF firewalls used with this book, this is accomplished by a file of addresses that are either private or not yet assigned by the IANA (Eastep 2005).

The other form of spoofing is where the source IP address is public and as such appears to be legitimate. To correct this alternate form of spoofing, you will need to employ one or both of two methods:

- Unicast reverse-path forwarding check (Cisco 2000)

- Reverse DNS lookup

Unicast reverse-path forwarding (RPF) is a check on the source IP address of a packet. Cisco Systems (**www.cisco.com**) is the dominant player in the network equipment market worldwide, making routers, switches, firewalls, and other capabilities. A solution according to Cisco (Cisco 2000, 2) is described below:

> "When Unicast RPF is enabled on an interface, the router examines all packets received as input on that interface to make sure that the source address and source interface appear in the routing table and match the interface on which the packet was received. ... If the packet was received from one of the best reverse path routes, the packet is forwarded as normal. If there is no reverse path route on the same interface from which the packet was received, it might mean that the source address was modified [spoofed]. If Unicast RPF does not find a reverse path for the packet, the packet is dropped."

This check then determines if, in the router's opinion, the packet coming into the same router interface matches a packet sent back to that IP address. Note that if a packet is spoofed with an actual IP address of a true host somewhere in the Internet, this check might not prevent the attack, since the router's default route probably covers the packet. On the other hand, if the packet came from the internal network bearing the source IP address of some real (or non-existent) machine on the Internet, the check should work.

IP Route Tables

Examining IP route tables can help you understand unicast reverse-path forwarding, as well as route filtering. (Route filtering—a topic we take up later in this chapter—closely resembles unicast RPF.)

The study of route tables is essential to every student of networking and can enhance many activities you may undertake, such as network configuration and troubleshooting. Every host computer, router, or firewall has a route table. Route tables provide information about how the IP layer will forward (route) every packet that comes through the machine. In Figure 4.2, we show a scenario of a network with several routers and hosts. The network is connected to the Internet. This figure illustrates how route tables contain a set of hop-by-hop linkages that accomplish correct forwarding for each possible packet.

Figure 4.2 shows host P sending two hypothetical packets, one to the IP address of google.com and another to host L on a different subnetwork.

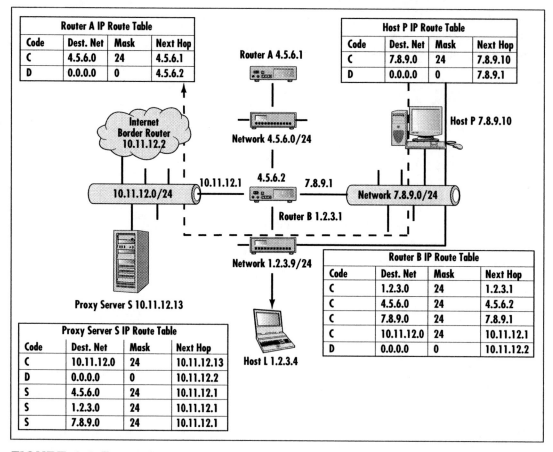

FIGURE 4.2 Forwarding operation of IP route tables.

The route tables involved are those of host P and router B. The dashed arrows in Figure 4.2 illustrate the operation of the default route (Code D) for the packet destined for google.com from host P. The solid arrows represent the operation of the default route in host P's IP route table and a directly connected network (Code C) in router B's IP route table.

IP route tables must contain several fundamental types of rows. Each row in an IP route table represents one step in a path toward a particular destination network. In Figure 4.2, if you trace the method by which packets get from any host or server to another host, there are linkages in each router's IP route table that forward the packet one hop closer to its destination. IP forwarding is a hop-by-hop method which relies on correct configuration, especially of routers.

The process of packet routing by the IP layer proceeds as follows:

1. Each packet passing through the IP layer has its destination IP address extracted from the packet header.

2. The IP layer proceeds through each row in the route table with the same procedure:

    a. The mask in the route table row is ANDed (binary AND operation) with the packet's destination address.

    b. This result is compared with the Destination Network field.

    c. If a match is successful, the row is added to a temporary table of successful matches.

3. When all rows in the route table have been scanned, the IP layer looks through the temporary table of all successful matches and chooses the row with the longest mask length. This is known as the "longest matching prefix" rule, since the rule chooses the most specific route in the table.

4. If there are two rows with equal mask lengths, then the metric field (not shown in Figure 4.2) is used as a tie-braker.

For the IP protocol to accomplish its purpose, the source and destination IP addresses must remain constant throughout the path across any inter-network (this of course includes the Internet itself). The only exception to this is when source IP addresses are changed by Network Address Translation (NAT). When the packets from host P in Figure 4.2 reach router B, the destination IP address is not changed. Rather, the destination MAC address is set to router B's MAC address on both packets from host P to google.com and to host L. Router B relies critically on the destination IP address remaining intact to make forwarding decisions based on router B's IP route table. All routers in the path rely on the destination IP address in a similar way.

Let us look through the IP route table of host P in Figure 4.2 and analyze the details of each route. This is a simple route table with only two rows.

- The directly connected network (Code C) shows the destination network is 7.8.9.0/24. We observe:

  - The next hop field is host P's IP address, 7.8.9.10. This indicates that the network 7.8.9.0/24 is directly connected.

  - Another interpretation of the next hop field in this row, 7.8.9.10 is "local," meaning any packet destined for a machine on network 7.8.9.0 can be sent directly by consulting host P's ARP table.

- The default row (Code D) shows a destination network of 0.0.0.0 and a mask of length 0. The CIDR notation /0 equates to a mask of 0.0.0.0. This row is the only other row in host P's table, so it must properly direct all packets not destined to network 7.8.9.0/24. According to the procedure for IP routing above, only packets destined to 7.8.9.0 will match the first row in host P's table. All others will match the default row, since a binary AND operation of 0.0.0.0 with any packet's destination address will produce the result 0.0.0.0. The IP routing procedure will successfully match this packet with destination network of the default row. We observe:

- Default rows are a "catch-all" for packets not matched by any other row.

- Host P's default row relies on the next-hop router (router B, 7.8.9.1) to have a correctly configured route table.

We now examine the route table of Server S. Unlike hosts P and L, server S does not have a default route that works for all packets that server S may need to send. Note that the IP route table of server S in Figure 4.2 needs static routes (Code S) in order to be able to communicate with machines on the interior of the network. This is because server S has a default route that sends packets toward the internet, via the border router. S has one directly connected subnetwork, but it needs to know how to forward packets to the hosts on other subnets. Since the default route will not carry packets in the right direction, toward router B, server S needs static routes to allow communication with the other subnets.

We have simplified the illustration of Figure 4.2 somewhat when compared to route tables displayed from real computers. Most computers do not display a code beside each row. Codes are not actually associated with rows of a route table; rather the IP routing procedure outlined above determines how packets will be forwarded.

IP networks are typically larger than those of Figure 4.2 and will usually be running a routing protocol to make subnets on distant routers known to all routers in a network. One such routing protocol is RIP, and another is OSPF. In the case of Cisco routers, each route learned via the routing protocol has a letter (R for RIP, O for OSPF) identifying the source of the route.

We now will look at two real-world route tables to provide more detail. A typical route table for Windows is shown below in Table 4.1. The route table on any Windows machine can be displayed with the route print command. We have suppressed the metric column for brevity, but have added the MAC address of the interface, which can be obtained via the ipconfig -all command. The route table shown in Table 4.1 can best be understood by having the output of the ipconfig command, which is displayed next:

```
C:\>ipconfig

Windows IP Configuration

Ethernet adapter Wireless Network Connection:
```

```
Connection-specific DNS Suffix : private.network

IP Address : 192.168.1.3

Subnet Mask: 255.255.255.0

Default Gateway: 192.168.1.254
```

The interpretation of the columns in a route table is as follows:

- Network Destination: A destination subnet that a packet's destination address can be matched against.

- Network Mask: (shown in Table 4.1 in CIDR notation) The network mask in each row will be used in the computer to perform a binary AND operation with each destination IP address of every packet.

- Gateway (Next Hop): The next hop IP address that will be used to forward the packet if that row is the successful winning match.

- Interface: The interface from which that packet will be sent. Windows and most operating systems display this as the IP address of the interface, but a MAC address is added in Table 4.1.

- Metric (not shown): A numerical value used to break ties between two rows of the route table.

As Table 4.1 shows, the default gateway displayed in the ipconfig output above is in the first row in the gateway column. Now consider the second row in Table 4.1. Recall from chapter 1 that the address block 127.0.0.0/8 is reserved for local loopback interfaces. The default configuration on virtually every computer, router, or firewall is to assign 127.0.0.1 to the loopback interface. Since the loopback has no actual physical NIC, we use a dummy MAC address "L0" instead.

The function of the loopback interface is to take outbound packets and turn them into inbound packets. The loopback interface is very similar to a

TABLE 4.1 Table 4.1 Windows route table.

Dest. Network	Network Mask	Gateway, or Next Hop	Interface	MAC address of Interface
0.0.0.0	/0	192.168.1.254	192.168.1.3	00- … -F3
127.0.0.0	/8	127.0.0.1	127.0.0.1	L0
192.168.1.0	/24	192.168.1.3	192.168.1.3	00- … -F3
192.168.1.3	/32	127.0.0.1	127.0.0.1	L0
192.168.1.255	/32	192.168.1.3	192.168.1.3	00- … -F3
255.255.255.255	/32	192.168.1.3	192.168.1.3	00- … -F3

mirror. There are two rows in Table 4.1 that involve loopback interfaces, row 2 and row 4.

We will focus on row 4. This row matches only the exact IP address assigned to this machine, since the mask length for the loopback row is 32 bits. This is important for purposes of testing server programs (daemons) running on the local machine.

Let's use the example of a single machine running a Web server. It is common to test a new Web page by opening a browser on the same machine. When using a domain name in the Web browser, the DNS system will map the domain to the local IP address 192.168.1.3. It is also possible to type the IP address 192.168.1.3 directly into the Web browser.

Since the rules of IP routing will select the longest matching prefix (32 bits is the longest possible prefix), row 4 will be the only one selected.

The packet with destination address 192.168.1.3 will be sent to the loopback interface and be transformed to an incoming packet. The IP layer will then forward this to the Web server application, and the Web browser should see the rendered Web page.

Next is a representative set of interfaces from a Linux system and the corresponding route table in Table 4.2. The information about interfaces and routes is available via the ip command in linux systems. There are many capabilities of the ip command. We use the command ip address show, which displays the interfaces and their IP and MAC addresses.

```
firewall: -root-

# ip addr sho

1: lo: <LOOPBACK,UP> mtu 16436 qdisc noqueue

link/loopback      00:00:00:00:00:00

brd                00:00:00:00:00:00

inet 127.0.0.1/8 brd 127.255.255.255

scope host lo

2: dummy0: <BROADCAST,NOARP> mtu 1500 qdisc noop

link/ether         00:00:00:00:00:00

brd                ff:ff:ff:ff:ff:ff

3: eth0: <BROADCAST,MULTICAST,UP> mtu 1500 qdisc
pfifo_fast qlen 100

link/ether         00:02:e3:13:02:78

brd                ff:ff:ff:ff:ff:ff

inet 1.2.3.89/26 brd 1.2.3.127

scope global eth0
```

```
4: eth1: <BROADCAST,MULTICAST,UP> mtu 1500 qdisc
pfifo_fast qlen 100

link/ether          00:02:e3:12:7d:94

brd                 ff:ff:ff:ff:ff:ff

inet 192.168.1.254/24 brd 192.168.1.255

scope global eth1
```

The interpretation of the display above is similar to what is obtained via the ipconfig –all command in a Windows environment. Each physical or logical interface is represented by a number and a mnemonic, for example "1: lo:" and "3: eth0:". All lines between successive numbers are for a single interface, as we have formatted the lines to fit this page.

First, the loopback interface is listed. In the ip addr command, the MAC address (if any) is shown in the line beginning with "link/". In the case of the loopback row above, the line begins with "link/loopback" and shows a fictitious MAC address of all zeros. As expected, the loopback IP address is 127.0.0.1, indicated by the inet keyword. This indicated that the IP address is an IP version 4 address.

The next line is an interface called "dummy0" which also indicates fictitious MAC address of all zeros. This interface is used to discard packets.

Briefly, the remainder of parameters of the ip addr show output are as follows. There are various terms indicating the status of the interface (for example BROADCAST, MULTICAST, UP). The UP keyword indicates that the interface has an IP address and is active. The mtu keyword is followed by a number that indicates the maximum transmission unit for the interface. The phrase "qdisc pfifo_fast qlen 100" indicates other parameters, including queueing discipline for the interface is first-in-first-out (fifo) and the queue length for the interface is 100 packets.

We use the ip route list table all command, resulting in a display of the route table in Table 4.2, with some rows removed for brevity. (For a shorter list of main active routes use the command ip route.) In Linux, there are two basic IP route tables, local and main. (There are other route tables that can be created by other routing protocols.) The table all key-phrase indicates that all tables should be displayed. In table 4.2 we have suppressed some repetitive information. We have also represented the ip route command output "default via 1.2.3.65 dev eth0" as a row with the typical destination network and mask for a default route.

Table 4.2 uses square brackets for items that do not appear in the ip route output, but can be inferred. We show items in parentheses that correspond to the columns or keywords in the ip route output. We do this so that a comparison can be drawn with other route table output, such as the Windows route table in Table 4.1. The characters B, L, and D stand

TABLE 4.2 Table 4.2 Linux firewall route table.

B/L/D (1st Col.)	Dest. Net (2nd column)	Mask	Next Hop (src)	Inter-face (dev)	Table	Scope
L	1.2.3.64	/26	1.2.3.89	Eth0	[Main]	[Link]
L	10.1.2.0	/24	10.1.2.254	Eth1	[Main]	[Link]
D	[0.0.0.0]	[/0]	1.2.3.65	Eth0	[Main]	[Link]
B	1.2.3.64	[/32]	1.2.3.89	Eth0	Local	Link
B	10.1.2.0	[/32]	10.1.2.254	Eth1	Local	Link
B	127.255.255.255	[/32]	127.0.0.1	LO	Local	Link
L	10.1.2.254	[/32]	10.1.2.254	Eth1	Local	Host
L	1.2.3.89	[/32]	1.2.3.89	Eth0	Local	Host
B	10.1.2.255	[/32]	10.1.2.254	Eth1	Local	Link
B	127.0.0.0	[/32]	127.0.0.1	LO	Local	Link
B	1.2.3.127	[/32]	1.2.3.89	Eth0	Local	Link
L	127.0.0.1	[/32]	127.0.0.1	LO	Local	Host
L	127.0.0.0	/8	127.0.0.1	LO	Local	Host

for broadcast, local, and default, respectively. For more information on Linux route tables, see the manual page for ip route.

The process that IP uses to route packets, described in the numbered list above, can be illustrated by referring to Table 4.1 and by imagining what happens when the Windows machine tries to send a web page request to the IP address 4.5.6.7. This IP address would be in the destination IP address field of any packet from a browser once the domain name was resolved. This IP address matches no row in Table 4.1 except the default route, which is the first row.

The default route is extremely important in any route table since, without it, you could not contact any machine except on a directly connected interface. The reason that the IP address 4.5.6.7 matches the default route can be seen by the following calculations. Following the procedure above, we quickly see that ANDing the address 4.5.6.7 will only match the default row:

```
4.5.6.7 AND 0.0.0.0 = 0.0.0.0
```

The result 0.0.0.0 matches the destination network field of the default row. Since that row is the only successful row added to the temporary table, there is only one choice. The mask length is 0, the shortest possible mask length. That is the strategy of the default row, to be a last resort when no other row can be matched.

At this point, the packet will be sent to the next-hop address, 192.168.1.254.

Finally, you will see three rows in a Linux local route table that are associated with true broadcast IDs (127.255.255.255, 10.1.2.255, and 1.2.3.127). Keep in mind that the subnet ID 1.2.3.64/26 contains a binary 1 in the 7th bit position (representing 2^6) of the last byte, leaving 6 host bits. That makes the broadcast IP address 1.2.3.127. We also see three rows marked broadcast (B) that represent subnet IP addresses. Why are these rows in the table? How can they be associated with broadcast addresses?

The explanation lies with a facility in the firewall used with this book to block certain Denial of Service (DoS) attacks. In a Linux system, there is a directory /proc/sys/net/ipv4 where many files relating to features of the system are located. Several of these control functions such as IP forwarding by the presence of a single numeric ascii value: 0 or 1. For example the file ip_forward in that directory contains a 1 if the system is allowed to forward packets between interfaces. Another file is icmp_echo_ignore_ broadcasts. This file, when set to the single character 1, causes any ICMP echo request sent to the broadcast address to be ignored. This would defeat an attack known as "ping-of-death" where ICMP packets are sent as fast as possible. You learned in Chapter 3 about such an attack. One way to defeat this type of attack is for a system to ignore ICMP echo request packets sent to the broadcast address.

There are other ways to send broadcasts. For example, sending a ping to a subnet IP address like 1.2.3.64 will result in a single echo reply instead of as many as 60, as would be the case if an ICMP echo request were sent to a broadcast address like 1.2.3.127.

Now that we have discovered the function of the extra three broadcast rows, we are ready to resume our discussion of Unicast RPF and DNS reverse lookup.

More on Unicast RPF and DNS Reverse Lookup

As we saw in the example in the previous section, a route table determines where a packet is forwarded during the routing process. The opposite of forward is reverse! Unicast reverse path forwarding is a procedure that asks the question, "Given the source IP address of this packet, could it possibly come from any device on my directly connected interfaces?"

This question must be answered considering each row in a route table. In the Web browser example above, once the Web server responds, the source IP address in the packet will be 4.5.6.7. In Table 4.1, that is quite clearly not an IP address on any directly connected interface, but it is a legitimate IP address if it comes from the interface associated with the default route.

We now turn our attention to DNS reverse lookup. In a DNS reverse lookup, the application has an IP packet in hand and wants to know if the source IP address (which could be an address chosen at random by the attacker) maps to an actual host with an Internet name. This is accomplished by the use of a ***DNS reverse zone*** and DNS record types called ***pointer (PTR)*** records (Arbitz and Liu 2001; Kopparapu 2002; Bernstein 2004). Essentially, an application can take the source IP address of any packet and do a reverse look-up for the host name using the DNS system. This procedure is analogous to having someone's phone number and looking up their name in the phone book. In the case of the phone system, this process would be tedious, but DNS supports this feature.

The LEAF firewalls are capable of the reverse DNS look-up, but the result varies depending on the application being used. An example is the difference between using a secure shell service (SSH) versus a Web server on the firewall. In the former case, the reverse DNS is checked, and if a different source IP is found, then the session is allowed to continue, although a message is placed in the authentication log noting the discrepancy. In the case of LEAF Web server—a utility that allows the access to the firewall, logs, and other data—a failure of the reverse DNS look-up will result in a refused connection, logged in the daemon log file. Daemons, in Linux terminology, are server programs that perform different functions. For example, a Web server or a mail server is a daemon.

FYI: Linux Log Files

In Linux systems, including LEAF firewalls, there is a directory /var/log that contains log files. Depending on what log utilities are being used, additional log files may appear. (See Chapter 9 for more on log records.) The common log files appearing in this directory are:

- auth.log—authorization of users and other secure protocols
- cron.log—the cron facility runs regular background jobs, such as daily backups or log file rotation
- daemon.log—services in Linux are called daemons, and a service may put records in this file
- debug—a file for debugging purposes
- messages—general messages
- syslog—messages logged by the syslog daemon
- ulogd.log—messages logged by the ulogd daemon

Unicast RPF must ascertain for every source IP address if it is possible that it is a legitimate address given all rows in a route table. This includes the default row, which must exist on every router. It is certainly possible for source IP addresses from distant, unknown (and unknowable)

IP addresses in the Internet at large to come into an internal network. Unicast RPF may still allow spoofed IP addresses into a network, since many such addresses may map to the default row of the IP route table.

Reverse DNS look-up is a way to map an IP address to a host name. However, reverse DNS look-up does not provide an absolute guarantee that an IP address is legitimate since a DNS database may be filled with many incorrect records. (See "Case Study" at the end of this chapter.)

The reverse situation—packets originating from within the internal network—is a little easier to determine. In addition to reverse DNS lookup, it is possible to search the routers Address Resolution Protocol (ARP) table. The latter method, however, will only determine if the source IP address exists on one of the router's directly connected interfaces.

In summary, reverse DNS lookup, as well as using the ARP table for IP address validation, have several limitations as does unicast RPF. We will return to the subject of source IP address verification later when we discuss route filtering.

Denial of Service Attacks (DoS)

A DoS is an attack where a large volume of network requests are generated, thereby degrading performance on the attacked server to the point where it is difficult or impossible to use. DoS's usually use IP address spoofing and have a number of colorful names including ***Smurf attacks*** (otherwise known as ping-of-death attacks), ***Fraggle attacks,*** and SYN floods (Cisco 2004). All of these types of attacks are generally known as packet floods.

The Smurf attack simply inundates a site with ***Internet Control Message Protocol (ICMP)*** echo requests and the resulting echo replies—simulating a rapid sequence of commands like the popular ping utility. The Fraggle attack uses a similar facility in the UDP protocol that induces echo requests and replies.

Figure 4.3 shows the basis of the Smurf and Fraggle attacks.

TCP Vulnerabilities: SYN Flood Attacks and Connection Hijacking

The ***SYN flood attack*** is based on the TCP protocol. Recall from Chapter 2 that TCP works by several methods to achieve connection orientation and reliable data transfer. These are:

- three-way handshake for connection setup

- sliding window flow control, and several congestion control algorithms during data transfer

- four-way handshake for connection close

TCP has 6 bits that control different phases of the TCP connection (setup, data transfer, and close). These bits are used as flags. They are ***SYN,***

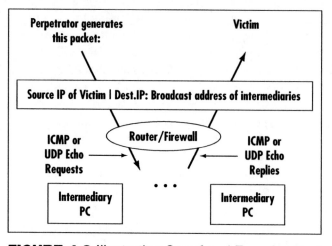

FIGURE 4.3 Illustrating Smurf and Fraggle attacks.

FIN, URG, PSH, ACK, and *RST.* Several flags are only valid in the data transfer phase (URG, PSH, ACK), while the SYN and FIN flags are only valid in connection setup and close, respectively. The RST flag is valid in any phase of TCP.

An attacker could try to generate a rapid sequence of SYN packets without ever responding to the return SYN from the opposite end, resulting in a half-open connection. However, every machine, even a large server, has finite resources. Each TCP connection uses a portion of the machine's memory called a TCP Control Block (TCB), where the state of the connection is maintained. The objective of the SYN flood attack, therefore, is to drive the available resources so low that new connections are impossible.

Another attack on TCP is known as the *"Christmas Tree" attack,* in which a TCP header with all flags set to 1 is sent. The intent is to exploit bugs in TCP implementations that cause crashes by gaining unauthorized access or causing DoS. Checking the validity of TCP flags, given the state or phase of the TCP connection, is part of the operation of a stateful firewall.

This leads to a TCP state called *invalid,* which we will discuss later (see the section on stateful firewalls). There are many invalid combinations of TCP flags, for example, setting SYN and FIN in the same TCP header.

Another attack on TCP is called the SYN flood attack. In this attack, the perpetrator initiates as many TCP segments with the SYN flag set as possible in a short amount of time. Frequently, this attack is used in a Distributed Denial of Service (DDoS) attack. It requires a substantial number of computers issuing connection requests to accomplish the goal, which is to deplete as many resources as possible, making new connections impossible or very slow to establish. Each TCP connection requires the receiver to maintain a TCB that keeps track of all parameters of the connection.

Since TCBs are usually kept in memory, a sufficient number of connections will exhaust the available memory.

Another issue in several operating systems is the number of available ports for client applications. If TCP SYN flood is performed using a server application as a perpetrator, the attacked machine (usually a single computer) will have its ephemeral ports exhausted. Windows and BSD Unix constrain the number of ephemeral ports used by client programs to about 4,000 ports. Once these are exhausted, no further connections can be opened.

FYI: The IETF and IANA Standards for Ephemeral Ports

The original set of TCP and UDP port numbers was determined by the Internet Engineering Task Force (IETF) RFC 1700. Later, the task of assigning port numbers was given to the Internet Assigned Numbers Authority (IANA). You can find the most up-to-date list for port number assignments at **www.iana.org/assignments/port-numbers**.

The standardized port numbers for TCP and UDP are divided into three categories:

- **well-known ports,** 1 to 1023
- **registered ports,** 1024 to 49151
- **ephemeral ports,** 49152 to 65535

These ranges are intended for the most frequently used services (well-known), less widely used services (registered), and for client software use (ephemeral).

Many operating systems do not comply with the IETF/IANA ephemeral port number assignments. These are:

- Windows, Linux kernels below 2.4, BSD Unix, default ephemeral range: 1024 to 5000.
- Linux kernel 2.4 and above, default ephemeral range: 32768 to 61000.

These operating system discrepancies can make identification of registered services, as opposed to client ephemeral port usage, ambiguous. To resolve these problems, it may be necessary to check the port range in use for each operating system. See **www.ncftpd.com/ncftpd/doc/misc/ephemeral_ports.html** for more information.

CONTINUED ON NEXT PAGE

4

CONTINUED

The command netstat –a –n can be used on any system to obtain information about open connections, both TCP and UDP. Because of the noncompliance we just noted—especially Windows, BSD Unix, and Linux prior to kernel 2.4—it may be ambiguous whether a connection displayed by netstat is a client connection using an ephemeral port or a registered service operating on the local machine. This is only the case if a valid IP address and port are identified at the foreign end. Otherwise, a registered TCP service will show the foreign address as 0.0.0.0:0, state LISTENING, and a registered UDP service will show the foreign address as *:*.

Another threat to TCP is called connection hijacking. In this scenario, a third party intercepts a connection, possibly redirecting the connection to a new port on the hijacker's machine. The hijacker may present her machine as the intended destination or place herself in the middle of the connection, becoming an MITM.

Man-in-the-Middle Attacks (MITM)

An MITM involves interception of packets somewhere between a legitimate sender and receiver. There are at least two forms of this attack:

- MITM using forged, commonly known, or intercepted security keys (Barrett 2003, 72-87)

- MITM using protocols without authentication, like ICMP (Holden 2004, 111)

MITMs are particularly difficult to detect. They are an active attack in which the attacker impersonates each of the legitimate players in a protocol to the other.

Before we continue, there are certain commonly used names for participants and attackers in describing security scenarios. These are:

- Ariel   First Participant

- Bob   Second Participant

- Carol   Third Participant

- Dave   Fourth Participant

- Eve   Eavesdropper

- Mallory   Malicious Attacker

- Sara   a server

If Ariel and Bob are negotiating a key and are not using authentication to be certain they are talking to each other, an attacker can insert himself in the communication path and can deceive both participants. Call the attacker Mallory. For Bob, he pretends to be Ariel. For Ariel, he pretends to be Bob. Two keys are then negotiated, Ariel-to-Mallory and Bob-to-Mallory. Ariel and Bob each think the key they have is Ariel-to-Bob.

A message from Ariel to Bob then goes to Mallory who decrypts it, reads it and/or saves a copy, perhaps altering the contents. Mallory re-encrypts the message using the Bob-to-Mallory key and sends it along to Bob. Bob decrypts it successfully and sends a reply which Mallory decrypts, reads, re-encrypts and forwards to Ariel.

Attacks are generated while the keys, authentication data, or certificates are being intercepted. As you recall from Chapter 1, there are two types of security keys—public/private keys and symmetric keys.

Certificates are the best defense against MITM. A certificate is an object from a trusted third party that can verify digital signatures from anyone. Many encryption technologies use a combination of public/private keys and symmetric keys. Some will also use digital signatures and possibly certificates.

An example of one technology that is vulnerable to MITMs in certain situations is the *Secure Shell (SSH)* version 2 protocol. SSH has evolved through two versions, SSH1 and SSH2. (The use of SSH standards, while widespread, are implemented as Internet drafts, which are working documents in the process of becoming standards-track Internet Engineering Task Force (IETF) RFCs.) A backward compatibility feature in SSH2 allows SSH1 clients to connect to a SSH2 server, and a possible vulnerability exists in the backward compatibility scheme (Securiteam 2002).

SSH2 uses an object called a host key, which is the public key for the server that is sent to the client for verification. The host key can be verified by a certificate if that feature is enabled in the SSH configuration file. It is also possible to use password verification for the SSH client; however, the SSH2 server is normally required to use *Rivest-Shamir-Adelman (RSA)* and *Digital Signature Algorithm (DSA)* security techniques.

The MITM scenario described above begins with the MITM sniffing a network segment through which the SSH transmission passes. A tool such as Dsniff (Loeb 2001) or Ettercap (Norton 2004) can be used for this purpose. During this phase, several things will occur:

- First, the client initiates the connection, and a secure channel is set up.
- On the first connection attempt, the public key of the digital signature (perhaps in the form of a certificate) is sent across the connection.
- If the client accepts the signature, the client is asked for the password.
- The password is sent across the connection.

Despite the fact that the entire connection is encrypted, a hacker can intercept encrypted packets and use them to pose as a legitimate server. Therefore, an important concept implemented in SSH2 is host-key verification. This means that the server's public key needs to be verified, and if the client is providing a public key, it must also be verified. However, when an SSH client first initiates a connection to a server, it is presented with an option to accept the server's host key. This then allows the client to decrypt the digital signature of the server (which the server signs with its private key).

In this scenario, an MITM can quickly intercept the initial exchange of traffic, set up a connection to the client machine, and subsequently set up a connection to the true server. In this way, the MITM is posing as the real server to the client and as a client to the true server. The MITM can do whatever it wants at this point.

A principal document describing SSH2 is Lonvick 2004 which discusses the possibility of MITMs. As a quick method of host-key verification without certificates, Lonvick advises the use of host-key *fingerprints.* Fingerprints are simply a checksum of the host-key that can be used to verify the key without distributing the public key in an insecure way.

Replay Attacks

A *replay attack* is similar to the MITM but involves capturing a set of critical data, usually for access to a computer system such as a database server. A typical scenario involves a legitimate user on a client machine using an **authentication protocol** to an authentication server, where the authentication server is running the authentication protocol. An authentication protocol is something every computer user has experienced when using a password and user-id to login to a computer. Most authentication protocols use one-way encryption. When the password is entered at a login prompt, the authentication protocol encrypts it and sends it to the authentication server. There, the encrypted password is compared to the contents of a password file—which contains encrypted values only—until a match is found.

The replay attack is perpetrated by a third party, who "sniffs" data across a communication link. The object of a typical replay attack is to capture a set of authentication data—for example, a user ID and password. Then the attacker resends (replays) the data to allow unintended access to a server.

An example of an authentication protocol vulnerable to replay attack is the **Password Authentication Protocol (PAP).** In this protocol, an encrypted password and user ID are sent over a communication link. The problem with PAP is that, while the password is encrypted, the communication link is not (Kay 2003). A normal login would require the legitimate user to type a cleartext password that would then be encrypted and sent over the communication link. A hacker can initiate a conversation using the encrypted version of the password. All the hacker needs is the user ID and the location (IP address) of a server. By sniffing the traffic using tcdump or other programs, the hacker can obtain all of this data.

So how can replay attacks be prevented? One solution is to use the ***Challenge Handshake Authentication Protocol (CHAP),*** which is much more secure than PAP. CHAP uses a method of periodic, random challenges to re-authenticate the user during the communication session. The CHAP Protocol on the authentication server periodically sends a random value to the client machine where the legitimate user is located. This random value is combined with two predefined items rather than a preshared secret key (PSK) and a hash algorithm that is known only to the client and authentication server. The client then uses the hash algorithm to combine the random value, the user ID and password, and the PSK. This object is then sent back to the authentication server.

4

FYI: RSA, DSA, Certificates, and Hash Functions

The MITM and replay attacks may intercept RSA and DSA keys. The RSA security method involves a public and a private key pair for any entity—a client, a server, or a certificate authority. This is the basis of the public key system that you learned about in Chapter 1, which implements the confidentiality aspect of security.

The DSA is an algorithm that uses public/private key pairs to form digital signatures. Digital signatures are used for authentication and nonrepudiation components of security. They are especially valuable when used in conjunction with digital certificates, since the certificate verifies a public key.

Hash functions provide the integrity feature of security. They have an interesting property that produces a unique, fixed-length identifier (called a digest) when the function is applied to an object of any length. Hash functions are used in security technology to produce the digest, which is a fixed-length mini-document related directly and uniquely to a file or message to which the hash function was applied. The two most prevalent hash functions in use today are the MD5 and SHA1 algorithms.

Hash functions can be used as part of the DSA. They can be encrypted using the sender's private key, making the digest a ***keyed hash.*** The encrypted digest is then attached to the end of the main document—which is encrypted with the receiver's public key. This technique—using a combination of public and private keys—is one of the most powerful features of the public key infrastructure.

Refer to Chapter 1 for the definitions of the confidentiality, authentication, and integrity functions.

The Main Types of Firewalls: Stateless, Stateful, Proxy, and Content-Aware

Now that we have discussed several kinds of threats and have added the zone concept to Defense in Depth (DiD), we are ready to discuss the main types of firewalls.

Stateless Versus Stateful Firewalls

Stateless firewalls examine the header of the packet and determine whether to allow or drop the packet, which makes them very fast and efficient. They compare the protocol, source/destination IP addresses, and source/destination port numbers to a set of rules to determine what to do with a packet.

However, stateless firewalls have no "memory" of previous packet information. They have no way to determine if:

- a packet is a response to a network request by a local internal host

- a packet is a response to an external host

- a packet is the first packet of connection or part of a long, pre-existing stream of packets

Stateless firewalls must rely on detailed rules that identify which packets to let in and to let out. These rule-sets can be long and difficult to manage.

Stateful firewalls, on the other hand, have a greater degree of intelligence. Not only do they analyze more information in the packet header, including TCP flags for example, but they also look at information in the content of the packet.

Stateful firewalls keep track of connections by using tables. A row in the table will keep the "state," whether it is new or previously established, as well as other fine details for each connection that is simultaneously active.

Stateful firewalls can open up ports that an application needs and then close them back down when the application is finished. A stateful firewall tracks each packet to determine whether it belongs to an existing connection and whether to allow or deny the traffic.

The stateful firewall must search a table for each incoming or outgoing packet. This process slows the firewall down to some extent. Also, once connections have been closed, the row for that connection must be removed from the table. This maintenance actually adds a burden to the firewall processor. As a result, large organizations often use an initial border router or stateless firewall to do basic packet filtering for the Internet zone, as shown in Figure 4.1. Finally, a stateful firewall may also have stateless rules, thereby covering the situations where a stateless rule will suffice.

More about Stateful Firewalls

As you recall, the goal of *packet filtering* is to keep undesirable packets out while allowing packets in for certain services. These services fall into two general categories:

- external services outside the firewall
- internal services (e.g., Web servers) inside the firewall

Virtually all packet transfers are bidirectional (packets need to be allowed in both directions), falling into these categories:

- New connections, defined by the TCP three-way handshake. There are two sub-cases:
  - new packet conversations that begin outside the firewall—the firewall needs to allow reverse traffic back out
  - new packet conversations that begin inside the firewall—the firewall needs to allow reverse traffic back in

- *Established connections*–connections that are ongoing and have entered TCP's established phase

- *Related connections*–the familiar case of FTP where there is a data connection and a control connection

- *Invalid connections*–the situation where the TCP three-way handshake is flawed, or a TCP header appears with invalid combinations of TCP flags during the established phase

In the first situation, where conversations are already established, packets can be filtered by stateful firewalls. Naturally, a firewall knows the state of the connection by observing the table of all tracked connections. Ordinarily, firewalls will insist that new connections begin from the internal network, inside the firewall. To allow the conversations to begin outside the firewall requires additional security policies and special rules to accept traffic from only a handful of acceptable external IP addresses.

The second situation or related connections are more interesting. How can we know which connections are related to other connections? In the case of File Transfer Protocol (FTP), for example, two TCP port numbers are used, port 20 for data and port 21 for the control, or command, channel. The table of connections in the stateful firewall for this FTP session would first include the control channel associated with port 21, because the client machine will always initiate the session. Then, between the same two IP addresses on port 20, the server would initiate a connection for data transfer. The stateful firewall realizes the data connection is related to the control connection and permits the connection coming into the firewall.

A stateless firewall is likely to refuse the data connection in this FTP scenario. Even with a stateful firewall in place, many organizations have an overriding policy that no connections may originate in the Internet zone, outside the firewall. One solution in this case is for the client, which initiates the FTP control channel inside the firewall, to issue the PASV command, which stands for the word "passive." Another is to allow it to set up FTP connection tracking, which iptables supports. Both of these solutions allow the client inside the firewall to initiate the data connection.

The third situation is the most dangerous. The conversations have begun outside the firewall, either from the Internet zone or the DMZ, depending on the DiD architecture used. We need to make these rules the strictest. The best practice to follow is to be very specific about which IP addresses and which ports are allowed through the firewall from the Internet or DMZ zones.

The last situation–allowing packet flows back out from conversations begun inside the firewall–is a normal "permit" policy in a firewall.

Traceroute and Stateful Firewalls The popular utility traceroute (and its counterpart tracert in Windows) illustrates the properties of stateful firewalls. Traceroute uses a variety of protocols, including ICMP, UDP, and of course the IP protocol (Stekolshchik 2005; Stevens 1994, 97–110).

A few typical traceroute commands on a Linux system are shown below, illustrating the use of either an IP address or a valid DNS host name:

```
traceroute 137.55.22.11

traceroute interesting.server.com
```

A traceroute utility will usually originate inside one firewall and perhaps pass through another firewall on the way to the destination IP address. Both firewalls need to allow the protocols that traceroute uses to pass unimpeded.

Recall that ICMP echo requests are used by the popular ping utility. ICMP works by using two numbers in the ICMP header: types and codes (Stevens 1994, 82). ICMP echo requests are identified in the ICMP header by the type 8, code 0. The response to any ICMP echo request is an echo reply, type 0, code 0.

To allow the *ping and traceroute utilities* to work from outside the firewall (the Internet side), we need to allow ICMP type 8 packets into the firewall. Since by default any reverse packet stream is permitted, you do not need any corresponding permission for ICMP type 0 packets to go back out to the Internet.

Traceroute uses an additional facility of the IP header: the Time to Live (TTL) field. The TTL field is an 8-bit field that can assume values between 0 and 255. Traceroute's method is to use a series of ICMP echo request packets embedded in IP packets with TTLs ranging from 1 to 30 (this is the default). One of the required behaviors for any IP layer is to discard a packet when the TTL reaches 0 or 1, and every IP layer will decrement the TTL field once before forwarding. (An IP packet with TTL=1 can only be sent to an application on the current machine, hence a TTL=1 IP packet cannot be forwarded.)

When a TTL field reaches 0, in addition to discarding the packet, an ICMP time exceeded packet (type 11, code 0) is sent back to the originator. Most default firewall settings will not allow ICMP type 11 packets back through the firewall.

Traceroute does not rely on these ICMP type 11 packets even though the source IP address of these ICMPs could be compared with the traceroute command line to verify that the destination had been reached. This is because they will have originated outside the firewall and might be blocked. In fact, there might be a stateless rule or policy that prevents these ICMP packets from entering the internal network.

To get around the ICMP type 11 problem, traceroute also uses UDP. If we never receive an ICMP type 11, the traceroute program cannot truly determine if it has reached the destination. The traceroute program only knows the path, since the IP layer will have discarded the ICMP packet when its TTL is expired.

Traceroute sends a UDP datagram to the IP address of the traceroute destination—that is, the IP address or host name on the traceroute command line. Traceroute uses a destination UDP port number, by convention 33434, to be sure that no application is running on the destination host. (See the "FYI" on ephemeral port numbers to understand why this port number is used.) This will result in an ICMP port unreachable error message (ICMP type 3, code 3) being generated by the destination host.

This is where the stateful firewall does its work. Although UDP is a connectionless protocol, iptables can track UDP traffic as well as TCP connections. Since a UDP packet originated from inside the firewall, the ICMP port unreachable message counts as a "related" packet flow. The traceroute program can now decide to stop when the source IP address of the ICMP time exceeded message matches that of the port unreachable message. Finally, traceroute actually uses a range of UDP port numbers beginning at 33434 and adding one to this number for each hop in the path. This allows for the possibility that the host at that hop could be busy or that the UDP packet is lost.

This discussion returns us to the Smurf and Fraggle DoS attacks described earlier. How will network administrators defend the network from the Smurf attack if they wish to use ping and traceroute for legitimate purposes? We discuss this issue in later chapters, where we cover the topic of rate limiting. For now, however, suffice it to say that the firewall will be able to limit the average rate of ICMP echo requests and also limit the size of the bursts. Any IP conversation that exceeds either of those parameters will have packets dropped.

The ping and traceroute utilities generate ICMP requests at a very slow rate, such that reasonable rate limits are very effective at defeating the Smurf attack, which would attempt to generate ICMP requests as quickly as possible. As a second layer of defense, the firewall will never accept requests to the broadcast address of the internal network. It is a common feature of Smurf DoS attacks to elicit as many responses as possible.

What can be done about the Fraggle attack, which uses **UDP Echo Requests**? If you allow some UDP packets into the firewall to support traceroute, how can you defeat the Fraggle attack UDP echo requests? The UDP echo request is UDP port 7, and the ports used by traceroute are completely different. So under those conditions, we should never see a UDP echo request entering the firewall. If you wish to allow UDP echo requests for "peaceful purposes," you can use rate limitations. Ping and traceroute can still be used for network troubleshooting. Additionally, it is good practice to reject packets bearing the broadcast address from entering via the Internet.

Route Filtering and Packet Filtering *Route filtering* is the process of deciding which packets to accept based on a route table, and in this regard is similar to Cisco's Unicast RPF. Route filtering applies to firewalls and routers equally. Guidelines are found in RFC 1812 (Baker 1995). Section 5.3.8 of RFC 1812 says:

"A router SHOULD IMPLEMENT the ability to filter traffic based on a comparison of the source address of a packet and the forwarding table for a logical interface on which the packet was received. If this filtering is enabled, the router MUST silently discard a packet if the interface on which the packet was received is not the interface on which a packet would be forwarded to reach the address contained in the source address. In simpler terms, if a router wouldn't route a packet containing this [destination] address through a particular interface, it shouldn't believe the address if it appears as a source address in a packet read from this interface."

In Linux, route filtering is performed in the Linux kernel, so there are no iptables rules. By identifying interfaces, a series of files determines how route filtering is applied. The files pertinent to the firewall used in this book are:

- /proc/sys/net/ipv4/conf/eth0/rp_filter
- /proc/sys/net/ipv4/conf/all/rp_filter

If other interfaces than eth0 are connected to routers, then additional files will be necessary. To allow route filtering, these files must all be set to single character, the number 1.

It is perhaps a misnomer to call the facility described in section 5.3.8 of RFC 1812 "route filtering," which has a different meaning in section 7.5 of that document. What the rp_filter files will do at a minimum is cause packet filtering to be performed based on source address verification of each packet. If routing protocols are implemented on the firewall, then filtering of route information will also be performed.

One of the purposes of route filtering is to prevent invalid next-hops from being taken for certain destination network addresses. These have the colorful name *martian addresses* (Baker 1995, section 5.3.7), resulting in the occasional *martian next-hop* error.

Route filtering is also related to IP address spoofing. It is desirable to implement the following features in a firewall to control several anomalies that can arise during packet forwarding:

- Source IP address filtering: checking that the source address of an IP packet coming from a specific interface would actually exist on that interface. This practice defeats IP address spoofing.

- Source IP addresses should only be unicast addresses. Multicast or broadcast addresses should never be found in the source IP address field. This practice, when added to source IP address filtering, defeats DoS attacks using the broadcast address of a subnet.

- Loopback addresses should only be received from and/or forwarded to the loopback interface.

In RFC 1918, Baker requires routers and firewalls to compare a source IP address to the forwarding table and determine whether, if such an address were a destination IP address, it would be sent to the same interface from which the original packet came. This is not the same as simply checking that such an IP address could exist on the interface, because paths in an inter-network can be asymmetrical.

Proxies, or Application Firewalls

As part of a good DiD strategy, it is wise to have several layers of firewall protection, and proxies can be one of those layers. Application firewalls, also called application-aware firewalls or *proxies,* are specialized firewalls that are tailored for specific services, such as Web or mail servers. In the firewall used with this book, a proxy called "squid" is available. An example of a commercial proxy is Microsoft's ISA Server.

In a Web proxy, all Web service requests from clients to well-known port 80 (Web service) are sent to the proxy first instead of directly to the web server. The proxy may inspect the contents of the HTTP protocol payload (usually a GET request for a Web page) to ensure the safety of the request. If the request passes various tests, it is forwarded on to the actual Web server. The response from the server is checked for safety and the page is cached. The purpose of the normal, or forward, proxy (also known as a transparent proxy) is to serve the client and protect the server. Once a page is cached on the proxy, the next request from a client will find that page, thus off-loading the Web server. Figure 4.4 illustrates this process.

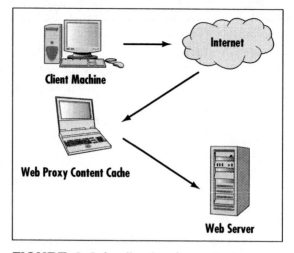

FIGURE 4.4 Application firewalls (proxies).

Another form of proxy is the ***reverse proxy.*** A reverse proxy serves the server by offering load-balancing and geographic distribution of content as well as security services. In this case, the HTTP GET request is inspected and, possibly, the response from the Web server. Caching accomplishes a load-balancing purpose and has a similar effect to caching in forward proxies. (A good description of commercial tools for reverse proxies is found in Cisco 2002.)

FIGURE 4.5 Reverse proxies.

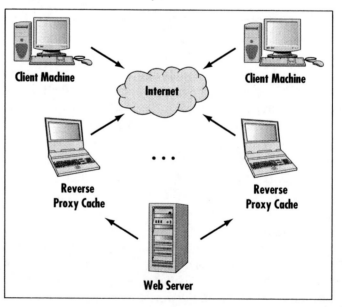

A good example of reverse Web proxy service is Akamai Corporation (Nottingham 2000). Akamai provides a service that allows content replication and distribution around the globe. Akamai's service also provides on-demand content replication when unusual peaks in Web page requests occur.

Figure 4.5 illustrates reverse proxies that distribute content to points on the Internet that are topologically closer to groups of users. Clients are "nearer" the reverse proxy caches in the sense of hop count—the number of telecommunications links between a client and a proxy.

FYI: Using Proxies to "Stealth" Your Web Connections

A common use of a proxy is to effectively replace your computer's source IP address with that of the proxy. With a proxy in place, the client's IP address cannot be known. For more information about "stealthing ports" and proxies see **stealthinfo.lockdowncorp. com/**. However, there are vulnerabilities in HTTPS proxies that use digital signatures. Loeb (Loeb 2001, 1) says "digital signatures were at risk of so-called 'man-in-the-middle' (MITM) attacks. ... webmitm implement active monkey-in-the-middle attacks against redirected SSH and HTTPS sessions by exploiting weak bindings in ad-hoc PKI." It may be wise to check with any HTTPS proxies to ensure they are immune from this vulnerability.

Content-Aware Packet-Filter Firewalls

General-purpose, content-aware firewalls are firewalls that inspect the contents of any packet for suspicious material. We will use the example of a firewall that inspects the content of an FTP session. Since FTP has a control connection and separate data transfer connection, a firewall can inspect either or both the control and data connections, making appropriate decisions whether the content is safe. FTP is unfortunately an insecure protocol, and if passwords are required to log in to an FTP server, they are sent "in the clear," meaning as cleartext without encryption.

A problem can arise when FTP is made secure by using encryption protocols like IPSec or Transport Layer Security (TLS, sometimes called Secure Socket Layer, SSL). When encryption protocols like IPSec and TLS are used to secure a data transfer, a content-aware firewall can no longer inspect the contents. A recent IETF draft calls attention to this problem (Ford-Hutchison 2004). Likewise with another insecure protocol, telnet, content-aware firewalls will be left blind by the encryption of telnet sessions.

Other content-aware firewalls exist as research (Lockwood et al. 2004), open-source, and commercial products. One such commercial product is Inventigo (Lockwood 2004). The approach taken by Inventigo is somewhat unique and based on standards published by the Object Management Group (OMG). This method is based on defining sensitive data policies implemented by policy definition points (PDPs). Elements of data models (think of tables and columns in database schemas) are formed into a profile to define the sensitive data. The content-aware firewall serves as the policy enforcement point (PEP) with the data store on an internal network. Content from packets are scanned and compared with the profile. When matches are found, the firewall converts cleartext elements into sensitive data elements (SDEs) by encrypting and/or aliasing the data elements on the way to the client program. The firewall-aware data access library on the client machine receives blocks of keys from the firewall and decrypts the element, allowing cleartext access.

This approach sends the encrypted SDEs over an insecure channel without requiring a Virtual Private Network (VPN). The reverse process is performed after a client program updates the data. The updated data is encrypted to form a new SDE and is sent back to the firewall. The firewall then decrypts the data before sending it to the data server.

More about Using Nessus

You have been exposed to Nessus in previous chapters. Nessus is an open-source vulnerability scanner available from **www.nessus.org**. Nessus goes beyond nmap in that it not only provides information on open ports, but it tries to determine what service is running on each port and then probes to determine if there are any vulnerabilities for that service. Anyone in the open-source community can develop new plug-ins for Nessus using NASL (Nessus Attack Scripting Language). Therefore, when new vulnerabilities are released, a plug-in for Nessus to detect the vulnerability quickly becomes available. Nessus even includes the nessus-update-plugins script, which can be used to download all new plug-ins. This makes Nessus a very powerful tool for testing the weaknesses of a system.

Starting Nessus

Nessus is much more complex than the basic nmap port scanner. Nessus is a client server application composed of two parts:

- Nessusd—the server daemon running on port 1241 by default

- Nessus—the graphical client available for a Windows and Unix

The nessusd server daemon is started on TCP port 1241 on the Nessus server when the system boots and listens for clients to connect. The

Caution

Crashing Remote Services or Hosts

Nessus uses a methodology to scan systems that may crash or create a DoS attack on some systems. These potentially hazardous plug-ins are turned off by default for Nessus scans. You should be very careful when running Nessus against production servers or systems with all plug-ins enabled.

FIGURE 4.6 KDE desktop–Nessus GUI icon.

4

graphical Nessus client program makes a connection to the server daemon and requires the user to enter a valid Nessus login and password to access the Nessus scanning engine. Once this has been completed, the graphical interface allows you to easily determine which plug-ins to use for the scan and which target hosts or network to scan.

The SLAX image available on the book Web site already has the Nessus server daemon installed and running when you boot from the CD. The client program is also installed on the SLAX image, making it very easy for you to use Nessus. Since the server daemon starts automatically when the SLAX image boots, it is only necessary to start the graphical client program. Because

FIGURE 4.7 Nessus host login.

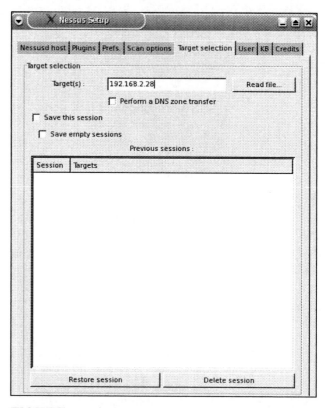

FIGURE 4.8 Nessus target selection tab.

the client relies on the X-Windowing system, you must first enter the graphical mode of SLAX by entering gui at the SLAX command prompt:

```
root@slax:~# gui
```

Once you have entered the graphical mode, the Nessus GUI icon should appear at the top of the desktop, as shown in Figure 4.6.

Once you click on the Nessus GUI icon to start the Nessus Client, the Nessusd connection screen (Figure 4.7) will appear for you to login to the server daemon. The login and password for the Nessus server on the SLAX image is the word *nessus*. Be sure to click on the login button to complete the login:

```
Login: Nessus

Password: Nessus
```

After you successfully connect to the server, the next step is to configure the scan parameters. Complete this task by using the Plugins, Preferences,

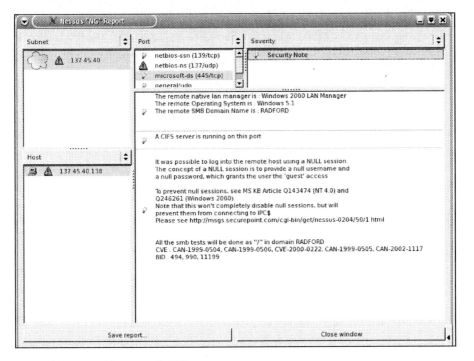

FIGURE 4.9 Nessus "NG" report.

Scan Options, and Target Selection tabs. The Target Selection tab as shown in Figure 4.8 is the screen you will modify based on the hosts or network you wish to scan.

The following are valid entries for the Target(s) field:

■ 192.168.2.28

```
Scan the host 192.168.2.28
```

■ 192.168.2.100, 192.168.2.101, 192.168.2.102

```
Scan the three listed hosts
```

■ 192.168.2.0/24

```
Scan the entire 192.168.2 Class C subnet
```

After the appropriate Plugin settings and the Target Selection have been entered, you may click on the "Start the Scan" button at the bottom to begin the scan process. Depending on the number of hosts selected to scan, the scan may take several minutes to complete. Once the scan has completed, a Nessus "NG" Report window as shown in Figure 4.9 is available so you can review the results of the scan.

Summary

At this point, you should have a detailed understanding of several common threats. The protocols used by many common attacks are ICMP, UDP, and TCP. IP address spoofing is a serious threat, and although there are various techniques for avoidance, including reverse path forwarding, route filtering, and reverse DNS look-up exist, none are foolproof by themselves. Used in combination with other firewall methods, such as ignoring ICMP echo requests sent to broadcast addresses, it may reduce the impact of DoS attacks in which IP address spoofing is prevalent.

The MITM attack is more difficult to interdict, since the machine in use may be trusted or commonly known keys in operating system distributions are not changed. However, strong authentication methods can be successful defeating the MITM attack.

Reverse DNS look-up is not totally foolproof in ensuring the validity of source IP addresses, and it may be time-consuming. Reverse path forwarding ("Source Address Validation" in the RFC 1812 terminology) is faster because it involves a check of the local forwarding and/or route tables. It is prone to errors, however, due to asymmetrical paths in internetworks, as well as the vast quantity of public IP addresses that will map to the default route of any route table.

The exercises and projects in this chapter should give you a detailed understanding of nessus. Ultimately, Virtual Private Networs (VPNs), discussed in chapter 8, will provide greater security and better protection from several of the threats reviewed in this chapter.

Test Your Skills

MULTIPLE CHOICE QUESTIONS

1. The kinds of security vulnerabilities include which of the following?

    A. software bugs

    B. configuration errors

    C. social engineering

    D. all of the above

2. Which of the following are basic network attacks?

   A. IP address spoofing

   B. Denial of Service (DoS)

   C. TCP SYN floods

   D. Man-in-the-Middle (MITM)

   E. All of the above

3. DNS reverse zones allow translation of records called:

   A. CNAME

   B. A

   C. PTR

   D. MX

4. Man-in-the-Middle (MITM) attacks can involve:

   A. forged or commonly known keys

   B. protocols without authentication

   C. forged or commonly known keys and protocols without authentication

   D. getting in between a user and the computer he is working on to deny him use

5. Defense in depth (DiD) involves:

   A. multiple layers of security

   B. a single layer of security

   C. special electronic filters on telecommunications lines

   D. using a router as a firewall

6. Since packet transfers are bidirectional, it is important to enable:

   A. established connections

   B. established and related connections

   C. marital relations

   D. route filtering

7. Which capabilities in some firewalls and routers allow legitimate ping and traceroutes but disallow DoS and DDoS?

   A. crowbarring

   B. switch-throwing

   C. rate limit and burst limits

   D. unplugging

8. Which of the following does RFC 1812 discuss?

   A. source IP address filtering

   B. martian addresses

   C. when loopback addresses are permissible

   D. all of the above

9. There are several ways to determine the validity of an IP address. What is the only completely foolproof method?

   A. using ARP

   B. reverse DNS look-up

   C. reverse path forwarding

   D. none of the above

10. The IANA defines these several kinds of TCP/UDP ports:

   A. well-known, registered, and vestigial

   B. popular, registered, and ephemeral

   C. well-known, registered, and ephemeral

   D. most popular, popular, and private

11. Application firewalls or _____ are specialized firewalls tailored for specific services, such as Web or mail servers.

   A. SOHO routers

   B. proxies

   C. routers

   D. host-based firewalls

12. Which of the following can act as a firewall?

   A. Cisco routers

   B. a computer with firewall software

   C. a proxy server

   D. all of the above

13. Stateful firewalls can use _____ to decide the state of the connection.

   A. port numbers

   B. flags in the header

   C. addressess

   D. all of the above

14. In general, stateful firewalls should distinguish between:

    A. new connections

    B. established and related connections

    C. related connections

    D. all of the above

15. An example of an authentication protocol immune to replay attacks is:

    A. PAP

    B. null authentication protocol (NAP)

    C. CHAP

    D. all of the above

16. The LAND attack:

    A. is an early form of IP address spoofing

    B. results in DoS

    C. uses identical IP address and port numbers for source and destination

    D. all of the above

17. Route filtering is the process of:

    A. finding a reverse path for a packet that needs to be returned to sender

    B. looking at the system route table and using a packet's source IP address, deciding if a packet could legitimately come from the interface it was received

    C. indicating whether an alternate path back to the send exists in the route table

    D. none of the above

18. The traceroute program uses the following protocols:

    A. ICMP

    B. IP

    C. UDP

    D. all of the above

19. Some advanced sniffing tools include:

    A. DogNose and weasel

    B. Dsniff and Ettercap

    C. ethereal and commercial sniffers

    D. C and D

20. The zone concept is:

    A. an architectural method to provide layers of security

    B. a method of defining forbidden zones in networks where no traffic may go

    C. a way to stealth an entire subnet

    D. all of the above

EXERCISES

Exercise 4.1: DNS Reverse Look-up

1. Use nslookup with type=PTR and look up 1.2.10.128.in-addr.arpa. To do this, open a command window in Windows (e.g., Start ⟶ Run ⟶ cmd) or a new terminal on a Linux or Unix. In either operating system, type the command nslookup. A prompt (>) appears. Type ? to see all the alternatives sub-commands.

2. Type the command set type=PTR. Then, at the next prompt, type the name 1.2.10.128.in-addr.arpa. The result should be the host name associated with the IP address 128.10.2.1. As you can see, the reverse look-up requires an IP address typed in reverse.

3. At the next prompt, type set type=ANY. Compare the results of the reverse look-up to looking up the name arthur.cs. purdue.edu.

Some campus networks block DNS queries of certain types. If using nslookup on a host results in timeouts, try using a Web-based service like **www.kloth.net**.

Exercise 4.2: Study IP/TCP/UDP Vulnerabilities

1. Do a search through your favorite Internet search engine and/or use the **sans.org** site (or any site) to discover and document the causes of *at least two* of the following categories:

   A security exploit attacking the IP layer

   An attack of the TCP or UDP transport layer

   An attack of an application (such as a Web server or FTP server)

   Other security exploit (i.e., describe the operation of a recent worm or virus)

2. You may use Internet sources of description for each of your chosen categories, but you *must cite the Web page or other source (magazine article, book, etc.) that you used as references.*

3. Copy and paste into your solution document any Web pages that you used, and for magazines and books use standard reference annotation, providing title, author/editor, date of publication, and page numbers. If citing a magazine or journal, you must also provide the volume and number. Your report should involve at least one single-spaced page for each category, and a page for references.

Exercise 4.3: Route Filtering

1. Read RFC 1812, focusing on sections 2 through 2.2.3, sections 5.3.7 and 5.3.8, and section 7.5.

2. Write a two-page paper on the implied implications for firewalls and routers addressing these questions:

   Is a firewall a router with added security features?

   Is a router with ACLs acting as a firewall?

   Is it necessary to filter packets, based on their source address (see 5.3.7 & 5.3.8), as well as routing protocols like RIP and OSPF (section 7.5).

Exercise 4.4: DNS Host Name Conflicts

ResTech University recently hired a new network administrator, and among his duties is to resolve some long-standing issues with DNS. The problem occurs when users try to use FTP, SSH, and various applications to connect to other systems both on and off campus. The remote system often gives an error message that the reverse DNS name is not valid or that the name of the host cannot be resolved. DHCP is used throughout the network to allow dynamic configuration of IP addresses. Apparently, when ResTech University switched from static IP addresses to DHCP addresses, many of the old entries were just left in DNS, while some of the entries in the DHCP range were not added to DNS.

1. What tools and information would you need to determine what host entries should be in DNS?

2. What tool would you use to check for the existence of each host entry in DNS, and how would you go about doing this?

3. What tool would you use to verify the reverse DNS name for each host?

Exercise 4.5: Elementary Route Tables

1. Go to any computer (Windows or Linux) and use one of the following commands to obtain the route table:

   `route print` (Windows)

   `route` (some Linux and other Unix operating systems)

   `ip route show` (Linux with the iproute command installed)

2. Explain the purpose of the loopback rows and the default row.

Exercise 4.6: Advanced Route Tables

This is a moderately advanced project for students with a prior background in networks, or students who can obtain help from the instructor.

1. First, look for routing protocol tutorials on the Internet using a search engine. A good introduction to RIP is found at **www.cisco.com/univercd/cc/td/doc/cisintwk/ito_doc/rip.pdf**

RIP works by taking a copy of the route table on a router and broadcasting the several pieces of information to its neighbors. The most important information is the destination subnetwork that the router knows, its subnet mask, and a hop count to get to the subnet. These broadcasts are called distance vectors, because the hop count is a distance to the subnet. A router initially comes up knowing only its directly connected subnetworks, but after several exchanges distance vectors, every router that runs the RIP protocol will learn of all subnets in an internetwork.

Another source of information is **www.infosyssec.net/infosyssec/netprot1.htm**

2. Refer to the GM.COM diagram in Figure 4.10. Assume that all routers are using RIP, active on all interfaces. Assume that none of the hosts are using the routing protocol RIP. Construct the route tables for two devices: the Host aztec.gm.com; and Router 4.

3. Be sure to show all routes (table rows) learned by the Router from RIP to subnets in GM.COM. Show the default route for the Router, as well as routes to directly connected subnets (you need not show *loopback* or *multicast routes* for a Router).

4. Be sure to show the *default route* and the *loopback route* for the Host, as well as routes to directly connected subnets (you need not show *multicast routes* for a Host). Mark the entries with the following codes:

   C = Directly connected subnet

   S = Static route (e.g. loopback)

   R = Learned route through the routing protocol

   D = Default route

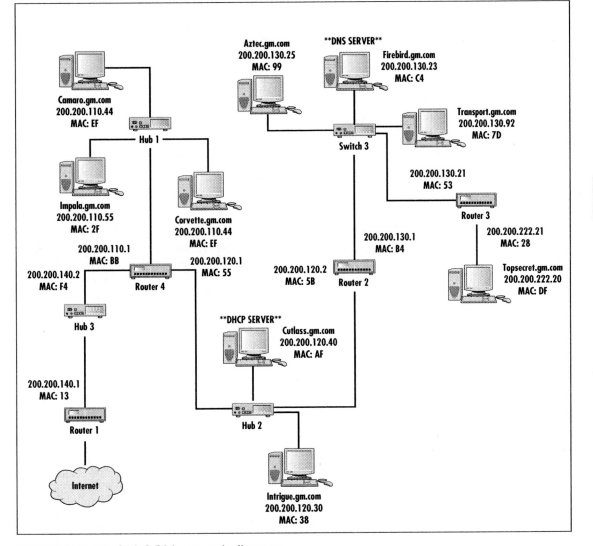

FIGURE 4.10 GM.COM network diagram.

5. Suppress the metric column for this exercise. For the Destination, Mask, and Next Hop fields, use IP address dotted-decimal notation.

Remember that for the Destination network field, your route table must successfully (and efficiently) route packets destined for any subnetwork of gm.com or destined for the Internet. Remember that the mask for all gm.com subnets is /24 (255.255.255.0), but of course the mask for a loopback entry of a Host route table will be different. The Next Hop field *must be a specific IP on one of the directly connected subnets* of the device (Router or Host).

6. For the Interface column, use the MAC address annotated on the GM.Com diagram (two-letter Hex code). Remember that the interface column contains only MAC addresses for the device itself.

7. To express your solution, use the following table format for the Router, and another for the Host.

PROJECTS

Project 4.1: Use Netstat Utility to Identify Active Connections on Any PC

Row#	Code ID	Dest Net (/n)	Mask	Next Hop	Interface (2-digit hex MAC)

Phase 1, No Applications Active

1. Go to any PC on campus, or your own PC at home. Close all windows and reboot the PC (on Windows, Start->Shutdown->Restart), and log back in. If you are at home, connect to the Internet. Make sure there are no open applications—for example, if you have an application like instant messaging that comes up when you start your computer, exit the application.

2. Now open a command window (on Windows, Programs->Accessories->Command prompt) and type netstat –a –n. You should see a collection of active TCP and UDP connections, their IP addresses, port numbers, and the state of the connection.

3. If you have a Linux PC, reboot and close all active applications. Open a terminal window and type netstat –a –n. If you have Windows XP SP2 or beyond, you might have more meaningful output for active connections using netstat –b; however, the –b option will not show services that have no client connected.

4. Copy the text from the command windows to your solution document, and use Chapters 2 and 3 as well as the following resources, to explain the local address column port numbers and the state of the connection for TCP.

   RFC 1700 (Assigned Numbers—a bit old and out of date)

   RFC 3232 (points you to **www.iana.org**, particularly **www.iana.org/ assignments/port-numbers**, for an online database of the most up-to-date assigned TCP/UDP port numbers)

   RFC 793 (defines TCP) and RFC 768 (defines UDP)

   (To access RFCs, see **www.ietf.org**, click on RFC pages, and type in the RFC number.)

   Or, you can find several resources on the Internet that have greater information than the RFCs describing the TCP/UDP port numbers and what they do, for example:

   www.seifried.org/security/ports/

5. Also use your favorite search engine to find resources for port number identification by typing "TCP/UDP port numbers" or similar keywords.

6. In your explanation, make sure you explain why an operating system would open this port without any applications running, and explain the state the connection is in for TCP.

Phase 2, Browser and Mail Applications Active

7. Open up a browser (Internet Explorer, Netscape, Mozilla, or other) and point it to a Web site of your choice. Then open up a mail client (e.g. Eudora, Netscape mail, Outlook—or if you don't have a mail client on your computer, open a separate browser window to a Web mail facility and access your mail there.) Now run the command netstat –a –n again. Copy the text output from this command to your solution file and explain the additional connections that come up.

8. Finally, remember that several operating systems begin ephemerals in the "registered" range 1024 to 4999. Explain if it is not possible to decide whether an open port is an ephemeral port or actually a service that is open on your machine.

Project 4.2: How Would You Harden Your System?

Based on the results of Project 1, you might be surprised to find so many ports opened up on your system. The process of closing down undesirable services is called "hardening." If you run a Web or mail server, it is known as "server hardening." Services that are not intended to be available represent a risk to your machine.

1. First, make sure a software firewall is running. Choose Zone Alarm, BlackICE, or Windows XP firewall and make sure it is active on the interface connecting your machine to the Internet.

2. Then, use PC Flank's advanced port scanner to scan your machine. You can find the port scanner at **www.pcflank.com/scanner1.htm**. This should expand the information that was obtained in Project 1.

3. Try the methods that you discovered during your research to close down unwanted services. Would you resolve some vulnerabilities through the software firewall? Show your instructor your results.

Project 4.3: Use ARP with SLAX and Windows

1. Open a command window in Windows, or a terminal in Linux or Unix. (You can use the SLAX Live Linux CD on any machine for this purpose.) Type the command arp. This will result in a display of options. Then type arp -a. This command should list all the ARP associations between IP addresses and hardware addresses that the machine knows.

2. Now do a reverse DNS look-up on one of the IP addresses shown in arp list (see Exercise 1). Does the IP address have a domain name (host name)? What does the arp –s command do?

Project 4.4: Using Nessus to Scan your Machine

This project is a follow on to Projects 1 and 2. After you have hardened your machine in Project 2, it is now time to rescan your machine to test the results.

1. Use nessus to scan your machine. Go to any machine except the one you hardened and use the SLAX CD for this chapter. At the boot prompt, quickly type boot: linux server.

2. Login as root, and on the next prompt type gui. This will automatically bring up nessus in an icon on the desktop of the SLAX gui.

Alternatively, there is a Nessus installer for Windows from **www. nessus.org**, if you would prefer to use a Windows machine as the attacker.

You may use the SLAX live Linux distribution from the book Website for this project. Make sure the machine you use has plenty of memory. If you use all the nessus facilities, this will take up quite a bit of memory. Alternatively, if you have a hard-drive installation of any Linux OS, that will work as well.

3. Use a crossover cable to put the two machines back-to-back. This will result in Nessus on one machine as an attacker, and your hardened machine as the other. This is to isolate the Nessus attacker machine from any other network components.

4. Compare the results of Nessus against your hardened machine, given what you expected after scanning with PCFlank. Did Nessus find any new vulnerabilities? If so, how would you improve the hardening of your machine? Write this up in a one- or two-page paper, using the Web to discover how to resolve any new vulnerabilities. Document any information you find on the web by citing the URLs as references.

▶▶ Case **Study**

In this case study, we still explore the ResTech University's DNS conflicts, as seen through firewall log records.

The firewall administrator of ResTech U., Sheila Bocquet, wants to view the log information on a Linux firewall. There is a convenient Web page hosted by the Web server program `sh-httpd`. This Web page is available from the internal inside the firewall, where hosts have no entries in the university's DNS server.

Sheila is on the main campus network, outside the firewall. She attempts to open the same Web page, but it does not render in her browser.

To find out what happened, she uses a secure shell client program and logs into the firewall. She goes through several logs, trying to determine what happened. The file auth.log show these messages:

```
Sep 2 20:02:08 firewall sshd[13220]: Accepted pass-
word for root from 127.54.192.80 port 3117 ssh2
```

CONTINUED ON NEXT PAGE

CONTINUED

```
Sep 2 20:02:09 firewall sshd[31878]: reverse mapping
checking getaddrinfo for cpsc-da-atrl06.restech.edu
failed - POSSIBLE BREAKIN ATTEMPT!
```

Although her secure shell login succeeded, the log message surprises her. She continues, examining the daemon.log file, and finds out why her firewall Web page did not come up.

The daemon.log records are:

```
Sep 2 20:02:16 firewall sh-httpd[29100]: warning:
/etc/hosts.deny, line 9: host name/address mismatch:
127.54.192.124 != cpsc-da-coop03.restech.edu

Sep 2 20:02:16 firewall sh-httpd[29100]: refused
connect from 127.54.192.124

Sep 2 20:02:44 firewall sh-httpd[7650]: warning:
/etc/hosts.deny, line 9: host name/address mismatch:
127.54.192.124 != cpsc-da-coop03. restech.edu

Sep 2 20:02:44 firewall sh-httpd[7650]: refused con-
nect from 127.54.192.124

Sep 2 20:03:47 firewall sh-httpd[2792]: warning:
/etc/hosts.deny, line 9: host name/address mismatch:
127.54.192.124 != cpsc-da-coop03. restech.edu

Sep 2 20:03:47 firewall sh-httpd[2792]: refused con-
nect from 127.54.192.124
```

Please answer the following questions:

1. Why do you suppose the secure shell session succeeded while the Web page would not?

2. Do you think it is possible for two machines with different host names to have the same IP address in a DNS server?

3. Why do you think the DNS server would find an incorrect host name for the IP addresses in the displays?

4. What should Sheila do to make sure this never happens again? (*Hint:* See solution to Exercise 4.)

Chapter | 5

Illustrated Exercises in Basic Firewall Installation

Chapter Objectives

After reading this chapter and completing the exercises, you will be able to do the following:

- Demonstrate knowledge of basic Linux firewall operating principles.
- Install and configure initial parameters for a Linux-based LEAF firewall.
- Upgrade the packages in a Linux firewall.
- Test the firewall using selected tools.

Introduction

This chapter works with the book Web site in detail. We describe a major laboratory exercise that requires three PC-based machines and a few cables, at a minimum. We also describe a more diverse setup that requires one or more low-cost Ethernet switches and optional operating systems, such as the Windows 2003 server. In the lab exercise, you will create an isolated network comprising the machines. You will need several blank CD-R discs that are suitable for creating bootable and/or data CDs. You will also need CD-burning software.

In this chapter's exercises and projects, one machine represents the outside world, which we call the external machine. This machine hosts various services the machines on the internal network will want to access. The external machine will also test the adequacy of the firewall by using several tools. Another machine is the internal server, which will nominally run DNS, Web, and mail services. The third machine, with two network interfaces, will be the firewall.

Finally, the exercises and projects will guide you through the testing process, which will assess your firewall configuration. Then, you will be able to connect your firewall to the Internet safely.

Laboratory Overview

The projects in this chapter require three machines, as shown in Figure 5.1. The internal machine is a platform for typical services inside the firewall, such as Web and mail servers. The external machine will represent the outside world (the Internet) and will host a number of applications that simulate attacks, as well as common applications the internal machines want to access. See Appendix A for more detailed information on burning CD-ROM and floppy diskette images.

The firewall must be a machine with two Ethernet interfaces. These interfaces are needed to allow connection to the internal and external machines. At a minimum, you will need a pair of crossover cables; however, two small Ethernet switches (or broadcast hubs) and four ordinary Ethernet cables can substitute for the crossover cables. Crossover cables will be the cheapest alternative for this laboratory.

Two kinds of Ethernet cabling are available:

- crossover cables
- straight-through (ordinary or regular) cables

Crossover cables are used to cable two computers back-to-back, avoiding the necessity for an Ethernet switch. Crossover cables swap the position of two wires called, transmit and receive, reversing the position of those wires on the opposite end of the cable. *Straight-through cables,* as the name implies, deliver every wire to an identical position on the destination connector.

FIGURE 5.1 Illustrating the laboratory configuration.

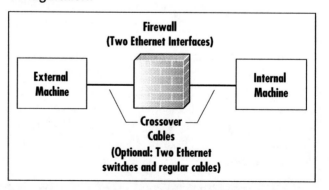

Two forms of shielding are available for Ethernet cable to improve immunity to *electromagnetic interference (EMI).* These are:

- unshielded twisted pair (UTP)

- shielded twisted pair (STP)

Unshielded twisted pair cables are the most common in use for LAN cabling. *Shielded twisted pair* is rare, used only for extreme EMI environments.

Firewall PC Requirements

For this project, you will need a PC for the firewall with these minimal capabilities:

- 32 Mbytes RAM

- CD-ROM boot is preferred. Refer to Chapter 7 and Appendix A for more details on floppy boot options

- A floppy drive for storing configuration changes

- Pentium 1 or better

- Two PCI slots and two Ethernet PCI NICs (or, if the PC has a NIC integrated into the motherboard, just one additional PCI slot and one additional PCI NIC)

This chapter assumes in great part that you have a machine capable of CD-ROM boot. The only problem with CD-ROM boot is that packages must be updated with configuration changes for each firewall's unique environment. With CD-ROM boot, a "helper" floppy is used to store configuration changes, a standard MS-DOS formatted, 1.44 Mbyte media.

In the Linux world, hardware devices are associated with directories under /dev. An MS-DOS 1.44 Mbyte floppy is the sub-folder /dev/fd0. A de-facto standard for LEAF floppy boot is the device /dev/fd0u1680, which is a floppy formatted to hold 1,680 Kbytes, or 1.68 Mbytes.

If your machine does not support CD-ROM boot or does not have a CD-ROM, you must use a floppy boot. Although a floppy boot method can support a basic Linux operating system on an MS-DOS 1.44 Mbyte floppy, it has no room for additional packages that make Linux into a firewall. You will usually need to use the device type /dev/fd0u1680.

It will help if both NICs are of the same type in the firewall computer, since you will need only one *NIC driver module* that instructs the operating system on how to access the NIC.

You will need two more PCs for the internal and external machines. These can be either Windows PCs or Linux PCs with one Ethernet port. It will also be useful if one PC can burn a CD from an image file (or find any additional PC with such a capability).

5

> **Caution**
>
> **Use the Correct Linux Floppy Device!**
>
> Make sure you are using the correct floppy device. /dev/fd0 indicates a 1.44-Mbyte floppy and /dev/fd0u1680 indicates a 1.68-Mbyte floppy. If you must boot from a floppy, you will use /dev/fd0u1680 to get the most files on your floppy.

Using the book Web site, copy the SLAX ISO image to a directory on a PC with CD-burning software. Then insert a new CD-R or CD-RW media into the CD drive and burn the image. Take a permanent marker and make a note of the SLAX image and date on the printed side of the CD.

Implementation Issues for Services on the Internal Network

Typical services that are desirable on the internal machine are DNS, Web, and mail servers. Normally, a firewall is used to protect an enterprise such as a business, a university, or a government agency. An enterprise usually will have a domain name. We will use the example of **mydomain.com**. From previous chapters, we know what TCP/UDP ports are used by DNS, and an enterprise with a domain name has two choices:

- allow a separate company to host the domain name, providing a DNS server

- implement an internal DNS server for the domain name

A similar set of choices exists for Web and mail servers. Often broadband ISPs will offer several mailboxes included in the price of the service. However, the mail address will be "joe@isp.net" rather than "joe@my domain.com." As a result, many enterprises take another approach called *virtual hosting.* There, a third party (neither the ISP nor the enterprise) hosts the domain, providing access to the domain, and Web and mail servers for the domain. This solves the problem of appearances, since now the mail names appear to be hosted by the domain.

The only problem with the virtual hosting approach is the cost. For a growing enterprise, virtual hosting may not scale well, especially if the company plans on being a participant in *e-commerce,* which involves conducting business transactions over the Internet. The next alternative after virtual hosting is *dedicated hosting* from the same third party; however, costs are generally even greater for dedicated hosting, and it often requires sharing domain, mail, and Web servers with other domains. Eventually, a more cost-effective solution with more local control may be preferred.

In light of these factors, the enterprise may wish to begin with *internal hosting* by installing and maintaining its own servers to reduce costs and avoid increasing dependence on a third party. This is the scenario we describe in this chapter.

The first step in bringing up these services on the internal machine is to insert the SLAX CD image for this chapter into any machine. Then, there is a very brief opportunity during the SLAX boot process when the boot: prompt occurs to type:

```
boot: linux server load=internal
```

Typing any character will cause the boot process to wait for **kernel parameters** at the boot: prompt. The kernel parameters provide special instructions to the operating system setting specific values in the kernel during the boot process or instructing the operating to load specific modules during boot. The parameters above will start the DNS program called named (name daemon), otherwise known as the bind 9.3 program. The command also starts the sendmail and procmail mail servers and the so-called "monkey" Web server during the ensuing boot process. Most configuration tasks will be done by the internal module that you activated. (Refer to Appendix A for more SLAX boot options and look through Exercise 5.3 at the end of the chapter.)

Installing a LEAF on the Firewall Machine

When beginning your LEAF installation, make sure the firewall machine has the minimum requirements for a LEAF firewall, as mentioned previously (see *Firewall PC Requirements*). If the machine chosen has an Ethernet NIC integrated into the motherboard, you will need to add a PCI bus Ethernet card. The simplest method is to check the type of integrated NIC, and purchase a PCI NIC that uses the same driver module. Another alternative is to disable the integrated NIC and purchase two identical PCI NICs. The purpose of having identical NICs is to simplify the loading of modules, which are drivers that work with each NIC. The book Web site has a collection of modules for most available NICs. However, a machine with different NICs can function as a firewall.

Using the book Web site, copy the firewall ISO image to a directory on any PC with CD-burning software. Next, insert a new CD-R or CD-RW media into the CD drive and burn the image. Take a permanent marker and make a note of the firewall image and date on the printed side of the CD. You may be burning multiple copies of the CD, so using a date and time will help keep track of the different versions. Then, obtain the Chapter 5 leaf.cfg file from the book Web site and transfer it to a standard 1.44-Mbyte floppy. If your machine does not support CD-ROM boot, do Exercise 5.1 at the end of the chapter now using the CD-ROM you burned above.

By default, the firewall CD image assumes that the interface eth0 is the external interface connected to your external machine. It also assumes that eth1 is the internal network. Linux and other Unix operating systems for the PC use a **network interface numbering** system based on the location of the interface on the PCI bus. PCI buses on PCs tend to order the interfaces in a descending order, going farther down the bus away from the CPU. For a tower PC, this is toward the bottom, but for a desktop PC, you may need to experiment to find which interface is eth0 versus eth1. Figure 5.2 illustrates a tower PC with an integrated NIC and two PCI cards.

5

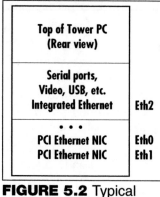

FIGURE 5.2 Typical ethernet NIC numbering scheme for a tower PC.

(For this project, you only need two total NICs on the firewall, but it is clearer to show an integrated NIC and two PCI cards to understand the numbering scheme.)

Initial Installation

By following the procedure above, you have burned a CD with a ***bootable image.*** A bootable image is a single file containing software and programs that can be copied to a CD or a floppy containing everything necessary to boot the computer to a running operating system.

First let us review the basics of any Linux system that uses the syslinux ***boot loader.*** The boot loader is a program located on the master boot record of the hard disk or, in this case, a CD or a floppy and is the first program to execute when a computer is turned on and tells the system how to load the OS kernel. The packages that are loaded are controlled by a file called syslinux.cfg. An example is shown in Figure 5.3. (Although the last line beginning with "default" in Figure 5.3 appears to wrap, it is actually one continuous line).

FIGURE 5.3 A typical syslinux.cfg file.

```
display syslinux.dpy

timeout 0

default linux initrd=initrd.lrp init=/linuxrc rw
root=/dev/ram0 LEAFCFG=/dev/fd0:msdos
PKGPATH=/dev/fd0:msdos,/dev/cdrom:iso9660 syst_size=12M
log_size=4M
LRP=root,etc,local,modules,iptables,pump,keyboard,shorwall,ul
ogd,dnscache,daemontl
```

There are several features of this syslinux.cfg:

- There is a *package path* variable that identifies two possible devices (CD-ROM and floppy).

- There is reference to a file named leaf.cfg — this is to get around a 254-character limit on the last line of syslinux.cfg.

- A (partial) list of packages to load—the rest can be specified in the file leaf.cfg, an example of which is shown in Figure 5.4.

- The parameter syst_size changes the /dev/root partition to 12 Mbytes of memory, and the parameter log_size changes the size of the /var/log partition to 4 Mbytes.

Obtain a high-quality floppy disk and copy the appropriate leaf.cfg file from the book Web site to the floppy, or simply cut and paste a leaf.cfg configuration using a free editor like editpadlite (**www.editpadpro.com**), editing as needed. For a first laboratory exercise you should not need to edit leaf.cfg.

When you look at Figure 5.3, notice the LEAFCFG= parameter. This means that the LEAF CD image is configured to look for a leaf.cfg file on a standard DOS-formatted 1.44 Mbyte floppy disk. Further, notice that the first preference for package source is the same type of floppy, with CD-ROM as the backup device. This means that if a package exists on the floppy, when LEAF loads, it will find it there first, and only load other packages from the CD-ROM. Finally, note that the entire text beginning with "default linux …." through "daemontl" must be on a single line, with a 254-character limit.

Since you may want to add other packages later, you must name them in the leaf.cfg file if the line in syslinux.cfg has insufficient room. The first

FIGURE 5.4 A typical leaf.cfg file.

```
# This file is parsed as a shell script
# < other comments deleted for brevity >
# Other variables you might want to set in this file include:
# LRP          Packages to load
# PKGPATH Device(s) to load packages from
# syst_size    Size of root ramdisk
# tmp_size     Size of /tmp ramdisk
# log_size     Size of /var/log ramdisk
# Example:
log_size=12M
LRP="$KCMD_LRP dhcpd"
LRP="$LRP weblet"
```

Caution

Editing Key Linux Configuration Files

Many people will use Windows machines to generate their LEAF boot diskettes or boot CD-ROMs. This will require editing syslinux.cfg and/or leaf.cfg files. Windows editors can insert unacceptable end-of-line (EOL) characters into these files. There are two options to overcome this problem:

- using the dos2unix utility (available for either Windows or Linux/Unix operating systems)

- using a low-cost editor like editpad lite (**www. editpadpro.com**)

LRP= line must use the string keyword $KCMD_LRP, while the remaining must use only $LRP.

You can make changes to the packages you need, saving them to the same floppy with your leaf.cfg. Clearly, you will need a good, high-quality floppy disk, since each student or SOHO environment will be different with respect to many features, including the internal and external IP addresses, and the VPNs you would like to implement. Notice in Figure 5.4 that the size of the log file partition, /var/log, is changed to 12 Mbytes. This overrides the 4 Mbyte specification of the syslinux.cfg file in Figure 5.3, when a floppy with this file is inserted in the floppy drive.

The reason for this increased size for logging is that the "daemon tools" package, daemontl.lrp, was loaded by syslinux.cfg. This package, along with certain dnscache parameters, turns on logging of all DNS requests. Just a few active hosts on the internal network might produce hundreds of records daily.

With no specification of the parameter tmp_size, the LEAF system will take the remainder of available memory for use by the /tmp partition. This is the memory that is used for package updates by the backup menu in lrcfg.

Note also in Figure 5.4 that two additional packages are added. One is the Dynamic Host Configuration Protocol (DHCP) daemon, dhcpd.lrp. This facility allows hosts on an internal network to acquire IP addresses, the default gateway, and the default DNS server automatically via the firewall. The SLAX Linux image from the book Web site normally uses DHCP to acquire its IP address. However, for the specifications you will select from the boot prompt, static IP addresses will be set up on the SLAX machines. There is no conflict in having a DHCP server available to the SLAX machines. For these projects, it will simply never be used.

The last package mentioned in leaf.cfg is weblet.lrp. This facility is a small Web server that hosts a status page for the firewall.

For CD-ROM boot, once you have burned a bootable CD-ROM, you should need only a single 1.44-Mbyte floppy to save your updated packages. Make sure you include the appropriate leaf.cfg file on the floppy.

If your machine does not support CD-ROM boot, refer to the book Web site and select one of the alternative boot methods. The simplest of these is to use a 1.44-Mbyte boot floppy while reading the packages from CD-ROM. These images are available from the book Web site.

Locating Your NIC Module

You must locate a module for your Ethernet cards. To do this, look on the book Web site to download the appropriate module. These are modules in the Linux sense (/sbin/lsmod, /sbin/insmod, and other commands are included with LEAF), but they will be loaded upon bootup; you will not manually load them.

For example, a common network card is the 3COM 3c509Tx. For that NIC (and several others), you would use a module file called 3c59x.o. On the CD-ROM-boot image, the modules.lrp package will contain these modules:

- 3c59x

- 8390

- eepro100

- natsemi

- tulip

When you first boot your firewall, there may be no module for your NICs (all the images from the book Web site will load 3c59x.o driver module). These module files live in the directory /lib/modules in the LEAF distributions. Check by logging into the firewall as root using the password Rootr00t. Initially, the system will put you into the ***leaf-router-configuration (lrcfg)*** menu as shown in Figure 5.5. Exit this by typing q. You should then see the command prompt #. Type the command:

```
ip addr show
```

If you see no interfaces except loopback and dummy, then the correct module needs to be obtained. If you see eth0 and eth1 with IP addresses assigned to them, then you probably have 3com NICs. For all other NIC modules listed, it is only necessary to edit the file /etc/modules.conf, as described in the next section. If your NIC requires a different module than those listed, you will have to use the complete procedure in the next section (*Installing a Different NIC Module*).

A package called modules.lrp is included that is a compression of the modules you have chosen and the etc/modules.conf configuration file. The modules.conf file determines which modules are loaded. There are also several Point-to-Point protocol (PPP) modules and several connection-tracking modules. Only 3c59x.o is loaded for your NICs, however.

Two directories are involved in the process of module selection and loading in a Linux system. They are:

- /etc and the file modules.conf

- /lib/modules

The directory `/lib/modules` contains all the ".o's" that are loaded by /etc/modules.conf.

If the module that you need is not included in the /lib/modules directory, you will have to download it from the book site. Another resource to find the appropriate module is the installation guide: **leaf.sourceforge.net/doc/guide/bidownmod.html** (Nilo and Wolzak 2003). Another resource is the user guide for the LEAF firewall (Nilo 2003)

You may have to check with the manufacturer of your network card, since some of the modules go by the chipset that is used—for example, natsemi.o is a module for most cards using the National Semiconductor Ethernet chipset.

Installing a Different NIC Module

Once you have identified the module that your Ethernet NICs require, edit the configuration of your firewall by entering the lrcfg utility. This utility has a main menu, shown in Figure 5.5.

Option 3 in lrcfg is the Packages Configuration option. Select this and then select Modules. This brings up a submenu containing a single item: modules. Select modules to edit the /etc/modules.conf file. If the module for the NICs in your firewall machine is present in the /lib/modules directory (see the previous bulleted list), then you need only edit /etc/modules. conf. Otherwise, proceed completely through this section.

This will bring up an editor that that will allow you to modify the /etc/modules file. Use the editor to comment out any unnecessary NIC modules and load the ones you need. Note that some modules will require the pci-scan module to be loaded first. Alternatively, the vi editor is available, or the command "edit" brings up the lrcfg editor.

Next, you will need to put the module on your floppy. Download the module from the book Web site on any machine and copy the module to the floppy that you used for your leaf.cfg file. (Alternatively, you may use any floppy that is MS-DOS 1.44 Mbyte formatted.) Once you have copied the module to the floppy, return to the firewall machine and insert the floppy into the firewall drive. Then issue the commands:

```
mount -t msdos /dev/fd0 /mnt

cd /lib/modules
```

FIGURE 5.5 The lrcfg main menu.

```
              LEAF configuration menu


   1 ) Network configuration
   2 ) System configuration
   3 ) Packages configuration

                              b) Back-up a package
                              c) Back-up your LEAF disk
                              h) Help
q) quit

 ------------------------------------------------------------

    Selection:
```

```
cp /mnt/yourmodule.o /lib/modules
```

```
umount /mnt
```

(Substitute the actual module name for *yourmodule*.) This will copy the module to the directory /lib/modules.

The method of attaching **permanent storage volumes** in Linux and other Unix variants begins with the command mount. A permanent storage volume is a drive or volume where data can be retrieved, files can be updated, or new files can be stored on the media. The media can be a **removable storage volume,** such as a floppy or usb drive, that can be removed from the computer. The umount command de-associates the device /dev/fd0 with the directory /mnt in the examples above.

Devices in Linux and Unix variants are represented by files in the /dev directory. There will be numerous devices that are not yet attached to the machine in the /dev directory. The device /dev/fd0 in the commands above is such a device and represents a standard 1.44-Mbyte format. The –t parameter specifies an MS-DOS file system. Another device that will appear in /dev is /dev/fd0u1680. This represents a floppy formatted at 1.68 Mbytes. (It is not well known that most floppy drives can be formatted reliably at this density.) The other element of the umount command is a "substitute" directory for the device. In the commands above this is the directory /mnt.

You are now ready to backup your modules.lrp package. Previously, you edited the /etc/modules file to specify the module to load. Now, at a command prompt on the firewall type:

```
lrcfg
```

Then select the backup option b.

A menu will be displayed that lists all the packages that were loaded when you first booted the image. Unless you have previously saved the package to a floppy, this list will indicate the CD-ROM as the *package destinations* for all packages. The package destination indicates the media or location where a specific LEAF package resides. You must change the destination of the module option by typing:

```
d modules
```

If you do not see [fd0] available, select the custom destination and specify /dev/fd0, indicated by the [fd0] option. Also choose the [msdos] file format. (Your 1.44-Mbyte floppy with leaf.cfg should still be in the floppy drive.) This should return you to the main backup menu. Then type:

```
b modules
```

This will place the new modules package onto your floppy. The backup procedure will ask you if there is enough space on the floppy disk. There should be, so type **y**. The backup process should then say, "backup of modules completed."

Caution

Don't Forget to UMOUNT

Until the umount command is executed, partial contents destined for the media are held in a disk cache in the system memory. It is important to umount the floppy before removing it from the drive, or data may be lost. If you forget the umount command and remove the floppy disk, put it back in the drive and issue the umount command.

5

Now, type q until you come to a Linux prompt (the #). Then reboot your machine by activating a ***restart sequence.*** Usually this can be done by the reboot command or, alternatively, by using the Ctrl-Alt-Del sequence.

In some rare cases you must type the command shutdown -h now because a Ctrl-Alt-Del sequence doesn't work. When a "Power Down" prompt appears, the usual Ctrl-Alt-Delete will reboot your machine. Even more rarely, you may need to press the power button once to power off. Then press the power button again to power on.

Once rebooting is completed, you should be able to log in as before. Check again to make sure the interfaces eth0 and eth1 are present by using the ip addr show command.

Upgrading an Installation

Initially as you read this chapter and install the LEAF firewall, you will not need to upgrade to newer versions of the packages on the CD. However, this section provides information that will be necessary if you do decide to upgrade the packages on the CD. Of the two primary packages that are used with this book, Shorewall and FreeS/WAN, Shorewall is still under active development, and there are later versions of FreeS/WAN. See Chapter 8 for more details on these packages. As new features are added or bugs are fixed, upgrading is inevitable.

So far we have discussed the two commands associated with the backup menu: the backup destination and the backup command itself. A third command that we have not discussed is called "the type." In the backups you have done so far, the type was "***full backup***" that backs up all of the packages. There is another type called "***partial backup***".

The purpose of the partial backup is to allow packages to be upgraded easily. The partial backup saves only the configuration files. For some packages, there are quite a few configuration files (for example, Shorewall). It would be tedious to make a copy of each configuration file (shorewall.conf, interfaces, zones, policy, rules, etc.), so the partial backup provides a simple way to get all the configuration files associated with a package in one step. The other benefit is that partial backups provide compression of these files.

For example, to upgrade Shorewall, the command to change the backup type is:

```
t shorwall
```

This command will put the configuration files on a floppy, assuming the destination has been directed there. Once the configuration data files are separated from the rest of the package, it's an easy matter to upgrade the package while keeping your current configuration. There are a few exceptions when certain old configuration files will not have acceptable configuration statements, but these should be rare and well documented by the package providers.

Below are the step-by-step instructions to upgrade your package while keeping your configuration intact. These instructions assume a conventional CD-ROM-boot LEAF system with updated packages and leaf.cfg on a separate floppy.

1. Make a backup copy of your firewall diskette. The backup copy is the disk to which you will add the upgraded package. You can do this by option c from the main lrcfg menu, "backup your LEAF disk." (This option works whether the diskette is a boot diskette or helper diskette used with a CD-ROM boot.) Mark your original boot or helper diskette "OLD" and mark the backup copy "NEW." Put the OLD diskette in a safe place and do not use it during the upgrade process. This way, in case something goes wrong, you have a fallback.

2. Format a floppy (or obtain a preformatted MS-DOS 1.44-Mbyte floppy) to use as a temporary location for your configuration files. Label this diskette "XFER."

3. Remove your current firewall configuration disk and replace it with the XFER disk. Use the lrcfg backup menu to make a partial backup of the package you want to upgrade, being sure to backup the files to the XFER diskette. Make sure the destination of the package you are upgrading is floppy.

4. From the backup menu, type:

   ```
   t shorwall

   p
   ```

5. Then type:

   ```
   shorwall
   ```

6. Quit from the lrcfg menu system so you have a Linux prompt. Then type:

   ```
   # umount /mnt
   ```

7. Take out the XFER disk. Download and copy the package(s) you want to upgrade onto the NEW diskette.

8. Since the package names will be something like "shorwall 2.0.9.lrp," rename the file to shorwall.lrp and copy to the NEW disk. Otherwise the boot process will not find the package. Put NEW disk into the floppy drive of the firewall.

9. In our cases so far, the helper diskette is a 1.44-Mbyte standard MS-DOS floppy, with leaf.cfg and the new shorwall.lrp file. This way, you could download the new package on a Windows machine and transfer it to the floppy.

10. Reboot your firewall using the NEW diskette and login. At this point your upgraded package will have the default configuration, not your configurations from the old package. As usual, upon login lrcfg will be executed. Exit lrcfg to get to a Linux prompt. Remove your NEW diskette and insert the XFER diskette.

11. Mount the XFER disk by typing:

    ```
    # mount -t msdos /dev/fd0 /mnt
    ```

12. CD to the root directory by typing:

    ```
    # cd /
    ```

13. Manually extract configuration data for each package you upgraded:

    ```
    # tar -xzvf /mnt/shorwall.lrp
    ```

14. Unmount the XFER diskette:

    ```
    # umount /mnt
    ```

15. Remove the XFER disk.

16. Put the NEW diskette back in the floppy drive.

17. Using lrcfg, do a full backup of your upgraded package. From the backup menu type:

    ```
    t shorwall
    ```

    ```
    f
    ```

    This will make the backup full. Then type:

    ```
    b shorwall
    ```

18. Reboot, verifying the firewall works as expected. One way to do this is to make sure you can load any Web page from an internal machine if you are connected to the Internet. Alternatively, if you are still in the configuration of Figure 5.1, try to load the pages **www.intexample. com** and **www.extexample.com**. For whichever package you upgraded, you should test various features.

FYI: Making a Bootable CD using WinISO or MagicISO

Although the images from the Web site are bootable, and any CD-burning software will burn a bootable CD from them, you may want to provide a more reliable boot mechanism. This is true whether you use floppy boot or a "helper" floppy with CD-ROM boot. The CD plus updated packages on a floppy are somewhat vulnerable, since floppies occasionally fail. Combining

CONTINUED ON NEXT PAGE

CONTINUED

the updated packages and the packages from the CD that have not been updated to create a new CD allows you to create a customized CD with your packages and updates providing a reliable boot mechanism. The goal is to copy the packages from your floppy onto any machine—even Windows, if you use a 1.44-Mbyte floppy and then update the original firewall image. If you use floppy boot, use the Winimage batch assistant or another tool to import your 1.68-Mbyte floppy to a Windows OS. To do this, you will need to update the ISO image that you downloaded. A program is required that can:

- open the existing firewall ISO image and allow you to overwrite the packages with those on your floppy
- create a new bootable image

Note that you may use a bootable CD-ROM even if you use floppy boot. Some ISO image software may restrict you to creating an ISO image from scratch. In that case, you will have to make it bootable.

The popular, modestly priced utility MagicISO (**www.magiciso.com**) or WinISO (**www.winiso.com/**) is an easy way to make a bootable CD. In MagicISO, a bootable CD dialog box is under the Tools menu. (MagicISO has more options for boot file information.) Each product has the option to load boot information from a bootable file. In the LEAF firewall image you obtained, there is a file named bootdisk.bin. You can extract this file from any firewall image and use it as the boot information file.

These software utilities are for Windows. Others may be available for Linux. We recommend trying to open the original firewall ISO image with whatever software is available and see if it allows overwriting the packages that you have updated so far. Then, save the new ISO image as a different filename, and burn a new firewall boot CD.

Installing Linux on the External Machine

To install Linux on the external machine, we will again burn a SLAX CD-ROM for booting the external machine. You can use the same image for the internal machine. To bring up services on the external machine, there is a *very brief* opportunity during the SLAX boot process to type:

```
boot: linux server load=external
```

This starts all services and configures the IP addresses correctly for the external machine. The load=external line activates a module named external. You should take time to learn about modules in Linux, since it is a powerful feature.

After logging in as root, at the next command prompt, type:

```
#: route add -net 0.0.0.0/0 -gw 192.168.1.254
```

This adds a default route to the system route table. In general, a default route catches all the traffic not destined for directly connected networks. In the case of the projects for this chapter, the internal and external machines have just one directly connected network. The firewall has two directly connected networks.

In the most recent command, the phrase `-gw 192.168.1.254` says "take any packets that match this row and forward them to 192.168.1.254." This, as you will discover, is the IP address on the other end of the cable from the external machine if you have successfully connected your cables to the right NIC.

This command also specifies a destination network of 0.0.0.0 and a network mask of length 0 by the phrase `-net 0.0.0.0/0`. The IP layer on the external machine will take each incoming packet from any application and go through all the rows of the route table using the following recipe:

- Take the destination IP address from the packet.

- Create a mask of the appropriate length from the current route table row.

- Use a binary AND operation on the mask and the destination IP address.

- Check if the result matches the destination network field of the current route table row.

- If so, save the gateway (gw) as a possible next-hop for the packet.

- Once all route table rows are scanned, select the possible next-hop by using the row with the longest network mask.

The way a default route works is by representing the shortest possible network mask: length zero! Therefore, the default route will never be chosen except as a last resort.

Even in a completely simple network such as the three-machine network in this chapter, each machine needs a default row in its table to function. When you do the exercises and projects in this chapter, you will be loading a Web page from a machine on the other side of the firewall. The default row you add is the only way that packets destined for that Web site will ever be successfully routed.

Services and Tools on the External Machine

We have looked at DNS through the bind program and the Web server monkey. We now turn to the mail server sendmail.

Sendmail has been a staple of Unix and Linux operating systems for many years. Its main Web page is **www.sendmail.org/**. Sendmail has a few restrictions, which we will discuss in the general context of mail services.

Mail services rely on three protocols:

■ Simple Mail Transfer Protocol (SMTP)

■ Post Office Protocol (POP)

■ Internet Mail Access Protocol (IMAP)

Each of these protocols requires a client program and a server program, or daemon. SMTP is mandatory for any mail server or client; it is defined in RFC 821 (Postel 1982). POP is defined in RFC 1725 (Myers and Rose 1994), and IMAP is defined by RFC 2060 (Crispin 1996).

While sendmail implements only SMTP, the other two protocols will fetch the mail. Most mail client software supports either IMAP or POP. They are alternatives with different properties. With POP, a mail client on a PC will actually download all mail messages to the hard drive of the PC, and they are removed from the mail server. With IMAP, only the titles of the mail messages are downloaded, and the mail messages stay on the mail server until they are deleted. The advantage of IMAP is that a person can use any machine—possibly even Webmail—to continuously check e-mail without having the mail messages spread over several machines.

Other mail servers implement SMTP, IMAP, and POP in one facility. There is the Mercury32 mail server for Windows (**www.pmail.com**) and the Courier mail transfer agent for Linux (**www.courier-mta.org**). These facilities are open-source and freely downloadable.

Finally, there are two tools that the external machine will use to attack the firewall and try to obtain access to the internal machine(s): Nmap and Nessus. You have learned about these testing tools in previous chapters, and a few exercises and projects in this chapter will use Nessus and Nmap in more detail.

IN PRACTICE: Using Any Linux OS to Create LEAF Boot Diskettes

Occasionally, the situation arises where a machine has no CD-ROM boot capability. Now that you have a couple of SLAX Linux machines available, it may be easier to create boot floppies for LEAF from these machines. To do this, go to a SLAX machine (any Unix or Linux machine should be suitable) and insert a high-quality floppy disk into the floppy drive.

▶▶ CONTINUED ON NEXT PAGE

> **▶▶ CONTINUED**
>
> First, download the LEAF floppy boot image of your choice from the book Web site. If you chose a 1.44-Mbyte boot floppy (using CD-ROM for your packages), then replace the phrase `/dev/fd0u1680` with `/dev/fd0` in the following commands.
>
> Start by opening the Web browser by clicking on the globe icon in the GUI, and download the image of your choice.
>
> Open a terminal window or, from the command prompt (if you are unable to run the SLAX GUI), type the following commands:
>
> ```
> fdformat /dev/fd0u1680
> ```
>
> ```
> dd if=<image file name> of= /dev/fd01680
> ```
>
> Substitute the actual file name, including full path if you are not in the directory where the image file resides, for the text `<image file name>`.
>
> You should see the following for a 1,680-Kbyte floppy following the previous dd command:
>
> ```
> 3360+0 records in
> ```
>
> ```
> 3360+0 records out
> ```
>
> This indicates the transfer of the image was successful. Note that certain Windows operating systems, including Windows XP and Windows 2000 SP4, will not format a diskette on a USB floppy 1.68 Mbytes. Linux cannot format a USB floppy at all.

The Blackhat/Whitehat Scheme: Using Tools to Assess Your Firewall's Capabilities

Your firewall is all that protects your internal machine(s) from the true Internet, especially in the case of broadband connectivity like DSL or cable modem service. The tools available to test your firewall—Nessus and Nmap—are included on the SLAX CD image. At the end of this chapter, you will put your newfound knowledge to work on Projects 5.1 through 5.3 and then test your firewall by doing Project 5.4.

The scheme of all four projects is to use your external machine as the blackhat (the attacker) and your internal machine as the whitehat. Your firewall stands between the two machines and should protect your internal machine from most attacks.

Once you have tested your firewall from the external machine with these tools, you will be ready to connect your firewall to the Internet or campus network.

Connecting Your Firewall to the Internet or Campus Network

Now it is time to take the next big step—connecting your firewall to the Internet or campus network. But first, you will need to make a few changes to your firewall's configuration.

First, disconnect the external machine, which has been playing the role of the external network (by convention in the firewall, the interface eth0). Replace the crossover cable with a straight-through Ethernet cable and plug one end into your eth0 NIC, and the other into an Ethernet port leading to your campus network or ISP (for example, a cable or DSL modem).

Second, activate the DHCP server on the internal interface of your firewall. This is a wise change if you plan to add more machines on the internal subnet. This optional step is described in the next section.

FIGURE 5.6 The Interface eth0: transition from static IP address to DHCP.

```
Before editing /etc/interfaces

#auto eth0
#iface eth0 inet dhcp
# ...
auto eth0
 iface eth0 inet static
 address 192.168.1.254
 masklen 24
 broadcast 192.168.1.255
# gateway


After editing /etc/interfaces

auto eth0
iface eth0 inet dhcp
# ...
#auto eth0
# iface eth0 inet static
# address 192.168.1.254
# masklen 24
# broadcast 192.168.1.255
# gateway
```

Third, the firewall image you used to create your firewall had static IP addresses on each interface. Most ISPs and campus networks will require you to use the DHCP client on the external interface to get an IP address from your ISP. This will require you to make a few additional changes to the firewall, as described below in *Configuring for Your Environment*.

FYI: Static IP Addresses for Your Campus Network or ISP

If you are interested in hosting your own Web server, mail server, and even a DNS server, it is usually preferable to have a static IP address. This is because occasionally your IP address on the external firewall interface might change if you obtain it via DHCP from your ISP or campus network. Once that IP address changes, references to DNS, Web, and mail servers will be in error until you change the entries in various files in /var/named/ on the SLAX internal machine. (You may keep your internal servers running on the internal machine, if your campus will allow it.)

You will need to use port-forwarding to allow DNS, Web, and mail traffic to be mapped from a public IP address on the external side of your firewall to the private IP addresses on your internal network.

Your ISP will normally require a public IP address rather than the private ones we have been using. The same may be true of campus networks, unless the campus is using private IP address space and NATing the private addresses to public ones at the boundary of the campus network. Check with your ISP or campus network administrator if you want a static IP address. If you are allowed to have one, proceed as follows. (An ISP may charge a monthly fee for a static IP.)

You must determine several items from your campus network or ISP:

- the static IP address(es) that are allowable
- the subnet mask for the subnet you will be connected to
- the gateway router for your subnet
- the DNS servers available (preferably two DNS servers)

Once you have determined these parameters, keep the static IP declaration on eth0 in the figure above, and edit the parameters accordingly.

The next change you must make is to determine which DNS servers are available to you. You must edit the files /etc/resolv.conf and etc/dnscache/env/DNS1. This will be described in the next section.

The requirement to edit /etc/dnscache/env/DNS1 assumes your campus network does not allow direct contact with the DNS root servers. You must then alter the forwarding configuration by editing the dnscache package configuration files.

Forwarding is already configured in your firewall image, but the DNS server IP addresses being used by dnscache are the internal and external DNS servers on your SLAX machines. You will need to change those addresses to one or, preferably, two DNS servers on your campus network or ISP. The following explains the procedure.

Configuring for Your Environment

There is a general process that must first be carried out to make your firewall fully functional. By now, you will have successfully loaded the appropriate modules for your NICs and updated the etc package. Next, you must take the following steps to allow the firewall to function correctly:

1. Insert the CD and floppy (with leaf.cfg and updated modules package) into the firewall and reboot, if the machine is not up. Alternatively, enter the lrcfg menu at any firewall prompt.

2. If you rebooted, use the password Rootr00t to login as root. (Later, from a command line, use the passwd command to change your password, and backup the /etc package.)

   The firewall will initially place you in the lrcfg program, a menu-based facility to configure the firewall. There are several major options, as Figure 5.5 shows.

3. First, update your firewall to forward DNS queries to a server other than your internal and external machines. We will do this first through the DNSCACHE feature of the firewall. Enter 3 for Packages Configuration at the lrcfg prompt. You should see a list of all possible packages. Select DNSCACHE.

4. Select the ISP DNS addresses option. This reveals a simple file that allows you to change the DNS addresses that will be used to resolve new names. This could be your college DNS server, and you may add multiple DNS servers, one per line. If you are a SOHO firewall user, use the DNS address(es) that your ISP gave you. When changes are complete, type ctrl-Q. A prompt at the bottom of the display requires you to type a Y to update the file.

5. Enter q (quit) twice to get back to the main lrcfg menu. Type 1, Network configuration. Type 5 to edit resolv.conf. Put the same DNS IP addresses in the resolve.conf file. Type ctrl-Q and Y to save.

6. Enter q (quit) twice to get back to the main lrcfg menu, and type b (backup). The Backup Packages menu is displayed. Make sure the destination for the DNSCACHE package is /dev/fd0 (standard 1.44-Mbyte MS-DOS floppy). If not, change the destination using the d option. For DNSCACHE this is accomplished by typing d dnscache. This will result in a menu that includes the ISO9660 CD-ROM option and an option for a custom destination. Choose custom, and use /dev/fd0 with MS-DOS file system.

7. Backup DNSCACHE by typing b dnscache. The backup process will compare the former package size (if any exists on the floppy) and ask whether there is enough space. There should be, so type y. Type q (quit) to exit until you obtain the usual command prompt (#).

   Note: There is currently a bug in lrcfg that does not allow you to change the destination of multiple packages. However, you can change the destination of all packages by the d e command, although it is rarely useful.

8. You will have to reboot (Ctrl-Alt-Delete).

9. Now, you must put the same DNS server IP address into the etc package as you did the DNSCACHE package. To do this, select item 1), Network Configuration from the main lrcfg menu. Select 5), resolv.conf. Enter nameserver statements for the DNS server that you want to use on the external machine, using the external machine's IP address.

10. Change the destination for etc to /dev/fd0 and backup the etc package. Once several packages have the appropriate destinations, you can backup each package in one lrcfg session if you need to make further changes.

11. Reboot.

12. You can choose to offer DHCP service to your internal network, and this is already configured in the images for this chapter. Check the DHCPD package under the packages menu. You will see two options, one for DHCPD daemon config file, /etc/dhcpd.conf, and another for the startup script. Select the DHCPD config file. Notice the IP addresses in the 192.168.10 range. Your internal machines will have an address in that range when you boot any machine (e.g., SLAX with no options at the boot: prompt).

13. One option is to leave your internal server in place, with its static addresses. Obtain another machine and an Ethernet switch, replacing

the internal machine's crossover cable with a straight-through cable to the switch. Also place a straight-through cable between your firewall's internal NIC and the switch.

14. Test: using a client machine (e.g., SLAX) booted on the internal network, check the IP address by opening a command terminal and typing `ifconfig`. If SLAX has obtained an IP address, then open a Web browser and go to your favorite Web site.

15. If you have used DHCP from your ISP or campus network, log in to your firewall and check that the IP address has been set for the external interface by typing `IP addr show` at any firewall prompt.

The above procedure is the general method for making any changes to configuration. Once you have made all the necessary changes and backed up packages, you will need to reboot.

The Web page provided by the weblet package is very useful; you can access it by simply typing the firewall's internal IP address in a browser on a machine on the internal network. We recommend that you explore the links, especially the RAM disk icon, and the various log files. When viewing the weblet log file selections, notice that several archives are numbered 0 through 3. Since logs will accumulate as a firewall operates — and Linux firewalls are so stable that many will run for years without rebooting — the log files are gnu-zipped and rotated. There are a total of four archives in addition to the current log.

You are now ready to enjoy access to the Internet and/or your campus network. You have completed a major milestone in configuring a successful firewall project. Enjoy your firewall!

5

IN PRACTICE: The /etc/fstab File

Most Unix and Linux systems have a file called /etc/fstab that lists static file system mount information. The LEAF systems have an fstab file with only a single entry for the proc file system, expressed in these lines:

```
<files      <mount    <type>    <options>    <dump>
system>     point>                            <pass>


proc        /proc     proc      noauto       00
```

You can add lines to your fstab file if you are highly familiar with Linux, including auto-mounting through the options parameter.

Summary

By now, you should have a basic understanding of installing and configuring a LEAF firewall and using SLAX to bring up the internal and external machines. The configuration of basic firewall operations should be clear, and you should be able to implement services on the internal machine.

Additionally, you should be able to use firewall testing tools on the external machine. Nessus and Nmap are the primary capabilities that you need to test the firewall. Burning a bootable CD can be done from any CD-burning software.

You can revise the contents of a bootable CD with several low-cost software packages. The process for modifying a bootable image involves software that can manipulate ISO images.

The process for making configuration changes to the packages in LEAF is a repeatable general process. It is advisable to occasionally take the updated packages from a floppy and update the CD image to improve the reliability of the boot process.

Test Your Skills

MULTIPLE CHOICE QUESTIONS

1. Cables suitable for Ethernet include: (choose all that apply)

   A. straight-through Ethernet cables.

   B. crossover Ethernet cables.

   C. twisted sister Ethernet cables.

   D. unshielded twisted pair.

2. To link two computers' Ethernet NICs without using an Ethernet switch, you would use

   A. straight-through Ethernet cables.

   B. twisted sister Ethernet cables.

   C. unshielded twisted pair.

   D. crossover Ethernet cables.

3. To use an Ethernet switch between two or more computers, you would use

   A. straight-through Ethernet cables.

   B. twisted sister Ethernet cables.

   C. unshielded twisted pair.

   D. crossover Ethernet cables.

4. The choices for Web and DNS hosting include: (choose all that apply)

    A. virtual hosting.

    B. redundant hosting.

    C. dedicated hosting.

    D. internal hosting.

5. Each type of Ethernet NIC requires a unique

    A. boot loader.

    B. module.

    C. Ethernet switch.

    D. kernel parameter.

6. Cables that are most resistant to EMI are

    A. STP.

    B. UTP.

    C. twisted sister.

    D. crossover cables.

7. You may lose data on a permanent storage device in Linux unless you

    A. remount the device.

    B. mount the device.

    C. unmount the device.

    D. reboot the computer.

8. Which of the following is a possible format for a 3.5-inch floppy disk?

    A. 720 Kbyte

    B. 1.44 M byte

    C. 1.68 M byte

    D. All of the above

9. When you are backing up a LEAF package, it is important to check the correct

    A. destination.

    B. file system and format.

    C. package.

    D. All of the above

5

10. To restart a PC running Linux, you can
    A. press Ctrl-Alt-Del.
    B. shut down –h now.
    C. press the power button.
    D. All of the above

11. Upgrading a LEAF package requires: (check all that apply)
    A. saving a backup copy of your original boot diskette or package diskette.
    B. having a new boot or package diskette.
    C. creating a storage area network for the old configuration files.
    D. using a transfer floppy for the configuration files.

12. To modify the packages and the configuration of a boot CD-R, it is necessary to
    A. perform a full backup to the existing CD-R.
    B. use Winiso or MagicIso to modify the contents of a boot image.
    C. perform a partial backup of the existing CD-R.
    D. it is impossible to create a modified boot CD-R.

13. A high-density 3.5-inch floppy can be used at this capacity to provide the maximum space for a boot diskette:
    A. 1.44 Mbytes
    B. 1.68 Mbytes
    C. 1.2 Mbytes
    D. 720 Kbytes

14. The identity of packages loaded by a LEAF system is contained in which of the following?
    A. syslinux.cfg
    B. syslinux.cfg and leaf.cfg
    C. leaf.cfg
    D. modules.conf

15. The size of the log partition is specified in this file:
    A. /var/log
    B. /etc/syslinux.cfg
    C. /etc/modules.conf
    D. shorewall.lrp

16. The following is a scanner that can be used to test the open ports on a firewall:

    A. Nessus

    B. Ping

    C. SMTP

    D. telnet

17. Linux can be used to format which of the following?

    A. Only 1.44-Mbyte floppy diskettes

    B. Both 1.68- and 1.44-Mbyte floppy diskettes

    C. Only 1.68-Mbyte floppy diskettes

    D. Linux cannot be used to format a floppy disk.

18. For a boot floppy or package floppy, you should use

    A. the cheapest floppy available.

    B. a high-quality floppy.

    C. a floppy that came with a software distribution.

    D. a low-density floppy.

19. The SLAX live-Linux CD contains the following service daemons:

    A. DNS

    B. DNS and Web servers

    C. DNS, Web and mail servers

    D. None of the above

20. A good test to see which IP addresses are on any Unix or Linux machine NICs is to issue this command:

    A. ipconfig

    B. ifconfig

    C. mount

    D. ping

21. On LEAF systems, to identify which IP addresses are available on each interface, you should use this command:

    A. ipconfig

    B. ifconfig

    C. ip addr show

    D. netstat

EXERCISES

Exercise 5.1: Format a 1680 KB Boot Diskette

This exercise will help walk you through creating a 1.68-Mbyte LEAF boot diskette. This is especially useful if your computer is unable to boot from a CD-ROM. You may use either a Windows computer or a SLAX/Linux computer to create the boot diskette.

In the case of a machine with no CD-ROM, an alternative is a dual-floppy system where both floppies are 1.68-Mbyte formatted and the first contains the basic boot information, while the second contains the packages. You will learn in Chapter 8 that this is often necessary when many packages are required—for example, with VPNs.

Windows Computer Boot Diskette Creation

1. Visit the book Web site and choose the 1,680-Kbyte floppy image for this chapter.

2. On a Windows computer, use WinImage to transfer the image to a floppy.

SLAX/Linux Computer Boot Diskette Creation

1. Boot a computer that is connected to the Internet using the SLAX CD.

2. Start the graphical interface with the gui command.

3. Use the Web browser to download the floppy image from the book web site.

4. Follow the instructions from the *In Practice: Using Any Linux OS to Create LEAF Boot Diskettes* earlier in this chapter and use the fdformat and the dd commands to create the boot floppy.

5. After creating the boot diskette using either a Windows or Linux computer:

   Obtain a computer with two NICs and a floppy drive to serve as the firewall.

   Use the boot diskette you just created to boot the firewall and answer the following questions:

   - What do the devices /dev/fd0, /dev/fd0u1680 refer to in terms of format?

   - How would you specify an MS-DOS file system in a Linux mount command?

Exercise 5.2: Use SLAX to View the Unix Manual (man) Pages

For this exercise, use a SLAX CD to boot any machine. You do not need to type anything at the boot prompt.

1. Login as root and start the gui, if you wish. At the command prompt type:

```
man fdformat
```

2. What does the -n parameter do?

3. Now type:

```
man dd
```

4. What do if and of refer to in the dd command? What effect does the noerror parameter have?

Exercise 5.3: Leaf.cfg Effects

1. Refer to Figure 5.4. What would the line syst_size = 12M accomplish in a leaf.cfg file?

2. Why is the size of the partition /var/log changed?

3. On a machine with 32 Mbytes of RAM, *given the Linux kernel requires 2 Mbytes of Ram,* what will the size of the /tmp partition be for the case of syslinux.cfg and leaf.cfg in Figures 5.3 and 5.4? Will this be enough if the file system /tmp should have at least 750 Kbytes?

Exercise 5.4: The Sizes of Your Packages

1. Use SLAX or any Linux or Windows machine. If you're booting SLAX, at the boot: prompt issue the kernel parameters:

```
boot: linux nolock
```

This will allow the SLAX CD to be removed.

2. Load the firewall CD that you have built onto any machine.

3. If it is a Linux machine, look at the /etc/fstab file to see if there is a line that mounts the CD-ROM. If so, when you put the firewall CD in, it will automount. You should be able to issue the command:

```
cd /mnt/cdrom
```

```
ls -l
```

4. If you use floppy boot with no CD, take your 1,680-Kbyte floppy(ies) and use the SLAX CD to mount using the command:

```
mount -t msdos /dev/fd0u1680 /mnt
```

5. Of the packages loaded by syslinux.cfg or leaf.cfg, which is the largest package in Kbytes?

PROJECTS

Project 5.1: Install the Firewall

1. Visit the book Web site. If the machine you have chosen for the firewall supports CD-ROM boot, download the CD-ROM ISO image.

2. Use a CD-burning software package on any computer to burn a bootable CD.

3. Obtain a computer with two NICs and a floppy drive to serve as the firewall.

4. Insert the CD into the firewall machine and reboot. Remember to check the PC BIOS settings to ensure that the CD-ROM is the first boot device.

5. Alternatively, if only floppy boot is supported, download a floppy boot image from the Web site for this chapter. You can still use a standard MS-DOS 1.44-Mbyte floppy disk for the boot disk as long as you have a working CD drive. (Refer to Exercise 5.1 for detailed information on creating a boot floppy.)

6. If you have only Windows machines, you will have to use a program such as WinImage to transfer the image to the floppy. You may use the same bootable CD-ROM image as a repository for the major packages. In this mode, you will have a single boot floppy, a CD, and a separate ordinary MS-DOS 1.44-Mbyte formatted floppy to collect updated packages, as you change the configuration of the firewall to suit your needs. It will be necessary to update packages to the update floppy and reburn the CD each time and reboot. To do this you will use WinImage to copy the updated packages from the floppy overwriting the package on the original image. Once this has been completed you can use WinImage to burn a new customized CD.

There are a few slightly easier alternatives that do not require reburning the CD each time a LEAF package is updated. These alternatives require a machine that can create floppies at 1.68-Mbyte format. Any Linux-based machine should be able to format floppies as long as the floppy drive is of sufficient quality. Some bargain PCs may not be up to this task. For

Windows machines, a program such as WinImage is capable of formatting floppies at 1.68 Mbytes.

The first and easiest of these options is to format a single 1.68-Mbyte floppy and load a few essential packages on it. There is a limit to what a single floppy can hold, and using IPSec or other VPN packages will not be possible.

The second of these options is a dual-floppy system where both floppies are 1.68-Mbyte formatted, and the first contains the basic boot information, while the second contains the packages.

All of these options are available as images from the book Web site. Whichever you choose, obtain a machine with two NICs and use it to boot the firewall.

Project 5.2: Install and Configure the External Machine.

1. Using the same process that was used to create the firewall boot CD in Project 5.1, create a bootable SLAX CD for the external machine using the SLAX image you download from the book Web site.

2. Obtain a computer with a NIC and a bootable CD-ROM to serve as the external machine.

3. Using a crossover cable, connect the external machine to the external interface on the firewall computer.

4. Insert the CD-ROM into the computer and boot the computer. Then at SLAX boot: prompt quickly type:

   ```
   linux server load=external
   ```

   Or, if you want to be able to remove the CD, type:

   ```
   linux server copytoram load=external
   ```

   That line will start the services on your external machine, only one of which is necessary: the monkey Web server. It will also allow you to take the CD out to use in another machine, if necessary.

5. Login as root. If you prefer GUI interface, from the next command prompt type:

   ```
   gui
   ```

6. Proceed to Project 5.3.

Project 5.3: Install and Configure the Internal Machine.

1. Using the same process that was used to create the firewall boot CD in Project 5.1, create a bootable SLAX CD for the internal machine using the SLAX image you download from the book Web site.

2. Obtain a computer with a NIC and a bootable CD-ROM to serve as the internal machine.

3. Using a crossover cable, connect the internal machine to the internal interface on the firewall computer.

4. Insert the CD-ROM into the computer and boot the computer. Then at SLAX boot: prompt quickly type:

```
linux server load=internal
```

Then login as root. If you prefer a GUI interface, at the next command prompt type:

```
gui
```

5. Start the Konqueror Web browser from the GUI interface.

6. Test from the internal and external machines to bring up the Web sites **www.internalenterprise.com** and **www.externalenterprise.com**.

Project 5.4: Use Weblet to See the Status of Your Firewall

You must complete Project 5.1 through Project 5.3 before completing this project.

1. Open a browser on the internal machine.

2. In the URL window, type the IP address of the firewall on the internal network. This is normally 192.168.10.254 from any of the images for this chapter.

3. First look at the traffic light icons. Are any of them red or yellow? Why would weblet ever show a red light for the memory or RAM disk traffic lights?

Project 5.5: Use Nessus from the External Machine to Attack the Firewall

The SLAX images for both internal and external machine have the Nessus server daemon running when they boot up.

GUI Method

1. If you have GUI running, you will see a Nessus icon on the desktop. Click it and the login pane will be presented.

2. The login and password are both the word *Nessus*.

3. After logging in, you may select the Target tab and specify 192.168.10.0/24 as the host(s) to scan and then proceed with the scan. View the results to determine which services are running.

Command Line Method

1. Alternatively, if you prefer to use the command line also known as batch mode for Nessus, you will first need to create a file that lists the target host(s) you wish to scan.

   ```
   vi /tmp/targets.txt
   ```

2. Add a line 192.168.10.0/24 to this file, save, and exit.

3. After you have created a file containing the targets you wish to scan (/tmp/targets), you will need to run Nessus with the –q option, which tells Nessus to use batch mode. To start Nessus in batch mode, use the following syntax:

   ```
   /usr/local/nessus/bin/nessus -V -q localhost 1241
   nessus nessus /tmp/targets.txt /tmp/results.txt

   nessus -V -q host port login password targetFile
   resultFile
   ```

4. After the scan is complete, look at the scan /tmp/results file. Records should appear as in the display below, perhaps with different IP addresses:

   ```
   192.168.2.1|http (80/tcp)|10919|NOTE|This port was
   detected as being open by a port scanner but is now
   closed.;This service might have been crashed by a
   port scanner or by a plugin;;

   192.168.2.1|general/icmp|10114|INFO|;The    remote
   host answers to an ICMP timestamp request. This al-
   lows an attacker ;to know the date which is set on
   your machine. ;;This may help him to defeat all
   your time-based authentication protocols.;;Solu-
   tion : filter out the ICMP timestamp requests (13),
   and   the   outgoing   ICMP   ;timestamp   replies
   (14).;;Risk factor : Low;CVE : CAN-1999-0524;

   192.168.2.1|http (80/tcp)|10330|NOTE|A web server
   is running on this port;

   192.168.2.1|http (80/tcp)

   ....
   ```

5. Verify that services are still available between the internal machine and external machine.

Magic City Quality Solutions

Magic City Quality Solutions is a struggling consultancy in rural Drofdar County in the deep South. The principal of Magic City Quality Solutions is Dr. Rebop Kwaku Bah, who recently obtained his doctorate. He was hired by large, virtual DeepFry University and finds time to run a consulting business on the side. Dr. Bah lives in Magic City, which has recently had digital subscriber line (DSL) capability available. He uses virtual hosting with stupendousnetworks.com for his Web site.

Although Bah is a world-renowned expert in network quality of server (QoS), he has little hands-on experience with networks. DeepFry offers its faculty one free course per semester, so he has taken a firewalls course that uses this book. He has just read this chapter and is about to create his first LEAF firewall. The problem is, Bah has an antiquated computer with no CD-ROM boot, but it has a working CD-ROM and a high-quality floppy drive.

Bah anticipates many updates to his packages until he can get his firewall working. He wants to complete the course and include VPN capabilities, so he is sure that he will need a leaf.cfg file for the extra packages that syslinux.cfg cannot hold. For this reason, he needs to have /dev/cdrom/ as one component of his PKGPATH parameter in syslinux.cfg, since it is doubtful that one or even two 1,680-Kbyte floppies could hold all the packages.

Bah does not look forward to the prospect of using a separate 1.44-Mbyte floppy to save updated packages, nor to wasting new CD-R media every time he has an updated package to test, since it is possible the updated package won't work! He has the following idea, which he explains to you, a fellow student in the firewalls class.

"I think I can use a 1,680-Kbyte boot floppy, read most packages from the CD-ROM, and update a few packages to the boot floppy. I can test these packages to make sure they work before transferring them to a new CD-ROM. Do you think the scheme will work?" Bah asks.

You explain that you need to think about it and you will get back to him.

Can he do it? What will he have to do to make this solution feasible, and what will his syslinux.cfg file look like?

Chapter **6**

Determining Requirements for the Firewall

Chapter Objectives

After reading this chapter and completing the exercises, you will be able to do the following:

- List and describe the basic components of a firewall policy.
- Design a network to improve the effectiveness of firewall rules.
- Determine the network services a company or organization will need to allow external users to access.
- Analyze and document the Internet services employees need to access.
- List and restrict vulnerable network services which should not be permitted to enter or leave the network.
- Design a network to utilize port forwarding and NAT where appropriate to enhance security.

Introduction

This chapter will focus on understanding and creating a firewall policy and a set of rules to guide the configuration of the firewall. First, you will need to make some decisions regarding the services that will be available from both sides of the firewall. Two of the main functions firewalls provide are:

- protecting the internal network from external attacks
- controlling access of internal machines to the Internet

The first step the network administrator must take is to determine what services the internal network will provide to the outside world. A typical business or enterprise usually makes its Web site available to the outside world. In addition, the enterprise will likely have a domain name and a mail service for its employees. If a company hosts its own Domain Name Service (DNS), Web service, and e-mail service, then the firewall needs to allow external Internet users to access these resources.

The second step is to determine what Internet services internal users will be allowed to access. Will employees be allowed to access anything on the Internet or only a predefined set of resources? These decisions are often driven by the type of business and the security and confidentiality threats created by employees' having free and open access to the Internet.

Firewall Policy

In recent years, information security, or cyber security, has become a major concern for companies and organizations. The dependence on the network and Internet for daily business activities makes it imperative for computer systems and networks to be operational 24 hours a day, seven days a week. Due to this reliance on technology, companies need to create a firewall policy to clearly state the intent and goals of the firewall in protecting the internal network from external attacks.

As with any technology initiative, proper planning and documentation are essential to successful deployment of a firewall. The effectiveness of the firewall can drop to less than 30 percent if it is not managed properly (Greeff 2003). At the outset, companies should develop a policy to guide decisions about the rules and configuration of the firewall. The *firewall policy* is a high-level document describing acceptable incoming and outgoing network traffic and requires very little understanding of technology. During the setup of the firewall, the firewall administrator will have many decisions to make about how to secure the network. The firewall policy will serve as a guide in making these decisions.

Management Support

Successful development of a firewall policy and deployment of a firewall requires the understanding and support of upper management. Properly configured firewalls often prevent users from performing activities that are not necessary for daily activity of the business. Managers and supervisors must be willing to support the policy rather than bend to meet user requests. Without this support, it is difficult to maintain the integrity of the firewall.

In order to establish management support, a group of managers and users should be involved in the creation of the firewall policy. This group must understand the importance of the policy and the role it plays in the efficient and reliable operation of the corporate network and computer systems. Getting stakeholders involved early in the development of the policy will help ensure the firewall rules will not restrict normal business activities.

One way to achieve this involvement is to give management a few scenarios and ask them how they might react. An example would be: "How will you react when the Vice President's personal assistant can no longer use NetMeeting to talk with his brother in another state during lunch?" The responses will indicate the level of understanding and support management will provide for the firewall policies.

Firewall Policy in Depth

A firewall policy clearly states the intent of the firewall and provides information about its configuration. This policy should be available for internal users to access and review regularly. Most of the policy should be readable by average nontechnical users so they can understand what activities are allowed and denied by the firewall. At a minimum, the firewall policy should include the following key components (Wack 2002):

- the purpose of the firewall
- a basic explanation of how the firewall handles traffic
- information on the services or applications that are allowed
- information on the services or applications that are denied
- documented procedures for how changes to the firewall are requested and approved

Purpose of the Firewall The overall purpose of the firewall is to ensure that a secure and reliable network is always available. This is accomplished by:

- protecting the internal network from external attacks and threats
- controlling access of internal machines to the Internet
- ensuring that external Internet users only have access to those internal resources and services that are necessary to conduct business

The firewall policy should begin by describing why the company or organization needs to maintain a reliable network infrastructure and how the firewall will help meet this goal. The statement of purpose of the firewall may include a short overview of the technology and security goals of the organization.

How the Firewall Handles Traffic As an administrator, you would need to use a layered approach or defense in depth (DiD) to avoid daily threats successfully. Before implementing this layered approach, you must develop a strategy for how each layer will handle network traffic. Business rules and needs will dictate the basic premise for this aspect of the firewall policy.

Two opposing strategies can be adopted when determining the basis for how the firewall will handle traffic. These two design strategies are:

- allow everything and only block specific items and ports

- block everything and only allow traffic that is explicitly permitted

The first strategy often defeats the goal of the firewall. This strategy assumes a very open network, focuses on a few key servers and known threats, and leaves all other network resources open and free. This allows for maximum flexibility for the user community, but also opens the door for a number of external attacks.

Universities often adopt this open strategy so that educators and researchers can use and access various local and remote resources. In these environments, a firewall might protect the administrative and student records systems and key services like DNS, mail, and Web, and openly allow all other traffic. This strategy can result in a number of misconfigured systems fully exposed to the Internet. In this type of environment, when a new Trojan or vulnerability threatens, you may need to add a new rule to the firewall to protect the network from the immediate threat.

The second strategy, blocking everything and allowing only traffic that is explicitly permitted, produces a much more restrictive network and requires users to ask for permission to access new services on the Internet. This strategy, however, does a much better job of protecting the internal network from attacks and vulnerabilities because many of the holes used by new attack tools are blocked at the outset. In an environment where security and confidentiality are key requirements, this strategy will provide a much greater level of protection.

As we will see later in the chapter, good network design may aid us in isolating sections of the network, so we can implement this more restrictive strategy while still leaving other areas of the network more open.

FYI: HIPAA

In some organizations, laws and federal regulations dictate a large portion of firewall policy. In the medical industry, the Health Insurance Portability and Accountability Act of 1996 (HIPAA) provides a set of standards and regulations for the transmission, storage, access, and usage of patient records and information. Therefore, the network policy for a medical provider must ensure adequate protection of patient records and prevent unauthorized access. HIPAA helps network and firewall administrators gain the support of upper management. Since this is mandated, users understand the need for confidentiality of records and are usually willing to accept a more stringent firewall policy.

Allowed Services Services such as DNS, Simple Mail Transfer Protocol (SMTP), and Hypertext Transfer Protocol (HTTP) will be required of almost every network. As we will address later in the chapter, the firewall policy should also include information on whether instant messaging (IM), NetMeeting, and other potentially risky applications are allowed to exist on the network. If the firewall policy allows these applications, the company may need to implement some additional policies governing their acceptable use.

Denied Services Services such as Dynamic Host Configuration Protocol (DHCP), Trivial File Transfer Protocol (TFTP), Simple Network Management Protocl (SNMP), and Windows Browsing and File Sharing (ports 135–139 and 445) should be denied at the boundary of the network to prevent a wide variety of attacks. These are services that are very useful internally to an organization, but present a large security risk if access is allowed from outside the organization. The policy should indicate exactly which services will be denied.

6

Firewall Changes Proper documentation of the firewall configuration is extremely important. The firewall rules start out straightforward and simple and grow into a complex set of rules as new applications and exceptions are added. When administrators review or audit the firewall configuration, they should be able to easily review the documentation and determine whether to keep or delete a given rule. Without proper documentation, administrators may be unsure of how removing a rule might block network traffic that is essential for an application or may leave unnecessary rules or holes in the firewall.

There should be a formal procedure and approval process for requesting modifications to the firewall. A document or form is useful for allowing a user to request an exception to the firewall rules. This form can ensure the user gathers the appropriate information on the IP address, port, and protocol for the exception. It should also outline the process for approving the request. If the policy is driven by business rules, then managers should review the need for the exception and approve or deny the exception before it reaches the firewall administrator. Figure 6.1 provides a sample Firewall Change Request Form.

Approving a firewall exception presents an excellent opportunity for an organization's security officer to audit the configuration of a server or system before opening access to the Internet. The ease with which anyone can install and configure a Web server makes it quite possible that a department will create its own Web server and request a firewall exception without properly ***patching*** and ***hardening*** the server. Patching a server refers to the installation of all vendor related service packs or bug fixes to a server after the installation of the operating system. Hardening a server is the task

---

Firewall Change Request Form

Name (Last, First): _____   _____
Department: _____

Application Name:
Detailed Description of Business Need for Application & Firewall Exception

_____

_____

_____

_____

_____

	Source (*From*)		**Destination (*To*)**
IP Address:	____ . ____ . ____ . ____	**IP Address:**	____ . ____ . ____ . ____
or		**or**	
Address	____ . ____ . ____ . ____	**Address**	____ . ____ . ____ . ____
Range		**Range**	
	____ . ____ . ____ . ____		____ . ____ . ____ . ____
Port[s]	_____	**Port[s]**	_____
Protocol	TCP UDP ICMP	**Protocol**	TCP UDP ICMP

_____   _____
Requestor Signature   **Date**

_____   _____
Supervisor Approval Signature   **Date**

Notes:

_____   _____
Firewall Administrator Signature   **Date Rule Updated**

FIGURE 6.1 Firewall Change Request Form.

of removing any unnecessary services, user accounts, or other security vulnerabilities to help protect a system from attack. The firewall will help provide a layer of security for the unpatched and unhardened server, but network administrators should not rely on the firewall alone.

User Education

Once you have created a firewall policy, you will need to communicate it to all network users. The implementation of the firewall may change an employee's ability to perform non-business-related tasks she has become accustomed to doing at work, but if designed properly, it should not prevent her from executing normal business transactions. Communicating firewall policy might take the form of required training sessions or departmental meetings. However, it is important to present this information in person, rather than just through written communications. Users must understand the goal of the firewall and the importance of maintaining the security and reliability of the IT and network infrastructure. Without this type of education, employees may see the implementation of a firewall as a new set of restrictions that hamper their ability to use their computer or as management's attempt at blocking their Internet activities at work.

Educating employees on the firewall policy presents an opportunity to review other information security principles that will help expose the user to the DiD approach. Topics include choosing a good password, locking a workstation when not in use, properly updating virus software, safe and unsafe e-mail attachments, confidentiality of documents and information, and the difference between secure and insecure Web sites.

The firewall provides no protection at all, however, if a hacker uses social engineering techniques to gain access to restricted resources. *Social engineering* techniques involve a hacker finding a way to convince a company employee to provide valuable information that will allow access. As an example, a hacker may call the help desk and impersonate an employee, convincing the help desk to reset the employee's password. Other techniques may involve looking over someone's shoulder or even searching through trash. It is important for employees to have a strong understanding of how to properly guard and protect company information and documents. Employees should have a clear understanding of how to properly discard documents and what information can be shared with non-company employees. It is also important for employees to use a standard means of customer verification before any confidential or private information is discussed. For some organizations, this may mean that some transactions must be conducted in person where a photo ID can be presented.

FYI: Internal Attacks

Many organizations go to great lengths to protect the network from external attacks and pay little attention to the potential for internal attacks. Internal attacks can result from disgruntled or greedy employees, or accidents such as someone bringing in an

CONTINUED ON NEXT PAGE

CONTINUED

infected USB jump drive or a vendor plugging an infected system into the internal network. The network and firewall design should limit access as much as possible to reduce the threat of internal attack. However, the firewall cannot do everything. Policies regarding access of terminated employees and access to confidential information must be carefully followed.

Network Design

Network design plays an important role in how the firewall policy is structured. When designing a network from the ground up, you should consider security at each step along the way. With the availability of cheap, high-speed, layer-three routers and the possibility of Virtual Local Area Networks (VLANs) on most network switches, it is desirable to place key groups or departments on isolated subnets to provide a higher level of control. VLANs allow departments or groups that are split among several locations to be grouped together on the same VLAN, allowing the network administrator to treat this group as one common subnet for networking purposes. It is also beneficial to place servers on isolated subnet(s) that can allow for a greater level of both internal and external security.

Figure 6.2 represents a sample network design where separate subnets are used for the Sales, Accounting, and System Management groups, and a separate subnet is used for the servers.

If we review our firewall strategies for this scenario, we might adopt a different strategy for each subnet, based on the business needs of that department. Table 6.1 outlines those business needs.

The set of rules listed in Table 6.1 are more difficult to implement if the Accounting and Sales departments are on the same subnet, because the IP address of each machine would need to be entered to establish the rules. Each time a new machine is added, the rule set would need to be updated. By placing these similar groups on the same subnet or VLAN, administrators can easily create group-specific rules.

Firewall Rule Syntax

As a basis for discussing the specific services that will pass through the firewall, it is important to have a basic understanding for how firewall syntax typically appears. In this section, we introduce the syntax of rules for the LEAF Firewall and for Cisco routers.

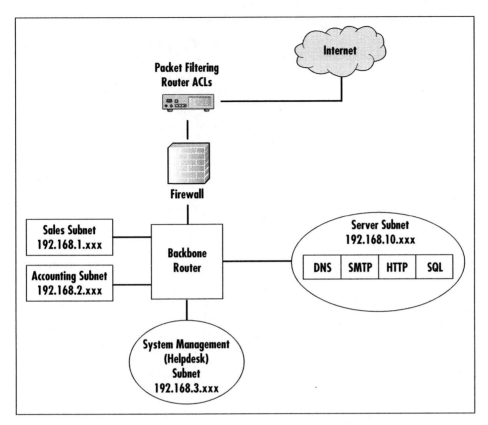

FIGURE 6.2 Network design for security management.

Chapter 3 provided a brief summary of the differences between IPTA-BLES and Cisco action control lists (ACLs); however, it did not focus on the specific syntax of each of these rules. The syntax of rules or exceptions is slightly different for every firewall, but the rules normally include:

- action
- source address and port
- destination address and port
- protocol

The LEAF Firewall distribution used throughout this book uses the shorewall for configuring the firewall. *Shorewall,* also known as the Shore-line Firewall, is a high-level tool for configuring the kernel-based Netfilter packet filter that comes with Linux 2.4 and later. As illustrated in the following examples, the Shorewall rules and Cisco access lists include the same basic information, using a slightly different syntax.

TABLE 6.1 Firewall strategies for subnets.

Department	Rules
Sales	Allow everything and only block specific items and ports. Provide an open subnet allowing sales force to use various tools to communicate with customers.
Accounting	Only allow connections to the server subnet. Restrict access to the Internet for the accounting staff, only allowing access to Intranet services. Users are allowed to send e-mail and connect to the corporate Web server.
System Management	Block everything and only allow traffic that is explicitly permitted or connections to the server subnet.
Server	Block everything and only allow traffic that is explicitly permitted. Allow ports 25 (SMTP) , 53 (DNS) , 80 (HTTP), 143 (IMAP), 443 (HTTPS), and 1521 (SQL) access, and block all other access.

Shorewall Rules

Shorewall uses a policy file (/etc/shorewall/policy) and a rules file (/etc/shorewall/rules) to configure most of the rules for the firewall. The rules file contains rules and exceptions to the policies and therefore is the primary file to focus on as we look at how rules are configured. Table 6.2 provides the syntax of a rule in the /etc/shorewall/rules file.

Thus, the following line is a sample rule to ACCEPT all incoming traffic from the external network bound to TCP port 80 on the local Web server 192.0.2.10:

```
ACCEPT      net   loc:192.0.2.10    tcp    80
```

Action   - ACCEPT

Source   - net   (Any external host)

Destination - loc:192.0.2.10 (Any external host)

Protocol   - tcp

Dest Port   - 80   (Well-known HTTP port)

Client Port -   (Any client port is ok)

TABLE 6.2 Shorewall rules syntax.

Action	Source IP Address	Destination IP Address	Protocol	Destination Port	Source Port	Original Dest
ACCEPT,	net	net	tcp	number or service	number (may be blank)	only for DNAT entries. address to forward to
DROP,	fw	fw	udp			
REJECT,	loc	loc	icmp	80		
DNAT,	loc:192.0.2.10 loc:192.0.2.0/24	loc:192.0.2.10 loc:192.0.2.10/24	all	low:high		
DNAT-,				http,		
REDIRECT, CONTINUE, LOG				smtp, dns		

Cisco Access List Entries

As discussed in Chapter 3, a router can serve as a packet filter and provides a basic level of protection. Cisco routers are the predominant router throughout networks on the Internet; therefore, it is beneficial to understand the basics of Cisco ACLs and how they are used to apply basic filtering. You will apply this understanding to examples later in this chapter.

Cisco provides three types of ACLs:

- standard ACLs

- extended ACLs

- dynamic ACLs (lock and key)

Extended ACLs are available on Cisco IOS 8.3 and later. They provide the most functionality and are the most commonly used; therefore, this section will include a brief introduction to the extended ACL syntax.

FYI: The Implicit DENY ALL in Access Lists

When ACLS are enabled on a Cisco router, the default is to deny traffic that is not explicitly permitted. Therefore, an ACL must have at least one permit rule. This default is accomplished by an "invisible" DENY ALL statement at the end of each ACL.

6

Extended ACLs Extended ACLs look at both the source and destination address of the packet to determine whether to permit or deny the packet:

```
access-list access-list-number {deny | permit} protocol
  source source-wildcard [operator[port]]

  destination destination-wildcard [operator [port]]
  [established]
```

access-list-number = 101-199 and 2000-2699

action = deny | permit

protocol = ip, icmp, tcp, udp

operator = eq, lt, gt

port = Port Number (23,25,53,80)

  Ranges (23-80)

  Name of Well Known Service (SMTP, DNS, WWW)

A sample Cisco access list entry to allow external hosts to connect to a Web server at IP address 192.0.2.10 is:

```
access-list 111 permit tcp any host 192.0.2.10 eq 80
```

Action	-	permit
Protocol	-	tcp
Source	-	any (Any External Host)
Destination	-	host 192.0.2.10
Operator	-	eq
Port	-	80

Access list entries are evaluated sequentially, so it is important for router and network performance to place the most heavily used rules first and the less frequently used rules last. In some instances, this may not be possible because a packet must be blocked before other traffic can be allowed.

Reverse masking The masking used in the access list entries to indicate a range of systems or an entire network is the inverse or reverse of the subnet mask. It is sometimes referred to as the *wildcard mask.* The netmask for the internal class C subnet 192.0.2. is 255.255.255.0. The inverse of this mask would be 0.0.0.255. Therefore, to write a rule that would apply to this subnet, the wildcard mask would be:

```
192.0.2.0 0.0.0.255
```

A sample access-list entry using this reverse mask is:

```
access-list 112 tcp permit 192.0.2.0 0.0.0.255 any eq 80
```

This rule would allow all hosts on the 192.0.2.0 subnet to connect to any external Web server:

Action   - `permit`

Protocol   - `tcp`

Source   - `192.0.2.0 0.0.0.255`

              (Any host on the 192.0.2 subnet)

Destination - `any (any external host)`

Operator   - `eq`

Port   - `80`

Flow of Traffic (Incoming and Outgoing)

As you begin to understand the syntax of rules, it is important to understand the direction in which traffic flows. This will help you comprehend what address should be listed for the packet's source address and destination address. We will refer to this throughout the remainder of this chapter as incoming and outgoing traffic. Figure 6.3 provides an illustration of a very simple network and compares shorewall rules to Cisco access-list entries.

Bering uses the keywords net, fw, and loc to help designate the flow of traffic:

- net—systems on the external network or Internet

- fw—the firewall

- loc—the local or internal network

In the example, incoming traffic from the Internet or with a source address of "net" and a destination address of the local Web server "loc:192.0.2.10" on port 80 will be accepted. Because of the stateful nature of the firewall, there is no real need to have a different rule set for incoming and outgoing packets.

Cisco ACLs can have an incoming set of rules and an outgoing set of rules on every interface on the router. Figure 6.3 indicates access list 101 is an incoming access list on interface 0, and access list 102 is an outgoing access list on interface 0. This is much more difficult to understand than the net, fw, and loc words from the shorewall configuration. Therefore, if we want to allow incoming traffic bound for the Web server into the network and allow the Windows Host 192.0.2.20 to connect to any external Web server, the rules would look like this:

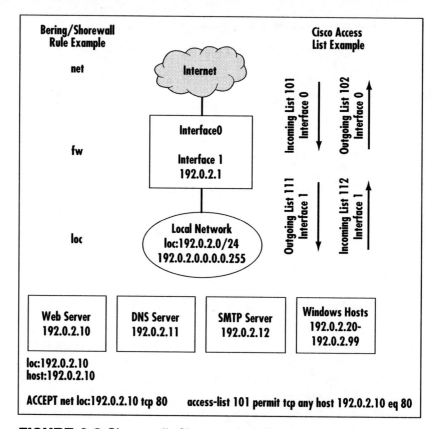

FIGURE 6.3 Shorewall–Cisco access list comparison.

Shorewall sample:

```
# allow incoming traffic from the Internet to the
# local Web server
ACCEPT net              loc:192.0.2.10     TCP      80
# allow the local machine 192.0.2.20 to connect to any Web
# server on the Internet
ACCEPT loc:192.0.2.20    net                TCP      80
```

Cisco ACL sample:

```
access-list 101 remark Allow incoming traffic from the Internet
access-list 101 remark to the local Web server
access-list 101 permit tcp any            host 192.0.2.10 eq 80
access-list 102 remark allow the local machine 192.0.2.20 to connect
access-list 102 remark to any external Web server
access-list 102 permit tcp host 192.0.2.20   any eq 80
```

In these examples, it is easier to understand the direction of traffic in shorewall because of the loc and net keywords. In the Cisco example, you must know access list 101 is processed on incoming traffic and access list 102 is processed for outgoing traffic to understand how this rule affects traffic. Note also the need for an incoming access list and an outgoing access list to accomplish this with the Cisco router. In the 101 example, any represents any computer on the external Internet. In the 102 access list, any represents any external Web server. This need for a separate incoming and outgoing access list helps demonstrate that devices intended to serve as firewalls are often easier to configure and maintain than using packet filtering techniques on routers.

Services to Offer to the Outside World

Understanding the syntax of firewall rules makes it easier to look at some examples of restricting traffic. It is a given that almost any company or organization will have a Web site and an e-mail address. Assuming that these services are hosted internally, you must configure the firewall to allow external Internet users to access these key services. You need to provide access to these Internet resources while at the same time protecting the internal servers from external attacks.

One common practice to help secure these services is to use a separate physical server for each service. This increases the number of servers but helps to enhance security and reliability by isolating each service on its own box. If the Web server runs on a server by itself, then there is no question as to how another service might be affecting performance. If the DNS server runs on its own box and someone breaks into it, that person will not have access to change the organization's Web server. Only one port on each of these servers will be available to external users, thus reducing the vulnerability of each server to attack.

The three main services to allow through the firewall are DNS, SMTP, and HTTP. Examining each of these carefully will help you develop an understanding of the rules necessary to allow these and other critical services through the firewall.

Domain Name Service (DNS)

DNS is a service that is invisible to most users, but is essential for communication with the outside world. Without DNS, the network becomes unusable because computers cannot find other computers on the network. A DNS problem often gives the appearance of a network outage because users are unable to connect to Web sites. It is similar to moving to a new city and not having a phone book. The phone works fine, but if you can't look up the phone number of the local pizza parlor, the phone is of little value.

DNS uses port 53 and operates over both TCP and UDP protocols. DNS uses TCP for zone transfers between the master and slave DNS servers. A typical organization will have one or more slave DNS servers that function as backups to the primary DNS server. These primary and slave DNS servers will need to transfer information using TCP port 53 for communication. If these servers are on opposite sides of the firewall, then the firewall will have to allow port 53 TCP transfers between these specific IP addresses.

Normal DNS queries from client computers to the server use the UDP protocol and port 53. Client computers will contact the DNS server each time they try to connect to a new host and look up the appropriate IP address for the given name. It is beneficial for all of the hosts on an Intranet to connect to internal DNS servers. This helps prevent a Trojan or misconfigured computer from using a rogue DNS server outside of the network. Because of this, some organizations restrict incoming and outgoing port 53 UDP connections to valid DNS servers, requiring everyone on the internal network to use the company's DNS server.

Sample Incoming Shorewall /etc/shorewall/rules Rule:

```
ACCEPT net   loc:192.0.2.11   udp   53
```

This rule allows all incoming UDP DNS traffic from the Internet to go to the local DNS server with the IP address of 192.0.2.11.

A sample incoming Cisco ACL entry for this same rule would be:

```
access-list 101 allow udp any host 192.0.2.11 eq 53
```

This set of rules allows external hosts to query the local DNS server 192.168.10.12. For the local DNS server to be able to perform look-ups of names on remote hosts, an outgoing rule must exist. Once the incoming rule is defined, an outgoing rule must be defined that will allow the internal DNS server to query external DNS servers for information.

Sample outgoing shorewall /etc/shorewall/rules rule:

```
ACCEPT loc:192.0.2.11    net    udp    53

DROP   loc               net    udp    53
```

The first entry allows the local DNS server 192.0.2.11 to make DNS queries of servers that are on the Internet or external network. The second entry denies all other internal hosts from making DNS queries of external servers. This will force all internal hosts to use 192.0.2.11 as their DNS server.

A sample outgoing Cisco access list entry for this same rule is:

```
access-list 102 allow udp host 192.168.10.12 any eq 53

access-list 102 deny udp any eq 53
```

Caution

DNS Restrictions

If the firewall restricts DNS traffic to only valid internal DNS servers, it must be updated if a new or test DNS server is installed on the local network.

Simple Mail Transfer Protocol (SMTP)

SMTP allows computers to connect to each other and send e-mail. SMTP remains one of the dominant protocols on the Internet for communications. It uses TCP port 25 for communication. Organizations will typically have some type of e-mail server that will need to access port 25 for sending e-mail. The firewall must allow both incoming and outgoing port 25 connections to the SMTP server.

Network and Internet security must ensure that only properly managed SMTP servers are allowed to send and receive e-mail. In a properly configured environment, all local e-mail clients should route their e-mail first to the local SMTP mail server. Many recent e-mail worms and Trojans set up their own SMTP engine on the host computer and begin sending out e-mail. This can result in a massive amount of spam or virus e-mails being sent from a single computer.

To provide a layer of protection against this type of threat, only the corporate SMTP server should be allowed to make outgoing port 25 SMTP connections. With this restriction in place, if a computer on the local network becomes infected with a virus, then all of the virus's attempts to propagate itself or send out spam will be rejected by the firewall.

Sample Incoming Shorewall Rule:

```
ACCEPT   net              loc:192.0.2.12     tcp    25

DROP     net              loc                tcp    25
```

Sample Outgoing Shorewall Rule:

```
ACCEPT   loc:192.0.2.12   net                tcp    25

DROP     loc              net                tcp    25
```

Web: Hypertext Transfer Protocol (HTTP) and HTTP over Secure Socket Layer (HTTPS)

The World Wide Web is the most widely used resource on the Internet, and virtually every organization will have at least one Web server. HTTP uses TCP port 80 for communication, and HTTPS uses TCP port 443.

Every Web server runs on port 80, and there are a limited number of Web server applications on the market. Therefore Web server administrators must patch the Web server on a regular basis to prevent attacks from newly released vulnerabilities.

Many software packages and Web development tools now install a personal Web server on workstations. To prevent the potential security threat created by these unmanaged installations, you should consider blocking all other incoming TCP port 80 and 443 connections to the network. This will ensure that only the corporate Web server is available to the general Internet community.

A department or group may bring up its own Web server that will be available to local users, but it should have to request a firewall change for this to be available from the Internet. Before you add an exception to the firewall to allow incoming connections to a Web server, you should audit the configuration of the server to ensure it has been hardened and that common Web vulnerabilities are patched. Hardening a server consists of removing any unnecessary services or accounts and modifying the system configuration to remove any weak default settings.

Sample Incoming Shorewall Rule:

```
ACCEPT      net    loc:192.0.2.10    tcp    80

DROP        net    loc               tcp    80
```

Structured Query Language (SQL)

Many organizations have a ***Structured Query Language (SQL)*** database server to store business information and transactions. This server is typically an Intranet server, meaning that only users inside of the company will need to interact with it. As an added layer of protection, the firewall should include a rule to block all access to the SQL server from the Internet. Many new applications are written using Web interfaces, and thus even the client computers inside of the organization will not need to directly connect to the SQL server. In this case, only the systems on the server subnet and possibly the Systems Management subnet will need to connect to the SQL server. In addition to the firewall rules at the network boundary, a packet filter placed on the backbone router to prevent direct access to the SQL server will provide a DiD strategy.

Each vendor uses a different port or range of ports for clients that will connect to the database. Table 6.3 provides the default ports for several common SQL databases. If an organization uses a given database, then it is advised to block traffic to these ports at the firewall. Users may also install versions of these databases on their own, so it might be wise to restrict in-

TABLE 6.3 Ports for common databases.

Database	Default Ports
IBM DB2	523(TCP), 50,000(TCP), 50,001(TCP)
Microsoft SQL	1433 (TCP) 1434 (UDP)
MySQL	3306(TCP)
Oracle	1521 (TCP)
PostgreSQL	5432(TCP)
Sybase	4100(TCP)

coming connections to all of these databases to prevent unknown vulnerabilities. Microsoft SQL, MySQL, and PostgreSQL are three common databases that might be installed by users who never realize they could be creating a security vulnerability.

Sample Incoming Rule

Reject incoming traffic from any Internet address to any local address with TCP port 523 or other common database ports.

DROP	net	loc	tcp	523
DROP	net	loc	tcp	50000
DROP	net	loc	tcp	50001
DROP	net	loc	tcp	1433
DROP	net	loc	udp	1434
DROP	net	loc	tcp	3306
DROP	net	loc	tcp	1521
DROP	net	loc	tcp	5432
DROP	net	loc	tcp	4100

FYI: SQL Slammer Worm

On January 25, 2003, at approximately 12:30 a.m. EST, the SQL Slammer began infecting computers around the world. After only 10 minutes, more than 90 percent of vulnerable hosts were infected. A set of rules to prevent unnecessary connections to the SQL server would have prevented many of these infections. This illustrates the importance of blocking everything and only allowing traffic that is explicitly permitted for server subnets.

Generalized Service Rules

Even though DNS, SMTP, and HTTP are three of the most commonly used services that will be listed in almost every firewall, it is important to include other services that will be available to the outside world in the firewall policy and firewall configuration. The following generalized rule sets recap the incoming and outgoing rules that must be installed on the firewall to properly secure these services and the servers they are running on.

Generalized incoming firewall rules for the server subnet:

- allow incoming DNS connections to the DNS server[s]
- allow incoming SMTP connections to the SMTP mail server
- allow incoming HTTP connections to the Web server
- allow incoming HTTPS connections to the Web server
- allow return traffic from established TCP connections from the server subnet
- DENY all other incoming Internet traffic bound for the server subnet

Generalized outgoing firewall rules for common services:

- allow outgoing DNS connections from the DNS server(s)
- deny all other outgoing DNS connections
- allow outgoing SMTP connections from the SMTP mail server
- deny all other outgoing SMTP connections

Order and Performance for Rules

Firewall rules are evaluated in a top-down fashion, making it important to think about placement of rules in the firewall configuration and the order of the rules for proper execution and firewall performance. Rules that will be hit the most should be placed near the top of the rule set. In the above example, the DNS rules are near the top of the list because they will be hit most often.

The first step is to allow or permit all of the valid connections for DNS, SMTP, and HTTP, and then deny all other connections. If the deny rule were moved to the top of the list, then all of the other rules would be useless because the first rule would say to drop any traffic bound for the server subnet.

Deciding What Internet Services Employees Can Access

Determining what services employees will have access to is the most challenging part of developing the firewall policy. In order to serve the needs of the business, these decisions should involve input from a group of stakeholders and managers. At the same time, it is impossible to make everyone happy and keep the network secure. There is a simple principle to keep in mind when determining how restrictive to be in configuring rules: Users will always let you know if they are unable to access something, but they will never let you know if they have too much access.

Some applications that users wish to access will create vulnerabilities for computers and the network. It is important for management to perform a risk analysis and determine what level of risk is acceptable. It is then up to management to weigh valid business needs versus employee desires. As discussed earlier, one solution provided by a good network design is to alleviate some of the risks by keeping confidential information and resources on a secure server subnet, allowing a more open environment on the user subnets.

Allowing All Outgoing Connections to User Subnets

Many organizations choose to have an open policy for outgoing network connections. As with the Windows XP firewall, the assumption is that the majority of outgoing connections are not dangerous. However, a computer infected with a Trojan may try to infect every other computer on the Internet. This will pass through the firewall with no trouble if all outgoing connections are allowed. We have discussed disabling outgoing DNS and SMTP connections for computers that are not servers. Later in this chapter, we will cover disabling outgoing connections for known Trojans and worms.

Generalized outgoing rules for an open environment:

- permit outgoing DNS and SMTP connections from servers

- deny outgoing DNS and SMTP connections

- deny common Trojan and worm traffic

- permit all other outgoing traffic

Allowing Limited Outgoing Connections

Some businesses do not want employees to have unlimited access to the Internet. To ensure employees focus on business activities rather than surfing the Web, it may be necessary to disallow some or all employees from accessing the Internet. This will require setting restrictions in the outgoing rules.

Web Access

On the other hand, many organizations want users to be able to establish outgoing HTTP and HTTPS Web connections so they can explore and use the Internet. Some organizations restrict Web access only from certain departments. The following is an example of allowing the sales department to surf the Web but denying the accounting department this access.

Allow the sales department to surf the Internet:

```
ACCEPT    loc:192.168.1.0/24    net    tcp    80
ACCEPT    loc:192.168.1.0/24    net    tcp    443
```

Do not allow the Accounting Department to surf the Internet:

```
DROP        loc:192.168.2.0/24    net    tcp    80

DROP        loc:192.168.2.0/24    net    tcp    443
```

There may be instances where it is preferred that employees be denied access to a specific Web site. As an example, a company may want to ensure employees cannot access eBay while at work. To accomplish this, the outgoing rules must include the IP address of the host(s) that will be restricted. If the IP address of the destination hosts change, the rule will need to be updated.

Instant Messaging (IM)

Instant Messaging (IM) is a technology whereby users are notified when their friends are online and can chat with their friends using text messages. IM has become a common tool for real-time synchronous communications on the Internet. It is becoming as popular as e-mail for short communications between friends, family, and coworkers. Many businesses are adopting IM as a communication tool for employees and customers.

The basic chat feature of IM possesses less of a security concern than the advanced features. Advanced IM functionality allows users to share files and establish video and audio compunctions. However, these same popular features allow the introduction of viruses and Trojans into the corporate network.

A company or organization's policy on IM should be clearly stated in the firewall policy. Although an organization may attempt to block access to IM ports, many IM clients are *port-agile* and can search for other open ports to establish connections. Port-agile applications try to use a default TCP or UDP port. If the default port is blocked, port-agile applications search for other TCP or UDP ports that are not blocked.

Without completely blocking user access to the Internet, it is difficult to prevent use of IM clients. This makes it even more important to properly educate users about the security threats in the file sharing, voice, and video components of the IM clients. Adopting a corporate policy that allows IM but places specific guidelines on how IM clients should be configured and what types of communications are acceptable is important for the organization's overall security.

TABLE 6.4 Ports for common instant messaging clients.

Common IM Clients	Standard IM Ports
AOL Instant Messenger (AIM)	5190
MSN Messenger	1863
Yahoo Instant Messenger	5050

NetMeeting

H.323 is a standard protocol for audio and video transmission. NetMeeting, one of the most widely available H.323 applications used for audio and video conferencing, is available for every Windows-based computer. NetMeeting dynamically allocates an incoming port between 1024 and 65535 for the audio and video features. It is nearly impossible to use the audio and video features of NetMeeting without opening access to over 60,000 ports. This requires conducting a careful risk analysis of the benefits of NetMeeting before determining whether to allow it on the corporate network. In many instances, it may be acceptable for a predefined set of hosts while it is a considerable security risk to provide this capability to all hosts on the network.

The rules to allow incoming NetMeeting audio and video connections must be listed after the server subnet and services are locked down.

General rules to allow NetMeeting. Use with caution:

```
ACCEPT    net    loc    tcp    1024:65535

ACCEPT    net    loc    udp    1024:65535
```

6

FYI: Net Meeting and NAT

NetMeeting not only requires a computer to be able to use any port from the upper port range, but it also requires two computers to be able to contact each other directly. Without other special configuration, NetMeeting may not work in an environment where Network Address Translation (NAT) is used.

P2P Applications

Peer-to-Peer (P2P) applications became popular for sharing MP3 music files in 1999 when Shawn Fanning introduced a file-sharing application called Napster. Peer-to-Peer applications allow users to connect with each other over a common communications network and easily share resources. Today, there are a variety of P2P applications, including BitTorrent, eDonkey, Kazaa, Gnutella, and iMesh, that allow users to share files. These applications not only present issues of copyright and illegal distribution of copyrighted materials, but also allow for confidential corporate documents to be shared inadvertently if they are placed in the wrong folder. This could be a tremendous security risk.

Adopting a strict policy of blocking all incoming connections to user computers that are not established connections will still allow many of the P2P applications to function, but users will not be able to share files on their computer with others. If at all possible, the threats introduced by P2P software and file sharing in IM applications should provide a convincing argument for restricting incoming network connections.

Network and System Management Services

Network and system administrators must be able to manage devices and servers remotely, and a wide variety of tools are available for this. However, administrators must understand the security implications of the tools used to manage these devices. We recommend a Virtual Private Network (VPN) (see Chapter 8) connection be used for any administration that will take place from outside the corporate firewall.

ICMP The use of ICMP for network troubleshooting is a valuable tool for resolving and tracking down networking issues. The *ping* command utilizes the echo-request (ICMP Type 8 Code 0) and echo-reply (ICMP Type 0 Code 0) to provide a tool for testing network connectivity (Convery 2004). Unfortunately, the ability of these echo-request and echo-reply packets to be received by any computer on the Internet is also its greatest weakness. This type of ICMP traffic has become a common target of many *denial of service (DOS)* attacks and several worms. As a result of these weaknesses, many organizations have started blocking several of ICMP features including echo-request, echo-reply and echo redirect at the edge of the network. The overwhelming amount of infected computers has even caused some organizations to block this type of Internet Control Message Protocol (ICMP) traffic between subnets on the internal network. In this area, the risks of this type of ICMP traffic often outweigh the benefits.

Telnet and FTP Telnet is a common terminal-based application used to gain console access to servers and networking equipment. Telnet operates on port 23. File Transfer Protocol (FTP) is a common tool used to allow for the exchange of files between systems. Both telnet (TCP port 23) and FTP (TCP ports 20 and 21) send passwords across the Internet in an unencrypted, plaintext manner. Sniffers can easily capture the username and plaintext password in these applications. Therefore, you should avoid these two services where possible. Anonymous FTP access may be acceptable, since a password is not needed for logins. By blocking incoming telnet and FTP connections at the firewall, you can ensure network users cannot provide telnet or FTP services to the outside world.

SSH Secure shell (SSH) operates on TCP port 22 and offers a suite of tools that provide the same types of services offered by telnet and FTP. SSH, however, encrypts all traffic, including the password, eliminating the potential of someone sniffing the network traffic. Many organizations that still need terminal-based access have blocked all access to the telnet port and allow incoming and outgoing SSH connections instead.

More information on SSH and the available tools can be found at **www.openssh.com** (free implementation) and **ww.ssh.com** (commercial implementation). SSH is the recommended tool for any type of remote console managements for servers, switches, and routers. The FTP built into SSH is also far superior to FTP because of the encrypted communications.

Windows Terminal Services Windows Terminal Services is available with Windows 2000 and Windows 2003 servers and allows administrators to use the MSTSC.EXE client program to remotely manage servers. Terminal Services provides a full Windows login to a remote host, and almost anything that can be accomplished from the console can be accomplished via a terminal services connection. This service allows administrators to manage servers from anywhere, but it also opens the door to attack. Therefore, it is important to restrict the computers and subnets that can establish terminal services connections.

By default, Windows Terminal Services operates on TCP 3389. Only select management systems or computers located on encrypted VPN connections should be allowed to establish terminal services connections.

Services That Should Not Leave the Local Network

Several other common services on networks should be prevented from entering or leaving the firewall. Although important on the local Intranet, they can create additional unwarranted risks if allowed to pass through the firewall.

The most debated set of ports on this list is the Microsoft Networking ports 135-139 and 445. Although these protocols and ports can be used for useful business purposes, recent viruses and worms have exposed numerous vulnerabilities in these services. It is not recommended to let them through the firewall. If these services are absolutely necessary, then a VPN connection should be established for accessing them.

Table 6.5 provides a list of a few of the services that you will want to be sure do not leave or enter the internal network.

TABLE 6.5 Services blocked from leaving the internal network.

Port	Protocol	Service
67/68	UDP	Bootp/DHCP
69	UDP	TFTP
135,137,138,139	TCP and UDP	Netbios–Microsoft Networking
445	TCP and UDP	CIFS–Microsoft Networking
515	TCP	LPR
2049	UDP	NFS

IN PRACTICE: Blocking Trojan Ports

New worms and Trojans are released daily. As new threats arise, it is important to determine how they affect the security of the network. If ports above 1024 are open, allowing services such as NetMeeting and others to run, it is imperative to block the ports of common Trojans and worms. The port information provided at **isc.sans.org**, **www.cert.org**, and other security Web sites can provide a useful analysis of the top ports being accessed to help determine new ports that should be blocked. Table 6.6 provides a list of several ports used by Trojans that should be blocked.

TABLE 6.6 Common Trojan ports.

Port #	Protocol	Description
1080	TCP	MyDoom.B
1243	TCP	Sub Seven
1349	UDP	Back Orifice DLL
1999	TCP	Sub Seven
2041	TCP	W32.korgo
2745	TCP	Bagle.C
3067	TCP	W32.korgo
3127	TCP	MyDoom.A
3128	TCP	MyDoom.B
5554	TCP	Sasser – FTP server
6711	TCP	Sub Seven
6776	TCP	Sub Seven
8080	TCP	MyDoom.B
8787	TCP and UDP	Back Orifice 2000
9898	TCP	Dabber
9996	TCP	Sasser – Remote Shell
10080	TCP	MyDoom.B
12345	TCP	NetBus
12346	TCP	NetBus Pro
17300	TCP	Kuang
27374	UDP	Sub Seven
54320	TCP and UDP	Back Orifice 2000
54321	TCP and UDP	Back Orifice 2000

NAT and Port-Forwarding

With increasing numbers of systems connecting to the Internet, it has become extremely difficult for organizations to get their own Class C or B block of IP addresses. There simply are not enough IPV4 address ranges for every network-connected device on the planet to have its own unique IP address. This has created the need for companies and organizations to allow multiple computers on the internal network to access the Internet with a single IP address.

NAT allows computers on the internal network to use a private set of IP addresses for internal communication and share a single IP address for external Internet communications. RFC 1918 provides for several ranges of IP addresses that are available for private internet networks. The IP addresses for these private internets should never appear on the Internet. Therefore, the same IP private addresses can be used by multiple private networks. The NAT gateway serves as a bridge, forwarding external Internet traffic that is bound for its address to the appropriate computer on the internal network. Figure 6.4 illustrates a simple NAT configuration.

6

FIGURE 6.4 NAT example.

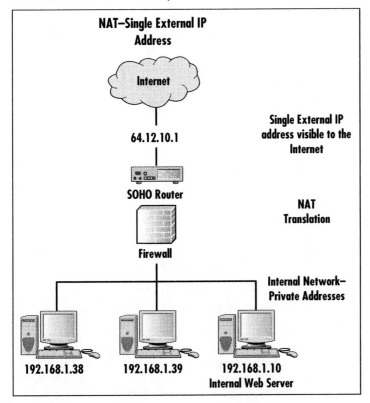

NAT

Most SOHO firewalls and home office routers use NAT because broadband providers typically only provide one dynamic IP address to a user. NAT allows users to connect multiple systems in their home and use a single IP address from the broadband provider. Some large companies that are only able to get a single set of Class C IP address assigned to them from the Internet Corporation for Assigned Names and Numbers (ICANN) may also use NAT. NAT allows these organizations to use the private address ranges defined by RFC 1918 to create an internal IP address scheme that allows the number of hosts and subnets required by a large business.

NAT provides an added layer of security by hiding internal systems from the Internet. This is useful for large companies and organizations that are sensitive to their exposure to the Internet. In a NAT environment, it appears that all traffic from an organization is coming from a single device. If a hacker tries to port scan the corporate network, he will only be scanning the NAT device, not the internal systems.

FIGURE 6.5 NAT–IP header changes.

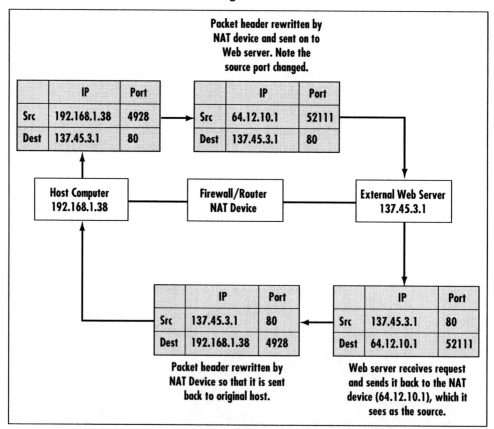

Figure 6.5 illustrates how the source and destination address in the IP header are modified as the packet passes through the NAT device. The NAT device keeps a table in memory containing all of the local IP address and ports in use so it always knows to which local host to send the return traffic.

NAT works well until an organization wants to provide e-mail, Web, or other services to the outside world. Since the organization only has one external IP address, if someone tries to connect to port 80 on this IP address they are actually connecting to port 80 on the NAT device. Therefore, the NAT device must be configured to forward port 80 to an internal host. This is known as port forwarding.

Figure 6.6 shows an example of how port forwarding allows a Web page to be displayed on the external network. When the NAT device receives a packet destined for port 80, it rewrites the packet header and forwards this packet to the internal systems that are providing Web services.

The NAT device can be configured to forward different ports to different systems. A port 80 connection can easily be forwarded to an internal server running the Web service. NAT and port forwarding, along with the proper firewall configuration, can provide an additional layer of security.

The /etc/shorewall/rules file allows port forwarding to be set up through a simple rule entry. The following DNAT rule will forward all

6

FIGURE 6.6 Port forwarding.

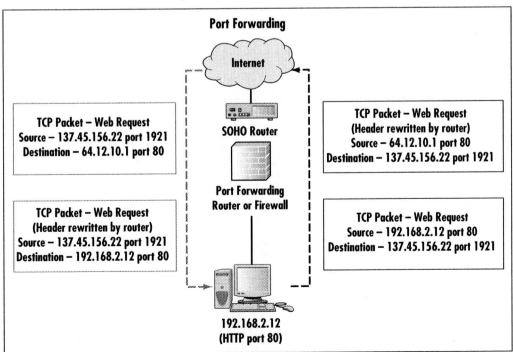

traffic destined for the Web server on IP address 192.0.2.100 and forward this traffic to 192.168.10.13:

```
DNAT  net   loc:192.168.10.13  tcp  80  -  192.0.2.100
```

Demilitarized Zone (DMZ)

The term *demilitarized zone,* or DMZ, originated with the military and refers to a buffer zone between two enemies. In the networking world, the term is used in much the same way. The DMZ is the zone between the Internet and the local network. Figure 6.7 represents a simple DMZ configuration that is often used in a SOHO environment. Many organizations go to great lengths to create an elaborate DMZ where DNS, mail, and Web servers can be placed and maintain a much greater level of security for the internal networks. Devices in the DMZ are susceptible to attacks from either side because the firewall does not provide protection for these hosts. Some SOHO routers have a single DMZ port, allowing a single computer to be placed in the DMZ.

In the SOHO example, placing a computer in the DMZ allows Net-Meeting and P2P applications to execute without any problems because all of the incoming ports are open and available. It is very risky to place computers in the DMZ, but it is necessary in some environments due to user needs.

FIGURE 6.7 DMZ—demilitarized zone.

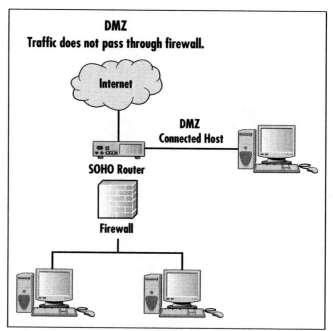

Review of General Firewall Rules

Once a firewall is put in place, it is essential to perform both internal and external testing and monitoring to ensure the intended level of protection. Without continued testing and updating, new vulnerabilities and threats can slip unnoticed through the firewall. There have even been instances when an administrator has accidentally disabled the firewall. Without proper testing and notifications, this could go unnoticed for several hours or even days.

Also, remember that to provide adequate protection, firewall rules may change weekly to address new threats and vulnerabilities. The following provides a sample set of generalized firewall rules for an organization that has a fairly open firewall policy. This is by no means an exhaustive or universal set of rules.

Incoming traffic rules:

- Block any incoming packets that appear to have originated from the local network. These packets have spoofed source addresses.

- Block any incoming packets from the RFC 1918 private IP address ranges.

- Block any incoming packets with a source or destination address of 127.0.0.1 (localhost).

- Block any incoming packets with a source or destination address of 0.0.0.0. This indicates broadcast traffic and should never pass through the firewall.

- Permit the return traffic of any established TCP connections. Most stateful firewalls allow return traffic with no additional configuration.

- Permit or port forward traffic to services we will provide to the outside world. (DNS, SMTP, HTTP, HTTPS).

- Deny all other traffic to server IP addresses or subnets.

- Deny ICMP echo-request traffic unless specific outside servers need access to ping us.

- Deny incoming traffic that appears to be a Trojan.

- Block all incoming port 135 to 139 and 445 traffic. Microsoft Netbios and file sharing is a great feature but very risky.

- Block incoming server management connections (telnet, Terminal Services).

- Deny all other incoming traffic unless explicitly allowed.

Outgoing traffic rules:

- Block any outgoing packets that have a source IP address that does not originate from the local network. These packets have spoofed addresses or a source address from the private IP address range and should never be passed on the Internet.

- Permit SMTP traffic from the mail server only.

- Permit DNS traffic from the DNS server only.

- Deny outgoing traffic that appears to be a Trojan.

- Deny outgoing ICMP echo-reply traffic.

- Allow all other outgoing traffic.

One of the rules that should appear at the top of our list is the rule to block any spoofed traffic. Traffic entering the network from the Internet should never include a source address of one of the RFC1918 Private IP address ranges (10.0.0.0, 172.16.0.0, 192.168.0.0); therefore, any traffic with a source address matching this subnet should be blocked. Using Shorewall, this will be completed by adding a single keyword norfc1918 to the appropriate interface in the /etc/shorewall/interfaces file as follows:

```
net    eth0    detect    norfc1918
```

If using a Cisco ACL, this would require a separate ACL entry for every range of RFC1918 addresses. The following three lines show the first few access list entries that would be necessary to block this range:

```
access-list 101 remark --- Block any spoofed traffic

access-list 101 deny ip 192.168.0.0 0.0.255.255 any

access-list 101 deny ip 10.0.0.0 0.255.255.255 any
```

Local hosts that have established a TCP connection with other hosts on the Internet need their return traffic passed through the router. In a stateful firewall, this traffic would be allowed back in with no additional rules. In a stateless firewall such as a packet filter, a rule would need to be added to allow this traffic. This will be one of our heavily used rules; therefore, it should appear near the top of our access list to enhance performance, since rules are evaluated in order:

```
access-list 101 remark --- Allow return traffic

access-list 101 permit tcp any 192.168.2.0 0.0.0.255
established
```

IN PRACTICE: Configuring the LEAF Firewall

The LEAF firewall provides a menu driven interface for viewing and configuring the firewall. To login to the Bering firewall installed in Chapter 5, use root as the login and the Rootr00t password:

```
Bering V1.2 firewall tty1

firewall login: root

password: Rootr00t
```

After logging in, the LEAF Configuration screen shown in Figure 6.8 is displayed. This screen provides access to the various options available to configure the firewall.

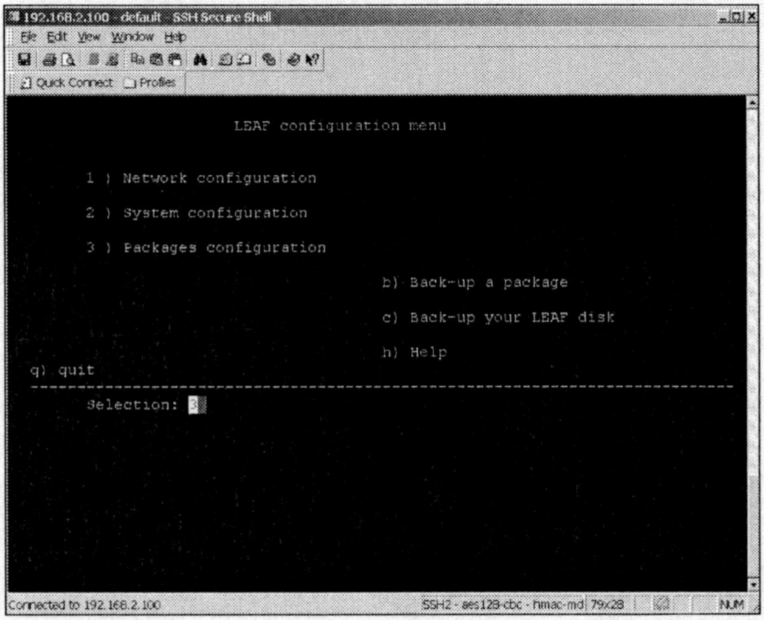

FIGURE 6.8 LEAF Configuration menu.

The Shorewall firewall is one of the packages installed on the distribution and therefore is accessed from the Packages menu option. Select option 3 to enter the Packages Configuration menu shown in Figure 6.9.

From the Packages menu, option 6 provides access to the Shorewall configuration. As shown in Figure 6.10, the Shorewall configuration files screen lists 24 files that are used to configure the firewall. Each of these files allows you to control a variety of settings for the firewall.

▸▸ CONTINUED ON NEXT PAGE

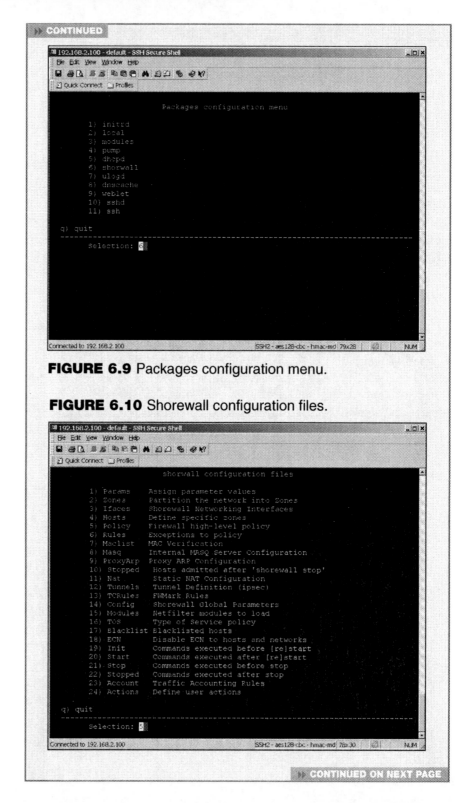

FIGURE 6.9 Packages configuration menu.

FIGURE 6.10 Shorewall configuration files.

CONTINUED ON NEXT PAGE

This chapter focuses on the policy and rules files. To edit the policy file, you select option 5 and the policy file appears. The top of the policy file includes comments and information on the proper syntax for entries in the policy file. Using the arrow keys allows you to scroll to the bottom of the policy file and observe the actual entries in the policy file. Figure 6.11 shows a sample policy file. Note that lines that begin with a "#" are comments and therefore are ignored.

```
# 192.168.2.100 - default - SSH Secure Shell                                    _ □ ×
 File  Edit  View  Window  Help
  ⊟ ⎙⎙  ⊿⊿  ⧉⧉⧉  ⎗  ⊟⊟  ⊗  ⊘❢
 ⊒ Quick Connect  ⊒ Profiles
#                      If you don't want to log but need to specify the          ▲
#                      following column, place "-" here.
#
#        LIMIT:BURST   If passed, specifies the maximum TCP connection rate
#                      and the size of an acceptable burst. If not specified,
#                      TCP connections are not limited.
#
#        As shipped, the default policies are:
#
#        a) All connections from the local network to the internet are allowed
#        b) All connections from the internet are ignored but logged at syslog
#           level KERNEL.INFO.
#        d) All other connection requests are rejected and logged at level
#           KERNEL.INFO.
#############################################################################
#SOURCE         DEST            POLICY           LOG             LIMIT:BURST
#                                                LEVEL
loc             net             ACCEPT
net             all             DROP             ULOG
# If you want open access to the Internet from your Firewall
# remove the comment from the following line.
#fw             net             ACCEPT
#
# THE FOLLOWING POLICY MUST BE LAST
#
all             all             REJECT           ULOG
#LAST LINE -- DO NOT REMOVE
     INS  /etc/shorewall/policy                         90:1  altH=help NE
Connected to 192.168.2.100                    SSH2 - aes128-cbc - hmac-md 78x30      NUM
```

FIGURE 6.11 Shorewall policy file.

The default editor used by the LEAF distribution is NEDIT. Pressing <ALT> <H> provides you with a list of commands available in NEDIT. From this help screen, you can see that pressing <CTRL> <Q> followed by the letter N, Y, or L is used to close the editor. The following list of commands provides a description of each of these commands:

<CTRL><Q> N   Exit without saving
<CTRL><Q> Y   Exit and Save
<CTRL><Q> L   Save and Load New

As with the policy file, the rules file can be viewed by selecting options 6 from the Shorewall configuration files menu. As shown

▶▶ CONTINUED ON NEXT PAGE

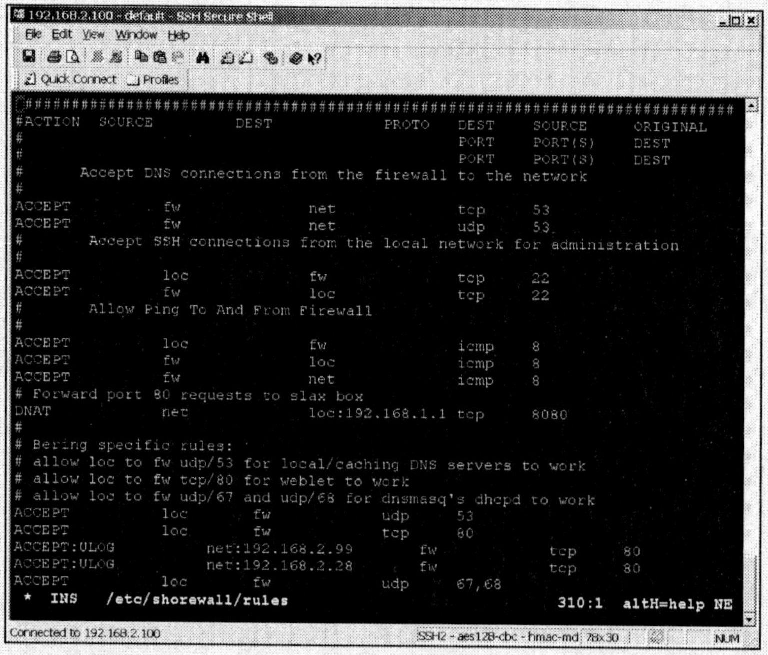

FIGURE 6.12 Shorewall rules file.

in Figure 6.12, because it includes exceptions to the firewall policy, this file will contain more entries than the policy file.

Summary

This chapter focused on creating a firewall policy and the configuration necessary to allow external and internal users to access only those resources that are necessary. Two of the main functions of firewalls are to protect the network from external attack and to control access of internal machines to the Internet. A well-thought-out and management-supported firewall policy should be in place before installing a firewall. This policy should clearly state the intent of the firewall and provide high-level information about the configuration of the firewall. User education is the key for understanding of the firewall rules and implementing a successful firewall.

Network design can impact firewall design and configuration, and should be considered if a new organization is being created. The firewall must allow external users to connect to key server resources including SMTP, DNS, HTTP, and HTTPS. At the same time, any potential threats should be blocked from entering the network. A more restrictive network policy will always result in less exposure to an attack.

Test Your Skills

MULTIPLE CHOICE QUESTIONS

1. The two key functions of the firewall are protecting the internal network from attack and controlling access of the internal machines to which of the following?

   A. intranet

   B. Internet

   C. servers

   D. World Wide Web

2. The firewall policy is a high-level document describing acceptable _____ network traffic and requires very little understanding of technology.

   A. incoming

   B. outgoing

   C. incoming and outgoing

   D. TCP

3. Properly configured firewalls often prevent users from accessing resources that are

   A. necessary for daily business activities.

   B. nice to access but not necessary for business activities.

   C. available to anyone on the Web.

   D. internal servers.

4. The firewall policy should be available for _____ to review.

   A. anyone on the Internet

   B. hackers

   C. only firewall administrators

   D. internal users

5. Which of the following is not accomplished by the firewall?

   A. Protecting the internal network from external attacks and threats

   B. Providing virus protection to user workstations

   C. Controlling access of internal machines to the Internet

   D. Restricting access of Internet users to a set of specified services

6. The firewall design strategy "Block everything and only allow traffic that is explicitly permitted" provides

   A. an open environment that does not provide a high level of protection.

   B. a means for users to easily set up their own Internet servers.

   C. an environment where users must ask for permission to access new external network services running on non standard ports.

   D. the ability of everyone to use P2P software.

7. _____ often adopt a more open firewall strategy.

   A. Government agencies

   B. Hospitals

   C. Universities

   D. Businesses

8. Once the firewall is configured and a set of rules are created, they should

   A. never need to be changed.

   B. change hourly.

   C. be quickly updated by the firewall administrator when users experience problems.

   D. be updated after careful review and management approval of exceptions.

9. By talking with knowledgeable employees, hackers can often use _____ to bypass the firewall.

   A. social engineering

   B. firewall vulnerabilities

   C. IP addresses

   D. modem connections

10. Placing key groups or departments on separate subnets or VLANs provides

   A. no advantage to network security.

   B. the ability to provide separate firewall rules to each department or group.

   C. the ability to place servers inside of each department.

   D. the ability to easily protect users from computer viruses.

11. Which of the following is *not* a key service to allow through the firewall?

    A. DNS

    B. DHCP

    C. SMTP

    D. HTTP

12. DNS uses port 53 TCP connections for _____, which may not need to pass through the firewall.

    A. client queries

    B. lookups

    C. zone transfers

    D. management

13. _____ should be allowed to make outgoing port 25 SMTP connections.

    A. All computers on the intranet

    B. Only client computers running Eudora, Outlook Express, or other mail clients

    C. The corporate mail server

    D. The corporate Web server

14. External connections to internal _____ servers can normally be denied to enhance security.

    A. Web

    B. DNS

    C. mail

    D. SQL

15. The order with which rules are entered into a firewall

    A. does not matter.

    B. only affects performance.

    C. requires deny rules to appear first.

    D. must be carefully planned for proper sequencing of deny connections, permit connections, and enhancing performance.

6

16. One of the hardest portions of setting up a firewall policy is
    A. determining to what servers access will be allowed.
    B. determining what services employees will be able to access.
    C. deciding which Trojan ports to block.
    D. determining the order of the rules.

17. Users will always let you know if they
    A. have access to something they shouldn't.
    B. are unable to access something.
    C. do not understand the security policy.
    D. are able to access restricted Web sites.

18. _____ is a useful troubleshooting tool, but the risks may outweigh the benefits.
    A. ICMP echo request and echo reply
    B. ICMP time exceeded
    C. ICMP destination unreachable
    D. SSH

19. _____ is/are used in Microsoft networks for browsing and sharing of files but have been the source of many attacks and should be blocked by the firewall:
    A. Ports 135 to 139 and 445
    B. Ports 67 and 68
    C. Port 515
    D. Port 80

20. _____ provides the ability for internal computers to use a single external IP address for communication with other systems on the Internet.
    A. Port forwarding
    B. NAT
    C. DMZ
    D. NUT

EXERCISES

Exercise 6.1: Restricting Access to eBay

ABC Computers has been having a problem with several employees spending time on eBay during work. The company wants to restrict the accounting group's access to eBay.

1. Use Nslookup to determine the ip addresses for eBay.

2. Review the Shorewall /etc/shorewall/rules file.

3. What specific entry would need to be added to the rules file to restrict access to eBay?

4. What changes at eBay might break this rule?

Exercise 6.2: Showing Management Sample Firewall Policy Exceptions

ABC Computers is in the process of developing a firewall policy. Stakeholders from each department and a management team are working together to evaluate business needs and create the firewall policy. Review each of the following requests and write a short response as to whether you think the service should be allowed and why. For each scenario, determine how allowing the service would affect the integrity of the firewall.

1. The marketing department would like to use Microsoft Netmeeting for online meetings with customers.

2. The Customer Support Center would like to use Instant Messaging as a means of providing live support.

3. The manufacturing department would like to use P2P software to download music that can be played on the factory floor.

Exercise 6.3: User Education of Firewall Policies

ABC Computers has just developed a new firewall policy. You are responsible for developing and teaching the user education training session.

1. How will you describe the firewall to the users?

2. What major topics should be covered in the training?

3. What steps should users follow if they are unable to access an external network service they think they should have access to?

Exercise 6.4: Developing Firewall Rules

1. Review Figure 6.3 and the incoming firewall rules for the server subnet under *Generalized Service Rules*.

2. Develop a detailed set of firewall rules that will permit incoming SMTP, DNS, and HTTP, and use the Shorewall rules syntax. Include whether the rule is a TCP or UDP rule.

3. Assume the following addresses:

   SMTP Server = 192.168.10.11

   DNS Server = 192.168.10.12

   HTTP Server = 192.168.10.13

Exercise 6.5: Is ICMP Ping Disabled?

1. Use ping to determine whether ICMP echo-request and echo-reply packets are enabled on your network. Can you ping anything on your network?

2. Write a short summary of your findings.

3. If ICMP ping is not disabled, find three popular external Web servers you can ping and three Web servers you cannot ping.

4. Write a brief summary of why you think each of these allows or does not allow ICMP pings.

PROJECTS

Project 6.1: Local Firewall Policy and Configuration

Use information available from your school or organization's Web site and other resources to learn about the local firewall policy and configuration of your network.

1. Does an acceptable use policy exist?

2. Does a firewall policy exist?

3. What type of firewall is used?

4. What incoming connections are allowed?

5. What incoming connections are denied?

6. What outgoing connections are allowed?

7. What outgoing connections are denied?

Project 6.2: SLAX Iptables Configuration

1. Boot the SLAX CD into normal mode. Do not use the server option.

2. Use the iptables command to view the configuration.

```
iptables -L -v
```

3. Now use the SLAX CD to boot into server mode.

4. Use the iptable list command to view the configuration.

```
iptables -L -v
```

5. From a firewall perspective, describe the differences between these two modes.

Project 6.3: Shorewall Policy Configuration

Boot the Shorewall firewall installed in Chapter 5 and look at the Shorewall policy file /etc/shorewall/policy.

1. What is the default firewall policy?

2. Write a short document describing this policy that you can provide to an end user.

Project 6.4: Shorewall Configuration

Boot the Shorewall firewall installed in Chapter 5 and look at the Shorewall rules file /etc/shorewall/rules.

1. What connections are allowed?

2. What connections are denied?

Project 6.5: Creating Policy and Rules Files

1. Using table 6.7, create a /etc/shorewall/policy file for the default incoming, outgoing, and firewall policy. Note that all traffic that is not explicitly permitted is blocked.

2. Create a /etc/shorewall/rules file based on the information in Table 6.7 below.

3. What additional information does Table 6.7 need to provide to restrict access to specific internal servers?

4. Create a modified version of Table 6.7 that includes any additional information you think should be included.

TABLE 6.7

Service	Outside to Firewall	Outside to Inside	Inside to Firewall	Inside to Outside
FTP	No	Yes	No	Yes
SSH	No	Yes	Yes	Yes
telnet	No	No	No	Yes
SMTP	No	Yes	No	Yes
HTTP	No	Yes	Yes	Yes
IMAP	No	Yes	No	No
HTTPS	No	Yes	No	Yes
ICMP Echo-reply	Yes	No	Yes	Yes

Case Study

You have been asked to design a network and firewall policy for a startup company that manufactures wooden toy cars. The company will have four major departments.

- Sales/Marketing—full Internet access with NetMeeting access

- Accounting—ability to browse Web sites and use AOL IM

- Manufacturing—intranet access only

- Shipping and Receiving—access to shipping vendors only: UPS, FedEx, USPS

    The company will have six servers:

- DNS server

- Linux Apache Web server for product and support information

- Secure order processing Web server for external customers

- Exchange mail server

- SQL server

- Intranet order entry and tracking Web server

    Create a one-page firewall policy, a set of rules to add to the firewall, and a separate network design for this network. Define the IP address to use for the servers and departments, and detail the ports each service uses.

6

Chapter 7

Introduction to Advanced Firewall Concepts and Terminology

Chapter Objectives

After reading this chapter and completing the exercises, you will be able to do the following:

- Use advanced firewall concepts and terminology, including rules, policies, and chains.
- Manage iptables/netfilter using the iptables command line utility.
- Implement rules, policies, and blacklisting in Shorewall.
- Recognize the uses of stateful and stateless rules in a LEAF firewall.
- Take advantage of LEAF firewall services available on the internal network.

Introduction

In general-use distributions of the Linux operating system, a simple software firewall called the *netfilter/iptables* package (**www.netfilter.org**) is available. As briefly introduced in Chapter 3, iptables is one of many independent open-source projects that may be integrated into the Linux operating system. Iptables has been part of the Linux kernel since version 2.4. A separate open-source project called Shoreline Firewall (Shorewall) is used with the LEAF firewall described in this book.

The LEAF we use here is based on the Linux 2.4 kernel, the same kernel used in the popular Red Hat 9.0 and other distributions of Linux. Although the specific version (version 2.4.20) of the Linux kernel is the same as many other distributions, the LEAF firewall described in this book operates using a specialized Linux 2.4 kernel based on the Debian open-source distribution, with several additional open-source packages. The Shorewall package, mentioned above, is integrated into the LEAF distribution to simplify the creation and management of the netfilter/iptables rules. In addition to Shorewall, the LEAF distribution provides two virtual private network (VPN) packages, as you will learn in Chapter 8. Because the LEAF distribution is stripped down to the bare minimum set of tools and utilities, it is not intended for general workstation or server use. For example, there is no graphical user interface with LEAF. Network administrators often choose LEAF instead of other full Linux distributions for several reasons:

- First, many of the full Linux distributions contain numerous programs that contain security vulnerabilities. These programs are unnecessary on the firewall.

- Second, the LEAF firewalls are intended to be "minimalist" operating systems. The fewer the programs the better.

- Third, LEAF installs completely into the system memory, leaving the hard drive untouched.

- Finally, even computers that would be useless for Windows and general Linux distributions can run LEAF.

FYI: Memory Requirements of LEAF

The most recent distributions of Windows require 128 Mbytes of RAM, while most general purpose Linux distributions require a minimum of 64 Mbytes. The LEAF system can be installed on a basic Pentium-1 machine with as little as 16 Mbytes of RAM. Realistically, for the inclusion of significant logging activities and VPNs on a LEAF firewall, a minimum of 32 Mbytes of RAM is required.

Several variations of LEAF firewalls are available at the LEAF Web site (**leaf.sourceforge.net**). The version of LEAF referenced in this book is Bering 1.2. Earlier releases of LEAF firewalls lacked stateful filtering and VPN capabilities.

In the first section of this chapter, we will focus on the command format and syntax of the netfilter/iptables facility in the LEAF firewall, also examining the associated Shorewall front-end. Once we have discussed the command format and syntax of the netfilter/iptables facility and the Shorewall facility, we will examine the difference between stateful and stateless rules and how they are processed. Finally, we'll turn our attention to other services LEAF can provide beyond its firewall capabilities.

Rule, Policy, and Chain Concepts

The Shorewall package used by the Bering Firewall is a high-level configuration utility that is used to build iptables entries. These entries are commands, as you will learn shortly. Shorewall uses several easy to manage configuration files to build a series of iptables commands for the firewall. This chapter will provide detailed information on the iptables entries that are created based on the Shorewall configuration files. Since you have set up and worked with the Bering Firewall in previous chapters, it may be helpful to use the iptables -L command as you read this chapter to better understand the relation of the iptables entries to the Shorewall configuration files. The -L flag instructs the iptables utility to list the rules in all chains or a specified chain.

The following are several examples of iptables commands that will be useful as your read this chapter:

```
iptables -L [chain]
iptables -L [chain] -n
iptables -L [chain] -n -v
iptables -L [chain] -n --line-numbers
```

The [chain] parameter in any of the preceding commands can either be left blank to view all configuration information, or [chain] can be replaced with a valid chain (INPUT, OUTPUT, FORWARD, net2loc, loc2net, loc2fw). The net2loc, loc2net, etc. chains have been defined by Shorewall, whereas INPUT, OUTPUT, and FORWARD are pre-defined chains in iptables. As an example, the command iptables –L net2fw displays all of the rules that are specified for traffic between the net (Internet) and the fw (firewall):

```
# iptables -L net2fw
Chain net2fw (1 references)
target    prot opt source          destination
ACCEPT    all   -  anywhere        anywhere      state RELATED,
                                                 ESTABLISHED
ACCEPT    tcp   -  192.168.2.99    anywhere      tcp dpt:ssh
ACCEPT    tcp   -  192.168.2.28    anywhere      tcp dpt:ssh
ACCEPT    icmp  -  anywhere        anywhere      icmp echo-
                                                 request
ACCEPT    tcp   -  192.168.2.99    anywhere      tcp dpt:www
ACCEPT    tcp   -  192.168.2.28    anywhere      tcp dpt:www
net2all   all   -  anywhere        anywhere
```

A simple definition of a *rule* is:

- a specification of some combination of protocol, IP address, and TCP or UDP header information that identifies a class of packets

- a target, which can be a direct action or a reference to another set of rules
- optionally, the state of a connection
- optionally, the content of a packet

All firewalls, whether commercial, open-source, software, or hardware, live and die by rules. Rules are matched against packet, frame, and TCP or UDP segment header contents before policies are applied. Furthermore, the terminology and syntax of iptables commands are more complicated than that of router ACLs covered in Chapter 3 and Chapter 6. Rules serve as the basis of filtering mechanisms.

Netfilter/iptables was the first stateful firewall capability integrated into Linux systems. It is specific to kernel version 2.4 and beyond, whereas prior versions had only a stateless system called ipchains available. Another important feature of netfilter/iptables is that because it is integrated into the Linux kernel, there is no need for a separate daemon to run on the firewall.

It is helpful to think of rules in terms of two categories: stateless and stateful. A rule is *stateless* if it can only be applied to each packet traversing the firewall one-at-a-time, without considering the preceding sequence of packets. Occasionally, you may use hardware or MAC addresses as criteria for rule matching. This is an example of a stateless rule because the firewall applies the rule based on the MAC address with no regard to the state of the connection.

A stateful firewall is capable of tracking the state of a connection and determining that return traffic is associated with an existing connection. Stateful rules consider the preceding sequence of packets, usually for a specific TCP connection and require additional resources to keep information—the state—of each connection. Iptables rules support state information by the characteristics *new, established, related,* and *invalid.*

The *new* characteristic refers to a new connection. How would iptables determine whether a connection is new or established? New TCP connections get an initial sequence number (ISN) by generating a random number and setting the SYN bit in the TCP header. It is easy for a firewall to use the TCP header information to detect new versus established TCP connections.

The *established* characteristic refers to an existing connection. For TCP, this would be a sequence of TCP headers with no SYN or FIN bits set. TCP uses sequence numbers to establish the order of TCP segments.

The *related* characteristic is the case where two or more connections are associated with a single application. For example, File Transfer Protocol (FTP) uses two TCP connections—port numbers 20 for data transfer and 21 for requests (i.e., the control channel). Another example of related TCP connections is Web server design. To increase responsiveness, multiple TCP connections are opened from a single Web page hit, perhaps transferring each image with an individual TCP connection. How would a firewall detect these connections are related? They would all bear the same source and destination IP addresses. In the case of FTP, the well known ports 20 and 21 should be found for one end of each connection. In the case of Web pages, the multiple connections should all have well-known port 80 directed toward the web server application.

Finally, the *invalid* characteristic matches any invalid combination of TCP flags. Several combinations of TCP flags are invalid. A few of these are:

- SYN and FIN bits set in the same header

- SYN and RST

- ACK and RST

In another such combination, all flags are set. This is invalid due to the cases cited above. This type of TCP header is sometimes called the Christmas Tree attack.

IN PRACTICE: TCP Sequence Numbers and RFCs 1948 and 1337

7

In earlier chapters, we introduced TCP SYN floods, where a system uses a stream of rapid TCP segments with the SYN bit set. This is the basis for a DoS attack during connection setup. It is important to note that, at the speed of modern day computers (now in excess of 2 gigahertz processor cycle times), an attack must use Distributed Denial of Service (DDoS) methods, infecting multiple machines. The fact that IP addresses from the attackers must change becomes the key to avoid SYN flood attacks, as described in the *FYI: Cookies and SYN Cookies.*

RFC 1948 and 1337 describe attacks on TCP during the established phase and during connection close, respectively. These attacks are described as connection hijacking and Time Wait Assassination, respectively.

RFC 1948 describes an attack used to predict TCP sequence numbers. Using the base guidelines for ISN selection from RFC 793, TCP sequence numbers are subject to certain forms of attack, generally called TCP connection hijacking. This is due to an all-to-simple method of determining initial sequence numbers (ISNs) specified in RFC 793 to avoid confusing sequence numbers from one connection with those of another. RFC 793 says:

▶ CONTINUED ON NEXT PAGE

"Initial Sequence Numbers: To avoid confusion we must prevent segments from one incarnation of a connection from being used while the same sequence numbers may still be present in the network from an earlier incarnation. We want to assure this, even if a TCP crashes and loses all knowledge of the sequence numbers it has been using. When new connections are created, an initial sequence number (ISN) generator is employed which selects a new 32-bit ISN. The generator is bound to a (possibly fictitious) 32-bit clock whose low order bit is incremented roughly every 4 microseconds. Thus, the ISN cycles approximately every 4.55 hours. Since we assume that segments will stay in the network no more than the Maximum Segment Lifetime (MSL) and that the MSL is less than 4.55 hours we can reasonably assume that ISN's will be unique."

The idea expressed in RFC 793 is to allow initial sequence numbers for new connections to be generated by the approximately four microsecond updates of the system clock. This translates into 250,000 increments each second. A new connection arising at some random time in any second therefore obtains an approximately random initial sequence number. However, this has an obvious flaw as described in RFC 1948 (Bellovin 1996), and confirmed by others, which allows a hacker to guess the next sequence number. This is accomplished by using a sniffer and obtaining copies of the all packets (including the source and destination IP addresses, as well as the TCP headers) between a host and a server. In this way, a third party—an intruder—can "hijack" the TCP connection.

Once the source and destination IP addresses, as well as the source and destination port numbers, and the sequence numbers are known, the so-called hijacker can then inject TCP segments containing viruses or other malware. The true host may be sending data with identical sequence numbers, but if that arrives later than the hijacker's segments, the receiving TCP will drop those segments believing it has already received them.

To have complete control, the hijacker must silence the true host. To do this, any convenient DoS attack that causes the host to run out of available TCP connections would do the job.

Most systems including Linux have implemented RFC 1948 and segmented the ISN numbers across the 32-bit ISN range to insure that the ISN from one connection yields little or no information

▸▸ **CONTINUED ON NEXT PAGE**

» CONTINUED

about the ISN for another connection. There is a Web site dedicated to analyzing different operating systems and the ISN attack probability of each (**http://alon.wox.org/tcpseq.html**). Linux is among those with the lowest "ISN guess" likelihood, and from Linux kernel 2.2 and beyond, there is strong protection from ISN prediction. However, it may be necessary to modify a file in the directory /proc/sys/net/ipv4 in general-purpose Linux and Unix distributions. This directory contains several files and one of these is files is tcp_syncookies, which, if set to the single character "0," indicates RFC 1337 is not to be implemented. By issuing the following command you can turn on RFC 1337 effects:

```
echo "1" > tcp_syncookies
```

You will have to reboot after this command, or issue the command:

```
/etc/rc.d/init.d/network restart
```

Note that, in LEAF, these options will not be set since a firewall is not intended to host a Web server accessible from the Internet. Other operating systems, including Solaris prior to Solaris 9 and Berkeley Standard Distribution (BSD) prior to 4.3, have an implementation, but it is either turned off by default or has weak random number generation (Sun Microsystems 2002).

On Solaris 2.6, Solaris 7, and Solaris 8 systems, RFC 1948 ISN selection is not enabled by default. To enable RFC 1948 sequence number generation on these systems, the file /etc/default/inetinit must be modified by setting the variable TCP_STRONG_ISS to 2:

```
TCP_STRONG_ISS=2
```

Once the above line is modified or added to the /etc/default/inetinit file, the system must be rebooted to complete the change.

Under the Berkley distributions prior to 4.3, there is no way to change the algorithm used for ISNs. Therefore, to gain the added security of RFC 1948, the system must be upgraded to a newer version.

Another threat called TCP Time-Wait Assassination (TWA) is described in RFC 1337 (Braden 1992). There, the threat occurs when TCP connections close, via the four-way handshake (for example, the *In Practice: Using TCPDUMP* in Chapter 2). This attack works based on the possibility of old duplicate segments that have been delayed by network equipment, or have been injected by

» CONTINUED ON NEXT PAGE

▶ CONTINUED

attackers. The result of the TWA phenomenon is one end of the TCP connection sends an RST flag to the other. The solution suggested by RFC 1337 is to modify TCP to ignore RST segments when in the close-wait state. Once again, the solution is a file in the directory /proc/sys/net/ipv4. This file is tcp_rfc1337, which, if set to the single character "0," indicates RFC 1337 is not to be implemented. By issuing the following command you can turn on RFC 1337 effects:

```
echo "1" > tcp_rfc1337
```

TWA can be successful because TCP's time-wait state upon connection close is designed to wait a very long time, defined as twice the Maximum Segment Lifetime (MSL). This is known as the 2MSL timer, and on some systems the 2MSL timer may be as long as 240 seconds. An attacker can generate many of these and exhaust the system resources, therefore achieving denial of service.

Firewalls can help by filtering undesirable TCP connections and protecting systems from SYN floods. However, it must be the client and server systems that are configured to implement RFC 1948, since those are the systems that originate TCP connections.

IN PRACTICE: Cookies and SYN Cookies

The feature that guarantees immunity from SYN floods relates to the common Internet term *cookie*. A cookie is most commonly associated with Web servers making practical improvements to the experience of client computers using Web browsers.

According to the Computer Incident Advisory Capability (CIAC, **www.ciac.org/ciac/bulletins/i-034.shtml**):

"Cookies are short pieces of data used by Web servers to help identify Web users. The popular concepts and rumors about what a cookie can do has reached almost mystical proportions, frightening users and worrying their managers."

On the other hand, the SYN flood attack has been observed since 1996 by CERT (**www.cert.org/advisories/CA-1996-21. html**). A number of commercial firewalls, including Cisco, Checkpoint, and other products, used SYN cookies as a means of defeating SYN floods.

▶ CONTINUED ON NEXT PAGE

Let us pose the question: "How would a single Web server, say amazon.com, uniquely identify each Web client's browing habits, considering a single user may have multiple Web browsers open at any time, or multiple users may be connected through a Network Address Translation (NAT) device?" The solution to this problem is to produce a small, fixed-length item called a cookie that takes a variable amount of information (for example, a sequence of Web page URLs) at a minimum:

- The Web Server's IP address and well-known port number.
- The client Web browser's IP address and ephemeral port number.
- Optionally, for e-commerce support, a user password, e.g. to support online banking or access to credit card account information.

The above characteristics are the requirements for a hash function. That is in fact what cookies are: a unique way to identify a particular user. One of the benefits of cookies is that the user, if authenticated to online banking, does not have to re-authenticate on every new Web page.

Cookies are used by Web servers to track patterns of browsing by client computers, but how can they be used to defeat a SYN flood attack? The way a SYN flood is initiated is from one or multiple computers, a series of identical TCP connection attempts as follows:

```
Client           -------------->        Server
"SYN, ISN"                          (server receives SYN)
                 <-------------
(client receives SYN,ACK          (SYN, ACK, ISN)
                                  Server waits ...
```

If the client is an attacker and never sends the final ACK to complete the three-way handshake, then the result is the so-called "half-open connection." If the server waits—sometimes as long as five minutes—while allocating the TCB, memory resources will eventually fill to capacity. This results in denial of service.

SYN cookies are an idea generated by Daniel J. Bernstein (see the e-mail correspondence at **http://cr.yp.to/syncookies/ archive**) and Eric Schenk at the University of Toronto in 1996. This was in response to incidents of SYN flooding in the early 1990s.

» CONTINUED ON NEXT PAGE

▶▶ CONTINUED

By the late 1990s, the problem was essentially solved. The final result in most operating systems was the use of an MD5 hash function of the preceding bulleted list, including an arbitrary secret.

With SYN cookies, the Server sends back a SYN,ACK,ISN using the hash function above for the ISN. The server does not allocate TCB resources until the originating client ACKs to complete the three-way handshake. The final ACK in the three-way handshake contains both ISNs, one from the client the ISN field, while the acknowledgment field of this ACK segment contains the server's hashed ISN. Therefore, the server does not need to save any state information about the connection until the client's final ACK of the three-way handshake, since the server can reverse the MD5 hash and have all the state information necessary to set up the TCB.

The above scenario explains how normal operation for a legitimate connection would succeed. How would SYN cookies help defeat SYN floods? Since multiple SYNs from the same or multiple clients with the same source port don't make sense, the server can discard the connection information unless a valid ACK with the hashed information is returned. Furthermore, no resources have been reserved, preventing a DoS attack.

Continuing with our discussion of rules, policies and chains, a policy is a generic action to be taken by a firewall after inspecting a packet. A policy can be viewed as a generalized rule that is applied to traffic between two zones (see Figure 7.1, which displays the Shorewall policy file). Recall from Chapter 4 that zones refer to areas in a network with a variety of levels of trust. Refer to Figure 4.1 and Figure 6.3 for more illustrations of the zone concept. At a minimum, general purpose firewalls implement one of three actions for any policy: accept, reject, or deny.

The iptables facility implements many additional actions, called *targets,* beyond accept, reject, and deny. Using the iptables command line, an example of a simple iptables command is:

```
iptables -P FORWARD DROP
```

This command illustrates another feature of iptables, that of setting a policy, signified by –P. The action to be taken is to drop the packet. Other policies implemented by commands issued previously to the one above permit valid packets to traverse the Linux system. The chain FORWARD (see Figure 7.2) is after the routing process, when a packet is being forwarded.

The iptables -L FORWARD command will allow you to view the existing FORWARD policy:

```
# iptables -L FORWARD
Chain FORWARD (policy DROP)
target     prot  opt  source      destination
DROP       !icmp  —    anywhere    anywhere      state
                                                 INVALID

eth0_fwd  all   —    anywhere    anywhere
eth1_fwd  all   —    anywhere    anywhere
Reject    all   —    anywhere    anywhere
reject    all   —    anywhere    anywhere
```

A *chain* is a sequence of rules that is associated with a location in the packet filtering process shown in Figure 7.2. Chains are so named because they refer to a series of statements, such as iptables rules. Statements in a chain are order-dependent. A central concept in firewalls, as with router ACLs, is the *first-matching rule* concept, which means that the first rule (as created by an iptables command) that matches a packet will have the appropriate action or target applied. Typically, no further statements in the chain will be processed. Therefore, the order of statements in chains is very important. An exception to this is when the log directive is used without any other action. In this case, processing proceeds with the next rule. When the log directive is used with no other target, the information is logged to the appropriate log facility and no other action is taken.

The Shorewall facility included in the LEAF firewall has a feature for specifying policy. This is the file/etc/shorewall/policy. A display is shown in Figure 7.1.

The source and destination columns in the figure are called zones. Each zone corresponds to a general area:

- `loc` refers to the local network being protected
- `net` corresponds to the Internet

FIGURE 7.1 Shorewall's policy file.

#SOURCE	DEST	POLICY	LOG LEVEL	LIMIT:BURST
loc	net	ACCEPT		
loc	vpn1	ACCEPT		
vpn1	loc	ACCEPT		
net	all	DROP	ULOG	
all	all	REJECT	ULOG	

- vpn1 refers to a virtual private network

- all refers to all traffic.

The features of the Shorewall policy file include the policies *accept, drop, reject, continue,* or *none.* Two other conveniences, a log level and limit:burst parameter pair, can specify a maximum average rate and maximum burst size for TCP connections.

To activate limit and burst parameters directly in iptables, you can use the following rule command:

```
iptables -A INPUT -p icmp —icmp-type echo-reply -m
limit —limit 3/minute —limit-burst 5 -j DROP
```

Each rule command has a target specified by the –j (sometimes called the "jump") parameter. The target options for iptables rule commands are less restricted than for policies, and they are *accept, drop, reject, redirect, DNAT, queue, log,* or *return.* The target *queue* actually allows a user-space program to access the packet.

A brief description of each parameter in the above command is:

- `-A INPUT` appends the rule to the INPUT chain

- `-p icmp` indicates the protocol must match the protocol type field in the IP header for ICMP

- `—icmp-type echo-reply` indicates that the ICMP type is echo-reply, type 0

- `-m limit —limit 3/minute` indicates an average of 3 ICMP echo-replies per minute is allowed, and the `—limit-burst 5` allows 5 back-to-back packets

- `-j DROP` indicates the packet should be silently discarded

The previous command is rather complex and can be prone to error. Another example of a complex iptables command is:

```
iptables -t nat -A POSTROUTING -o eth0 -s \!
192.168.1.0/24 -j MASQUERADE
```

Briefly, the parameters of the command above are:

- `-t nat`, indicating the nat table

- `-A POSTROUTING`, indicating the rule should be added to the end of the POSTROUTING chain

- `\!` is a continuation escape sequence to the command to be continued on the next command line

- `-s 192.168.1.0/24` indicates the source IP address is on the 192.168.1.0 subnet

- -j MASQUERADE indicates the target (or jump) parameter is dynamic NAT (also called NPAT, PAT, many-to-one NAT, etc.)

This command involves network address translation (NAT) (see Chapter 6) and is added to thePOSTROUTING chain. Recall that NAT changes a private IP source address to a public IP address by altering the IP packet header. The –j MASQUERADE parameter indicates that iptables should perform dynamic NAT, that is, using a single public IP address and multiple unique TCP or UDP port numbers for each active flow.

The NAT/NPAT function has been embedded within the netfilter/ iptables package. Furthermore, the target is Masquerade, indicating dynamic NAT.

The effect of this last iptables command is to append a rule to the end of the POSTROUTING chain (see Figure 7.2).

After all previous rules are processed (which may result in dropping the packet), a surviving packet will have its source IP address changed to the IP configured on eth0. This could be either a private or a public IP address, but most often it is a public IP address. Then, a unique source port number, different from any ongoing connections, will be substituted for the original source port of the TCP or UDP header. A table entry will be created to associate the machine's original source IP address and source port number and new source IP address and port. When return traffic comes back into interface eth0, the reverse translation will be made.

7

FIGURE 7.2 Illustrating Linux with netfilter/iptables.

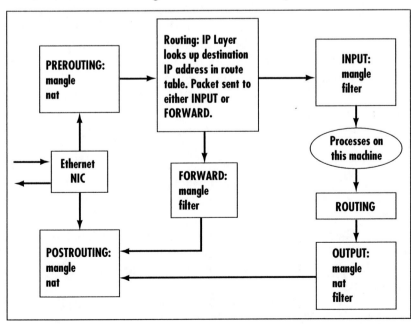

For more detail on the netfilter/iptables environment, see Figure 7.2, which illustrates the opportunities available for packet filtering within the netfilter/iptables worldview. The Shorewall worldview shields the firewall administrator from these details.

In Figure 7.2, notice that there are several "locations," that have associated chains, where rules and policies can be appended. We have already discussed the FORWARD and POSTROUTING chains. A chain is associated with each of these locations:

- PREROUTING
- INPUT
- FORWARD
- OUTPUT
- POSTROUTING

As you can see in Figure 7.2, each chain in the list has several associated tables—or equivalently, each table as an associated chain. For example, the PREROUTING chain has a ***mangle table*** and a ***NAT table.*** The purpose of the mangle table is to change the header contents regarding flags—for example, to change the TOS or TTL fields. The NAT table changes the IP address and/or the port number of the encapsulated TCP or UDP segment. Similarly, the output chain has mangle, NAT, and ***filter tables.*** Each table is addressed using the –t option.

The routing process illustrated in Figure 7.2 is the standard IP layer routing decision process in Linux associated with the iptables facility. As you learned in Chapter 4, the IP layer program looks up the destination address of the IP packet in the route table present on the machine. The boxes in Figure 7.2 titled "Routing" refer to the process described in detail in Chapter 4.

Note that there are two locations in Figure 7.2 that bear the title Routing—one for input to the machine and one for output. As with any machine —a host or a firewall—processes on the machine may receive IP packets as input, or generate them as output. The IP routing procedure described in Chapter 4 is the same in both cases.

In Table 7.1 we describe the operations of each table and its associated chains.

Table 7.1 describes the functions of each table—filter, nat and mangle. The associated chains and their functions are described. Tables are also called queues, since packets must wait to be filtered on one of the associated chains.

An iptables command can define other chains in addition to the ones in the previous list. These are called user-defined chains. To create a user-defined chain, you need to think of a unique name and create the chain by a command such as:

```
iptables -N block
```

TABLE 7.1 Iptables table functions, chains, chain functions, and typical applications.

Table, or Queue Type and Function	Associated Chains	Chain Function
Filter (Packet Filtering)	FORWARD	Filter packets to machines on one of the firewall's NICs.
	INPUT	Filter packets destined to a process on the firewall.
	OUTPUT	Filter packets originating from a process on the firewall.
NAT (NAT, NPAT, etc.)	PREROUTING	Address translation occurs before routing. Typical use: modification of the destination IP address, i.e., DNAT.
	POSTROUTING	Address translation occurs after routing. Typical use: modification of the source IP address, also called SNAT.
	OUTPUT	NAT for packets generated by the processes on the firewall.
Mangle (TCP header modification, e.g. TOS field)	PREROUTING, POSTROUTING, OUTPUT, INPUT, and FORWARD	Modification of the an IP packets header fields. Typical use: classify packets for different Quality of Service (QoS).

This command creates a user-defined chain called "block," and the –N parameter indicates it is a new chain. Subsequently, more rules can be added to the chain. See the section on dynamic stateful rules in this chapter for more about this feature of iptables.

Shorewall provides some additional features beyond iptables, one of which is *zones*. Zones help to define policy, as you learned earlier. However, each pair of zones mentioned in the /etc/shorewall/policy or /etc/shorewall/rule files defines a new user-defined chain. In addition, there will be an input, forward, and output chain defined for each interface. You can view these chains by issuing the command:

```
iptables -L
```

```
# Shorewall 1.4 -- Sample Zone File For Two Interfaces
#        /etc/shorewall/zones
#
# This file determines your network zones. Columns are:
#
#        ZONE              Short name of the zone
#        DISPLAY           Display name of the zone
#        COMMENTS          Comments about the zone
#
#ZONE    DISPLAY           COMMENTS
net      Net               Internet
loc      Local             Local Network
```

FIGURE 7.3 Shorewall's /etc/shorewall/zone file.

At a minimum, a firewall needs two zones: net and loc. These refer to the Internet and the local network, respectively. The local network is usually given a set of private IP addresses, and it is the network the firewall is supposed to protect. The LEAF firewall used in this book includes the Shorewall 2.09 package, which contains a file of zones located at /etc/shorewall/zones. In addition to the zones in the following display, an implicit zone fw defines the firewall itself.

Figure 7.4 shows a zone associated with a virtual private network called vpn1. Zones need not be associated with a strictly physical context. Shorewall needs to know which interface (usually an Ethernet NIC) to associate with each zone. This is contained in the file /etc/shorewall/interfaces, displayed in Figure 7.4.

The net and loc zones are associated with two Ethernet interfaces, eth0 and eth1. The zone vpn1 is associated with a "logical" interface, ipsec0. The topic of VPNs is covered in greater detail in Chapter 8.

The interface eth1 has the Dynamic Host Control Protocol (DHCP) option specified. See the section on Dynamic Host Control Protocol below for more information on this option. Finally, interface eth0, associated with the Internet, has the norfc1918 option. RFC 1918 (Rekhter et al. 1996)

FIGURE 7.4 The /etc/shorewall/interface file.

```
#ZONE         INTERFACE        BROADCAST        OPTIONS
net           eth0             detect           norfc1918
loc           eth1             detect           dhcp
vpn1          ipsec0
```

specifies the inadmissible source and/or destination IP addresses for general Internet routing. Among these are the private addresses, in addition to certain IP addresses like 0.0.0.0, 255.255.255.255, that should not be found in packets coming from the Internet. The norfc1918 option relieves the firewall administrator of several iptables rules that would be necessary to block private IP addresses and certain additional addresses as mentioned above.

FYI: The RFC 1918 File

In older versions of Shorewall, the file /etc/shorewall/rfc1918 specifies two objectionable classes of IP addresses. The first is the private address space identified in RFC 1918. The second is the set of all reserved and unassigned public addresses. These latter address blocks have never been assigned by the Internet Assigned Numbers Authority (IANA), or were returned to IANA when a company no longer needed them. A firewall should suspect any packet with a source IP address from those blocks. Since version 2.0.1 of Shorewall, the unallocated and reserved public IP address spaces have been moved to /etc/shorewall/bogons. (You only need this file if you use the "nobogons" parameter in Shorewall.) The name bogons is a colorful term for IP addresses "from an unknown world" derived from the atomic physics concept of bogons, which explains atomic particle interactions. Naturally, the term *bogons* could be read as "bogus ones," indicating an IP address that should not exist.

An additional layer of protection can be provided by the /etc/shorewall/hosts file, which can further define which hosts (optionally including MAC addresses) are allowed on each zone and interface. Most network applications do not require this level of protection.

A display of the Shorewall rules (/etc/shorewall/rules) file is shown in Figure 7.5.

This file shows a typical scenario for connections from the firewall (zone fw) and assumes the firewall is providing a DNS service. The first two rules, shown below, are for DNS server traffic on port 53. DNS protocol may use either or both of UDP or TCP (Refer to Chapter 2 for more information on DNS and see the section below on Domain Name Service).

```
ACCEPT    fw    net    tcp    53
ACCEPT    fw    net    udp    53
```

It is necessary for dnscache to use ISP or campus network DNS servers to resolve names; hence, the traffic must be allowed from the fw

#ACTION	SOURCE	DEST	PROTO	DEST PORT	SOURCE ORIG PORT(S) DEST
#					
#					
# Accept DNS connections from the firewall to the network					
#					
ACCEPT	fw	net	tcp	53	
ACCEPT	fw	net	udp	53	
#					
# Accept SSH connections from the local network for administration					
#					
ACCEPT	loc	fw	tcp	22	
ACCEPT	net:37.49.9.73	fw	tcp	22	
ACCEPT	net:37.49.9.77	fw	tcp	22	
ACCEPT	net:37.49.9.86	fw	tcp	22	
#					
# Allow Ping To And From Firewall					
#					
ACCEPT	loc	fw	icmp	8	
ACCEPT	net	fw	icmp	8	
ACCEPT	fw	loc	icmp	8	
ACCEPT	fw	net	icmp	8	
#					
# Bering specific rules:					
# allow loc to fw udp/53 for dnscache to work					
# allow loc to fw tcp/80 for weblet to work					
#					
ACCEPT	loc	fw	udp	53	
ACCEPT	loc	fw	tcp	80	
DNAT	net	loc:192.168.1.2	tcp	http	
DNAT	net	loc:192.168.1.2	tcp	imap	
DNAT	net	loc:192.168.1.2	tcp	smtp	
DNAT	net	loc:192.168.1.2	tcp	domain	
DNAT	net	loc:192.168.1.2	udp	domain	
ACCEPT	net	loc:192.168.1.0/24	udp	500	
ACCEPT	net	loc:192.168.1.0/24	50		
ACCEPT	net	loc:192.168.1.0/24	51		
ACCEPT	loc:192.168.1.0/24	net	udp	500	
ACCEPT	loc:192.168.1.0/24	net	50		
ACCEPT	loc:192.168.1.0/24	net	51		

FIGURE 7.5 Shorewall /etc/shorewall/rules file.

zone to the net (Internet). Those servers must be specified in /etc/ resolve.conf. In addition, a pair of rules in Figure 7.5 allows the same traffic from the local network to the firewall, so Web browsers on hosts can function:

```
ACCEPT   loc  fw   udp   53
ACCEPT   loc  fw   tcp   53
```

The target options in the Shorewall rules file are called "actions" and are slightly more limited than with the iptables command. The available targets are *accept, drop, reject, redirect, dnat, continue* and *log*.

Another series of rules allows secure shell (SSH) connections from various locations, including the local network and several specific IP addresses from the Internet. These should be applied with care, but they are often a useful troubleshooting method for solving problems before VPN functions are successful. The next set of rules allows the popular application ping. The ping application generates ICMP echo requests, which are an ICMP type 8 packet.

Finally, several additional rules in the display below allow a separate DNS server for a business domain, a Web server, and a mail server to operate on the local network. The rules for a basic SOHO operation with its own DNS, mail, and Web servers are shown below. The machine running these services is 192.168.1.2:

```
DNAT   net   loc:192.168.1.2 tcp   http
DNAT   net   loc:192.168.1.2 tcp   imap
DNAT   net   loc:192.168.1.2 tcp   smtp
DNAT   net   loc:192.168.1.2 tcp   domain
DNAT   net   loc:192.168.1.2 udp   domain
```

Figure 7.5 shows what the ***destination NAT (DNAT)*** rules accomplish. Unlike SNAT, where the source IP and/or port can be changed, here the destination IP address and optionally the destination port can be changed. Most small- to medium-size enterprises can save money using a private address space, and one or more public IP addresses from their ISP. To run a Web server inside a firewall with a private (nonroutable) IP address, an organization will need to associate a public IP address from their ISP with the Web, mail, and DNS servers for that domain. In the example file in Figure 7.5, all services run on a single machine at 192.168.1.2, so each packet with a well-known port for those services coming to the public IP (which shorewall knows when you specify the source as the net zone) needs to be port forwarded to the appropriate machine.

You learned about port forwarding in Chapter 6, but there is a specific way to do this with Shorewall. The internal Web server, mail server, and DNS server in Figure 7.5 are all running on the usual well-known ports, but that need not be the case. For example, the Web server could use TCP port

8080, in which case the destination port must be changed. The DNAT line would then become:

```
DNAT net:your.pub.lic.ip:http loc:192.168.1.2 tcp 8080
```

The equivalent iptables command for this would be as follows:

```
iptables -t nat -A PREROUTING -p tcp -i eth0 -d
your.pub.lic.ip —dport 80 —sport 1024:65535 -j DNAT —to
192.168.1.2:8080
```

- -t nat identifies the nat table
- -A PREROUTING identifies the PREROUTING chain
- -p tcp identifies the protocol to be matched is tcp
- -i eth0 indicates the interface that the packet is coming from
- -d indicated the public IP address of your machine
- -dport 80 indicates the destination port should match 80

As you can see, the equivalent iptables command is quite complex when compared with the Shorewall equivalent. The remaining lines in Figure 7.5 allow IPsec VPN traffic to traverse the firewall. These are IP protocols 50 and 51 and UDP port 500. You will learn more about VPNs in Chapter 8.

As a final remark, to appreciate what Shorewall achieves for the firewall administrator, issue the command iptables -L. This command will take several seconds to run, but it will provide a complete list of all the rules of all chains that are currently operating in the firewall kernel.

More About Stateless Rules

As described earlier, stateless rules deal with packets on a "one-at-a-time" basis. There is no identification of any previous stream of packets from or to the same source or destination. Some simple stateless commands are displayed here:

```
iptables -A FORWARD -s 202.54.6.1 -j ACCEPT
```

This command specifies that after the forward chain, if the source IP address is 202.54.6.1, that the action should be accept. (Note that the iptables command, like most Linux commands, is case sensitive.) Next we illustrate how an iptables command matches a particular protocol, specifically TCP:

```
iptables -A INPUT -p tcp -dport 80 -j ACCEPT
```

This command matches any packet whose contents is a TCP segment, via the -p (p stands for protocol) parameter. As described in Chapter 2, a TCP segment contains two port numbers, a source port number and a destination port number. The destination port number often identifies a service, such as a Web server. The default port number for Web service is port 80, so this rule only matches TCP segments with destination port 80, via the -dport parameter. The action is to accept these packets.

Notice that the INPUT chain is specified in the iptables command above. This command implies that the destination of the packet is a process on the machine itself (since the next bubble after the INPUT chain in Figure 7.2 is titled "processes on this machine"). An example of the previous command is that the LEAF firewall includes a small Web server called "weblet" that provides a Web page giving overall status of the firewall and easy access to log files. However, due to Shorewall's policy file such an iptables command is not necessary.

Although not shown in Figure 7.1, the Shorewall policy file will always allow access to the fw zone from the loc zone via an ACCEPT policy. If you type the IP address of the internal interface of the LEAF firewall (usually 192.168.1.254) into a browser, you will see the "weblet" interface. This will allow you to see a number of status indications about the firewall. If an iptables command were necessary to allow this access, it would be:

```
iptables -A INPUT -p tcp -i eth1 -dport 80 -j ACCEPT
```

The usual interface on the internal network is eth1, so the -i eth1 parameter indicates that only packets from the internal interface can view the weblet status page.

In reference to the example of a Web server or a mail server behind a firewall, the command above applies to only the firewall itself. Another facility of iptables, called destination network address translation (DNAT), must be used, as illustrated below. Many applications of firewalls in a SOHO environment would have a single public IP address from an ISP, while using private, nonroutable IP addresses on the internal network. A Web or mail server would have one of these private IP addresses, however, and would therefore be inaccessible from the Internet. The solution to this problem is to use the DNS system to map the public IP address obtained from the ISP to the domain name in question (e.g., mycompany.net). Then, the scheme is to use the following iptables commands to accomplish port forwarding:

```
iptables -A PREROUTING -d 203.200.144.114 -dport 80 -j
DNAT -to 192.168.1.68:80
iptables -A PREROUTING -d 203.200.144.114 -dport 25 -j
DNAT -to 192.168.1.68:25
```

These two commands use the PREROUTING chain because we do not want the firewall router to redirect the traffic elsewhere and these iptables commands assume that the public address 203.200.144.114 is in the IP destination address field (-d parameter). The destination port numbers found in the TCP segment must be 80 and 25, belonging to Web service and Simple Mail Transfer Protocol (SMTP), respectively. Finally, these commands assume that the Web and mail servers are running on the same machine at 192.168.1.68.

However, in this scenario, mail clients for the employees of this SOHO or other environment can only access their mail from the internal network. To allow these individuals to access their mail from the Internet at large, we must add one or two additional rules, depending on the type of mail client service being provided by the mail server. Two popular client mail protocols are Post Office Protocol (POP) and Interactive Mail Access Protocol (IMAP), whose well-known service ports on the mail server are 110 and 143 respectively. Commands for these applications to traverse the firewall are:

```
iptables -A PREROUTING -d 203.200.144.114 -dport 110 -j
DNAT -to 192.168.1.68:110
iptables -A PREROUTING -d 203.200.144.114 -dport 143 -j
DNAT -to 192.168.1.68:143
```

More About Stateful (Dynamic) Rules

Stateful rules identify and store a "track record" of what went on before the current packet is inspected. This means that some kind of state must be retained for certain connections, usually in the form of a table in the firewalls memory. An example of stateful commands is provided in Figure 7.6.

The first command in Figure 7.6 flushes the iptables system (-F), and deletes all rules. The second command creates the user-defined chain called block. The next command accepts any packet for which a pre-existing connection is established. Despite the fact that TCP is connection-oriented,

FIGURE 7.6 Stateful commands and command ordering.

```
/sbin/iptables -F       # Flushes the iptables chains

/sbin/iptables -N block    #Creates a new chain called block
/sbin/iptables -A block -m state --state ESTABLISHED,RELATED -j ACCEPT
/sbin/iptables -A block -m state --state NEW -i ! ppp0 -j ACCEPT
/sbin/iptables -A block -j LOG
/sbin/iptables -A block -j DROP

# These rules tell the INPUT and FORWARD chains to jump to block.
/sbin/iptables -A INPUT -j block
/sbin/iptables -A FORWARD -j block
```

stateful operations in iptables can work for such connectionless protocols such as UDP. Finally, the last two commands have added a jump (-j parameter) to the block chain from both the input and forward chains. If any other rules in the input or forward chains follow the jump rule to the block chain, after the block chain is executed, processing continues with the rest of the input or forward chain statements.

As mentioned previously, the possible states of a packet are *new, established, related,* and *invalid.* The Shorewall facility takes care of setting up the most desirable configurations, that is, accepting *new, established,* and *related* packets, and rejecting or dropping *invalid* ones.

Virtually all capabilities can be accomplished through configuration with Shorewall. Occasionally, a special circumstance may arise that requires an actual iptables rule to be used. Shorewall provides a facility called *extension scripts* that are accessible through the lrcfg utility. See the documentation at **shorewall.net/shorewall_extension_scripts.htm** before proceeding.

IN PRACTICE: Blacklisting in Shorewall

Many attacks may originate from a small handful of IP addresses. Some may emanate from inside the local network. Shorewall has a facility for **blacklisting.** Blacklisting is the practice of denying access from certain locations by IP address or, in the case of the directly connected networks, by MAC address. This facility is found in the file /etc/shorewall/blacklist. A sample blacklist file is displayed below:

```
# /etc/shorewall/blacklist
#
#
#####################################################
###############
#ADDRESS/SUBNET        PROTOCOL      PORT
#
# Block all connections from IP 192.168.10.32
#
192.168.10.32
#
#  Block all connections from the following MAC
   address
#
```

CONTINUED ON NEXT PAGE

```
▶▶ CONTINUED

~00-A0-C9-15-39-78
#
# Block dns queries from 192.0.2.126
#
192.0.2.126          udp          53
#
#
# LAST LINE — ADD YOUR ENTRIES BEFORE THIS ONE —
  DO NOT REMOVE
```

One application of blacklisting is to avoid secure HTTP tunnels (HTTPS protocol, port 443) associated with Web proxies. These are sometimes dangerous because each tunnel carries a virtually unknown content. As mentioned in previous chapters, tunnels appear to be trustworthy because they protect the traffic from interception and avoid many threats. However, what if the tunnel leads to a network that is not under your control?

In this situation, you need to take special care. For example, suppose you are using a forward Web proxy for a Web site that you frequently visit. Suppose further that the proxy has been compromised. There may be any number of threats waiting on the other end of the tunnel. You will not be able to determine the health of the proxy because another organization is in charge of its maintenance. A solution is to add to /etc/shorewall/blacklist the IP addresses associated with such sites, and the firewall will refuse the connection.

Other Services the LEAF Firewall Can Offer to the Internal Network

The LEAF firewall is also a router and, like most routers, offers several other services. To understand how these services are installed on the firewall, we will look at two files that are central to every LEAF firewall:

- syslinux.cfg

- leaf.cfg

As you learned in Chapter 5, these files, called *firewall configuration files,* control which packages are loaded when booting the firewall. Each package is called by a package name followed by the suffix .lrp, which stands for *Linux Router Project.* The Linux Router Project was the original name of the open-source project, which was later changed to Linux Embedded Appliance Firewall (LEAF).

As an example, the package iptables is contained in the file iptables.lrp. These files are simply gzipped (***Gnu-zip utility***) ***Tape-Archive-Retrieval*** (TAR) files. A gzipped file is a file that has been compressed with the gzip utility found on most Linux systems. (This is identical with utilities on Windows systems, such as WinZip™.) TAR files are a different compression method, but one that is complimentary to zip files. The combination of gzip and TAR allows greater compression of binaries, and as a consequence more binary programs can fit on a single floppy diskette.

In fact, most utilities on Windows will be able to extract gzipped and/or tared files. The normal extensions for these files is ".tgz." The extensions ".tgz" and ".lrp," are identical. The only exception to this is the file initrd.lrp, which is just gzipped (its normal extension would be ".gz"). The syslinux.cfg file determines where the initial Linux system for boot is found and where packages can be found, offering options including:

- Single 3.5-inch floppy boot at 1,680-Kbyte format, all packages on the floppy

- Dual floppy at the same format, when more packages than can fit on a single floppy are needed

- CD-ROM boot, if supported by the machine

- Floppy boot, plus packages read from a CD-ROM

A diagram of several syslinux.cfg files is shown in Figure 7.7 and illustrates the options above. The first file shows three lines. The syslinux.dpy file contains a small graphic that will display upon bootup. The timeout=0 parameter means never timeout. We suppress these two lines in the remainder of the files in the figure, showing only the line beginning with the word *default*. This indicates the operating system to be Linux and indicates several parameters. We will focus only on the LEAFCFG, PKGPATH, diskwait=yes, and LRP=parameter strings.

One aspect of the kernel command line of syslinux.cfg is that it has a line length limit of 254 characters. As more packages have become available, it is necessary to use a separate file called leaf.cfg to specify additional packages when the syslinux.cfg file cannot provide sufficient space to name them all. (In Figure 7.7, no carriage returns are in the individual lines. They have been wrapped to fit the page margins.)

In Figure 7.7a, the syslinux.cfg file for a basic single floppy boot is shown. All necessary executables and packages are on a single floppy. Many older machines have no capability to boot from CD-ROM, so Figure 7.7b shows a way to add a second floppy with more packages. When you want quite a few conveniences with your firewall, such as adding secure

```
display syslinux.dpv

timeout 0

default linux initrd=initrd.lrp init=/linuxrc rw root=/dev/ram0
LEAFCFG=/dev/fdu1680:msdos PKGPATH=/dev/fdu1680:msdos  syst.size=12M
log_size=4M
LRP=root,etc,local,modules,iptables,pump,keyboard,shorwall,ulogd,dnscache
,dhcpd,ipsec,mawk
```

a. Single floppy boot

```
default linux initrd=initrd.lrp init=/linuxrc rw root=/dev/ram0
LEAFCFG=/dev/fdu1680:msdos diskwait=yes PKGPATH=/dev/fdu1680:msdos
syst_size=12M log_size=4M
LRP=root,etc,local,modules,iptables,pump,keyboard,shorwall,ulogd,dnscache
,dhcpd,ipsec,mawk
```

b. Dual floppy boot

```
default linux initrd=initrd.lrp init=/linuxrc rw root=/dev/ram0
LEAFCFG=/dev/fd0:msdos PKGPATH=/dev/fd0:msdos,/dev/cdrom:iso9660
syst_size=12M log_size=4M
LRP=root,etc,local,modules,iptables,pump,keyboard,shorwall,ulogd,dnscache
,dhcpd,ipsec,mawk
```

c. CDROM boot

```
default linux initrd=initrd.lrp init=/linuxrc rw root=/dev/ram0
LEAFCFG=/dev/fd0:msdos PKGPATH=/dev/fd0:msdos,/dev/cdrom:iso9660
syst_size=12M log_size=4M
LRP=root,etc,local,modules,iptables,pump,keyboard,shorwall,ulogd,dnscache
,dhcpd,ipsec,mawk
```

d. Floppy boot with CDROM

FIGURE 7.7 Several possible syslinux.cfg files.

shell daemons (SSHD.lrp) to a system with VPNs, then you might run out of space on two floppies.

If this happens, it might be best to transition to a CD-ROM boot, as depicted in Figure 7.7c. As a convenience, the LEAFCFG=/dev/fd0:msdos parameter allows a standard 1.44-Mbyte floppy to be used for updated packages. The PKGPATH=/dev/fd0:msdos,/dev/cdrom:iso966 specifies that the boot process should look first for packages on the standard floppy (which also contains the leaf.cfg file). The PKGPATH specification indicates that if a package specified in syslinux.cfg is not found on the floppy, then search for it on the CD-ROM.

It is still possible to get plenty of packages loaded from a CD-ROM, even if you can't boot from it. This process is shown in Figure 7.7d, where the syslinux.cfg file looks identical to 7.7c. The difference is where the file's Linux (the basic Linux operating system) and initrd.lrp reside. In the case of Figure 7.7c, these files will be on a floppy, whereas with Figure 7.7d they will be on the CD-ROM.

FYI: The Original Bering Configuration File

The first Bering 1.2 version used a file called lrpkg.cfg, playing the role of syslinux.cfg. If you have already worked with such a version, you can continue to use that file.

IN PRACTICE: Using 3.5-Inch Floppies at Sizes Larger Than 1.44 Mbytes

In Figure 7.7, notice that some examples show the parameter LEAFCFG=/dev/fd0:msdos, while others show LEAFCFG=/dev/fdu1680:msdos and/or PKGPATH=/dev/fdu1680:msdos. The first specifies a standard 1.44-Mbyte floppy in normal MS-DOS format, while the second specifies a floppy formatted to contain 1.68 Mbytes of data. This floppy may have only the single file leaf.cfg, specifying additional packages to those listed in the LRP= parameter of syslinux.cfg. If all packages fit on a single floppy, the leaf.cfg file will be on the same floppy as packages. In this case, there is a single bootable floppy.

While it is not well known, even a Windows-based PC can format a floppy as large as 1.722 Mbytes. The 1.68 Mbyte format has become a de facto standard for the LEAF firewalls, since it is quite reliable. We recommend using new, high-quality floppies rather than reusing floppies that were distributed for program installation purposes—such floppies are intended to be read only a few times, for installation purposes, and are often low quality.

The book Web site contains images of such floppies, for the situation in which CD-ROM boot is not available. Several low-cost programs can be used to manage the packages as you learn to add or

▶▶ CONTINUED ON NEXT PAGE

7

> ▶ **CONTINUED**
>
> subtract from the capabilities of your firewall. Two that are particularly useful are the programs magiciso (**www.magiciso. com**), winiso (**www.winiso.com**), and winimage (**www.winimage.com**). If you are trying to "recycle" an old PC that does not support CD-ROM boot as a firewall, you may wish to invest in winimage or a similar program to generate floppies of 1680 Mbytes.
>
> Another option is to use a small Disk on Module (DOM) that fits into the IDE connector in place of the hard drive. DOMs are quite inexpensive but require the IDE modules, and packages are then located on the DOM.

```
syst_size = 12M
log_size = 12M
LRP = "$KCMD_LRP sshd"
LRP = "$LRP weblet"
```

FIGURE 7.8 Example leaf.cfg file.

Figure 7.8 shows a typical leaf.cfg file.

Dynamic Host Configuration Protocol (DHCP)

DHCP is a service that provides IP addresses, gateway router addresses, and DNS server addresses. DHCP is offered through the program dhcpd (DHCP daemon). This daemon looks at the file /etc/dhcpd.conf in the Linux 2.4 environment to obtain its configuration. This file can be accessed and edited through the lrcfg utility supplied with the LEAF firewall by selecting option 3, packages configuration, from the main menu.

In a small network, the firewall can serve as the DHCP server. In this situation you load the dhcp daemon via the package dhcpd.lrp. This daemon has two files that affect its behavior. One is /etc/dhcpd.conf, which contains several directives. A sample dhcpd.conf file is shown here:

```
dynamic-bootp-lease-length 604800;
max-lease-time 1209600;
subnet 192.168.1.0 netmask 255.255.255.0 {
option routers 192.168.1.254;
option domain-name "private.network";
option domain-name-servers 192.168.1.254;
range 192.168.1.3 192.168.1.199;
}
```

This file sets several options:

- `dynamic-bootp-lease-length 604800;` indicates that the lease length on an IP address for any host is one week in seconds.

- `max-lease-time 1209600;` identifies the maximum lease period as 2 weeks before the host refreshes it. This means the host lease will expire in one week via the lease length parameter, but, since a host might be "out of the office" (e.g., a laptop) there is a second week of grace period before the IP address is available for another host.

- `subnet 192.168.1.0 netmask 255.255.255.0{...}` indicates the subnet and several options

FYI: DHCP Lease Time

If enough IP addresses are available, it is useful to set the lease time so that a computer will typically maintain the same IP address. This makes it much easier to track a computer if a problem occurs because it will likely have the same IP address.

- `option routers 192.168.1.254;` tells the host the default gateway is 192.168.1.254 which is the firewalls IP address on the internal NIC.
- `option domain-name "private.network";` gives the basic domain name. If a host named "yadda" is added to a DNS server, then the host has a domain name yadda.private.network.
- `option domain-name-servers 192.168.1.254;` indicates that the host should use 192.168.1.254 as a domain name server—thus the host is using LEAF's dnscache facility (see the next section on DNS).
- Finally, `range 192.168.1.3 192.168.1.199;` indicates that the range of IP addresses to be used for DHCP begins at 192.168.1.3 and continues to 192.168.1.199, allowing for 196 unique IP addresses. The addresses 192.168.1.1 and 192.168.1.2 are reserved, and are typically used as static IP addresses for servers.

The other file that controls dhcpd's behavior is /etc/init.d/dhcpd. A small portion of this file is shown below:

```
#!/bin/sh
# <material deleted ...>
RCDLINKS="2,S30 3,S30 6,K30"
# Add interfaces, separated by a space
#(ie "eth0 eth1")
# Typically your internal interface: eth1
# <material deleted ...>
ifs="eth1"
```

The main option available in /etc/init.d/dhcpd is identifying which interfaces the DHCP should serve. The most important feature is the ifs="eth1" parameter. This identifies eth1 as the interface the DHCP will serve, which is usually the internal interface.

There is one situation in which you may need to add an additional interface to the list. In the case where you need to use a third interface—for example, to host a wireless hot-spot with DMZ characteristics, the usual convention is for eth0 to be the interface leading to the Internet, and eth1 to be the internal (most trusted network). In this case, interface eth2 is the DMZ interface. The expression above becomes:

```
ifs="eth1 eth2"
```

indicating that DHCP should serve both eth1 and eth2.

Finally, remember that dhcpd is a daemon. Therefore, as such, it is a server providing IP addresses, and provides the identity of the default gateway and DNS server for the internal network(s).

The DCHP client in the version of LEAF used with this book is called pump, obtained by loading the package pump.lrp. The pump package works on a configuration file /etc/pump.conf. We show a typical configuration here:

```
retries 3
script "/etc/pump.shorewall"
device eth0 {
nodns  }
```

The purpose of pump is to obtain IP addresses from a campus network or ISP. Unless you have obtained static IP addresses, you will need to use pump on the interface leading to your campus network or ISP. The configuration file above indicates two important parameters:

- device eth0 indicates the device for which pump should obtain an IP address is eth0. You must also specify the dhcp option in /etc/shorewall/interfaces and in /etc/network/interfaces.

- nodns indicates that no DNS service is required of the campus network or ISP. This is because dnscache will be providing DNS to the internal network, and will be using a campus or ISP network DNS server as a "forwarder," as you will learn in the next section.

Domain Name Service (DNS)

The LEAF firewall includes a package called dnscache. This package, authored by D.J. Bernstein, is available separately from the Web site **http://cr.yp.to**. The package is actually more secure than most other DNS servers and is substantially more stable than the Unix bind program, according to Bernstein.

DNS service from your firewall to the internal hosts depends on two configurations: The first is the file /etc/resolv.conf, which can be edited using the lrcfg utility in LEAF. Select the first option on the main menu, Network configuration. Then, select the resolv.conf file to obtain an editor session. You must supply one or more DNS server IP addresses from your ISP or campus network for the dnscache deamon to use.

The second set of configuration items is in several files in the directory/etc/dnscache. These can be edited by using the lrcfg utility selecting option 3, Packages configuration, followed by the dnscache selection.

The /etc/dnscache directory has a number of subdirectories that cover several options, including logging DNS activity and forwarding. The only option we will cover here is the issue of forwarding. Logging will be covered in a later chapter. Most DNS servers need a "forwarder" as found, for example, in Windows Server 2000 and 2003 environments. The principle behind forwarders is simple. Most DNS servers are responsible for a single domain or subdomain. This corresponds to a small set of machines, as compared to the entire Internet. The other option is to use root servers directly by a set of "root hints"—the IP addresses of the 13 root servers that have global authoritative information on all domains. These are found in the file /etc/dnscache/env DNSO.

Many campus networks and some ISPs only allow direct DNS queries to propagate beyond their network boundaries from their own DNS servers. If this is the case, you must specify forwarding by editing the file /etc/dnscache/env/QUERYFWD, and replacing the single phrase NO with YES. It is necessary to repeat the DNS server IP addresses that were used in /etc/resolv.conf in the file etc/dnscache/env/DNS1. These options are numbers 4 and 5 in the dnscache configuration menu.

Network Address Translation (NAT) and Masquerading

We have looked at an example of the NAT facilities embedded in iptables, which illustrate port forwarding, or excluding certain addresses from treatment by NAT. An additional facility of the iptables facility is called *masquerading.* As mentioned previously, this is called Port Address Translation (PAT), dynamic NAT, or ***Network Port Address Translation (NPAT).*** These terms all refer to the same facility.

Masquerading can be used as a money-saving tool. Specifically, with broadband services such as cable Internet and digital subscriber line (DSL) becoming widely available and affordable, there is commonly only one public IP address allowed per subscriber. Obtaining additional IP addresses requires additional expense. Masquerading allows a single IP address to be mapped to multiple IP addresses on the internal network by using different unique source ports for each active connection or session.

Broadband services also lack security. Unlike dial-up modem service, broadband connections to homes and businesses have to deal with a plethora of attacks generated from the Internet. ISPs are often simply unable (or unwilling, due to the effort involved) to police their networks. As a consequence, a firewall is an absolute necessity for broadband connections. An additional layer of security can be provided by masquerading because it masks the identity of internal IP addresses from the Internet.

Summary

After reading this chapter, you should understand the basics of the LEAF firewall and the relationship between netfilter/iptables and the Shorewall facility. You should also have an understanding of several services— DHCP, DNS, and dynamic NAT (also called masquerading or port address translation.)

You have been given a detailed overview of the capabilities for the firewall to perform Destination NAT (DNAT), where services that need to be available to the outside world—Web, mail, and DNS services—are given explicit rules for port forwarding. Finally, you have learned about blacklisting, a technique for blocking specific sites by IP or MAC address.

On a final note, the LEAF firewall's executables are compiled using the glibc 2.0 libraries. This refers to the Gnu Libraries for C code. There are newer versions of LEAF that are based upon the uclibc—University of California libraries for C code. Since the uclibc LEAF versions were not stable when we began writing this book, we used a glibc version of LEAF. By the time this book is published, however, the uclibc versions may be quite stable. The main advantage of uclibc versions of compiled source code is the small size of the resulting binary executables, when compared to glibc. This enhances both memory use and certain applications such as Disk-on-Chip.

Test Your Skills

MULTIPLE CHOICE QUESTIONS

1. You have a mail server running on the internal network behind a firewall. Which protocols do you need to allow from the Internet?

   A. DNS

   B. SMTP and IMAP

   C. DNS, SMTP, POP, and/or IMAP, depending on the types of mail clients you wish to support

   D. DNS and SMTP

2. You need to provide DHCP service to client computers on the internal network. In which file is the configuration for this found?

   A. /etc/interfaces file

   B. /etc/dhcpd.conf file

   C. /etc/dhcpclient.conf file

   D. /etc/shorewall/masq file

3. You need to provide DNS service to client computers on the internal network. In which file is the configuration for this found?

   A. /etc/interfaces file

   B. /etc/resolv.conf file

   C. /etc/resolv.conf file and etc/dnscache/env directory

   D. /etc/dnschache/env directory

4. The majority of configuration tasks for the LEAF firewall can be carried out using which of the following?

   A. The lrcfg utility

   B. Iptables commands

   C. Direct editing of all the files in /etc and it subdirectories

   D. The telnet protocol to access the firewall and editing the files remotely

5. You decide to add or delete a package to your firewall. You will need to edit which of the following?

   A. syslinux.cfg

   B. syslinux.cfg and/or leaf.cfg

   C. only leaf.cfg

   D. None of the above. Use the telnet utility to access the firewall, enter the directory where the package exists, and delete the binary. Reboot.

6. You are having problems with rules. To find out what rules are actually operating with iptables, you should issue which command?

   A. iptables –L

   B. iptables –N INPUT

   C. iptables –F

   D. iptables –X INPUT

7. What kind of rule target (or *action*, in Shorewall terminology) would you use to accomplish port forwarding?

   A. DROP

   B. REJECT

   C. DNAT

   D. FORGET

8. A rule that looks at a single packet at a time is called

   A. stateful.

   B. forgetful.

   C. stateless.

   D. clueless.

9. A set of actions taken after rules are processed in iptables is called

   A. targets.

   B. chains.

   C. DNATs.

   D. policies.

10. What are the equivalent acronyms for Dynamic NAT?

    A. DNAT, NAPT

    B. DHCP, NPAT, PAT

    C. PAT, NPAT, MASQUERADE

    D. DNS, DHCP

11. A zone can be a specification of
    A. a physical interface or a logical interface.
    B. a physical interface, a logical interface, or an arbitrary collection of hosts.
    C. only a physical interface.

12. The process of identifying unwanted IP addresses is called what?
    A. linecutting
    B. blacklisting
    C. wiretripping
    D. blackhatting

13. What does the suffix .lrp stand for?
    A. Linux Root Project
    B. Linux Project for Root access
    C. Linux Router Project
    D. A Real Linux Project

14. Which are the most important configuration files for the LEAF firewalls?
    A. shorewall.lrp
    B. syslinux.cfg, leaf.cfg
    C. linux.cfg, syslinux
    D. iptables

15. A LEAF firewall can provide the following services to the internal network:
    A. DNS and DHCP
    B. DNS, DHCP and NAT
    C. DNS, DHCP and static bridging
    D. DNS, PCHD and ANT.

16. What does dhcpd.lrp implement?
    A. DNS server
    B. DHCP client
    C. DHCP server
    D. DNS client

17. What does pump.lrp implement?

    A. DNS server

    B. DHCP client

    C. DHCP server

    D. DNS client

18. What does dnscache.lrp implement?

    A. DNS server

    B. DHCP client

    C. DHCP server

    D. DNS client

EXERCISES

Exercise 7.1: Adding an IPTABLES Rule to the Shorewall Package

It is occasionally necessary to enter direct iptables commands for special purposes, either for temporary debugging or simply to avoid rebooting a firewall. It is also convenient to have such rules become permanent, surviving across reboots, power outages, or other failures.

You find it necessary never to apply NAT or masquerading to packets from a certain machine, 192.168.1.3, within the local network behind a firewall.

1. Refer to the iptables tutorial at **www.faqs.org/docs/iptables/ index.html**.

2. Outline the iptables command to accomplish this.

3. Decide which extension script to use, consulting the link **www.shorewall.net/1.4/shorewall_extension_scripts.htm**.

Exercise 7.2: Configuring an Internal Web Server in Shorewall

You want to create a Web server running in the local network behind the firewall. The internal network uses the Class C private IP subnet 192.168.10.0/24, and the Web server will be running on 192.168.10.11. You have DNS service from the registrar where you registered your domain, **www.mynewco.com**. In addition, you are paying for a Web forwarding service that takes requests from the Internet to your domain name on port 80 and sends them to the public IP address on the external interface of your firewall.

For security reasons, you have configured your internal Web server to respond only to destination port 8888. Write the appropriate rule for the /etc/shorewall/rules file that will allow requests on port 80 to pass through the firewall and be directed to the Web server.

Exercise 7.3: Configuring an Internal FTP Server in Shorewall

Using the same IP address from Exercise 7.2, now you want to add an FTP server to the machine running the Web server. Two ports are associated with FTP: one for data and one for commands. These are TCP ports 20 and 21. Write the additional rules to enable FTP on the machine.

Exercise 7.4: Configuring an Internal Mail Server in Shorewall

Using the same IP address from Exercise 7.2, now you want to add a mail server to the machine running the Web server and the FTP server. Naturally, your mail server must support SMTP and also support Post Office Protocol (POP) for POP client programs operating from the Internet. Write the additional rules to enable these mail applications on the machine.

Exercise 7.5: Restricting Access for a Specific MAC Address

Someone has been using a machine on the internal network to access illicit Web sites. You have blacklisted the Web site IP addresses, but the employee has found new sites. You have sniffed the traffic and know the MAC address. Before confronting the employee, you want to stop all access to the Internet. Describe the rule to do this and discuss the shorewall files involved.

PROJECTS

Project 7.1: Set Up a LEAF Firewall to Support Internal Web Services and Attach to Your ISP or Campus Network

For this project, you will need a PC for the firewall with these minimal capabilities:

> 32 Mbytes of RAM
>
> Pentium 1 or better
>
> Two PCI slots and two Ethernet PCI NICs (or if the PC has a NIC integrated into the motherboard, just one additional PCI slot and one additional PCI NIC)

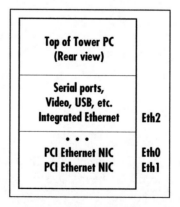

It will help if both NICs are of the same type, since then you will need only one driver module. You will need a second PC to act as a client on an internal network. This can be either a Windows PC or a Linux PC with one Ethernet port. It will also be useful if the second PC can burn a CD from an image file (or find any PC with such a capability).

1. Using the book Web site, copy the firewall ISO image for this chapter to a directory on a PC with CD-burning software.

2. Insert a new CD-R or CD-RW media into the CD drive, and burn the image.

3. Using a permanent marker, make a note of the firewall image and date on the printed side of the CD. You may be burning multiple copies of the CD, so using a date and time will help keep track of the different versions.

By default, the CD image assumes that the interface eth0 is the external interface connected to your ISP or campus network. It also assumes that eth1 is the internal network. PCI buses on PCs tend to order the interfaces in a descending order going farther down the bus away from the CPU. For a tower PC, this is toward the bottom, but for a desktop PC you may need to experiment to find which interface is eth0 and which is eth1.

The following diagram illustrates a tower PC with an integrated NIC and two PCI cards. (For this project, you only need two total NICs, but it is clearer to show two PCI cards to understand the numbering scheme.) Because you need to identify the correct NIC for the Internet, or campus network side of your firewall, this needs to be done correctly. Otherwise, you might connect the Internet to your internal network NIC, which is always

FIGURE 7.9 Typical ethernet NIC numbering scheme for a tower PC.

Top of Tower PC **(Rear view)**	
Serial ports, **Video, USB, etc.** **Integrated Ethernet**	**Eth2**
• • •	
PCI Ethernet NIC	**Eth0**
PCI Ethernet NIC	**Eth1**

trusted, and this could lead to disaster. By default, LEAF assumes the NIC called eth0 is connected to the Internet, e.g. to cable or DSL modem. LEAF assumes eth1 is connected to the internal network. This is because the default /etc/shorewall/interfaces file will associate the net zone with eth0, and the loc zone with eth1. The /etc/shorewall/policy file will define policies that trust the machines on the internal network, and distrust the machines on the Internet (net) zone. Of course, you can edit/etc/shorewall/interfaces file to reverse the association.

Project 7.2: Set Up a LEAF Firewall for Traceroutes

For this project, you will need the firewall that you installed in Project 7.1. To begin, do not make any modifications to your firewall. You will need to connect your firewall to the Internet. You may have problems if your campus network or ISP blocks ICMP protocol (a.k.a. ping) going in or out of the campus. Try to ping an off-campus Web site to make sure.

1. Using traceroute under Unix or Linux, or tracert under Windows, trace a route to any location. You should get output from a command prompt similar to Figure 7.10.

FIGURE 7.10 Tracert output from a Windows machine before modification.

```
C:/tracert www.radford.edu
Tracing route to infolink.radford.edu [137.45.3.1]over a maximum of 30 hops:
  1     *         *         *        Request timed out.
  2    45 ms    56 ms    45 ms    64-4-124-1.dmt.ntelos.net [64.4.124.1]
  3    47 ms    47 ms    47 ms    216.12.1.209
  4    54 ms    47 ms    48 ms    1-120.atm-1-0.wbo-gsr.core.ntelos.net
[216.12.22.209]
  5    52 ms    48 ms    47 ms    1-120.atm-1-0.wbo-gsr.core.ntelos.net
[216.12.22.209]
  6    51 ms    51 ms    51 ms    POS2-3.GW3.RIC2.ALTER.NET [157.130.56.101]
  7    54 ms    53 ms    52 ms    506.at-0-2-0.CL2.DCA1.ALTER.NET
[152.63.37.250]
  8    57 ms    58 ms    56 ms    194.ATM7-0.GW2.RIC2.ALTER.net [152.63.37.233]
  9    56 ms    78 ms    56 ms    owl-covanetmci-oc3.customer.alter.net
[157.130.57.78]
 10     *         *         *        Request timed out.
 11    85 ms    96 ms    94 ms    igw.radford.edu [137.45.227.55]
 12    92 ms    87 ms    86 ms    infolink.radford.edu [137.45.3.1]
Trace complete.
```

ACCEPT	loc	fw	icmp	8
ACCEPT	net	fw	icmp	8
ACCEPT	fw	loc	icmp	8
ACCEPT	fw	net	icmp	8
ACCEPT	loc	fw	icmp	11
ACCEPT	net	fw	icmp	11
ACCEPT	fw	loc	icmp	11
ACCEPT	fw	net	icmp	11

FIGURE 7.11 Adding support for traceroute.

2. Notice two lines with asterisks and the message "request timed out." The first one of these is your firewall. While your firewall allows ICMP type 8 packets—part of tracert's method—it does not allow an additional necessary option that tracert uses.

3. Using the lrcfg utility in the LEAF firewall, add four new rules to the /etc/shorewall/rules file, as shown in Figure 7.11. This figure shows four rules that allow ICMP packets of type 8 (echo request) to pass among the local, firewall, and Internet zones (loc, fw, and net, respectively). These four rules should already be in the rules file. The next four allow traceroute (or Windows tracert) to work. Traceroute uses two ICMP types to trace a route: type 8 and type 11. The popular ping command only uses type 8.

4. Once this is done and the rules file is saved, make sure to back up your Shorewall package and reboot.

5. Try the traceroute (or Windows tracert) again.

6. Compare your results to the traceroute (or Windows tracert) done before implementing the support for ICMP type 11. You should see the hop corresponding to your firewall identified properly, rather than timed out. Try the traceroute from behind the firewall as well as from some point on the Internet side of the firewall. Of course, different IP addresses corresponding to the internal and external addresses will show up in the traceroute output.

Project 7.3: Set Up a LEAF Firewall to Allow Secure Shell from Specific Internet IP Addresses

For this project, you will need the firewall that you installed in Projects 7.1 and 7.2. Again, you may need to make sure your campus or ISP network does not block incoming secure shell traffic, which is TCP port 22. For this project, you must load the following packages: SSHD.lrp, sshkey.lrp, libcrypt.lrp, libz.lrp, and libnsl.lrp. You must add these to syslinux.cfg and, if necessary, use leaf.cfg if you run past the 254-character line limit in syslinux.cfg.

You will also have to add the appropriate rule to Shorewall's rule file to allow access from a specific machine. (*Hint:* What zones will be involved if the SSH client is running somewhere on the Internet or campus net, and the SSH daemon is running on your firewall?) If your campus network blocks SSH from the Internet, you may have to use an on-campus machine's IP address for testing purposes.

1. Create a new CD-ROM and/or floppy, depending on your boot method that loads the packages we mentioned, in addition to all the packages you have used so far.

2. Reboot your firewall using the new media.

3. Once the packages are loaded, you must run two commands in the /etc directory:

```
ssh-keygen -t dsa
ssh-keygen -t rsa
```

4. Each of these commands will generate a public/private key pair. They will prompt you for a filename. Simply press Enter to accept the default filename.

5. The commands will prompt you for a passphrase. This is a separate password that is used in addition to a user password when logging into the SSH server. Press Enter (twice, since the command will ask you to enter the passphrase again) to indicate no passphrase.

6. Next, configure the SSH daemon running on your firewall. To do this, type `lrcfg` at the firewall prompt and enter the Packages configuration menu.

7. If SSHD has been successfully loaded, you will see an entry for SSHD. Select this item and, on the next menu, select the SSHD config file.

8. Set PermitRootLogin to yes, and RSAAuthentication and PubkeyAuthentication to no for this exercise.

9. Set PasswordAuthentication to yes. All other configuration should be sufficient.

10. Now you have generated public keys that an SSH client can accept and configured the SSHD daemon. You must use the Backup Packages option on the lrcfg main menu to backup your SSHD package.

11. Reboot the firewall. You should issue the command ps –A at the Linux command prompt to verify the SSH daemon is running.

Now you are ready to try your SSH client. If you don't have one available, there is a free package called PuTTY (**www.chiark.greenend.org.uk/~sgtatham/putty/**). Download this executable and install it on the machine you chose to allow SSH into the firewall.

Case Study

The Coffee Mall is a growing business in rural Drofdor County in the Deep South of the United States. Nearby is DeepFry University, and although the Coffee Mall enjoys repeat business from many of the faculty of DU, it wants to attract more students. The owners have decided to put in a wireless HotSpot so that the students can bring in their laptops and surf the Internet. They have broadband service that provides an Ethernet port into the ISP's network. The Coffee Mall also has some business computers that need to access the Internet. They are worried about the lack of security in wireless networks, having seen on the Internet several recipes to break Wireless Equivalent Privacy (WEP), which is the 802.11 standard for encrypting traffic over wireless networks, and they want their business machines protected from their wireless customers. They also want protection from the threats present in their broadband connection.

You have been retained as a consultant to advise Coffee Mall on matters of security. As you are an expert in the LEAF firewall system, you begin studying the problem with that firewall in mind. Since there needs to be three zones—the local zone where the business computers are protected, the wireless zone, and the Internet zone—you decide a three-interface setup is necessary.

Refer to Figure 7.9. How will you configure rules and policy on the LEAF firewall to satisfy the needs of each zone? Which zone will be assigned to each interface eth0 through eth2? What services will be offered to the business machines? What services will be offered to the wireless customers? Describe in detail the policies and rules that you will apply to each interface by specifying segments of the appropriate Shorewall and other LEAF files. Make sure you discuss the issues of wireless security with your client (Sorensen 2004; Dornan 2002; Berghel 2004).

Part Three

VPNs and Logging

Part Three *VPNs and Logging* covers virtual private networks and instruction for using log files to perform post-analysis of network events. The concepts in this part do depend to some extent on understanding the topics in Part Two, but you may choose to cover certain sections from Part Three even if Part Two isn't covered in the classroom.

- **Chapter 8:** Exploring and Using Virtual Private Networks

- **Chapter 9:** Integrating Firewall and System Logs

Chapter | 8

Exploring and Using Virtual Private Networks

Chapter Objectives

After reading this chapter and completing the exercises, you will be able to do the following:

- Implement virtual private networks (VPNs).
- Configure IPSec VPNs and NAT Traversal.
- Implement Transport Layer Security VPNs.
- Use VPNs to protect patient data in accordance with the Health Information Privacy and Authority Act.
- Understand Point-to-Point Tunneling Protocol VPNs.
- Use VPN and firewall technologies in industrial settings.

Introduction

Up to this point, this book has focused on the configuration of a firewall to keep unwanted traffic out of the internal network. As a byproduct of keeping unwanted traffic out, the firewall prevents employees and other valid users from accessing corporate resources when they are connected through a broadband connection at home or other Internet location. This chapter will turn our attention to virtual private networks (VPNs), which provide remote users with secure access to the internal network.

Companies can connect to the Internet for a relatively inexpensive monthly fee; therefore, the Internet has replaced complex private networks as the preferred means for connecting remote sites and remote users. The Internet is a shared public network, however, so there is no guarantee that someone isn't eavesdropping on the network activity passing between two sites. To securely connect two sites across the Internet or to securely allow an employee that is telecommuting to connect to confidential resources on the internal network, there must be a guarantee that the user is authorized to access the resource and that their network traffic is secure.

With a VPN connection, it is as if the user is passing through a secret door in the firewall and the remote user or site will have access to network resources just as if they were directly connected to the internal network. Thus, we have used the public Internet to create a virtual network between two hosts that is private and secure because only the hosts at each end can understand the traffic.

VPNs use authentication mechanisms and encryption to create a secure connection or tunnel between two sites or hosts on the Internet. During World War II, the U.S. Marines used the Navajo Indian language for radio and telephone communications because it was an unwritten language that was difficult to understand without extensive exposure and training (Molnar 1997). This allowed the transmission of tactics and troop movement over insecure radio waves. Because the Japanese did not know the language, it was impossible for them to decode the messages. In much the same way, VPNs use complex encryption algorithms to encrypt network traffic between two hosts. Even if someone can listen to the communication, they will be unable to decipher the message.

This chapter will cover Internet Protocol Security (IPSec), Point-to-Point Tunneling Protocol (PPTP) and Secure Socket Layer (SSL) also known as Transport Layer Security (TLS) based VPNs. Except for PPTP, these VPNs provide the highest level of security. For that reason we offer only projects for IPSec and TLS VPNs. These three VPNs are the most commonly used. After looking at these three VPNs, you will learn about troubleshooting VPN connections. Finally, this chapter will provide an example of how the IPSec VPN can be used in conjunction with LEAF to provide a highly scalable firewall and VPN environment.

The Growth and Popularity of VPNs

In Chapter 1, we discussed how connecting an internal network to the Internet is practically unavoidable for modern organizations, despite the risk posed by hackers and other dangerous elements. Likewise, enabling secure network access to remote users has become just as vital in business, industry, and academics. For instance, an employment specialist for a national temporary staffing agency in Des Moines may need to access a database of resumes stored on the network at the company headquarters in Chicago. An auto assembly plant manager in Nashville may need to access a part supplier's ordering system in another city. Or, a college student in a campus apartment may need to access her university's online registration program to enroll in classes.

Before the advent of the Internet, organizations provided access to remote users by setting up private wide area networks (WAN). A WAN functions similarly to an organization's local area network (LAN), only it is spread out over a larger geographical area. A WAN normally connects two or more LANs at different locations through an existing telecommunication infrastructure, such as digital lines leased through the telephone system. With leased lines, a company pays for exclusive use of a permanent telephone circuit between two locations. This includes time that the leased line is not in use, for example during night hours.

However, there are some drawbacks to leased line connections:

■ Leased lines can be expensive. The fixed monthly rate is primarily determined by the distance between connections and the speed of transferring data (companies can choose from a range of data transfer speeds; the faster the transfer, the more expensive it is.)

■ There is no secure access to or from the Internet, unless additional link encryption hardware or software is provided. This is so because you are leasing a circuit at a certain speed which is combined with many other circuits traversing the same communication links between two cities. For example, if company A has offices in the same two cities as company B, it is likely that the digital circuits are combined and ride the same telecommunications facilities between those cities. As a consequence, the communication is less secure. Link encryption hardware is an additional expense, added to the leased lines.

Another option for connecting remote users to an internal network is a packet-switched data network (PSDN). There are two main PSDN technologies:

■ Frame Relay (FR)

■ Asynchronous Transfer Mode (ATM)

Any PSDN can provide security through hardware link encryption devices or via encryption protocols such as the ones we discuss here.

Frame Relay (FR) is a PSDN technology that originated in 1984 by the Consultative Committee for International Telephony and Telegraphy (CCITT), now known as the International Telecommunications Union (ITU). According to Cisco System's Frame Relay Tutorial, (Cisco 2005) FR was standardized in the mid-1980s but did not become popular until a group of companies—Cisco, Digital Equipment Corp., Northern Telecom, and Stratacom—formed a consortium in 1990. This consortium developed a new FR standard that was compatible with the original one, but added many needed features. After that standard was released, FR became more

TABLE 8.1 Plesio-synchronous digital hierarchy.

Service Identifier	PDH Nomenclature	Kbps
FR (Frame Relay)	DS0, with signaling	56
FR	DS0, clear channel	64
FR	DS1/12 (fractional T1)	128
FR	DS1/6	256
FR	DS1/4	384
FR	DS1/3	512
FR	DS1	1544
HSFR (High Speed Frame Relay)	DS3/11	4000
HSFR	DS2	6312
HSFR	DS3/2	22000
HSFR	DS3	44736

popular. FR can operate at speeds including fractional T-1 through T-3 leased lines. T-1 and T-3 technologies are part of the Plesio-synchronous Digital Hierarchy (PDH). Table 8.1 shows the data rates associated with T-1 technology for North America. Europe and Japan have their own PDH with different bit rates. (See **www.speedguide.net/read_articles.php?id=115& print=friendly** for a complete set of rates for PDH and SDH.)

Another PSDN technology is Asynchronous Transfer Mode (ATM). ATM can operate at speeds greater than FR, using the synchronous digital hierarchy (SDH) and some of the nomenclature used for them. The SDH is defined by GR-253-CORE (Telcordia 2000) for North America. There is a separate standard called Synchronous Optical Network (SONET) defined by ANSI. As with the PDH, there is a separate but completely compatible set of standards from the ITU as follows:

- G.707 Network Node Interface for the Synchronous Digital Hierarchy

- G.781 Structure of Recommendations on Equipment for the Synchronous Digital Hierarchy

- G.782 Types and Characteristics of Synchronous Digital Hierarchy (SDH) Equipment

- G.783 Characteristics of Synchronous Digital Hierarchy (SDH) Equipment Functional Blocks

- G.803 Architecture of Transport Networks Based on the Synchronous Digital Hierarchy

TABLE 8.2 Synchronous digital hierarchy.

Optical Carrier	Synchronous Transport Module	Synchronous Transport Signal	Approximate Speed, Megabits/second
OC3-c	STM-1	STS-3	155
OC9-c	STM-3	STS-9	466
OC12-c	STM-4	STS-12	622
OC18-c	STM-6	STS-18	900
OC24-c	STM-8	STS-24	1244
OC48-c	STM-16	STS-48	2500
OC96-c	STM-32	STS-96	5000
OC192-c	STM-64	STS-192	10000
OC256-c	(N/A)	STS-256	13000
OC768-c	STM-256	STS-768	40000

Table 8.2 shows the SDH link types and speeds. There are multiple designations for each of the SDH bit rates, including Optical Carrier (OC), Synchronous Transport Module (STM), and Synchronous Transport Signal (STS). STM is called SDH by some authors.

Both FR and ATM have two kinds of virtual circuits: Switched Virtual Circuits (SVCs) and Permanent Virtual Circuits (PVCs). The difference is that SVCs, as the name implies, are circuits that are set-up on demand, closely resembling a common telephone call. Therefore, there is a set-up delay analogous to the delay when you make a long distance phone call. If there is only occasional use of the circuit, SVCs are acceptable, and they are less expensive than PVCs. PVCs are permanent, and stay up for the life of the FR network.

PSDNs have some drawbacks, however:

■ The PSDNs are not interconnected. For example, Verizon's FR network is not connected to AT&T's FR network. Similarly, Sprint's ATM PSDN is not interconnected with MCI's ATM PSDN. Therefore, only if you share an FR or ATM provider with another company can you interconnect with that company.

■ The company that uses a FR service must purchase a full period leased-line from each corporate location to the FR service provider's Point of Presence (POP). While less expensive than an owned network where the leased line must span the entire distance between corporate locations, there is a cost associated with these leased line segments.

- FR users must pay a certain price for the bit-rate of the connection, called the port charge. This is often the largest charge in the entire FR price structure.

- You must have the FR provider set up a PVC or SVC between some or all company locations and all the others, implementing at minimum tree-like topology or completing a "full mesh" topology where each location connects to every other location. Each PVC or SVC has an associated charge.

As a consequence of the cost and interconnection considerations of owned networks and PSDNs, the solution to providing secure access to remote sites and traveling personnel with the lowest "cost per bit transmitted" is using a VPN.

Implementing a VPN on a Firewall

Once you have a firewall in place that protects your internal systems, the next item to consider should be to provide secure access from remote locations. With the rise of the Internet, the most popular and least expensive option for providing remote access to an internal network is the *Virtual Private Network (VPN)*.

A VPN is two or more software programs communicating with a security gateway. All VPNs establish a trust between each of the endpoints, which are computers running the appropriate VPN software. VPNs can be generally divided into three categories:

- host-to-host, where a secure connection is between two specific host computers

- subnet-to-subnet, which allows all computers on one subnet to access those on another

- host-to-subnet, in which a single, sometimes mobile host accesses a remote subnet

Each of the categories above implements a secure connection called a tunnel. These tunnels can be chained together with the appropriate routing configurations, if desired. Along another general dimension, they can be classified as:

- point-to-point, in which each end is an equal peer

- client/server, where generally the server is the main authentication gateway

With these concepts in mind we can build different styles of VPNs. A VPN can be defined by the features it implements as follows.

- A secure link between two hosts or two IP subnets that provides some combination of:
  - Authentication
  - Integrity
  - Confidentiality
  - Non-repudiation

- The above properties can be negotiated from a set of:
  - available cipher algorithms, e.g., 3DES or AEP for the confidentiality property of security
  - available set of keyed hash codes such as MD5 or SHA1 for integrity
  - a choice of pre-shared secret key or certificates for the authentication and non-repudiation properties

A VPN can be thought of as a large, secure WAN that connects computers with the appropriate access privileges. A VPN works by first authenticating the endpoints followed by encryption of the contents of the data transferred. This feature protects the data from being revealed to unwanted observers.

We must protect the data from being modified. Data integrity is provided by a hash code. Optionally, non-repudiation can be provided by certificates as we describe in some of the projects. This feature structure is consistent for the VPNs that we describe in the book.

There are several varieties of VPNs. This book discusses IP Security (IPSec), Point-to-Point Tunneling Protocol (PPTP), and Secure Socket Layer (SSL), also called Transport Layer Security (TLS) VPNs. We cover these VPNs because they are the most widely used and because IPSec and TLS VPNs are the most secure. Specifically, we discuss implementation of IPSec and TLS VPNs, while giving an overview of the technology of PPTP VPNs. We then contrast IPSec and TLS with the less secure PPTP alternative. As you will learn, other VPNs exist besides these three, but either they lack security or apply to more general protocol environments that are somewhat rare today.

Our approach to IPSec and TLS VPNs is to provide sufficient detail for the reader to:

- Implement the available authentication methods

- Choose options for integrity, i.e. hash codes

- Choose alternative ciphers for confidentiality

- Implement optional non-repudiation techniques via Certificates

FYI: Other Types of VPNs

Several other types of VPNs exist, such as IP-in-IP tunneling, defined by RFC 2003. IP-in-IP is frequently used as an alternative to NAT. IP-in-IP used alone does not provide any encryption or authentication.

Another VPN protocol is Layer 2 Tunneling Protocol (L2TP). The advantage of L2TP over IPSec or TLS VPNs is that L2TP is independent of the network protocol. IPSec and TLS require IP as the network layer. L2TP is intended to support other network layers like IPX, since L2TP works with many data link protocols.

See Khanvilkar and Khokhar 2004 for an extensive list of these VPNs. In addition, there are specialized VPNs based on Multi-Protocol Label Switching (MPLS) and Border Gateway Protocol (BGP) (Pepelnjak and Guichard 2000). MPLS VPNs are not actually secured, i.e., there is no encryption, as is the case with IP-in-IP.

IP Security (IPSec) VPNs

IPSec Protocol Overview

IPSec is a technology developed by the IETF and defined by several RFCs and other documents. Internet Protocol Security (IPSec) is the accepted standard for Internet based VPNs.

- RFC 2401 Architecture of the IPSec system

- RFC 2402 Authentication Header protocol (AH)

- RFC 2406 Encapsulation Security Payload protocol (ESP)

- RFC 2408 (Maughan et. al. 1998) Internet Security Association and Key Management Protocol (ISAKMP)

- RFC 2409 (Harkins & Carrel 1998) Internet key exchange (IKE)

- RFC 2764 (a general framework document)

- RFC 2631 Diffie-Hellman Key Agreement Method

- SKEME (Krawczyk 1996)

We will focus mainly on the use of ESP for confidentiality and integrity. ESP provides a certain amount of authentication that does not involve authenticating each packet and is quite adequate without AH for most applications (see Figure 8.1).

TABLE 8.3 Features and modes of IPSec.

Feature\ Mode	Authentication Header (AH)	Encapsulation Security Payload (ESP)	ESP + AH
Access Control	Yes	Yes	Yes
Authentication	Yes		Yes
Message Integrity	Yes		Yes
Replay Protection	Yes	Yes	Yes
Confidentiality		Yes	Yes

The IPSec protocol has several modes (not to be confused with ISAKMP modes discussed below), provided by the AH and ESP protocols. The two protocols may be used in any combination. Table 8.3 shows the features achieved by different modes of IPSec. Possible applications include ESP alone, AH alone, or ESP and AH together.

Each protocol AH, ESP, or the combination of both may be used in either tunnel mode or transport mode. Tunnel mode places a secure channel between two IP subnets, allowing all users on each subnet to access services and hosts on the other. The transport mode is a method of providing a secure channel end-to-end between two hosts. In this case, authentication or confidentiality is protecting the entire path.

Tunnel mode is the condition when either or both endpoints of the secure channel are not the source and/or destination of the intended transmission. Tunnel mode is most logical between two firewalls, or between a mobile host and a firewall (the so-called *road warrior* configuration). Once again, depending on whether AH, ESP, or both are employed, the secure channel provides authentication, confidentiality, or both. In this book's hands-on projects, we do not cover cases where AH and ESP are used together, nor cases where AH is used by itself. This is because:

- NAT traversal only supports ESP. It is very common for machines using IPSec to be located behind NAT devices. (You will learn more about NAT traversal later in this chapter.)

- ESP has its own form of authentication.

- AH only authenticates the IP header, and provides no confidentiality so it does not add substantial value when compared to ESP.

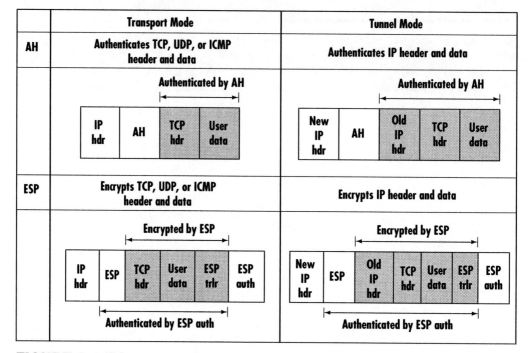

FIGURE 8.1 IPSec protocol components.

Differences arise between tunnel and transport mode when the AH or the ESP protocol are used. The position of the AH and/or ESP headers and what is protected differ in each mode.

Figure 8.1 illustrates the authentication and encryption issues in each mode and for each combination of protocols, including the portions of the original packet that are encrypted (shown as shaded areas). The IP trailers are suppressed for brevity.

IPSec Protocol Details

IP Security (IPSec) is a suite of protocols that accomplishes several different security objectives for the IP protocol. Generally, a secure channel (e.g., a stream of IP packets between a source IP address and a destination IP address) has several goals—authentication, confidentiality, integrity, and non-repudiation. IPSec is a complex protocol. One of the most complex elements is its key management system. We provide a detailed overview for the reader who wants to become more familiar with IPSec, but this section can be skipped on a first reading.

As you learned in Chapter 1, authentication is the process of determining who or what originated a communication. Confidentiality makes the contents private, usually through encryption. Hash functions make it very unlikely that the contents can be altered, ensuring integrity.

Non-repudiation is the property that establishes whether the sender was authenticated as having originated the communication, preventing the sender from claiming that a different individual or entity originated the content. Some authors call this property "repudiability."

Critical parts of IPSec include the ***Internet Key Exchange (IKE)*** defined by RFC 2409 and the ***ISA Key Management Protocol (ISAKMP),*** defined by RFC 2408. ISAKMP specifies the use of UDP port 500, but does not specify the key exchange protocol. While ISAKMP mandates no specific key exchange, it is common to use IKE in combination with the Oakley key determination method. This is where IKE becomes important. IKE goes through a series of negotiations using UDP port 500 between each IPSec endpoint to establish which ciphers (encryption algorithms) and keys will be used. IKE uses a set of four policies to determine four necessary elements:

- Encryption Algorithm Policy (what cipher algorithms are acceptable to this endpoint)

- Hash codes to use for integrity

- Diffie-Hellman groups

- Authentication method (see description of ISAKMP phase 1)

Diffie-Hellman is a key agreement method defined by RFC 2631. Diffie-Hellman was first established in 1976 (Diffie & Hellman 1976). Continuing our theme to point out Man In The Middle (MITM) attack scenarios, this early version had a vulnerability to MITM, that was fixed by Station-to-Station (STS) version of Diffie-Hellman (Diffie et al. 1992). The ***Oakley key determination method*** extends STS by adding Denial of Service (DoS) protection, and identity protection, i.e. the identities of the IPSec end-points are not disclosed. The Oakley key determination method also uses a part of the SKEME key exchange method, but it is not necessary to elaborate on it. Table 8.4 provides a list of the most common Diffie-Hellman groups and their properties. We recommend using Group 1 as 1024 key bits. For situations of extreme "paranoia," Group 2048 can be used.

There are other ways to configure Diffie-Hellman parameters than using Diffie-Hellman "well-known" groups. Refer to Project 8.5, where openssl is used to manually generate the parameters.

TABLE 8.4 Diffie-Hellman groups and their properties.

Group number	Key bits	Properties
Group 2048	2048	Strong Security
Group 2	1024	Medium Security
Group 1	768	Low Security

The goal of ISAKMP, via the IKE protocol, is to set up a *security association (SA)*. An SA is a relationship between two IPSec entities that establishes trust between two hosts. A pair of IPSec entities is a pair of hosts or firewalls that implement IPSec via either or both of the AH or ESP protocols. There may be multiple SAs that are active at any time between two IPSEC entities.

Figure 8.2-a illustrates the hierarchical relationship between IKE, ISAKMP, the Oakley key determination method, and SKEME by the solid arrows. However, IKE is the most specific document and unifies aspects of the Oakley and SKEME protocols while maintaining compatibility with the ISAKMP framework. The dashed arrows indicate IKE tailoring the Oakley and SKEME methods, while maintaining compatibility with the framework set down by ISAKMP. Figure 8.2-b illustrates the two-step process by which IKE generates an SA between two IPSec entities, followed the the IPSec protocol suite (AH, ESP or both) follow the "recipe" specified by the SA for securing the channel.

The IKE protocol is separate from AH and ESP, and accomplishes the initial authentication phase for the entire IPSec connection, as well as the exchange of keys to be used between the entities. ISAKMP provides for two phases of negotiation. RFC 2409 (IKE) describes a method for using the Oakley key determination protocol as defined in RFC 2412 (Orman 1998) in conjunction with *Perfect Forward Secrecy (PFS).*

FIGURE 8.2 Illustration of IKE

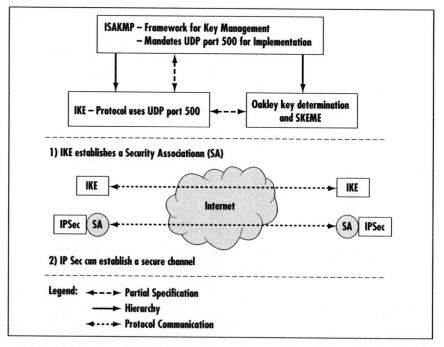

During a key establishment process implemented by IKE, several symmetric keys are exchanged. Recall that symmetric key methods are faster than public key methods for encryption and decryption of data, especially in the case of large file transfers. The types of symmetric keys involved are master keys and session keys. PFS has two methods, Master PFS and Session PFS. Generally, PFS ensures the compromise of a symmetric session key or long-term master key after a given session completes, but it does not cause the compromise of any earlier session. The principle involved is never to use a past session key to generate the key for a new session. If neither Master nor Session PFS is specified, then the master key is negotiated once, and all future session keys are generated from the master key. In most situations, we recommend using both Master and Session PFS. What this implies is that each new IPSec session will be begun first by re-authentication to establish a master key. Then, session keys will be determined and periodically renegotiated. The following scenario illustrates the effectiveness of this technique.

An attacker could collect a packet trace of all the encrypted traffic between two IPSec entities. The attacker could then apply a brute-force attack that tries to enumerate all possible keys during a session with the hope that, at some point long after the session is over, the data could be decrypted. PFS assures that, should such an attack succeed for any past session that it cannot succeed in decrypting future sessions. Therefore, the attacker must apply multiple brute-force attacks for each new session when a new session key is established, making it virtually impossible to achieve a complete breach of security. The PFS property allows periodic key re-negotiation to make it virtually impossible for an attacker to decrypt more than a small handful of sessions.

Oakley defines three modes that map to each of ISAKMP's phases, as follows:

- quick mode – phase 2 only
- main mode – phase 1 only
- aggressive mode – phase 1 only

There are many pros and cons of the above Oakley modes, too numerous to explore here. One example is that aggressive mode does not provide identity protection (Krawczyk 2003). That leaves aggressive mode vulnerable to the Man-in-the-Middle (MITM) attack. For that reason, it is common to provide main mode in phase 1 and quick mode in phase 2. However, if both Master and Session PFS are specified, then the re-authentication of new master key is done in main mode.

ISAKMP through IKE provides a mechanism for exchange of keys, including several options:

- Preshared Secret Key (PSK)

- Public/Private Key Infrastructure (PKI)

- Certificates for third-party verification of the identity of IPSec entities

Preshared Secret Key (PSK) is essentially a simple password method. Public/Private key systems and certificates are more detailed and are discussed below. A preshared key is a constant string (until someone changes it) that accomplishes authentication. Although PSK is used, there are other keys that must be negotiated during setup of the SA to provide confidentiality and integrity. When someone is building a security policy in Windows operating systems, it is common for them to use 3DES (triple DES) for authentication purposes. To avoid ***replay attacks,*** the 3DES keys are periodically renegotiated. It is also common to use ***Message Digest 5 (MD5)*** (Rivest 1992; Madson and Glenn 1998) keyed hash codes to verify the integrity of messages, and these keys must also be renegotiated. This process is called ***rekeying.*** A hash code like MD5 or SHA1 is applied to any original document or message and has the following properties:

- Fixed-length function of the original document

- Uniqueness for each original document

The importance of these features for implementing the integrity property of security is two-fold.

- Encryption by itself cannot ensure the integrity of the content since the encryption keys may have been compromised.

- Having a fixed-length item, regardless of the length of the original document but unique for that document, allows a separate item to be appended to the encrypted document during transmission. This is called the digest.

Some properties of the MD5 and SHA1 hash codes (Preneel et al. 1998) are presented in Table 8.5.

Using the PKI as certificates makes more sense from a security standpoint. In the case of IPSec in LEAF firewalls, there are two directories of relevance:

Caution

PSK and MITM Attacks

If your PSK is compromised, an attack such as the MITM can be successful. Windows security policies allow any length of PSK, with no requirement for elements such as special characters. It may be advisable to use an automatic generation of a long PSK to avoid dictionary attacks from the MITM. For a good discussion of the MITM attack, see Kaufman et. al. 2002, 167.

TABLE 8.5 Hash codes and their properties.

ESP + AH	Hash code bits	Speed (333Mhz PentiumII)
SHA-1	160	1740 Kbytes/sec
MD5	128	750 Kbytes/sec

- `/etc/ipsec.d/cacerts` for certificates

- `/etc/ipsec.d/private` for private key files

Certificates are objects that contain the public keys and other relevant information about other people or other objects such as computers. Certificates are documents that are signed by the certificate authority's private key. For example, we present a scenario in which two LEAF firewalls are using an IPSec tunnel to link two subnets behind the firewalls. One firewall is called "home" and the other is called "office." To establish trust between the two firewalls, we need a home-certificate file and a office-certificate file. Each of these certificates is signed by the certificate authority. How will each firewall verify (authenticate) the opposite firewall? As you learned earlier, the PKI offers the following unique properties:

- If a document is encrypted with a public key, only the private key can decrypt it.

- If a document is encrypted with a private key, only the pubic key can decrypt it.

Since certificates are documents that are encrypted with the certificate authorities private key, we need the certificate authorities public key to decrypt the certificate. Since public keys are freely distributed, each firewall must have a copy of the public key of the certificate authority.

Once the home and office certificates are decrypted, each firewall has the opposite end's public key. This can then be used to decrypt digital signatures and other data.

Authentication Header (AH)

AH is a protocol that authenticates each IP packet. AH forms a digital signature by using one of two methods. One is the use of Message Authentication Codes (MACs) based on symmetric encryption. The second is a two-step process that first involves hashing, which is a one-way encryption technique, and then encrypting portions of the IP header. We will use the second method for examples in what follows. (For a description of the digital signature generation process, see Atreya 2005.)

Notice in Figure 8.1 that the AH in either transport or tunnel mode has no trailer. Note also that the payload data itself is not encrypted, even though the digital signature identifies who it came from. Therefore, when AH is used alone, it does not provide confidentiality.

The AH is inserted between the original IP header and the IP payload. It authenticates both ends of the secure channel by hashing selected fields of the original IP header. The resulting hash value is of fixed length. The AH encrypts the hash value to create a digital signature, which is part of the

Version	IHL	TOS	Length
Identification		Flags	Fragment Offset
TTL	Protocol (type)	Header Checksum	
Source IP Address			
Destination IP Address			

FIGURE 8.3 The mutable fields of IP headers.

AH itself. (The actual fields of the IP header are not modified as a result of hashing.) The fields that are protected by the AH are known in security jargon as "immutable or predictably mutable" fields (Kaufman et al. 2002). Figure 8.3 illustrates the fields that are hashed as shaded.

The AH protocol differs in its behavior between the transport and tunnel modes. Although the AH covers the same fields of the original IP header in either transport or tunnel modes, when used in tunnel mode, the AH hashes (and thereby authenticates) the new IP header as well. This effectively prevents IP spoofing by an MITM attack that captures the original tunnel-mode packets and attempts to modify the source or destination IP addresses.

Note that in tunnel mode, the AH actually precedes the original IP header and a second encapsulation is performed, embedding the AH and the original IP packet (now authenticated) inside a completely new IP packet. The AH is detailed in Figure 8.4.

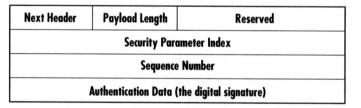

Next Header	Payload Length	Reserved
Security Parameter Index		
Sequence Number		
Authentication Data (the digital signature)		

FIGURE 8.4 The IPSec authentication header.

Encapsulation Security Payload (ESP)

ESP is a protocol that provides confidentiality by encrypting the IP packet payload. Since AH is independent of ESP, ESP has been extended to provide some minimal authentication features as well. ESP, as its name implies, actually encapsulates the original IP packet inside an ESP header and ESP trailer. Note that in tunnel mode, the ESP header actually precedes the original IP header and a second encapsulation is performed, embedding the ESP header, the original IP packet (now encrypted), the ESP trailer, and the ESP authentication field inside a completely new IP packet.

IPSec and Network Address Translation (NAT)

The IETF developed NAT, a capability defined by RFC 1631, to avert a shortage of IP addresses. Due to the explosive growth of the Internet, people feared that the supply of public, routable IP addresses would be rapidly exhausted. NAT was created to allow many organizations to use so-called "nonroutable" private IP addresses (the ranges 10.0.0.0/8, 172.[16-31].0.0/12, and 192.168.[1 . . . 254].0/24) in the organization's internal network. The NAT scheme allows a router or firewall placed between the organization's internal network and the Internet to translate the private IP addresses to a small number of public, routable IP addresses.

An incompatibility can arise when an IPSec host computer or IPSec gateway adds the AH and/or ESP header, and the resulting traffic passes through a device implementing NAT. The NAT process will try to replace the source IP address (usually a private address) with a public one. This will make the authentication at the destination fail, since the digital signatures—based on hash codes that include the IP header—will not match. If AH and/or ESP are used in either tunnel or transport mode, and the resulting traffic passes through a NAT device, authentication will fail.

You can use several methods to resolve this issue. The first option, which we highlight in this book, involves implementing the NAT and IPSec functions on the same device—in this case, a firewall. When this is done, the NAT process, which modifies the IP header, can precede the IPSec function, and you will avert the incompatibility. However, by doing this, we are inherently limiting the IPSec applications to tunnel mode, since normally a firewall is not the actual source or destination of the traffic.

The second option is to simply interchange the order of the IPSec and NAT devices, if they must be done on separate devices. Always perform NAT first, in the direction of traffic flow, and place the IPSec device further upstream.

In either of these two options, IPSec is working on public IP addresses, and they remain public throughout the secure channel. Once again, this usually allows only tunnel mode to be used.

A third option is under development in the IETF. It is called NAT traversal (NAT-T). The RFCs to perform this are not complete as of this writing, although many router and firewall vendors and some open-source packages support early versions of NAT-T. For example, Microsoft Windows Server 2003 supports NAT-T (CableGuy1), as does Windows XP, service pack 2 or beyond. In such a case, it may be possible to use transport mode and provide end-to-end security.

A scenario including road warriors and NAT-T is important, as shown in Figure 8.5. It is important to realize that each host, whether mobile or on an internal network, should have the appropriate NAT-T patch. For Windows XP and 2000 Professional, a patch "L2TP/IPSec NAT-T update for Windows XP and Windows 2000" is available (Microsoft 2004). NAT-T

8

uses UDP port 4500 and encapsulates the entire IPSec packet, whether AH, ESP, or both, in a UDP packet.

FYI: NAT Traversal

A firewall or router that implements IPSec can also implement a NAT-T facility. This facility is a solution for any NAT process downstream from the firewall or router. If your firewall or router implements NAT, then you must have a NAT-T configured on the host computer originating the IPSec transmission.

Figure 8.5 illustrates the mechanism of NAT-T in IPSec. The simple solution to the problem of NAT-T is to encapsulate the entire IPSec packet inside a UDP packet. Because the UDP packet is not encrypted, it can be modified by a NAT device, which will at a minimum change the IP address. With port address translation—often the solution in a SOHO environment—a single public IP address leads to the Internet. In that case, the source port in UDP packet will also be changed.

Applications of IPSec

The typical applications of IPSec VPNs are:

- road warrior configuration
- subnet-to-subnet, or site-to-site configuration

FIGURE 8.5 Illustrating NAT-T.

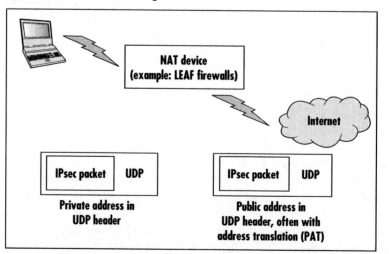

Many different VPN clients can use IPSec. There are too many to list here, but a number of configuration how-tos are available on the FreeS/WAN Web site, **www.freeswan.org**. This text covers two particular cases:

- road warrior using Windows 2000 Pro or Windows XP

- subnet-to-subnet using FreeS/WAN at both endpoints

In the case of Windows 2000 operating systems, an excellent setup guide for implementing a security policy is via a link on the FreeS/WAN site to **jixen.tripod.com/win2k-screen.html**. The Windows XP security policy setup is virtually identical to Windows 2000.

The LEAF firewall used in this book requires some additional configuration to host an IPSec VPN. As you have learned, you must load and configure two packages to make IPSec work: shorewall (shorwall.lrp) and FreeS/Wan (IPSec.lrp). The history of these two packages is rich; for more information, visit **www.shorewall.net** and **www.freeswan.org**, respectively.

Point-to-Point Tunneling Protocol (PPTP) VPNs

Point-to-Point Tunneling Protocol (PPTP) is defined by RFC 2637. PPTP VPNs are quite popular and are supported by many ISPs. These VPNs are less secure than IPSec or SSL VPNs, however. The basic operation of a PPTP VPN involves an unsecured control channel (using TCP port 1723) to set up the connection, followed by encrypted data transmission. Figure 8.6 illustrates this operation.

PPTP defines a client-server architecture that separates the authentication and connection setup functions, which in other VPNs are unified in a single technology (e.g., IPSec implements AH and ISP in the same protocol). PPTP defines three roles: the ***PPTP Access Concentrator (PAC),*** the ***Network Access Server (NAS,*** sometimes called RAS), and the ***PPTP Network Server (PNS).*** There are also, of course, a host PC or workstation and the desired internal corporate server. The purpose of the PAC is to collect all the incoming connections from mobile hosts, such as laptops. These are then concentrated through the GRE channel. Prior to allowing access to a remote host, the PAC contacts the PNS to establish security through the insecure TCP channel. Then, the NAS to PAC channel is secured, and the data transmitted over the Internet is encrypted.

Generic routing encapsulation (GRE) is used to provide the secure transmission of data between the remote PC and the corporate intranet. GRE is defined by IETF RFCs 1701, 1702, 2784, and 2890, and is

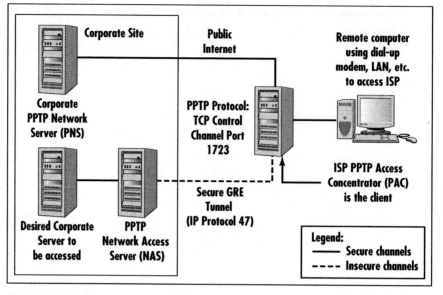

FIGURE 8.6 Illustrating PPTP VPNs.

identified by the IP protocol (or type) field value 47. The vendor support
for PPTP is quite broad, including Linux, Microsoft, Cisco, and others.

Part of the PPTP scheme is the use of *Point-to-Point Protocol (PPP),*
defined by RFC 1661. Several extensions to PPP allow additional protocols to nest inside a PPP frame. These include PPP Encryption Control
Protocol (ECP, defined by RFC 1968), PPP DES Encryption Protocol
(DESE-bis, defined by RFC 2419), and PPP Triple-DES Encryption Protocol (3DESE, defined by RFC 2420). The suffix "bis" is Latin for twice,
meaning a second version of the DESE protocol. A protocol can be given
minor modifications without creating a new version this way. The suffix
"ter" means third version.

The sole advantage of PPTP is that it is independent of the TCP/IP
protocol suite. PPTP can be used with Novell's IPX or even Microsoft's
NETBIOS protocols. However, since the vast majority of networks today
are based on TCP/IP, we focus only on IPSec and SSL for our exercises,
projects, and examples.

Khanvilkar and Khokhar (2004) compare the three VPNs that we describe in this chapter, as well as several others. They point out a drawback
of PPTP: the use of the proprietary *Microsoft Point-to-Point Encryption
(MPPE)* Protocol. In addition, there is the proprietary *Microsoft Point-to-
Point Compression (MPPC)* capability. Khanvilkar and Khokhar also point
out that compression significantly enhances the performance of VPNs,
since any VPN adds substantial amounts of overhead.

Secure Sockets Layer (SSL) and Transport Layer Security (TLS) VPNs

Secure Socket Layer (SSL VPNs), also called *Transport Layer Security (TLS)* VPNs, have been present since their definition and development by Netscape Corporation (Hickman 1995; Freier et. al. 1996). The IETF has retitled SSL as TLS (Dierks and Allen 1999). For all intents and purposes, SSL version 3 and TLS version 1 are identical. We will refer to this technology as TLS.

The most common use of TLS is in the HTTPS protocol (Rescorla 2000), (Khare and Lawrence 2000), which combines Web browsing protocol HTTP with TLS. This is the facility that is widely used when customers make purchases over the Internet or do online banking.

As with any technology, there are some minor risks. Levi (2003) points to an online banking session as an example. Browsers use TLS technology to show the famous "lock" icon as a signal that the URL in the browser matches that of a certificate from the bank's Web server. The certificate is verified with a trusted certificate authority (CA), but Levi points out that this could be subverted by IP address spoofing. The attacker would have to successfully mimic the root CA by verifying the certificate, a rather unlikely scenario. Newer browser technology can notify the user whether to accept a certificate and, with additional checks, whether a certificate has changed. Since the attacker would have to intercept the private key of the root CA, this is unlikely.

TLS is also available for use as a VPN technology. Occasionally, a company finds an improvement in cost and/or security by transitioning to a TLS VPN (Higgins 2004; Conry-Murray 2003). The major advantage for commercial versions of TLS VPNs, reported by Higgins and Conry-Murray, is the lack of a need for client software to manage and configure, whereas IPSec requires a security policy to be configured on each participating computer.

The additional effort required of IPSec may be its best strength, but it requires technical personnel to spend effort pursuing IPSec configurations that can apply to every computer that needs secure access. There are many ways to automate this process, but the total cost of ownership (TCO) will generally rise using IPSec VPNs.

In addition, any VPN will be dependent on the trustworthiness of computers connecting through secure tunnels. A secure tunnel has no defense against viruses, for example. Only active virus software can prevent these agents from reaching across secure tunnels into trusted networks.

The main advantage of TLS VPNs could also be its main weakness, as noted by Conry-Murray. The employees of a small company, for instance, can access their internal networks quite easily from anyplace where Internet access is provided. However, an Internet kiosk may host viruses—and

8

therein lies the problem. A public machine, at a location such as a cyber-café, may host unknown security threats. These threats, once the VPN connection is formed, can propagate inside the corporate perimeter. One solution to this dilemma is for businesses to enforce policies requiring employees to use their own computers or laptops with company-mandated virus software installed.

The Health Insurance Portability and Accountability Act of 1996 (HIPAA) has made many medical professionals rethink how patient records are managed. Our examples of TLS VPNs focus on the needs of the medical community to safeguard patient information. Several resources are available to allow security professionals to understand the demands of HIPAA, including **www.hipaa.org/** and the Web site of the U.S. Health and Human Services department at **aspe.hhs.gov/admnsimp/index.shtml**.

As stated in the federal register (FR Doc 03-3877, 2003, page 8335):

"The proposed standard consisted of four categories of requirements that a covered entity would have to address in order to safeguard the integrity, confidentiality, and availability of its electronic health information pertaining to individuals: administrative procedures, physical safeguards, technical security services, and technical mechanisms."

Two key terms mentioned in this quote—integrity and confidentiality—are the usual ones for electronic security, but they include separate issues:

- availability—the capability for authorized individuals to access the patient data

- authorized users—essentially authentication

Availability in this context is not necessarily the mathematical availability concept (see the *FYI* at the end of this chapter), but under some interpretations of HIPAA, it could be. Authentication, a key part of electronic security, is dealt with as follows (FR Doc 03-3877 2003, page 8356):

"... many different mechanisms may be used to authenticate entities, and this final rule now reflects this fact by not incorporating a list of implementation specifications, in order to allow covered entities to use whatever is reasonable and appropriate. 'Digital signatures' and 'soft tokens' may be used, as well as many other mechanisms, to implement this standard.

The proposed mandatory implementation feature, 'Unique user identification,' has been moved from this standard and is now a required implementation specification under 'Access control' ..."

With this overview of the requirements of HIPAA in the context of security, we are ready to evaluate TLS technology as a possible solution for satisfying HIPAA. Since TLS allows the use of digital signatures and certificates, this should be the best method of authentication. Figure 8.7 illustrates the TLS process during connection setup. As with most client-server methods, the client is the active member of the pair and opens the connection with a "client hello" message. The server responds with its own hello, the server's certificate, and optionally a request for the client's certificate.

FYI: Developing Certificates

The purpose of certificates is to verify the correct public key of the "applicant," a security term for a person seeking authentication. Certificates rely on a **certificate authority (CA)** to be a guarantor of the certificate's authenticity. This prevents imposters from assuming another person's identity.

CAs are public companies unregulated by any authority. They are based on a hierarchical organization that starts with a **root CA.** Other CAs may exist below the root CA. However, it is possible for you to act as your own private CA, in which case, a single root CA is sufficient.

In Chapter 7, Project 3, you were introduced to secure shell (SSH). (Once a VPN is successfully implemented, SSH access is no longer necessary, but is helpful for debugging purposes.) In that project, you recall, you were instructed to generate two different kinds of keys:

- RSA Keys
- DSA Keys

The algorithm invented by **Ron Rivest, Adi Shamir, and Len Adleman (RSA)** at MIT in 1977 is the basis for the **Public Key Infrastructure (PKI).** This scheme includes a public key, known to anyone, and a private key held in secret by a single individual.

The **Digital Signature Algorithm (DSA)** key generation is a separate method that generates a Digital Certificate. If you implemented Project 3 in Chapter 7 successfully, then when you logged in to the firewall the first time from an SSH client, you were presented with a dialog box asking whether to accept the SSH server's certificate from the firewall.

This process builds separate RSA and DSA key sets, each of which is a public/private key pair. The public key component of either of these key pairs could be used to build a certificate.

8

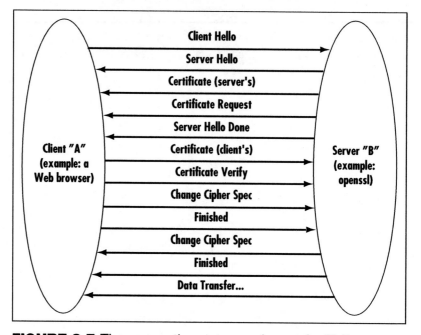

FIGURE 8.7 The connection setup exchange for TLS.

After the certificates are exchanged and verified, a change in the cipher specification is initiated. The change cipher specification methodology includes:

- a master key

- master key generates two session keys, Key(A->B) and Key(B->A)

- master key also generates two Message Authentication Code keys

FIGURE 8.8 The TLS protocol architecture.

TLS Handshake Protocol	TLS Change Cipher Specification	TLS Alert Protocol	HTTP	FTP
TLS Record Protocol				
Transport Protocol – TCP				
Network Protocol – IP				

Legend:
- TLS Protocols
- Application Protocols
- Other Protocols

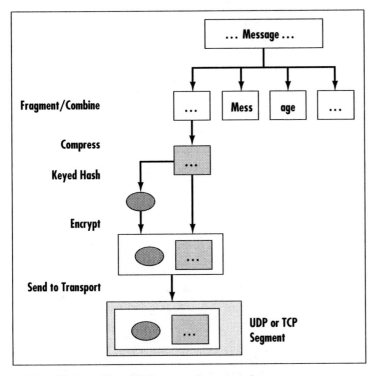

FIGURE 8.9 The TLS record protocol.

A ***Message Authentication Code (MAC)*** key is used to generate a keyed hash, as shown in Figure 8.9, for each TLS fragment. After the change cipher specification phase is complete, the TLS data transfer can begin. Figure 8.8 illustrates the overall TLS architecture.

The handshake and cipher change processes were illustrated in Figure 8.7. The Alert Protocol is only activated when a protocol failure is detected, which we hope is rarely. Figure 8.9 illustrates the TLS record protocol. The Record Protocol has several functions:

- Fragment or combine messages from applications

- Compress the fragments

- Use the MAC keys to provide a keyed hash of each fragment

- Encrypt the fragments and their hashes

- Give the results to the Transport layer

The TLS VPN solution we use for the following examples is based on the OpenVPN package (Yonan 2004). OpenVPN has a similar set of capabilities to that of IPSec in terms of protection for part or all of a path between two hosts. Essentially, we can place a tunnel between:

- two subnets

- a host and a subnet

- two hosts

This is similar to IPSec tunnel mode. There is no analog to IPSec transport mode in TLS VPNs, where an additional AH protocol exists. Another difference between IPSec and the OpenVPN implementation of TLS is that, whereas a single IPSec process can support multiple SAs, multiple OpenVPN process instances must be running to support multiple tunnels. This is not an issue for the LEAF firewalls we use, since they automatically create these instances during boot-up when they detect multiple OpenVPN configuration files. What is important is that the UDP port numbers used by the different tunnels are distinct and that routing is managed well.

An additional issue we cited in the previous discussion of PPTP is the involvement of proprietary protocols. The term proprietary essentially means "not standards-based," in the sense of Khanvilkar and Khokhar 2004. For a good discussion comparing OpenVPN, PPTP, and other VPNs such as Cipe and Vtun, see Gutmann 2003. It turns out that OpenVPN has a proprietary layer as well, having to do with its control channel. There is no conflict between open-source software like OpenVPN making a proprietary innovation. The control channel source code is available; in fact, Gutmann reviews the source code (Gutmann 2003).

The important difference between OpenVPN and VPNs like PPTP, Cipe, and Vtun, is that, in Gutmann's opinion, OpenVPN has more effective security. TLS-based VPNs are generally overtaking PPTP as a better alternative. OpenVPN also uses IPSec's ESP protocol and *US Secure Hash Algorithm 1 (SHA1)* for the MAC (Eastlake and Jones 2001). We have mentioned IPSec's use of MD5 hash codes. MD5 uses a 128-bit hash code to produce the digest of a document. SHA1 uses a 160-bit hash code. This makes SHA1 less vulnerable to the birthday attack.

Overall, OpenVPN is:

- a superior solution to many other open-source and commercial VPN solutions

- roughly equivalent to tunnel mode in IPSec, without a mode like IPSec's transport mode, yet capable of supporting host-to-host tunnels

- less complex to administer than IPSec

- capable of supporting Windows, Linux, and MAC OSX operating systems

For these reasons we choose OpenVPN for the following two examples.

IN PRACTICE: The Birthday Attack

The term "birthday attack" is derived from the statistical fact that if there are 23 people in a room, the chances are even (50-50 odds) that two of them will have the same birthday. This is sometimes called the Birthday Paradox. Let us present this in a hash code context.

1. Alice prepares two versions M and M' of a contract for Bob. M is favorable to Bob and M' is not

2. Alice makes several subtly different versions of both M and M' that are visually indistinguishable from each other by methods such as adding spaces at the ends of lines. She compares the hashes of all the versions of M with all the versions of M'. (She is likely to find a match because of the Birthday Paradox).

3. When she has a pair of documents M and M' that hash to the same value, she gives the favorable document M to Bob for him to sign with a digital signature using his private key. When he returns it, she substitutes the matching unfavourable version M', retaining the signature from M.

It is generally recommended to use at least 128-bit hash codes. The following table illustrates the time required to break a hash code by discovering the key via a brute force, complete enumeration attack.

Key Size (bits)	Number of Alternative Keys	Time required at 106 Decryption/µs
32	$2^{32} = 4.3 \times 10^9$	2.15 milliseconds
56	$2^{56} = 7.2 \times 10^{16}$	10 hours
128	$2^{128} = 3.4 \times 10^{38}$	5.4×10^{18} years
160	$b2^{160} = 1.46 \times 10^{48}$	4.63×10^{23} years

OpenVPN allows two modes of operation along two dimensions. The first dimension has to do with whether the endpoints are peers or not:

- point-to-point mode (default) where the endpoints are peers

- client/server mode

We will only use point-to-point mode in the following examples and in the exercises, projects, and case study.

8

On the second dimension, OpenVPN can operate in two more modes:

- routed mode (use of a tun device)
- bridged mode (use of a tap device)

We use both client-server and routed mode (see the dev tun configuration lines below), since the use of tap devices (i.e. bridged mode) generate more broadcast traffic. As a consequence, all of our OpenVPN configurations will lack server or client directives and will contain dev tun directives, making all tunnels routed and point-to-point. Client-server mode allows certificates and public/private key technology to be employed.

FYI: OpenVPN Tunnels on Windows Require a Virtual Adapter

When you install OpenVPN on a Windows operating system, either the Installation wizard will prompt you to add a new adapter or, once OpenVPN is installed, there is a menu item under OpenVPN to "Add a new tap-Win32 virtual adapter." Don't worry if you intend to use a `dev tun` directive; this tap-WIN32 adapter serves both purposes.

This will place an additional adapter under Start->Settings->Network Connections. Initially, its status will be "network cable unplugged." This is because OpenVPN is a manual service and must be started by using Start->Settings->Control Panel and selecting the Services icon. Scroll down to find OpenVPN service and click the Start button. Your tap-Win32 will be given an IP address at that time.

Once an OpenVPN tunnel targets a specific subnet or a single IP address, the OpenVPN configuration will usually cause a change to the route table in the LEAF machine. As a consequence, you will not be able to communicate (e.g., access Web pages) until two requirements have been met:

- The configuration of OpenVPN on the "client" machine—for example, wireless laptop or desktop—has been successfully configured.

- The rules of shorewall are updated to allow traffic between the local and/or network sides of the firewall (depending on your choice of protecting an internal machine on the local network or connecting two subnets together using OpenVPN between two firewalls).

Principles of Routing

Every computer, whether host or router, has an IP layer if the machine participates in the TCP/IP community. Several issues determine the success or failure of VPN connections. One is correct VPN configuration files, and another is correct administration of routing tables.

Every IP layer relies on a route table to determine the path of packets. The route table must have correct entries for all packets traversing, or packets may be silently discarded. When a NIC is configured, several items are required for the NIC and the IP layer:

- the IP address for the NIC
- the IP subnet mask
- the default gateway
- one or more DNS servers

The default gateway parameter causes a default route to be placed into the IP layer route table. This causes all packets not matched by any other row in the table to be sent to the default gateway, which is usually a router or firewall. In previous chapters, you learned to change the gateway parameter of LEAF firewalls when you were ready to connect to your campus network or the Internet. This parameter causes a change to the firewall's route table.

A route table will also contain a route for every NIC in the machine plus a route for the loopback interface. For a firewall, there will usually be two physical interfaces in addition to the loopback. A host usually has a single physical interface, and the loopback interface is a logical interface that simply takes packets inbound and changes their direction to outbound. This allows for two features: testing the IP layer in isolation, since the packets never go to the physical interface, and allowing a client program and a server program to run on the same machine. The following abbreviated display of route table entries from a Windows machine (via the route print command) illustrates several entries:

Destination	Netmask	Gateway	Interface
0.0.0.0	/0	37.45.19.55	37.45.19.69
127.0.0.0	/8	127.0.0.1	127.0.0.1
37.45.19.0	/24	37.45.19.69	37.45.19.69
37.45.19.69	/32	127.0.0.1	127.0.0.1

The first entry is the default route, the second is the loopback entry, and the third is the directly connected network that is connected to the NIC for the host. The last entry, in conjunction with the second, allows a Web browser to communicate with a Web server on the same machine. Note that the interfaces are identified by their IP addresses rather than hardware addresses.

Figure 8.10 describes the linkage between default routes between hosts and firewalls. The diagram shows forward paths in black arrows and reverse paths in dashed gray. For each host computer, a default route directs packets toward a gateway (in this case, a firewall). This only occurs for packets whose destination IP address are not associated with any machine on that host's IP subnet. The same principle holds for the reverse path—*there must be a chain of default routes for packets to successfully exit the local network leading to the destination.*

This is a general principle that also applies to packets directed to tunnels. Since VPNs encapsulate the original packets in alternative packets directed to tunnel IP addresses, there needs to be a consideration for similar routes in route tables at all points along a path.

FYI: Default Routes and IPSec Configuration

In IPSec configuration files, there are statements that determine routing issues and rely on correct configuration of route tables. For example:

```
left=%defaultroute
right=%defaultroute
```

These statements depend on the default route to be set correctly.

Figure 8.10 also shows two tunnels, X and Y. We will first focus on tunnel Y and look at the successful linkage to the two subnets behind firewalls A and B.

Avoiding routing loops is an objective in any network. We examine the issue through some configuration fragments from two abbreviated OpenVPN configurations for firewalls A and B in Figure 8.10. Firewall A has the private subnet 192.168.1.0/24 behind it, and firewall B has the subnet 192.168.10.0/24. For this reason, the firewall at the opposite end of the tunnel must have a route command for these subnets, if a machine on firewall A's subnet is intended to communicate with a machine on firewall B's subnet, and vice versa.

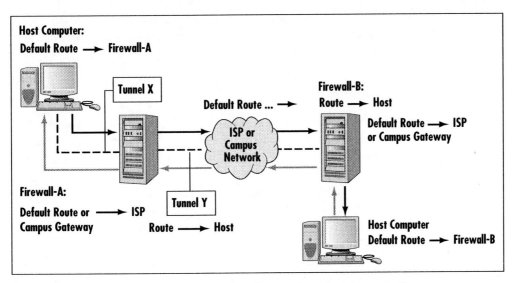

FIGURE 8.10 Routes that determine forward and reverse paths.

Firewall A:

dev tun

local 26.27.28.29

remote 35.36.37.38

ifconfig 10.1.10.1 10.1.10.2

route 192.168.10.0 255.255.255.0

secret static.key

Firewall B:

dev tun

remote 26.27.28.29

local 35.36.37.38

ifconfig 10.1.10.2 10.1.10.1

route 192.168.1.0 255.255.255.0

secret static.key

An explanation of several elements of the configuration for firewall B is as follows:

- dev tun identifies a tunnel device. The alternative is a tap device.

- The remote and local IP addresses identify the remote and local machine addresses, respectively. They are reversed for firewall A.

- The ifconfig directive identifies the tunnel endpoints as 10.1.10.2 and 10.1.10.1 for firewall B and A, respectively. They are reversed for firewall A.

- The route directive is described in the OpenVPN manual with the syntax route <destination net> [<mask>] [<next-hop>] as well as other parameters. The square brackets indicate optional parameters.

The route statements allow access to the subnets behind firewalls A and B. We will look at the mask and next-hop parameters. The default for the mask parameter is a 32-bit length mask—exactly one IP address. We have specified in the route commands that we want accessibility to the subnets behind each of the firewalls, which are /24 network masks. The default for the next-hop parameter is the second parameter of the ifconfig directive. We allow the next-hop parameter to take the default, because we want traffic destined for those subnets to use the OpenVPN secure tunnel.

These configurations are correct, but many examples exist on the OpenVPN Web site (openvpn.net) that illustrate a single tunnel between two hosts. Following those examples, it is tempting to use the following route commands on firewall A and B, respectively:

route 35.36.37.38

route 26.27.28.29

The route statements in this configuration, however, will, direct all tunnel traffic toward the opposite system. This will create a route loop and, after the IP packet's TTL field is decremented to zero, the packet will be discarded. No traffic will ever escape this loop.

Securing a Wireless LAN

Now that we understand routing between tunnel endpoints, we are ready to address a specific application of TLS VPNs: securing a wireless LAN (WLAN).

Now let's look at tunnel X from the previous section. Suppose tunnel X is protecting a WLAN. We would like the wireless subnet to be able to access a machine on the subnet behind firewall B. Suppose the tunnel endpoints for tunnel X are 10.1.1.2 on a wireless laptop and 10.1.1.1 on firewall A. The route entries we have for firewalls A and B are sufficient to route packets to a machine on the 192.168.10.0/24 subnet, but not to get them back. This is because these packets will be bearing IP addresses in the private range. Specifically, upon entry to firewall B, the original ping packets will be encapsulated in other IP packets bearing a source IP address of the original tunnel endpoint on the wireless laptop, 10.1.1.2. This fact, in conjunction with firewall B's route table, will prevent them from returning.

The lines in the following display are wrapped to fit the page, but each is a single row in firewall B's route table. On firewall B, with the OpenVPN configuration from the previous section, the route table, via the ip route command, is:

```
10.1.10.1          dev tun0 proto kernel scope link src
10.1.10.2

192.168.1.0/24 via 10.1.10.1 dev tun0

192.168.10.0/24    dev eth1 proto kernel scope link src
192.168.10.254

37.45.19.0/24      dev eth0 proto kernel scope link src
37.45.19.90

default via 37.45.92.55      dev eth0
```

The first entry of this route table for firewall B is the destination network "10.1.10.1," which we put in quotes because it is a network containing a single IP address, much like the last entry in the route table for the Windows host. This says that to get to 10.1.10.1, use device tun0, whose IP address is 10.1.10.2, as indicated by the "src" parameter. Then, due to firewall B's OpenVPN route directive, the 192.168.1.0/24 subnet is available through the same interface. You would think that this route table entry would ensure that packets destined for 192.168.1.5, for example, would get back successfully, but this is not the case.

The third entry is for firewall B's first directly connected subnet, 192.168.10.0/24. The fourth entry is for the second directly connected interface that connects the firewall to an ISP or campus network. The final entry is for the default route, which is similar to the first entry in the route table for the Windows host.

What is lacking is a way for packets destined to the wireless laptop to get back over tunnel X. The second entry in firewall B's route table says, "If a packet wants to get back to 192.168.1.0/24, encapsulate it with a packet destined for IP address 10.1.10.1." What will happen is the packet will make it all the way back to firewall A, but it will be silently discarded.

The solution to this is to add a second route directive to firewall B's configuration, namely:

```
route 10.1.1.2
```

This will cause an additional entry in firewall B's route table:

```
10.1.1.2 via 10.1.10.1      dev tun0
```

This entry says, "Take packets destined for 10.1.1.2 (the wireless laptop) and send them to 10.1.10.1." The result is that upon exit at firewall A, the packets are decapsulated and bear a new destination IP of 10.1.1.2. Firewall A will now be able to route those packets.

You might wonder why you should consider securing a WLAN in the first place. Wireless network administrators have many reasons to be concerned about security. Colorful names, such as wardriving and airjacking, abound for the art and science of making unauthorized use of WLANs. Most WLANs are unsecured, despite the existence of an encryption technology called *wired equivalent privacy (WEP)*. There are several reasons for this:

- MAC address registration for large quantities of wireless users is inconvenient or impossible.

- Public venues, such as conference halls and airports with wireless access points, cannot hope to use a registration procedure at busy times.

- The 802.11i security standard (a.k.a. WAP2) was finalized only in July 2004, so new products rarely support it.

- WEP has significant drawbacks and so is not widely trusted.

Berghal and Uecker point out several vulnerabilities of WEP (Berghel and Uecker 2004, second article). These are easily verified by searching the Web for ways to hack WLANs. One of the chief criticisms of WEP is the weak 3-byte *initialization vector (IV)*. The fact that there is an annual airjacking competition is enough to warn the user of a WLAN—especially a home wireless network—in which virtually anyone can get past WEP.

An initialization vector is a binary number that is used to initialize the encryption and decryption processes at two ends of a secure channel. Figure 8.11 illustrates the process. The initiator generates plain text that is sent through a security gateway (Security GW). The security gateway can be a separate device, or the user's own machine at either end. The security gateway acts to generate an initialization vector, which is fed into the key generator and the encryption process—usually an exclusive-OR (XOR) modulo-2 adder—that transforms the clear text into ciphered text. The security gateway at the opposite end recovers the initialization vector from the bit-stream and initializes its own key generator, as well as the decryption process (also an XOR device) to produce the original clear text. The clear text is then sent to the responder by the security gateway.

The WiFi Alliance (**www.wi-fi.org**) has information about *WiFi Protected Access 2 (WPA2),* which is based on recent amendments to the *IEEE*

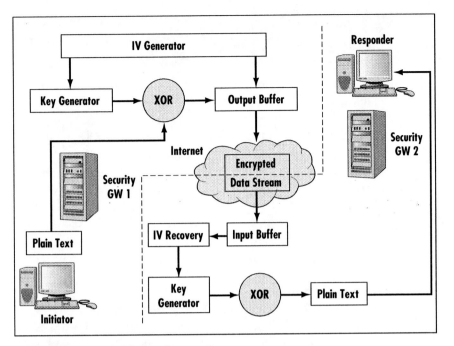

FIGURE 8.11 Initialization vector process.

802.11i security standard. IEEE 802.11i defines three methods to protect data transfer: Counter Mode with CBC-MAC Protocol (CCMP), Wireless Robust Authentication Protocol (WRAP), and Temporary Key Integrity Protocol (TKIP). We briefly review these protocols.

Recall that MAC stands for Message Authentication Code, and is based upon a hash function, providing the integrity feature of a secure channel. CCMP uses a Cipher-Block-Chain (CBC) mode MAC. In addition there is a 16-bit counter that provides the confidentiality property. CCMP uses a 6-byte IV for replay attack protection. In summary, CCMP provides a combined confidentiality and integrity feature set. WRAP has had problematic intellectual property issues and is being replaced by CCMP so we needn't discuss WRAP. Key management is based on the Extensible Authentication Protocol (EAP). EAP-TLS is the de facto authentication protocol for 802.11i. Here the acronym TLS stands for Transport Layer Security. EAP-TLS is just a TLS handshake (see Figure 8.7) over EAP.

The 802.11i amendment to the 802.11 standard was approved by the IEEE Standards Board on June 24, 2004 and published in July 2004. Due to the complexity of WPA2, (Cam-Winget et. al. 2002) it may be too early to expect WLAN products supporting 802.11i (or working correctly) at the time of this writing.

IN PRACTICE: Using a Wireless Tablet PC to Update Patient Records

OpenVPN, the solution we use here, has far better security than WEP, which is the only security available in most WLAN products purchased today. OpenVPN uses a stronger 8 byte IV. We illustrate a configuration that can be used between Windows XP or 2000 client operating systems (and even Windows 2000 and 2003 server operating systems) as well as Linux and several other varieties of Unix. Figure 8.12 relates to the case study in which the reader will implement an OpenVPN tunnel between a wireless laptop or other machine and a server with patient records and the OpenVPN package installed. OpenVPN is a free package under active development and improvement. It is a simple, low-cost solution to securing a WLAN.

We recommend that you implement Project 8.3, using static keys first, to establish a working OpenVPN connection over the WLAN between the wireless laptop and patient record machine. Then, transition to certificates by following this In Practice and following the steps of Project 8.5.

The first step in configuring OpenVPN for a high-security setting such as medical records is to use a popular Linux distribution (Red Hat or SLAX, etc.) and use the openssl facility available on most distributions. Openssl provides facilities for generating your own private certificate authority, generating certificates for other entities, such as the patient records machine and wireless laptop, and generating the private keys for each of these. Openssl has a configuration file called openssl.cnf. The location varies by distribution, but on any Linux or Unix™ machine you can type the commands:

```
cd /

find . -name openssl.cnf
```

The first command places you in the top directory of any Linux file system. The second command searches from the current directory "." to all subdirectories for a file named openssl.cnf. You should see the location after a few moments as the command searches the file system. If there is no result from these commands, then openssl is not installed on the system. You can download and install openssl from **www.openssl.org/**.

Once you locate openssl.cnf there are several items that need to be defined for your situation. First is the location of where

CONTINUED ON NEXT PAGE

openssl will locate certificates and private keys. This in a configuration line:

```
dir = /root/ssl # where everything is kept
```

This means that in the directory /root there must be a subdirectory /root/ssl. You must use the `mkdir` command to create this directory if one is not already there. Several other configuration lines, if left with their default settings, will require two other directories:

/root/ss/newcerts

/root/ssl/private

These directories are for new certificates and private keys, respectively. Recall that the certificates will contain the public keys.

Next, openssl.cnf contains several sections that can provide defaults for several necessary parameters, thereby easing the burden of generating certificates and keys at the command line. We display several here, starting the required Distinguished Name (DN):

```
[ req_distinguished_name ]
countryName            = Country Name (2 letter code)
countryName_default       = US
```

A DN is a set of information that forms a hierarchical path from the top of a directory structure. This hierarchy can be somewhat arbitrary, but a common method is using {country,state, city,email-address} combinations to provide a unique DN for each entity. The certificates you will be generating are called X.509 certificates, after the ITU standard by that name. The beginning of the DN must be at least a country. To be proper, if there the other end of a VPN tunnel is in another country, you should use that country's name. Here is the rest of a DN that resides in Radford, Virginia:

```
stateOrProvinceName     = State or Province Name
(full name)
stateOrProvinceName_default   = Virginia
localityName                = Locality Name (eg, city)
localityName_default          = Radford
```

▶ CONTINUED ON NEXT PAGE

▶▶ **CONTINUED**

```
0.organizationName                 = Organization Name
                                     (eg, company)
0.organizationName_default = RadfordUniversity
organizationalUnitName     = Organizational Unit
                                     Name (eg, section)
organizationalUnitName_default = ITEC
commonName                 = joe.student@radford.edu
```

Note that the common name (CN) is an email address. This is a common way to conclude the DN. The CN could also be a simple user-ID or the host name of a machine. The point is that you are generating a certificate, which needs to be specific to at least a machine name or individual to establish accountability for the certificate. There are other options that can be configured in openssl.cnf, such as a challenge password whenever a secure connection is opened, but that will not be necessary for laboratory exercises.

Finally, there is an important factor in generating certificates: For each certificate, the DN must be unique. Therefore, you must vary at least the common name or some other portion of the DN. When you use openssl as directed in Project 8.5, you will be prompted to override the defaults for the settings in the sample openssl.cnf file above. For each new certificate, you must vary the DN by at least one element or an openssl error will occur.

Although we illustrate a medical setting, any wireless network should have better protection than WEP.

FIGURE 8.12 OpenVPN securing a WLAN.

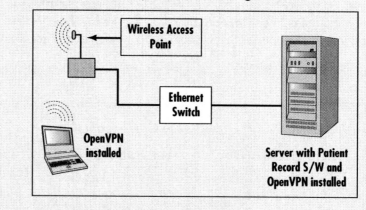

FYI: Using Traceroute to Verify a Path through Tunnels

With IPSec, it is obvious that packets are traversing a secure channel. The phrase "negotiating IP security" will appear when using a simple ping command to test an SA. With other secure protocols such as OpenVPN, there is no indication that the packets are traversing a secure channel. Here is an example of using traceroute, or tracert in Windows:

```
C:\>tracert 192.168.10.13
Tracing route to 192.168.10.13 over a maximum of 30 hops
    1    1 ms    1 ms    1 ms 192.168.1.254
    2   91 ms   90 ms   90 ms 10.1.10.2
    3   89 ms   90 ms   88 ms 192.168.10.13
Trace complete.
C:\>route -p add 192.168.10.0 mask 255.255.255.0 10.1.1.1
C:\>tracert 192.168.10.13
Tracing route to 192.168.10.13 over a maximum of 30 hops
    1    4 ms   12 ms    2 ms 10.1.1.1
    2   92 ms   95 ms   92 ms 10.1.10.2
    3   93 ms   92 ms   92 ms 192.168.10.13
Trace complete.
```

In the first trace, notice that the initial hop is over the firewall's private IP address, not the OpenVPN tunnel. Using the route command on Windows adds a persistent route (signified by the –p parameter) that will be preserved across reboots to ensure security.

8

Wired Networks and the HIPAA: Using Broadband Service to Transfer Patient Records Between Two Subnets

With a wired network in a single secured room in a doctor's office, the concern about unauthorized access to patient records is much less significant than with a WLAN. It would still be substantially important to protect patient records that are sent over the Internet using a broadband connection to a central patient record facility.

You might ask why patient record software isn't located in each office. The simple answer is cost. There would have to be multiple copies of the patient record software, as well as personnel in each office to process the insurance claims from each patient.

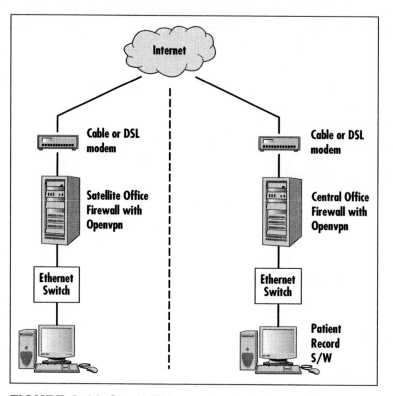

FIGURE 8.13 OpenVPN securing two subnets across the Internet.

A centralized approach is best from a cost standpoint, but it imposes security issues when multiple offices are all transmitting patient records to a central facility. Figure 8.13 illustrates the situation. As with WLANs, OpenVPN is a simple, low-cost solution to securing a wired network.

As in previous chapters, for this arrangement you will need two firewall machines with two PCI NICs. The application in Figure 8.13 is a medical office that has patient record software in the central office and one or more satellite offices accessing machines on the internal network. These machines may be using static IP addresses or may be obtaining IP addresses via DHCP provided by the broadband ISP. In the latter case, a dynamic DNS client (ddclient) is available with OpenVPN.

Troubleshooting VPN Connections

While we want to give you the tools to make your first VPN experience smooth, it would be unusual for a VPN connection to work the first time. In order to eliminate as many potential problems as possible for your first test of the VPN, it is useful to turn off the following services:

- Windows XP firewall

- Cisco VPN client stateful firewall

- Redhat firewall

- Any commercial or open-source firewall (e.g., Norton Personal Firewall, Zone Alarm, BlackICE)

With any or all of those items disabled, a VPN connection with significant delay may still have problems. Frequently, the ping command is used to test the connection. It may take six or eight ping packets before the firewall sets up the SA, especially on a congested network.

Using the college network scenario, the first step in checking a VPN connection would ideally be to place a small Ethernet switch on the network side of the firewall—that is, between the firewall and the campus network or between the firewall and the ISP. Figure 8.14 illustrates this configuration, which resembles a *demilitarized zone (DMZ)* architecture. In this case, you will not need a third interface, as in the CoffeeMall Hotspot case study of Chapter 7. Rather, you will need an additional Ethernet switch inserted between the firewall and the broadband or other modem, as shown in Figure 8.14. Connect any PC to the switch.

Preferably this PC is a laptop that you can easily move farther away from your firewall, to test across routers in your campus network, or across your ISP. In Windows, follow the instructions for defining a security policy with preshared key, to simplify the arrangement. Then make sure you can ping a machine on the internal network. This establishes that the SA is being successfully set up and that the Windows or other OS security policy is correctly set up.

The next important task in the firewall installation of our college scenario is to customize the configuration. As mentioned previously, there are several parameters that will be unique to every college or SOHO environment. You need to ensure that your firewall, as well as your campus network or ISP, will allow the following protocols and ports to pass in both directions:

- UDP port 500 (ISAKMP)

- ESP protocol (IP protocol type 50)

- AH protocol (IP protocol type 51)

A VPN for a road warrior configuration is quite useful for the traveling executive or technical individual. In that situation, the road warrior is often only required to deal with one or both of two elements:

- the firewall at a location such as a university or company headquarters

- the issue of NAT-T

However, VPNs are often placed between two company offices or two university campuses. This configuration requires two firewalls. Many SOHO (commercial or open-source) firewalls implement NAT by default, so using a NAT-T patch on a host PC will still be necessary.

Other problems may arise in unexpected areas. For example, you may find that an IPSec SA can be established over a wired network but no ISAKMP UDP packets arrive over a wireless network.

The other major VPN technology that we discuss in this chapter is TLS. By default, OpenVPN uses UDP port 5000 in most versions of the product. However, IANA has recently added a registered port, 1194 for OpenVPN. TLS VPNs can use either UDP or TCP with this port number. If you experience difficulty, it may be worthwhile checking with your ISP or campus network to make sure the ports and protocols you are using are allowed to pass.

The procedure in Figure 8.14 may require an additional IP address. If DHCP is provided by the ISP or campus network, then configuration of the VPN may have to be changed, but not necessarily. In IPSEC road warrior mode, the "%any" directive in /etc/ ipsec.conf should allow any IP address to connect. In OpenVPN, the "float" directive allows the opposite end of the tunnel to be any IP address.

If you have a static IP from your ISP or campus network, there are two choices:

■   Your campus network or ISP may still allow you to use DHCP for the laptop in Figure 8.14. In that case, you do not need to make further changes.

■   Most often, an ISP that assigns you a static IP address no longer provides DHCP service, especially if cable modem or DSL is used. In that case, you can temporarily disconnect the firewall in Figure 8.14 from the ISP and configure the laptop with the same address as the firewall.

FIGURE 8.14 Using an extra Ethernet switch and PC to test the VPN.

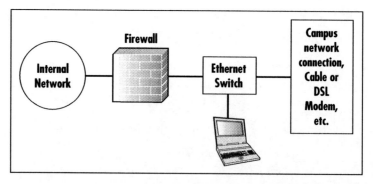

Testing can proceed normally once these options are determined. Once you have verified the successful operation of your VPN as shown, the next step is to proceed farther away from your firewall, across the campus network and the Internet. Taking an incremental approach is the best practice. The first challenge will be to take a laptop and move one or more routers away from your firewall.

As a final step before committing sensitive data to the connection across an untrusted network, you may want to ensure that the traffic is actually being encrypted. It may seem surprising, but even though you can connect, it is possible that the traffic is not being encrypted and authenticated for all or part of the path. It may be wise to invest in a broadcast hub or a switch with a monitor port and use a sniffer program to ensure that your data is not being sent in the clear.

Another troubleshooting tool is secure shell (SSH). It is often useful to have SSH service in your firewall for debugging purposes from distant locations. Once a successful IPSec SA is established, the SSH connection may not work anymore. This is because the SSH IP address is the campus or ISP network address of your firewall, usually a public IP address. In this case, there is a simple solution. Most LEAF firewalls come preconfigured to accept SSH connections from the internal network (usually a private address space). Simply change the destination address of your SSH session to the internal address of the firewall, usually 192.168.1.254 or 192.168.10.254. Your pre-existing SA will work to allow you to connect.

Finally, if you have ensured that your campus network and/or ISP allow the appropriate protocols to pass and your VPN still does not work, consider joining a list-serve for the open-source package that you are working with.

Industrial Applications of LEAF Firewalls and IPSec VPNs

The LEAF firewall used in this book is highly scalable and robust, extending to novel applications. In the following example, it is used in a large European Data Center (EDC). The EDC requires high reliability as well as high security, as illustrated in Figure 8.15. Consequently, the architecture could be called "dual-firewall with sparing," essentially a DMZ architecture with an additional backup firewall.

The EDC must allow access to dozens of internal servers that have application proxies in the DMZ zone. The Chameleon is a Bering firewall that can quickly assume the roles of either internal or external firewall via execution of a script. The EDC also serves a variety of VPNs for its clients.

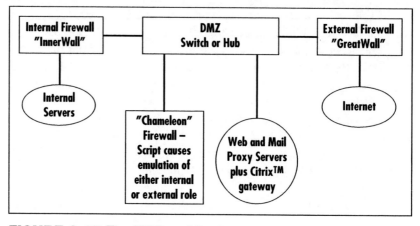

FIGURE 8.15 The EDC architecture.

The set of rules and policies for this EDC is so complex that instead of the shorewall front-end, it uses a graphical front-end called fwbuilder (**www.fwbuilder.org**) to manage the iptables facility.

FIGURE 8.16 The FWBUILDER display.

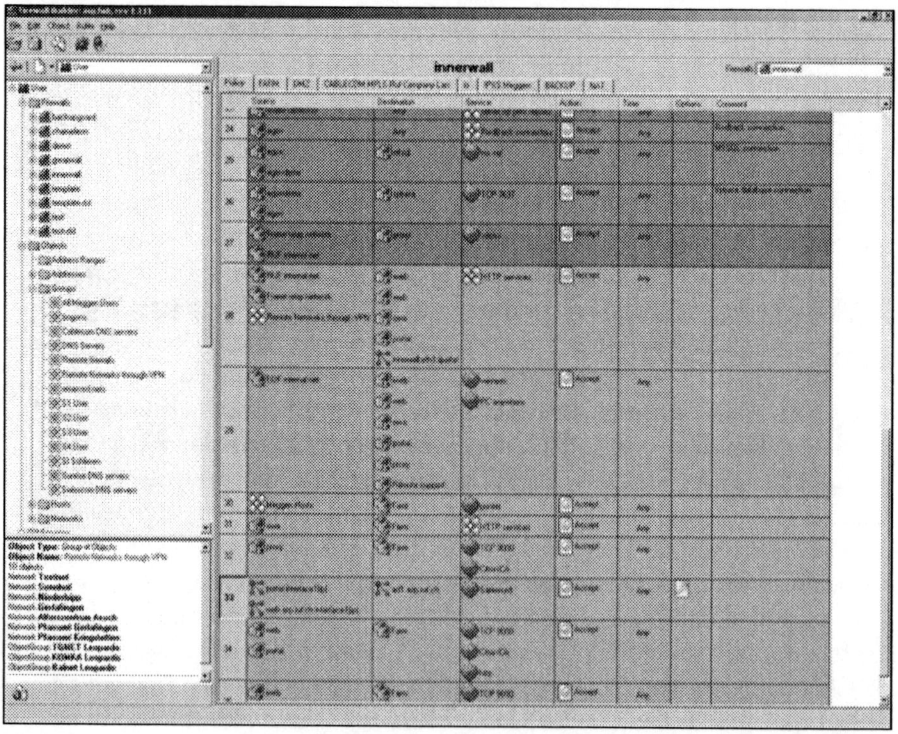

The EDC is an ***application service provider (ASP).*** The EDC hosts approximately 200 small companies, communities, and social institutions on blade servers. (Blade servers are small compact computers on a single printed circuit card that save space in a data center.) The workload of non-VPN connections is estimated at around 1,000 simultaneous connections. These connections must be served by both Innerwall and Greatwall. The VPN tunnels are estimated to be 20 in number, with an average of 3 ongoing connections inside the tunnels.

The DMZ switch HP Procurve 4000 series switch is used to connect the firewalls. All firewalls have all necessary interfaces connected to that switch. The shorewall configuration on Chameleon is an aggregate of Innerwall and Greatwall, with a script that tailors the configuration to assume either role.

We present some illustrations of the fwbuilder GUI and the data center equipment. Figure 8.16 shows the fwbuilder display for Innerwall, while Figure 8.17 shows the basic equipment rack in the EDC. The hardware supporting the LEAF firewalls is a NexGate NSA 1125 (**www.nexcom.com.tw**). Each NSA 1125 boots from Compact Flash Memory and contains 512 Mbyte of RAM.

FIGURE 8.17 The EDC equipment rack.

FYI: The Machine Repair Model and "k-for-n" Availability

The architecture of the EDC is an example of k-for-n availability, specifically 1-for-2. There are two firewalls, Innerwall and Greatwall. The Chameleon is capable of assuming either role. Availability is, by definition, the amount of time a system is up divided by all time, including down-time. Assuming a small switchover time (perhaps 10 minutes) for Chameleon to assume either role, knowing that it is extremely unlikely both Innerwall and Greatwall would go down simultaneously, we can compute the availability of the EDC architecture most accurately using the Machine Repair Model (Trivedi 1982, 385).

We need two parameters for any availability model, the **Mean Time To Failure (MTTF)** and the **Mean Time To Restore (MTTR)**—in this case, we estimate about 10 minutes. Although the permanent storage in all the firewalls is compact flash memory, there are other components, including the processor, power supply, and memory. We use 50,000 hours as a rough guess at the MTTF.

The simplest availability model, which does not account for a spare like Chameleon, is: $A = MTTF/ (MTTR + MTTF)$. From this formula (Trivedi 1982, 300), we would derive a rather impressive availability of 0.99999666667777774074086 419711934.

However, the Machine Repair Model would give even greater availability of 0.99999999997777785185209876296297. This gives the EDC an incredible expectation of survival, for the dual firewall plus spare system! It is more likely that one of the many servers behind Innerwall would fail first.

Summary

After reading this chapter, you should have a basic understanding of three types of VPNs: IPSec, TLS, and PPTP. You should also come to a deeper understanding of IPSec and TLS VPNs via the end-of-chapter materials, especially the projects and case study.

There are a large number of VPN solutions, including open-source and commercial VPNs. These VPN solutions vary in their level of security and complexity of administration. The most secure VPN solutions are arguably IPSec and TLS.

Test Your Skills

MULTIPLE CHOICE QUESTIONS

1. There are several major varieties of VPNs:
   A. IPSec, transport exchange, PPP
   B. TLS, IPSec, PPTP, L2TP
   C. twisted sister, IPSec, PPTP
   D. EAP, Protocol42, IPSec, TLS

2. IPSec VPNs include several additional protocols:
   A. authentication header (AH) and extra sensory perception (ESP)
   B. AH and encapsulation security protocols (ESP)
   C. AH, encapsulation security protocols (ESP), and ISAKMP
   D. AH, encapsulation security protocols (ESP), ISAKMP, and IKE

3. The goal of ISAKMP via IKE is to:
   A. establish a security authentication
   B. establish a security alliance
   C. establish a security association
   D. connect directly whether the channel is secure or not

4. The options available in IPSec include:
   A. PSK, certificates
   B. perfect secrecy key, certificates
   C. public/private keys, certificates and preshared key
   D. S&H certificates, public keys and digital signatures

5. The term *mutable fields* refers to (select all that apply):
   A. fields in the IP header that are allowed to change
   B. fields in the tunnel header that are allowed to mutate
   C. fields in the IP header that are exempt from hashing by AH
   D. TCP fields like ACK and sequence number that are encrypted and must be allowed to change

6. The relationship between IPSec and NAT is which of the following?

   A. IPSec is completely compatible with NAT.

   B. IPSec is incompatible with NAT.

   C. IPSec and NAT can work if either the NAT function is performed prior to the IPSec function or if NAT-traversal is implemented.

   D. IPSec is independent of NAT, NATP or any other modification of the IP addresses.

7. In security terms, the concept of a road warrior is:

   A. a mobile machine that must be prevented from accessing a corporate network

   B. someone who drives dangerously

   C. a mobile machine that needs VPN service with a fixed private IP address

   D. a mobile machine that needs VPN service but may have any unknown IP address

8. A subnet-to-subnet tunnel-mode configuration for an IPSec VPN:

   A. allows any machine on one subnet access to any machine on the other through a single tunnel between two IPSec gateways

   B. makes a separate tunnel for every combination of machines on the two subnets that are actively communicating

   C. provides random encryption service (RES) on packets from selected machines, providing high reliability that no one will see the contents

   D. takes the packets of each machine on one subnet, combines them, and encrypts the entire collection to save on protocol overhead

9. A host-to-host transfer-mode configuration for an IPSec VPN:

   A. allows any machine on one subnet access to any machine on the other through a single tunnel between two IPSec gateways

   B. makes a separate tunnel for any combination of machines that are actively communicating simultaneously

   C. provides random encryption service (RES) on packets from selected machines, providing high reliability that no one will see the contents

   D. takes the packets of each machine on one subnet, combines them, and encrypts the entire collection to save on protocol overhead

10. When compared to IPSec and TLS VPNs, PPTP is:

    A. more secure than IPSec

    B. more secure than TLS

    C. more secure than both IPSec and TLS

    D. less secure than both IPSec and TLS

11. PPTP uses the following additional protocols:

    A. PPP and GRE

    B. PPP, GRE, and TCP (port 1723)

    C. PPP, ECP, GRE, and TCP (port 1723)

    D. PAC, PNS, and NAS

12. There is no such thing as a VPN without encryption and/or integrity and/or digital signatures:

    A. True. Without confidentiality, messages can be read. Even if we want to use broadcast or multicast to spread a message with no confidentiality, we need the integrity function to prove no alteration was made to the message. We may need digital signatures for authentication/non-repudiation purposes.

    B. False. IP-in-IP has none of the features mentioned in the question.

    C. Partly true. Most VPNs need at least one of the features mentioned.

    D. Mostly false. Nobody needs anything beyond email privacy.

13. Microsoft's proprietary standards-based version of PPTP uses the protocols:

    A. MPPE and MPPC

    B. PAC, PNS, and NAS

    C. BGP, MPLS, and L2TP

    D. PPP, MPPE, MPPC, GRE, and TCP (port 1723)

14. TLS is used in:

    A. TLS-based VPNs

    B. IPSec VPNs

    C. HTTPS and TLS-based VPNs

    D. BGP, MPLS and L2TP VPNs

15. HIPAA requires:
    A. health professions to ensure the privacy of health information
    B. hippopotami to secure all health information
    C. all protocols to encrypt health information automatically
    D. availability and integrity

16. Certificates and verification of them is superior to preshared key because:
    A. false statement, PSK is better
    B. certificates are automatically verified
    C. PSK can be compromised by a MITM attack
    D. Neither certificates nor PSK is necessary

17. The connection setup exchange for TLS exchanges:
    A. master key
    B. master key and two session keys
    C. master key, two session keys, and two MAC keys
    D. No keys are necessary with TLS.

18. A TLS Message Authentication Code is:
    A. a keyed hash code of constant length added to each fragment in the record protocol
    B. a hash code of constant length added to each fragment in the record protocol
    C. a master key of constant length added to each fragment in the record protocol
    D. a session key of constant length added to each fragment in the record protocol

19. The OpenVPN package allows several modes. These are:
    A. point-to-point mode and client server mode
    B. point-to-point mode, client server mode, and routed mode
    C. there are no modes in OpenVPN, there are phases
    D. point-to-point mode, client server mode, routed mode, and bridged mode

20. The following are security standards available in WLANs:

    A. WEP, WAP2, and 802.11i

    B. WEP and WAP2, which is based on 802.11i

    C. WEP, WAP, WARP, and 802.11i

    D. all WLANs are unsecured

21. WLANs are:

    A. mandated to be secured by the FCC

    B. frequently unsecured because of lazy network administrators

    C. frequently unsecured in public places where registration of large numbers of people is impractical

    D. mandated to be secured by the IEEE

22. To troubleshoot a VPN connection, you should:

    A. automatically generate random configurations until one works

    B. check that no firewalls or security agents are active, and employ additional switches to isolate the trouble at increasing distances from the other end of the VPN connection

    C. obtain help from any person you can

    D. break into routers in the path of your VPN connection to ensure no traffic is blocked

23. Troubleshooting VPNs often requires:

    A. checking with a network administrator that the protocols involved are not blocked

    B. There are never any problems. All routers automatically pass VPN traffic.

    C. The only problems occur with IPSec VPNs. Make sure AH, ESP, and UDP port 500 are not blocked by routers.

24. Firewalls and VPNs are neither scalable nor reliable.

    A. true

    B. false

8

EXERCISES

Exercise 8.1: Analyze Logs for the IPSec Road Warrior Configuration

One of the features of IPSec is that it can be configured to try indefinitely to refresh a security association (SA). Go to the book Web site and access a copy of the initial IPSec firewall image. Burn a CD, or use floppy boot to get a firewall running. It does not matter for this exercise if the firewall has the correct interface drivers. The purpose is to look at the /etc/IPSec.conf file. Use lrcfg to access the packages menu and select IPSec. Then select the first entry, "IPSec main configuration file." Read through the section beginning with "conn %default."

Analyze the following segment of the auth.log file and answer the questions below about the entries:

```
Dec 3 13:00:39 firewall pluto[27302]: "road-
warrior" [1] 37.5.19.8 #45: ignoring Vendor ID pay-
load [MS NT5 ISAKMPOAKLEY 00000004]

Dec 3 13:00:39 firewall pluto[27302]: "road-
warrior" [1] 37.5.19.8 #45: ignoring Vendor ID pay-
load [4048b7d56ebce885...]

Dec 3 13:00:39 firewall pluto[27302]: "road-
warrior" [1] 37.5.19.8 #45: ignoring Vendor ID pay-
load [draft-ietf-IPSec-nat-t-ike-02_n]

Dec 3 13:00:39 firewall pluto[27302]: "road-
warrior" [1] 37.5.19.8 #45: Main mode peer ID is
ID_IPV4_ADDR: '37.5.19.8'

Dec 3 13:00:39 firewall pluto[27302]: "road-
warrior" [1] 37.5.19.8 #45: ISAKMP SA established

Dec 3 13:00:39 firewall pluto[27302]: "road-
warrior" [1] 37.5.19.8 #47: initiating Quick Mode
PSK+ENCRYPT+TUNNEL+PFS+DISABLEARRIVALCHECK

Dec 3 13:01:49 firewall pluto[27302]: "road-
warrior" [1] 37.5.19.8 #47: max number of retrans-
missions (2) reached STATE_QUICK_I1. No acceptable
response to our first Quick Mode message: perhaps
peer likes no proposal

Dec 3 13:01:49 firewall pluto[27302]: "road-
warrior" [1] 37.5.19.8 #47: starting keying attempt
2 of an unlimited number
```

```
Dec 3 13:01:49 firewall pluto[27302]: "road-
warrior"[1] 37.5.19.8 #48: initiating Quick Mode
PSK+ENCRYPT+TUNNEL+PFS+DISABLEARRIVALCHECK to re-
place #47

Dec 3 13:02:59 firewall pluto[27302]: "road-
warrior"[1] 37.5.19.8 #48: max number of retrans-
missions (2) reached STATE_QUICK_I1. No acceptable
response to our first Quick Mode message: perhaps
peer likes no proposal

Dec 3 13:02:59 firewall pluto[27302]: "road-
warrior"[1] 37.5.19.8 #48: starting keying attempt
3 of an unlimited number
```

If a laptop is connected to a network and establishes an initial SA, it is very likely that laptop will be leaving with its owner at the end of the day. Then, the SA will be refreshed by rekeying attempts. Explain:

- why there are so many re-keying attempts

- why the IPSec thinks that none are acceptable to the peer

- why the ISAKMP process indicates "ignoring Vendor ID payload [draft-ietf-IPSec-nat-t-ike-02_n]"

8

Exercise 8.2: Log Files: Multiple Road Warrior SAs

Consider the following excerpt from /var/log/auth.log:

```
Dec 3 20:32:22 firewall pluto[23610]: packet from
37.4.4.9:500: ignoring Vendor ID payload [MS NT5
ISAKMPOAKLEY 00000004]

Dec 3 20:32:22 firewall pluto[23610]: packet from
37.4.4.9:500: ignoring Vendor ID payload
[4048b7d56ebce885...]

Dec 3 20:32:22 firewall pluto[23610]: packet from
37.4.4.9:500: ignoring Vendor ID payload [draft-
ietf-IPSec-nat-t-ike-02_n]

Dec 3 20:32:22 firewall pluto[23610]: packet from
37.4.4.9:500: ignoring Vendor ID payload
[26244d38eddb61b3...]

Dec 3 20:32:22 firewall pluto[23610]: "road-
warrior"[1] 37.4.4.9 #1: responding to Main Mode
from unknown peer 37.4.4.9
```

```
Dec 3 20:32:23 firewall pluto[23610]: "road-
warrior"[1] 37.4.4.9 #1: Main mode peer ID is
ID_IPV4_ADDR: '37.4.4.9'

Dec 3 20:32:23 firewall pluto[23610]: "road-
warrior"[1] 37.4.4.9 #1: sent MR3, ISAKMP SA
established

Dec 3 20:32:23 firewall pluto[23610]: "road-
warrior"[1] 37.4.4.9 #2: responding to Quick Mode

Dec 3 20:32:23 firewall pluto[23610]: "road-
warrior"[1] 37.4.4.9 #2: IPSec SA established

Dec 3 20:36:02 firewall pluto[23610]: packet from
37.5.19.8:500: ignoring Vendor ID payload [MS NT5
ISAKMPOAKLEY 00000004]

Dec 3 20:36:02 firewall pluto[23610]: packet from
37.5.19.8:500: ignoring Vendor ID payload
[4048b7d56ebce885...]

Dec 3 20:36:02 firewall pluto[23610]: packet from
37.5.19.8:500: ignoring Vendor ID payload [draft-
ietf-IPSec-nat-t-ike-02_n]

Dec 3 20:36:02 firewall pluto[23610]: packet from
37.5.19.8:500: ignoring Vendor ID payload
[26244d38eddb61b3...]

Dec 3 20:36:02 firewall pluto[23610]: "road-
warrior"[2] 37.5.19.8 #3: responding to Main Mode
from unknown peer 37.5.19.8

Dec 3 20:36:02 firewall pluto[23610]: "road-
warrior"[2] 37.5.19.8 #3: Main mode peer ID is
ID_IPV4_ADDR: '37.5.19.8'

Dec 3 20:36:02 firewall pluto[23610]: "road-
warrior"[2] 37.5.19.8 #3: sent MR3, ISAKMP SA
established

Dec 3 20:36:02 firewall pluto[23610]: "road-
warrior"[2] 37.5.19.8 #4: responding to Quick Mode

Dec 3 20:36:02 firewall pluto[23610]: "road-
warrior"[2] 37.5.19.8 #4: IPSec SA established
```

- Can you guess to what #1, #2, correspond?

- To what do the numbers in brackets [1] and [2] pertain?

- Which Oakley modes are being used? Why? (Hint: Read RFC 2409.)

Exercise 8.3: Analyze Log Files for OpenVPN Protecting an Internal WLAN.

The following log files are from an OpenVPN installation on Windows XP. This is an OpenVPN 2.0 series log file, which may differ slightly from earlier versions:

```
Thu Dec 09 11:01:55 2004 us=532051 UDPv4 WRITE
[60] to 192.168.1.254:5000: DATA 724be2b9 4bb4c1bc
e230709c 411aea80 c9805a37 4edc2808 48e07e0a
2bcb807[more...]

Thu Dec 09 11:01:55 2004 us=532236 WIN32 I/O:
Socket Send immediate return [60,60]

Thu Dec 09 11:01:55 2004 us=532269 UDPv4 write
returned 60
```

The OpenVPN configuration file on the Windows XP machine is:

```
remote 192.168.1.254
port 5000
disable-occ
dev tun
tun-mtu 1500
tun-mtu-extra 32
mssfix 1450
ifconfig 10.1.1.2 10.1.1.1
route <insert public IP address on the campus or
ISP side of your LEAF firewall.>
secret secret.txt
# This section offers a more reliable
# detection when a system loses its connection.
# For example, dial-ups or laptops that travel
# to other locations.
ping-restart 60
ping-timer-rem
persist-tun
# keep-alive ping
ping 10
verb 9
mute 10
```

It may surprise you to know that this configuration file has no "local" configuration line. This is necessary since the Windows XP machine is a laptop playing the role of the road warrior. Therefore, the NIC will have an IP address that varies based on where it is located. OpenVPN can sense the active NIC and use that IP address as a local configuration directive.

Note also that several lines in the OpenVPN configuration file keep the connection alive for unreliable systems. This can help if a laptop is roaming on a WLAN network. Also note the configuration lines:

```
Verb 9
Mute 10
```

These lines control the "verbosity," that is, the level of logging information the OpenVPN produces. The mute 10 configuration allows that up to 10 repetitions of a similar log entry will be represented by a single log entry. Since verb 9 is the maximum logging level, the mute command can significantly reduce log file size.

Answer the following questions:

- Does the configuration file indicate that OpenVPN has successfully protected the connection?
- Is it possible to determine this, given only one log file from one end of the connection?

Exercise 8.4: Analyze Log Files for OpenVPN Connecting Two LEAF Firewalls

The objective of this exercise is to establish confidence in the operation of a subnet-to-subnet arrangement between two LEAF firewalls. This exercise should be done after Project 8.4. On both LEAF firewalls, look at the file /var/log/daemon.log, where the OpenVPN daemon will post its messages. Evaluate whether the tunnel is successful.

Exercise 8.5: Write a Two-Page Paper Describing the Uses of VPNs

In this paper, describe the advantages of VPNs for the variety of applications mentioned in this chapter. Discuss the advantages and disadvantages of the authentication methods:

Pre-shared Key

Certificates and digital signatures

Also compare the three VPNs 802.11i, PPTP and OpenVPN on the basis of the Initialization Vector (IV) that each uses. Which is more secure?

PROJECTS

Project 8.1: Install and Configure an IPSec VPN for the Road Warrior

For this project, you will need a single firewall machine with two Ethernet NICs and a laptop to act as your road warrior. Alternatively, you can use a desktop machine in a separate location, but a laptop is a better choice for debugging your configuration.

To proceed, you will need to edit two files: /etc/ ipsec.conf and /etc/ipsec.secrets. Initially, we will use a simple pre-shared key. A sample ipsec.conf file is shown below:

```
# /etc/ipsec.conf - FreeS/WAN IPsec configuration
file
# More elaborate and more varied sample configura-
tions can be found
# in FreeS/WAN's doc/examples file, and in the HTML
documentation.
# basic configuration
config setup
# THIS SETTING MUST BE CORRECT or almost nothing
will work;
# %defaultroute is okay for most simple cases.
interfaces=%defaultroute
# Debug-logging: "none" for (almost) none, "all"
for lots.
klipsdebug=none
plutodebug=none
plutoload=%search
plutostart=%search
# Close down old connection when new one using same
ID shows up.
uniqueids=yes
nat_traversal=yes
# defaults for subsequent connection descriptions
conn %default
# How persistent to be in (re)keying negotiations
(0 means very).
```

8

```
        keyingtries=0

        authby=secret

        left=%defaultroute

        leftsubnet=192.168.1.0/24  #  put  in  your  actual
        subnet ID

        leftfirewall=yes

        pfs=yes

        auto=add

        conn road-warrior

        right=%any
```

Then, once you can verify that ipsec is loading (hint: check the log files in /var/log) go to **jixen.tripod.com/win2k-screen.html** and follow the instructions for implementing a road-warrior configuration on a Windows machine using pre-shared key (PSK).

The PSK can be anything that you want—a simple passphrase is all that is needed for a laboratory exercise. In practice, you should use something at least 128 bits long in a real-world situation.

Last, you will need to edit /etc/ipsec.secrets and add lines of the form:

%any **your.firewall.IP.address** : PSK "**<your-passphrase>**"

your.firewall.IP.address %any : PSK "**<your-passphrase>**"

Substitute your chosen passphrase for the text **<your-passphrase>** above, and note that quotes are needed around the passphrase. Also substitute the IP address of the firewall for **your.firewall.IP.address.** Note that you need a PSK line for both directions of the connection. Finally, verify that your road warrior can connect by using several ping commands (it may take at least two pings from a Windows operating system before the SA is established). For troubleshooting, compare the contents of auth.log on the firewall with that displayed in Exercise 8.2.

Project 8.2: Add a Subnet-to-Subnet IPSec VPN

For this project, build on the activity of Project 8.1 by adding an additional firewall machine, again with two interfaces. The objective is to configure secure access between two separate subnets behind two firewalls. You may use pre-shared keys again in this exercise, as you did in project 8.1. If you have not completed project 8.1 refer to it, and make the appropriate changes to the other firewall. One firewall will be "left" and the other firewall will be "right." Therefore, the configurations for each need to be opposite-handed of the other.

Project 8.3: Install and Configure a TLS VPN for the Road Warrior

As with Project 8.1, this is a single-firewall, single-laptop operation in best practice. TLS VPNs may not work side by side with IPSec VPNs, so you may need to dismantle your IPSec VPN configuration.

1. First, ensure that the following additional packages are loaded, adjusting syslinux.cfg and/or leaf.cfg as necessary:

   - openvpn.lrp

   - libssl.lrp

   - libcrypt.lrp (should already be loaded if you did Projects 1 and 2)

2. Once you have added these packages to the appropriate .cfg files, reboot. Make sure that the OpenVPN, libssl, and libcrypt packages are loaded by using lrcfg to inspect the backup menu.

   The basic configuration we will use is a preshared key (PSK) generated by the OpenVPN command line as follows:

   ```
   cd /etc/OpenVPN
   /usr/sbin/OpenVPN —genkey —secret static.key
   ```

3. The above two commands will place a simple preshared key in the file static.key. This same key needs to be copied to the laptop. You can do this by mounting a separate 1.44 Mbyte floppy and transferring the file. Alternatively, if you have secure shell running on your firewall, you can use the copy and paste functions of secure shell.

4. Then you must edit the /etc/OpenVPN/OpenVPN.conf file on the LEAF firewall. To do this, enter lrcfg, navigate to the packages menu, and make the config file look as follows:

   (You are given the firewall openvpn configuration for this road warrior setup. You must supply the road warrior config on a laptop.)

   ```
   # Use a dynamic tun device.
   dev tun
   # For compatibility with 2.x openvpn uncomment
   these lines
   #tun-mtu 1500
   #tun-mtu-extra 32
   #mssfix 1450
   ```

```
local <insert public IP address on the external
side of your LEAF firewall.>
# Remote peer is a Road Warrior.
# The Road Warrior must "float" since it may have
# any IP address from DHCP
# The float directive is in lieu of the remote
directive
float
# 10.1.10.1 is our local VPN endpoint
# 10.1.10.2 is our remote VPN endpoint
ifconfig 10.1.10.1 10.1.10.2
route <insert public IP address on the campus or
ISP side of your LEAF firewall.>
# Our pre-shared static key
secret static.key
```

This file does several things. First, the local and remote commands identify a local firewall and a laptop or desktop machine playing the role of road warrior. Note that the local and remote commands call for public IP addresses; if your campus network uses a private address space, then use those IP addresses. Then the ifconfig command adds two new private IP addresses that are somewhat fictitious. The purpose of the 10.x.x.x IP addresses is to act as the endpoints of the TLS tunnel.

On the road warrior machine, you must reverse the ifconfig directive, and to access any of the machines on an internal network behind the firewall you must use an appropriate route command. Answer the following questions to complete your road warrior configuration:

How will you determine the local directive if you are given an IP address via DHCP?

Will you have to adjust your configuration if your IP address changes before starting the openvpn service?

Project 8.4: Implement a Subnet-to-Subnet VPN using OpenVPN

This project requires several computers, two as firewalls and at least two machines that can run SLAX or Windows. The simplest arrangement is to string the machines together as in the following diagram.

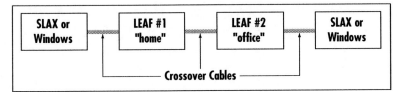

FIGURE 8.18 Project 8.4 equipment configuration.

1. Go to the book Website (**www.prenhall.com/security**) and download an image for the subnet-to-subnet OpenVPN configuration.

2. Install this image on two LEAF machines.

3. On one LEAF machine, reverse the ifconfig and route directives.

4. Test your configuration by pinging the opposite end of the tunnel from each firewall. (This is a 10.1.10.x IP address.)

5. Then use ping from the SLAX or windows machines to ping the IP address of the other machine. (This will be 192.168.x.y IP address).

Project 8.5: Generate Certificates for OpenVPN

1. On a firewall with a working OpenVPN installation, load the openssl.lrp package. Reboot the firewall and issue the commands (omit the lines beginning with #):

```
# Generate DH params
openssl dhparam -out dh1024.pem 1024
# Generate CA key/cert
openssl req -x509 -newkey rsa:1024 -keyout
private/cakey.pem \
-out cacert.pem
# Generate server key/cert
openssl req -new -nodes -keyout server.key -out
server.csr
# Generate client key/cert
openssl req -newkey rsa:2048 -keyout client.key
-out client.csr
# Remember to use different DNs for client and
server.
```

```
# Sign keys
openssl ca -in server.csr -out server.crt
openssl ca -in client.csr -out client.crt
```

2. Then configure your OpenVPN to transition from PSK to certificates. Change the OpenVPN configuration as follows. One machine must be the server and the other is the client. This can be used over a WLAN, as in the case of a patient records machine and a laptop, or between two firewalls. In the WLAN case it is most appropriate for the patient records machine to be the server, since the laptop may be mobile, and somewhat vulnerable.

```
# use certs on the Server
tls-server
dh dh1024.pem
ca ca.crt
cert my-server.crt
key my-server-private.key
#optionally use lzo compression
comp-lzo
# use certs on the Client—note no dh parameter.
tls-client
#dh dh1024.pem
ca ca.crt
cert my-client.crt
key my-client-private.key
#optionally use lzo compression
comp-lzo
```

Case **Study**

FixCrix Chiropractic is a small, high-quality practice. The doctor has a wireless access point and a wireless tablet PC. Networked to the wireless access point is the patient records server a few rooms away. The doctor would like to get away from her current system of recording patient treatments on card stock and then having the support staff record them in the patient record server. The doctor would like to access the patient records using the wireless tablet PC. The office needs a way comply with HIPAA regulations for protection of patient records.

Because you have read this book, you have formed the consulting company VPNs Inc., and FixCrix has retained you to solve their problems. You know that OpenVPN is one of the easiest and most secure VPN facilities to set up. The question is, how will you configure the OpenVPN installations at the doctor's office?

Describe your configurations for the wireless tablet PC and the patient records server.

8

Chapter 9

Integrating Firewall Logs and System Logs

Chapter Objectives

After reading this chapter and completing the exercises, you will be able to do the following:

- Define the relationship between firewall rules and log file entries.
- Configure the syslog daemon.
- List the fields present in the iptables and Windows XP firewall logs.
- Locate common problems in log files.
- Enable logging on the Windows XP firewall.
- Setup a centralized log server.
- Synchronize the time on servers to coordinate log events.

Introduction

Computer log files are like the black boxes found in airplanes. They record all of the transactions on a system or network and provide a historic log that can be reviewed to help determine what went wrong in the event of a system crash or intrusion. But logs are useful for more than just researching incidents. When configuring a firewall, you will rarely get everything correct on the first try. The log files provide a valuable source of information for troubleshooting initial configuration problems; therefore, you need to understand where the log files are located and how to decipher the information they contain. Once a firewall or VPN is implemented, the system maintenance cycle begins. One of the important responsibilities of a network administrator is to browse the log files daily to look for malicious activity. Finally, log files are essential to troubleshooting connection-related problems. Frequently, a network administrator will need to review the log files to determine what connections are being denied or what errors are occurring. For these and other reasons, it is essential to properly understand and configure a system to ensure adequate logging of activity.

This chapter will focus on configuring your log files to get the most out of the firewall and system logs. First, we will cover some general principles of logging: configuring, troubleshooting, monitoring, rotating, and archiving. Next, we will examine logging in both Unix/Linux and Windows. Finally, since many organizations run several different systems simultaneously, we will also cover time synchronization and centralization of log files as a method of enterprise level logging.

Logging: The Basics

Log files include information about:

- critical hardware and software error messages
- denied or dropped network connections
- invalid login attempts
- system modifications

In addition to these items, the level of logging can be modified to capture information based on business needs. This may include logging suspicious connections or connections to servers that employees have been instructed not to access. This might also include logging all connections to a server such as a critical database server to provide detailed access logs. Since log files contain a factual and historic log of transactions, they can also be used as forensic evidence to help in the prosecution of a hacker. This use as forensic evidence makes it necessary to archive and maintain highly secure log files. The log files should also be the first place to look when something goes wrong with the firewall. They will point you in the direction of a problem so you know where to begin to search for a solution. Without this information, you are often blindly trying to solve a problem without knowing what is wrong. When reviewing the log files, you must understand the following:

- location of the log file(s)
- format of entries in the log file
- how to search through the log file
- where and how old log files are stored

The format of the entries in the log file is comprised of the data fields that appear in the log file. It is important to understand what fields are present and the type of information available in each field. The Log Entries section later in the chapter will cover the format of log files in more detail. Searching and sorting through log files allows you to find information pertaining to a specific event, computer or time period. This topic will be covered under the log analysis sections later in the chapter. But first, effective use of logs for maintenance and troubleshooting begins with the firewall configuration.

How Log Files Relate to Firewall Rules

Each rule or policy of the firewall has an option that will allow for logging. If logging is enabled, an entry will appear in the log file for every packet that matches the rule. The default policy with the LEAF firewall is to log all incoming packets that are dropped. The excerpt below from the /etc/shorewall/policy file indicates that all packets from the Internet destined for the local subnet will be dropped and logged to the ULOG daemon.

```
#########################################################
#SOURCE      DEST  POLICYLOG    LIMIT:BURST
loc    net   ACCEPT
net    all   DROP  ULOG
```

Notice in this example that the accepted packets are not logged. Logging all accepted packets can generate tremendous amounts of data and should only be performed if absolutely necessary. The more acceptable practice is to log only the specific ports or protocols for which you need more information. As shown by the :info and :ULOG options in the following example, a log entry can be added to any of the rules in the /etc/shorewall/rules file to log specific traffic. This can allow additional data for accepted connections to be logged without logging all accepted traffic.

```
#########################################################
#ACTION         SOURCE          DEST    PROT    PORT
ACCEPT:info  net             fw      tcp     22
ACCEPT       loc             fw      tcp     22
### Allow computers to connect to web Server(weblet) on
Firewall
ACCEPT       loc             fw      tcp     80
ACCEPT:ULOG  net:192.168.2.99 fw     tcp     80
```

During the initial configuration, firewalls should be configured to log all denied or dropped connections and as much additional detail as possible. By initially using a high level of logging, you will find it easier to determine if the firewall rules are the source of a problem. However, once the rules are tested and everything is working, you may change the logging level so that less information is stored in the log files. You will need to be careful that you do not log more than necessary. Too much logging can have a performance impact on the firewall and quickly consume all of the available disk space.

Viewing Firewall Activity

Since dropped or rejected packets are normally logged, you will have to identify the location of the log information. Most Unix systems store all log information in the /var/log directory. Several files located in this directory provide log information for various functions and services. Figure 9.1 is a snapshot from the LEAF firewall weblet service that provides information about the firewall logs and allows the user to display the contents of the log file from a Web interface. Clicking on the appropriate log file or archive file will display the contents of the log file in the Web browser window.

As shown in Figure 9.1, a variety of files are in the /var/log directory, but the one that will be of most interest is the shorewall.log file that contains all of the log information for the shorewall firewall service.

The shorewall.log file will provide log information about the firewall policies. The following is a sample of two entries from the shorewall.log file, providing examples of the types of information available from the log entries:

```
Dec 15 17:27:05 firewall Shorewall:net2all:DROP:
IN=eth0 OUT=
MAC=00:01:02:2a:f5:cc:00:10:4b:87:46:e1:08:00
SRC=192.168.2.28 DST=192.168.2.100 LEN=48 TOS=00
PREC=0x00 TTL=128 ID=4930 DF PROTO=TCP SPT=3172 DPT=80
SEQ=3919991329 ACK=0 WINDOW=65535 SYN URGP=0

Dec 15 17:27:55 firewall Shorewall:net2fw:ACCEPT:
IN=eth0 OUT=
MAC=00:01:02:2a:f5:cc:00:10:4b:87:46:e1:08:00
```

FIGURE 9.1 LEAF firewall weblet log information.

Current	Archives				All	Description
:: Log Files ::						
shorewall.log	0	1	2	3	All	Shorewall messages
messages	0	1	2	3	All	System Messages
syslog	0	1	2	3	All	General log file - lots of info
auth.log	0	1	2	3	All	Who's logged in recently
debug	0	1	2	3	All	debugging information
daemon.log	0	1	2	3	All	daemon (server programs) messages
cron.log	0	1	2	3	All	cron log files
ppp.log	0	1	2	3	All	ppp log files
pslave.log	0	1	2	3	All	portslave log files
user.log	0	1	2	3	All	user log files
sh-httpd.log	0	1	2	3	All	weblet access log files

```
SRC=192.168.2.28 DST=192.168.2.100 LEN=48 TOS=00
PREC=0x00 TTL=128 ID=5245 DF PROTO=TCP SPT=3174 DPT=80
SEQ=3942843937 ACK=0 WINDOW=65535 SYN URGP=0
```

The other files in the log directory each provide valuable system error logs. You should view messages and syslog files regularly for major system problems.

Rotating and Archiving Log Files

Due to the amount of information stored in the log files, these files will grow rapidly. Early in the configuration of the firewall, it is important to configure the system to rotate the log files automatically. Depending on the size of the files and the business needs, you may need to rotate the log file weekly or daily. It is not uncommon for log files on a large network to reach sizes in excess of 200 Mbytes per day.

Fortunately, the LEAF firewall is configured by default to rotate the log files, but it is important to understand the rotation process. Without understanding how the rotation occurs, you may spend time searching for an event in the wrong log file. Rotating usually consists of deleting the oldest log file, aging all of the log files, and then resetting the new log file. For example, the LEAF firewall keeps, by default, four days worth of old log files online. These are:

- syslog (current log file)
- syslog.0 (yesterday's log file)
- syslog.1.gz (log file from two days ago)
- syslog.2.gz (log file from three days ago)
- syslog.3.gz (log file from four days ago)

A rotatelog script will generally perform the following actions:

- Remove the oldest log file – syslog.3.gz
- Rename the syslog.2.gz file to syslog.3.gz
- Rename the syslog.1.gz file to syslog.2.gz
- Compress syslog.0 file and rename to syslog.1.gz
- Rename the syslog file to syslog.0
- Create a new syslog file.

Although LEAF will compress these files using the gzip utility, LEAF uses a RAM drive as its file system, extensive logging can quickly fill up the /var/log RAM drive of the firewall.

Make it a practice to keep a copy of archived log files. These files are sometimes needed for forensic evidence or for other purposes. To maintain

9

Caution

Always Rotate Log Files

Improperly configured or missing rotations of log files can cause a system crash by filling up disk drives.

the integrity of these files, many organizations now archive log files to CD or DVD media at the end of each day or week to provide a method for maintaining the information in a read-only format.

Most Unix systems use the ***cron daemon*** to automatically execute a program at a given time hourly, daily, weekly, or monthly. The cron daemon reads information from a ***crontab*** file to determine when and what programs to execute. The following is a sample /etc/crontab file from the LEAF firewall. This crontab includes a daily, weekly, and monthly entry. The daily entry runs at 6:45 a.m. every day. The weekly entry runs at 6:47 a.m. every Saturday. The monthly entry runs at 6:52 a.m. on the first day of every month.

```
#Min   Hour  Day    Month  Day
#Hour  Day   Month  Year   Week  User  Program
#-------------------------------------------------------
45     6     *      *      *     root  run-parts —report
/etc/cron.daily
47     6     *      *      7     root  run-parts —report
/etc/cron.weekly
52     6     1      *      *     root  run-parts —report
/etc/cron.monthly
```

Logging in Linux/Unix

Unix and Linux systems use the ***syslog daemon*** (syslogd) as their primary mechanism for logging. The syslog dameon provides a single mechanism for the logging of events and information on kernel and system utilities. This can include hardware errors, software errors, and informational messages, among others. One of the features that has made the syslog daemon so popular is its ability not only to log information from the local machine, but also to accept connections from remote systems and write their log information, thus creating a centralized location for log files. Syslog was originally developed for Unix systems, but has become the standard logging mechanism for many networking devices, including routers, switches, printers, and a variety of other hardware.

Introduction to the Syslog Daemon

The syslog daemon is a service that starts at bootup on a Unix system to control the logging of messages. It uses the /etc/syslog.conf file as a configuration file to determine the type of information to log and the appropriate location or file to write the message to. Syslog error messages are broken down into two components:

■ facility–the part of the system the message originated from

■ level–the level of severity of the message or error

TABLE 9.1 Syslog log facilities.

Facility	Description
Auth	Security – authentication messages (login, SSH)
Authpriv	Security – authentication messages logged to a restricted file
Cron	Cron daemon messages
Kern	Kernel messages
Lpr	The print system
Mail	The mail system
Syslog	Messages generated by sylogd
User	User processes
local0 - local7	Local application and administrator-defined message facilities

The facility name helps categorize error messages based on the system or service the message originates from. Table 9.1 provides the common syslog facility names used by most Unix systems. There are additional facilities defined on some Unix systems that are not included in this table.

Notice that local0 through local7 are user-defined logging facilities. These facilities are commonly used by programs or other network devices that remotely record their syslog information. Programmers often define one of these levels in their applications as the logging level or provide an option to modify the logging level. As an example, Cisco routers write to local7 by default, but you can use a configuration parameter to change this to any of the local logging facilities.

The logging level indicates the severity of the error message to be written. This provides a greater level of granularity to help determine which events should be logged. Table 9.2 provides the levels of error messages.

Logging parameters are specified in the syslog configuration file as facility.level based on information from Tables 9.1 and 9.2. This indicates that each facility has eight levels of logging. As an example, the auth facility can send a message at any of these eight levels:

- auth.debug

- auth.info

- auth.notice

- auth.warning

- auth.err

- auth.crit

TABLE 9.2 Syslog log levels.

Level	Type	Description
0	Emerg	System error or panic conditions
1	Alert	A condition that must be handled immediately
2	Crit	Critical conditions such as hard drive errors
3	Err	Error condition
4	Warning	Warning condition
5	Notice	Normal condition but may be worth looking at
6	Info	Informational
7	Debug	Debug condition for debugging purposes; generates an extensive amount of detailed information

- auth.alert

- auth.emerg

A message written to auth.debug provides very detailed informational messages each time someone logs into the system. An auth.emerg message would potentially indicate that the authentication mechanisms are not working at all. The majority of shorewall messages are appropriate to be logged at the info level (Eastep 2004).

Syslog Configuration File The /etc/syslog.conf file is the configuration file that determines the name and location of the log files for error messages. The administrator must specify where the log file will be written for each facility.level combination. Because of the numerous combinations of facilities and levels, you can use an asterisk (*)as a wildcard character to represent either the facility or the level. The following entry would log all auth messages at any level to the /var/log/auth.log file:

```
auth.*      /var/log/auth.log
```

The following two entries would log all messages at the alert and higher levels to the console and /var/log/alert.log. Messages sent to *.alert would log all *.alert and *.emerg messages to the console and also to /var/log/alert.log since emerg is a higher or more critical error message.

```
*.alert     /dev/console
*.alert     /var/log/alert.log
```

TABLE 9.3 Syslog log format.

Example	Field	Description
Dec 19 22:13:51	Timestamp	The date and time of the event was logged. Note that the year is not recorded.
Firewall-host	Host	The name or IP address of the host that generated the message
SSHD	Program	The name of the program generating the message
1371	[Pid]	The system process ID of the program
Accepted password for root from 192.168.2.99 port 2053 ssh2	Message	The detailed log message

Syslog Output Syslog provides the date, time, originating host, program, and message as part of its output. Table 9.3 provides a sample of the fields for a log entry in the auth.log file.

```
Dec 19 22:13:51 firewall-host sshd[1371]: Accepted
password for root from 192.168.2.99 port 3052 ssh2
```

LEAF Logs

The LEAF firewall is based on shorewall, which provides a set of high-level tools for configuring the Linux kernel level netfilter parameters. Shorewall uses both syslogd and *ulogd* for logging information. Ulogd, an alternative logging mechanism, was developed as a replacement for syslogd in iptables-based firewalls (Welte 2004). Ulogd provides enhanced functionality over the standard syslogd dameon by allowing more detailed logging of packets to plaintext files and databases. Ulogd also makes it easier to separate firewall messages from other kernel-level messages. By default, the LEAF firewall is configured to use ulogd instead of syslogd and write information to the /var/log/shorewall.log file. The default configuration does not include the necessary plugins to allow for logging to a mysql or postgres database, but you could add this functionality.

When you configure the LEAF firewall, you should understand how to send log information to the syslog or ulog daemons and how to log specific entries in the policy and rules configuration files.

Updating the Shorewall Configuration File The first step in configuring logging is to update the configuration file /etc/shorewall/shorewall.conf appropriately. This file determines whether specific messages will be sent to syslog or ulog.

If the word ULOG in upper case is specified, the entries will be sent to the ULOG daemon. If a syslog level (info, notice, etc.) is specified, the entry will be sent to the kernel facility of the syslog dameon with the corresponding level.

FYI: shorewall and syslog

Since netfilter is a kernel module, firewall messages will be sent to the kern facility if syslog is used. This facility cannot be changed in the configuration file. The info level is usually the accepted norm for firewall messages.

The entries available for specifying the logging level in the configuration /etc/shorewall/shorewall.conf file are:

```
LOGNEWNOTSYN=info
MACLIST_LOG_LEVEL=info
TCP_FLAGS_LOG_LEVEL=debug
RFC1918_LOG_LEVEL=debug
SMURF_LOG_LEVEL=ULOG
BOGON_LOG_LEVEL=ULOG
```

In this example, the first two entries would be logged to syslog with kern.info, the second two entries would be logged to syslog via kern.debug, and the last two entries would be sent to the ulog daemon.

Configuring Logging for Policies The /etc/shorewall/policy file provides information on the shorewall policy. Every entry in this file has the option of including a log parameter, which can specify to write LOG information to either the syslog daemon or the ulog daemon. The LOG parameter in this file will contain either the word ULOG in all upper case letters or one of the syslog levels (info, debug, etc.). If nothing is specified for the LOG parameter, then no logging takes place when the policy is matched.

```
###############################################################
#SOURCE    DEST       POLICY LOG      LIMIT:BURST
loc        net        ACCEPT
net        fw         DROP            info
net        all        DROP            ULOG
```

Configuring Logging for Rules The /etc/shorewall/rules file contains exceptions to the policy file. Entries in the rules file take precedence over

Caution

Shorewall Restart

The shorewall restart command must be executed after the policy or rules files are modified to activate the updated configuration.

those in the policy file. Thus, if logging is specified in the rules file, it will be logged regardless of the policy logging level. Logging can be enabled for any entry in this file. As with the policy file, each entry may include no log parameter, the word ULOG, or a syslog level. In the rules file, the LOG parameter is specified directly after the action field by using a colon.

```
###########################################################
#ACTION            SOURCE            DEST     PROT    PORT
# Accept and log to syslog kern.info
ACCEPT:info     net                  fw       tcp     22
# Accept and do not log
ACCEPT          loc                  fw       tcp     22
# Accept and log to ulog
ACCEPT:ULOG     net:192.168.2.99     fw       tcp     80
# Drop without logging
DROP            net                  fw       tcp     80
```

IN PRACTICE: Dropping Packets Without Logging

The default policy of the firewall is to drop all incoming connections and log this information to the appropriate log file. If one service or port is being attacked, this can generate a large amount of log entries. The log parameter could be removed from the policy file to prevent the logging from occurring, but this would also prevent the logging of all dropped incoming connections.

For example, if the SQL Slammer worm were attacking port 1433 and generating a huge amount of log entries, you should disable logging of this traffic. The simplest way to do this is to add an exception to the rules file that drops all incoming port 1433 connections but does not log the traffic:

```
## Drop incoming TCP port 1433 SQL con-
nections but do not log.
DROP    net    fw     tcp     1433
DROP    net    loc    tcp     1433
```

The policy to drop and log all incoming connections remains intact, but this rule is an exception to the policy that drops the TCP port 1433 connections without writing anything to the log file.

9

Log Entries The information in the /var/log/shorewall.log file provides detailed information about accepted, dropped, or rejected packets based on the logging levels specified in the configuration files. Each field created by the firewall contains the field name and an = followed by the value. Thus, the key SRC=192.168.10.2 in the log file indicates that the SRC address of the packet was 192.168.10.2. This field name helps to easily identify each component of the log entry.

The entries below are samples of TCP and UDP log entries from the shorewall.log file:

```
Jan 3 11:29:53 firewall Shorewall:all2all:REJECT:
IN=eth1 OUT=
MAC=00:b0:d0:de:c1:22:00:50:04:a6:72:2d:08:00
SRC=192.168.10.2 DST=192.168.10.254 LEN=328 TOS=00
PREC=0x00 TTL=64 ID=0 DF PROTO=UDP SPT=68 DPT=67
LEN=308

Jan 3 19:43:04 firewall Shorewall:net2all:DROP: IN=eth0
OUT= MAC=00:01:03:e1:9c:3d:00:03:ba:12:4f:8f:08:00
SRC=137.45.192.100 DST=137.45.192.190 LEN=48 TOS=00
PREC=0x00 TTL=64 ID=47397 DF PROTO=TCP SPT=43672 DPT=81
SEQ=172715029 ACK=0 WINDOW=24820 SYN URGP=0
```

Table 9.4 (Bartz 2001) provides a breakdown of the fields in this log entry. Reference the TCP and UDP header information from Chapter 2 for more information on each of these fields.

Analyzing Syslog Files

Once logging has been configured to log the appropriate information to the log file, you must know how to analyze the logs and locate the needed information. This can appear overwhelming to new administrators because of the thousands of lines in each log file. This section will cover a few of the many methods you can use to search through and analyze log files.

Unix Command Line Tools The main tools provided with the LEAF firewall to assist with the analysis of the firewall logs are a small suite of Unix command line utilities. These are available with any Unix system, and you can download 32-bit DOS versions from the Internet to provide assistance in analyzing text-based log files on Windows systems. The cut, grep, sort, uniq, and wc commands are string processing utilities that are valuable tools for finding quick answers from the log files. Table 9.5 provides a brief description of each of these utilities.

These utilities can be used with the pipe symbol, "|" to combine several commands and quickly extract a wealth of information from the log files. Understanding the proper use of these utilities takes some time for

TABLE 9.4 Shorewall log fields.

Example	Description
IN=eth1	The interface the packet was received from
OUT=	The interface the packet was sent to
MAC=00:b0:d0:d3:c1:22	Destination MAC address
00:50:04:a6:72:2d	Source MAC address .
08:00	Type=08:00
SRC=192.168.10.2	The IP address of the source computer
DST=192.168.10.254	The IP address of the destination computer
LEN=328	The length of IP packets in bytes
TOS=00	The type of service Type field
PREC=0x00	The type of service Precedence field
TTL=64	The remaining Time To Live
ID=0	Unique ID for this packet
DF	Don't Fragment flag
PROTO=UDP	The TCP/IP protocol used: TCP, UDP, or ICMP
SPT=68	The TCP or UDP port of the source computer
DPT=67	The TCP or UDP port of the destination computer

9

TABLE 9.5 Command line text utilities.

Command Line Utility Name	General Function or Description
cut	Remove sections of a line.
grep "PATTERN"	Search for the specified pattern in a text file.
sort	Sort the output.
uniq	Remove all duplicate entries in the output. (Sort should be run prior to uniq.)
wc –l	Count the number of lines in the output.

most users. The following are examples of how these utilities can be used to examine log files:

Display all of the entries in the log file with a source IP address of 192.168.0.2:

```
grep "SRC=192.168.0.2" /var/log/shorewall.log
```

Count the number of entries in the log file with a source IP address of 192.168.0.2:

```
grep "SRC=192.168.0.2" /var/log/shorewall.log | wc -l
```

Display all of the TCP entries in the log file with a source IP address of 192.168.0.2:

```
grep "SRC=192.168.0.2" /var/log/shorewall.log | grep
"PROTO=TCP"
```

Provide a list of all source IP addresses that had dropped connections:

```
grep "DROP" /var/log/shorewall.log | cut -f5 -d"=" |
sort | uniq
```

The Unix manual pages provide additional information on each of these commands. You can access the manual pages from the SLAX system or other Unix system by entering man command at the command prompt. Due to limited space, these manual pages are not available on the LEAF firewall.

```
man grep
```

After entering the man grep command, the manual page or help screen for the grep command will be displayed.

Microsoft Excel for Log Analysis People with limited experience using Unix and the command prompt may find the Unix command line string processing utilities quite overwhelming. As with most technology tasks, however, there are multiple ways of achieving the same objective. Microsoft Excel, for example, can be used to provide a quick solution for sorting and evaluating log file data. Users can copy the shorewall.log file to a Windows-based system with Microsoft Office, open the file with Microsoft Excel, and then use all of the sorting and evaluation tools available in Microsoft Excel to analyze the data.

The standard File -> Open dialog box in Excel will automatically start the Text Import wizard if Excel is unable to recognize the file as an Excel document but can determine that it is an ASCII text file. By specifying a Delimited file as shown in Figure 9.2, Excel can determine the separation of fields in the log file.

Once Space is specified as the delimiter as demonstrated in Figure 9.3, Excel will separate the fields of the log file into columns. This will make it much easier to distinguish between fields.

After the file is loaded into Excel, it will look like the sample in Figure 9.4. From this point, you can use the Data->Sort option to sort by any or

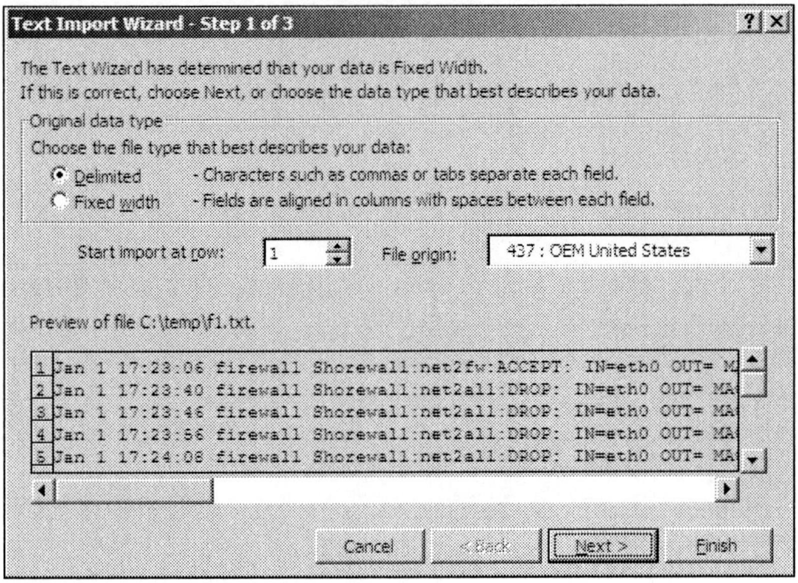

FIGURE 9.2 Importing into Excel.

several of the columns. Sorting by Protocol, IP, then by Destination Port (DPT) can help locate systems that have performed network scans. Sorting by Protocol, then Destination Port (DPT) can help find ports that are being heavily hit by network Trojans or other potentially problematic programs.

FIGURE 9.3 Importing into Excel—space delimiter.

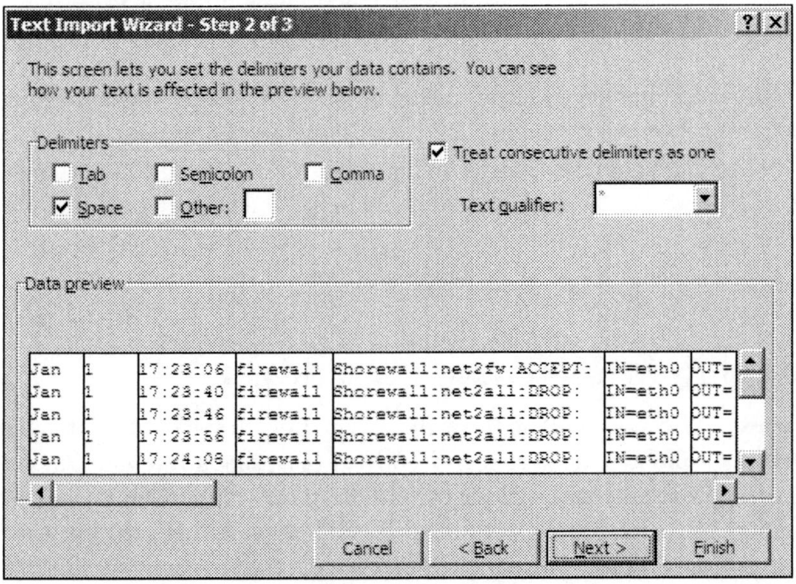

9

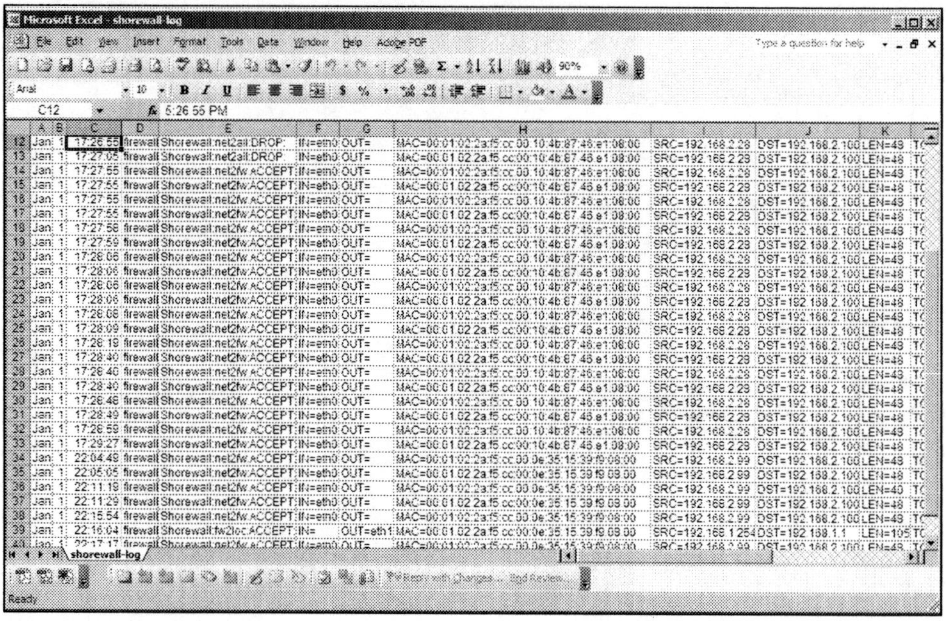

FIGURE 9.4 Excel view of log file.

Syslog and Cisco Routers

Like many other network devices, Cisco network equipment can log to a syslog server. If ACLs are used on Cisco routers to perform an initial layer of packet filtering, it is important to log any errors to a centralized log server. By default, Cisco network equipment is configured to log to the local7 facility. You can modify this by specifying a different facility in the router configuration:

```
logging facility local7
logging 192.168.1.1
```

Once the logging is configured properly, the word log can be added to the end of any access list entry, and it will be logged to the local7 facility on the logserver:

```
access-list 110 deny ip 192.168.0.0 any    log
```

Logging in Microsoft Windows

Microsoft Windows systems use the Event Log Service as their default mechanism for logging errors and notifications, much like Unix systems use syslogd. The Event Logs are broken down into three types of logs: Application, Security, and System logs. The Windows Event Log records information in a binary format and is only accessible using the Microsoft

Event Viewer. You can use the Event Viewer to export the log information to an ASCII file for further analysis.

The next section will cover enabling logging for the Windows XP firewall. The Windows XP firewall does not log its packet and connection information to the standard Event Log. Instead, when enabled, it logs packet information to a file much like Unix systems do. By default, the Windows XP Service Pack 2 firewall does not log any connection information.

Configuring Windows Firewall Logging

The default log setting for the Windows firewall is not to log anything. Although this setting might be acceptable once a system works properly, it is often useful to review the log information for dropped packets to determine why an application or connection is not working. The Windows XP firewall log setting can be reached via the Advanced tab from the Windows firewall configuration program. As shown in Figure 9.5, the Settings button corresponding to the Security Logging area should be selected to customize the logging settings.

FIGURE 9.5 Windows Firewall advanced Tab.

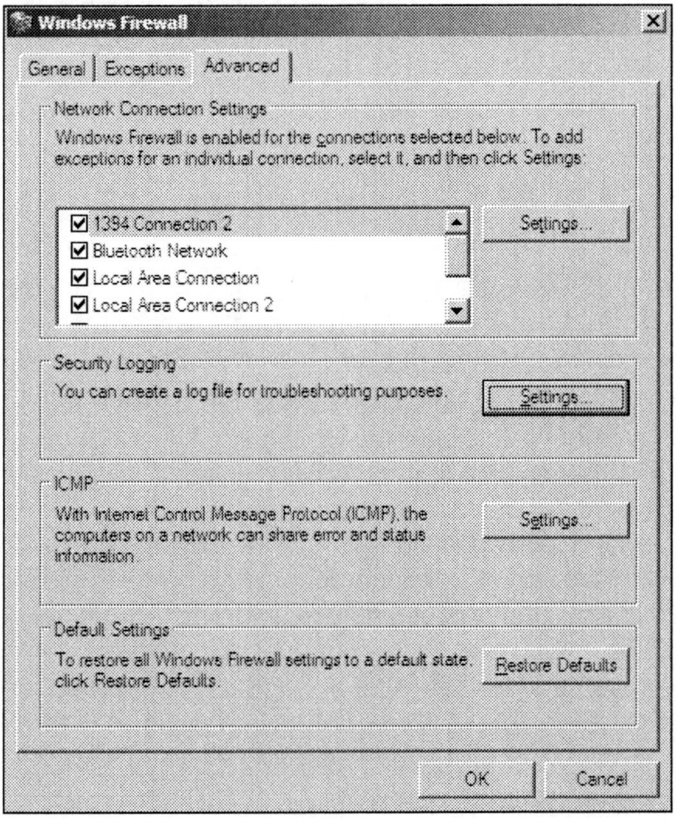

As indicated by Figure 9.6, placing a check in front of the Log dropped packets will turn on logging for all dropped packets. The default location for this log file is C:\WINDOWS\pfirewall.log, but you can change this location and filename to any location on the system. The default of 4096 Kbytes may be insufficient for keeping a detailed log of dropped packets, so you should consider increasing the size limit for this file. Unfortunately, however, the Windows firewall has a maximum firewall log file size of 32767 Kbytes. In busy network environments, this may be too small, and you may loose some of the log history unless you rotate the log file quite often. This limitation of the Windows firewall is another reason that you may need a more advanced firewall on a workstation.

Windows retains only one old log file. When the pfirewall.log file fills to the size indicated in the advanced firewall settings configuration, the file is renamed to pfirewall.log.old, and a new pfirewall.log file is created. If the pfirewall.log.old already exists, the previous file is deleted, thus providing no utility for archiving old log files.

If it is important to maintain an archive of log files, you will need to develop a script or batch file to rotate the log files daily. When the firewall is running and logging is enabled, the log file cannot be removed, renamed, or deleted; however, a small script program can be created that will change the firewall log file name each day.

FIGURE 9.6 Changing Windows Firewall log settings.

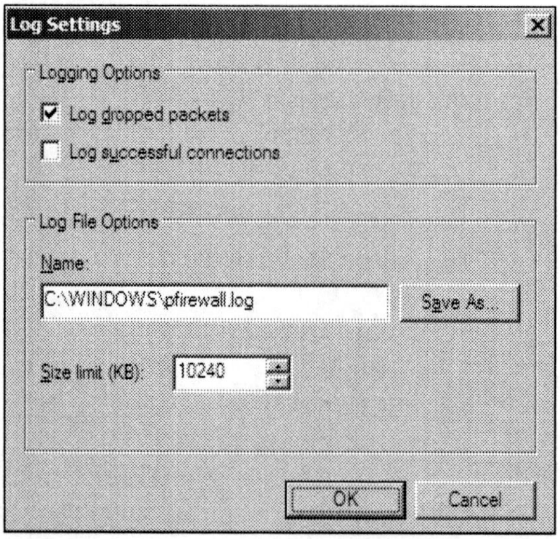

For example, the following command line sets the current log file to the name pfirewall.log.01212005. A script to rotate the log file could grab the current date and set the name of the log file to the current date at midnight each day:

```
netsh firewall set logging
filelocation=c:\windows\pfirewall.log.01212005
```

The ability to log all successful connections is also available, but you should use it with caution, as this could generate a vast amount of log information.

FYI: netsh Command

Windows XP includes a command line utility that allows you to view and modify network-related items such as routing, interface configurations, and the firewall. Execute the following commands to show the Windows XP firewall configuration:

```
C:\WINDOWS>netsh

netsh>firewall

netsh firewall>show config
```

9

Analyzing Windows Firewall Log

The information provided by the Windows firewall log is very similar to that provided by the shorewall.log file. Unlike the shorewall log file, each field does not include a designator to help identify the field, but a label row is written as the fourth line of the pfirewall.log file to provide a quick reference for the fields:

```
#Fields: date time action protocol src-ip dst-ip src-
port dst-port size tcpflags tcpsyn tcpack tcpwin icmp-
type icmpcode info path

2004-12-21 11:35:08 DROP TCP 192.0.2.151 192.0.2.10
58840 25 60 S 940735221 0 5840 - - - RECEIVE
```

Table 9.6 specifies the entries in the pfirewall.log file.

TABLE 9.6 Windows Firewall log fields.

Log Entry	Field	Description
2004-12-21	Date	year, month, day of the log entry YYYY-MM-DD
11:35:08	Time	time of the log entry HH:MM:SS
DROP	Action	action performed by the firewall OPEN,CLOSE,DROP, and INFO-EVENTS-LOST
TCP	protocol	TCP/IP protocol used: TCP, UDP, or ICMP
192.0.2.151	Src-ip	IP address of the source computer
192.0.2.10	dst-ip	IP address of the destination computer
58840	Src-port	TCP or UDP port of the source computer
25	dst-port	TCP or UDP port of the destination computer
60	Size	packet size in bytes
S	tcpflags	TCP control flags in the header. Ack, Fin, Psh, Rst, Syn, Urg
940735221	Tcpsyn	TCP sequence number of the packet
0	Tcpack	TCP acknowledgement number in the packet
5840	Tcpwin	TCP window size in bytes
-	icmptype	ICMP message type
-	icmpcode	ICMP message code
-	Info	
RECEIVE	Path	

Centralized Log Servers

In a network that consists of many servers and network devices, it is important to centralize the recording of log files to provide a single archive of log information and a single point from which to analyze it. Without this centralization, administrators must watch log files on many different systems. This centralization can make port scans and other attacks that hit several systems at once much easier to monitor and track.

Remote Syslog Servers

By creating a centralized log server, you can centralize the log output of servers and other network devices and provide a central point for secure log information that can be archived to appropriate media. This can be done by setting up a Unix or Linux server and enabling syslogd to receive log information from other servers on the network. Note that the remote logging feature of syslogd is turned off by default in all recent versions of Linux. To turn this feature on, you must start syslogd with the –r option:

```
syslogd -r
```

The server configured as the central syslogd server must be configured to start syslogd with this option enabled. Syslog uses UDP port 514 for the transfer of messages. If the Unix or Linux server is running any type of firewall or iptables, the firewall rules or iptables configuration must be modified to allow UDP port 514 incoming connections.

On the remote machines, the /etc/syslog.conf must be modified to send log information to the central log server. Make this modification by replacing the path for the logfile with @host where host is the name or IP address of the centralized log server:

```
auth.*; authpriv.*        @logserver.example.com
local1.*                  @logserver.example.com
mail.*                    @192.0.168.10
```

Time Synchronization for Correlation of Events

In the event of a system intrusion or attempted attack, you will often need to review the log files on many systems. To make accurate comparisons between log files on different systems, the time on both machines must be synchronized. Without this synchronization, you would have to adjust the times for every entry before any comparison can occur. Imagine trying to determine which system was attacked first if the log files from two separate systems are off by 4 minutes and 15 seconds.

The *Network Time Protocol* (NTP) is the most commonly used Internet protocol for synchronizing time on computers and network devices. NTP establishes connections to a network of systems that use atomic clocks to synchronize their time to *Coordinated Universal Time (UTC)* which is a worldwide time standard. It is important for all devices on a network to use some type of time synchronization to allow for easy correlation of events. Most organizations choose to set up an internal time server to assist in

> ## Caution
> **Syslog HUP**
>
> After making changes to the /etc/syslog.conf file, the syslogd process must be killed with the HUP (hangup) signal or the -1 option in order for the /etc/syslog.conf file to be reread.

9

synchronization of all network devices. The internal time server connects to one of the centralized NTP servers to adjust its time regularly. All servers on the local network can then connect to this time server to adjust their clock on a regular basis.

There is a facility in the LEAF firewall used with this book to set several parameters related to log files, and accomplish synchronization with a UTC time source. This file is /etc/lrp.conf. A display of several parameters is shown below:

```
# Log files in /var/log/ to rotate.
# DEPTH == Amount to keep.
lrp_LOGS_DAILY="daemon.log debug cron.log\
messages syslog user.log \
ppp.log pslave.log"
lrp_LOGS_WEEKLY="auth.log"
lrp_LOGS_MONTHLY="wtmp"
lrp_LOGS_DEPTH=4
# Email address to use for notices and alerts. If blank
alerts won't be sent.
#lrp_MAIL_ADMIN="admin@mydomain.net"
# Server that will be contacted via
#'rdate' for the time service daily.
# Turning this on also updates the CMOS clock
lrp_DATE_SERVER="time.nist.gov"
```

Notice that the phrase `lrp_LOGS_DEPTH=4` determines the number of days for which logs are kept. Also note the there are daily, weekly and monthly logs. Most are daily logs, but one log file, auth.log is rotated weekly. This indicates that we expect fewer entries in the auth.log file, which will contain logins from the console, via secure shell, and also for IPSec VPNs.

Another entry allows alerts to be sent to an email address. Finally, notice the phrase `lrp_DATE_SERVER="time.nist.gov"`. This allows the LEAF to synchronize with the National Institute of Standards time server. If you have a time server available from your ISP or campus network, it is preferable to use one close to your firewall. The farther away you are from the time server, the more error will occur in the time-stamps provided.

Daemon Tools (daemontl)

Where logging of Web site activity is desired, there is a package in LEAF called daemontl. For example, it may be desired to log access to certain Web sites containing pornography or other objectionable content such as Web sites of known terrorist organizations. Since the formation of the Department of Homeland Security, several ISPs have on-site FBI agents to monitor such activity. The daemontl package was first introduced in

Chapter 5 but no significant explanation of its benefits or purpose was made.

When daemontl is active, two additional processes are running on LEAF. Once is called svcan, and the other is multilog. Svscan and multilog work together to log Web page access from the internal network to a log file in the directory /var/log/dnscache. This log file is called "current." A sample of the file /var/log/dnscache/current is shown below, processed by the command tai64nlocal, which is provided by the daemontl package. If you visit the directory /var/log/dnscache and display the current file by use of the more command, you will see the date/time stamps represented as hexadecimal digits. IP addresses are left in hexadecimal form by the tai64nlocal command, as shown below. Use any calculator to convert each hexadecimal string to decimal:

```
# tai64nlocal < current
2005-04-24 21:22:57.566528500 query 266
c0a80a01:8001:c98e 1 download.fedora.redhat.com.
2005-04-24 21:22:57.566531500 cached 1 download.fedo-
ra.redhat.com.
2005-04-24 21:22:57.566533500 sent 266 76
2005-04-25 01:22:59.735197500 query 267
c0a80a01:8001:c98f 28 download.fedora.redhat.com.
2005-04-25 01:22:59.735203500 tx 0 28
download.fedora.redhat.com. . 892d1a13
2005-04-25 01:22:59.751738500 nodata 892d1a13 600 28
download.fedora.redhat.com.
2005-04-25 01:22:59.751740500 stats 267 18644 1 0
2005-04-25 01:22:59.751742500 sent 267 44
2005-04-25 01:22:59.752185500 query 268
c0a80a01:8001:c990 28 download.fedora.redhat.com.pri-
vate.network.
2005-04-25 01:22:59.752188500 tx 0 28
download.fedora.redhat.com.private.network. . 892d1a13
2005-04-25 01:22:59.760777500 nxdomain 892d1a13 3600
download.fedora.redhat.com.private.network.
2005-04-25 01:22:59.760780500 sent 268 60
2005-04-25 01:22:59.761152500 query 269
c0a80a01:8001:c991 1 download.fedora.redhat.com.
2005-04-25 01:22:59.761155500 tx 0 1
download.fedora.redhat.com. . 892d1a13
2005-04-25 01:22:59.779246500 rr 892d1a13 300 1 down-
load.fedora.redhat.com. 42bbe014
2005-04-25 01:22:59.779248500 rr 892d1a13 300 1 down-
load.fedora.redhat.com. d184b014
```

9

Notice that some of the lines are wrapped in the display above. There are several queries from the domain "private.network," which is the internal network domain name. Several of the entries are marked as "cached." This demonstrates the efficiency of the dnscache package which caches web pages for frequently visited sites. Notice that there are several "nxdomain" adjectives indicating that private.network is not a registered domain. Thus, the daemontl package provides more information than Web site access alone.

Software to Manage and Monitor Log Files

Due to the overwhelming size of log files on most networks, it is impossible for a network administrator to easily spot abnormal behavior, port scans, and other malicious activity in the log files. Several software packages have been developed to assist with the daily analysis of log files. Many of these packages can even send special alerts to the network administrator in the event of unusual activity.

Table 9.7 provides a list of several packages you should evaluate for assistance in managing and monitoring log files.

In addition to these utilities, the SANS (SysAdmin, Audit, Network, Security) Institute has created the Internet Storm Center (ISC) to provide a free analysis and warning service **http://isc.sans.org**. The ISC uses log file information submitted from sites across the Internet to help determine patterns of attack and warn against new threats. Sites can submit firewall log information to the ISC using a free and open source program called DShield (**www.dshield.org**). Since the ISC tracks activity across the globe, it is often useful to check the current port and activity on the ISC site and determine if this activity is affecting the local network or if firewall configuration changes should be updated to protect against a possible attack.

Summary

System log files provide a historical log of system activity and errors. The knowledge and skills you have learned throughout this book will be put into practice daily as you inspect the log files for malicious activity from the outside network, inappropriate activity from the internal network, configuration problems, and technical glitches. The log files should be the first point of reference for administrators trying to solve a problem. Understanding the format of log files and how to search the logs, along with an understanding of how the firewall works, will help you quickly locate and resolve problems.

TABLE 9.7 Log file tools

Package	URL / Description
fwAnalog	**http://tud.at/programm/fwanalog** A shell script that parses and summarizes firewall logfiles.
fwlogwatch	**http://fwlogwatch.inside-security.de** Produces log summary reports and analysis in plain text and HTML format for netfilter/iptables, ipchains, Cisco, Windows XP and other firewalls.
Logsurfer	**www.cert.dfn.de/eng/logsurf** Monitors text-based log files.
Swatch	**http://swatch.sourceforge.net** The Simple WATCHer and filter is a tool for monitoring log files and providing alerts in response to specific activity.
Wflogs	**www.wallfire.org/wflogs** A log analysis tool that can produce text or HTML reports or monitor firewall logs in real time.
Event Analyst	**www.eventanalyst.com** Examine cross sections of Windows event log records from multiple sources at once.
Event Archiver	**www.eventarchiver.com** Saves event log information from multiple machines into text logs and archives to an ODBC database.
Event Reporter	**www.eventreporter.com** Allows event log information to be sent to a syslog server.
Monilog	**www.monilog.com** Allows administrators to view digests of logs collected by Eventreporter or WinSysLog
WinSysLog	**www.winsyslog.com** Syslog server for windows.

9

Firewalls and VPNs provide a much needed layer of security to a company or organization's network. Through careful development of a firewall policy and installation and configuration of a Firewall and VPN, you will help shield the internal network from attack. Installation of software tools to monitor a centralized set of log files and alert you of suspicious activity will help you locate potential problems and update firewall rules before an attack can take place.

Test Your Skills

MULTIPLE CHOICE QUESTIONS

1. Log files provide a[n] _____ log of the transactions on a system or network.

   A. factual

   B. sequential

   C. historical

   D. all of the above

2. Log files do not include which of the following?

   A. invalid login attempts

   B. denied or dropped network connections

   C. critical hardware and software errors

   D. passwords

3. Log files are used for which of the following?

   A. troubleshooting dropped network connections

   B. forensic evidence

   C. providing a record of significant events

   D. all of the above

4. The _____ daemon is available on Unix systems to help automate the task of rotating log files.

   A. syslog

   B. cron

   C. NTP

   D. Event

5. Syslog uses the _____ name to indicate the part of the system the message originated from.

   A. level

   B. facility

   C. priority

   D. error code

6. Log files are normally found in the _____ directory on Unix systems.

    A. /etc

    B. /etc/log

    C. /log

    D. /var/log

7. _____ is the name of the configuration file for the syslog daemon.

    A. Syslogd

    B. Crontab

    C. Syslog.conf

    D. Shorewall.log

8. To change the log setting for policies in the LEAF firewall, what file should you change?

    A. /etc/shorewall/rules

    B. /etc/shorewall/policy

    C. /etc/shorewall/

    D. /etc/syslog.conf

9. Netfilter is a kernel module and therefore it uses the _____ facility for syslog logging.

    A. alert

    B. kern

    C. err

    D. info

10. Which of the following cannot be specified as a logging parameter in the shorewall policy or rules file?

    A. ULOG

    B. kern

    C. info

    D. debug

11. The DPT in the shorewall.log file indicates

    A. destination protocol.

    B. destination packet size.

    C. destination port.

    D. dropped packet.

12. _____ is a Unix command line utility that searches through a file for a given pattern.
    A. More
    B. Grep
    C. Vi
    D. Find

13. The firewall log can be imported as a _____ delimited file into Excel.
    A. tab
    B. comma
    C. space
    D. colon

14. Shorewall must be _____ each time the rules or policies are modified.
    A. stopped
    B. restarted
    C. killed with the HUP or -1
    D. enabled

15. If the log parameter in the shorewall rules or policy file is info, messages will be written to
    A. ulogd.
    B. syslog.log.
    C. kern.info.
    D. network.info.

16. By default, logging on the Windows XP firewall is:
    A. enabled
    B. disabled
    C. enabled for dropped connections only
    D. enabled for all connections

17. The default location of the Windows firewall log is
    A. c:\log\pfirewall.log.
    B. c:\WINDOWS\SYSTEM32\firewall.log.
    C. c:\WINDOWS\pfirewall.log.
    D. c:\log\firewall.log.

18. Syslog must be started with this option to allow it to receive connections from remote hosts:

    A. syslog -l

    B. syslog -n

    C. syslog -r

    D. syslog -s

19. Logging to a remote server is specified by using a _____ in front of the IP address or host name.

    A. &

    B. @

    C. ;

    D. #

20. _____ is a commonly used time protocol for synchronizing time on computers and network devices.

    A. Domain Time Protocol

    B. Universal Time Protocol

    C. Network Time Protocol

    D. Centralized Time Protocol

EXERCISES

Exercise 9.1: Analyzing Shorewall Logs with Excel

1. Load the example shorewall.log file for Exercise 9.1 from the book Web site into Excel.

2. Answer the following questions:

    When did the log file start?

    When does the log file end?

    How many entries are in the log file?

    How many packets bound to destination port 137 were dropped?

    How many packets bound to destination port 22 were accepted?

    How many computers ran port scans?

Exercise 9.2: Analyzing Windows Logs with Excel

1. Load the example Windows pfirewall.log file for Exercise 9.2 from the book Web site into Excel.

2. Answer the following questions:

   When did the log file start?

   When does the log file end?

   How many entries are in the log file?

   How many packets bound to destination port 137 were dropped?

   How many packets bound to destination port 22 were accepted?

   How many computers ran port scans?

Exercise 9.3: Viewing the Log Files from the Firewall Weblet

1. Reconfigure the firewall and SLAX network configuration so that you have a firewall and an internal SLAX machine.

2. Use a Web browser on the Internal machine to connect to the firewall weblet.

3. Download the shorewall.log file to the Web browser using the Web interface.

4. Import this file into Excel and submit the Excel file.

Exercise 9.4: Troubleshooting Firewall Problems

1. Determine the reason the packets were dropped for each of the following log entries. (What firewall rule, policy, or setting caused the packet to be dropped?)

```
/etc/interfaces
net eth0   detect   dhcp,routefilter,norfc1918
loc eth1   detect
/etc/policy
loc  net   ACCEPT
net  all   DROP   ULOG
all  all   REJECT   ULOG
/etc/rules
ACCEPT fw    loc    tcp    22
ACCEPT fw    loc    tcp    80
```

```
Dec 31 16:12:44 firewall Shorewall:all2all:REJECT:
IN=eth1 OUT=
MAC=00:10:4b:31:54:04:00:01:02:2b:21:59:08:00
SRC=192.168.1.1 DST=192.168.2.100 LEN=40 TOS=00
PREC=0x00 TTL=50 ID=22313 PROTO=TCP SPT=35030
DPT=165 SEQ=1308099071 ACK=0 WINDOW=3072 SYN
URGP=0

Jan 5 01:46:43 firewall Shorewall:net2fw:DROP:
IN=eth0 OUT=
MAC=00:01:02:2a:f5:cc:00:0e:35:15:39:f9:08:00
SRC=192.168.2.99 DST=192.168.2.100 LEN=48 TOS=00
PREC=0x00 TTL=128 ID=51592 DF PROTO=TCP SPT=3795
DPT=80 SEQ=3288664372 ACK=0 WINDOW=16384 SYN
URGP=0

Jan 2 03:29:00 firewall Shorewall:rfc1918:DROP:
IN=eth0 OUT=
MAC=00:01:02:2a:f5:cc:00:0e:35:15:39:f9:08:00
SRC=192.168.2.99 DST=192.168.2.100 LEN=48 TOS=00
PREC=0x00 TTL=128 ID=7711 DF PROTO=TCP SPT=3827
DPT=22 SEQ=2917628917 ACK=0 WINDOW=16384 SYN
URGP=0
```

Exercise 9.5: Review ISC port Activity

1. Connect to the ISC Web site.

2. Look at the port History and list the top five active ports.

3. Using knowledge from previous chapters, determine what services this traffic corresponds to.

4. What information should you look for in your log files for activity using these same ports?

PROJECTS

Project 9.1: Enabling Windows Firewall Logging

1. Enable logging in the Windows firewall.

2. Modify the settings to capture all information.

3. Use the computer to browse the Web for 15 minutes.

4. Load the pfirewall.log file into Excel.

5. Analyze the log file and provide the following information:

How many Web servers were visited?

What was the IP address of each Web server?

How many connections were dropped?

Why were they dropped?

Provide a log entry that includes a TCP SYN number.

Project 9.2: Observing a Port Scan

1. Set up the firewall and attach one system to eth1 that can be booted with SLAX.

2. Boot the SLAX system.

3. From the SLAX system, perform an nmap scan of the firewall box.

4. Review the shorewall.log file and determine how you can tell an nmap scan took place.

Project 9.3: Configuring Remote syslog Logging

1. Enable syslog remote logging on SLAX. Log from firewall to SLAX.

2. Set up the firewall and attach one system to eth1 that can be booted with SLAX.

3. Boot the SLAX system with the "SLAX server" option.

4. Use ifconfig to determine the IP address of the SLAX host.

5. Login to the SLAX system and enable sysylogd to receive network syslog messages.

Use ps –ax syslogd to find the syslog process:

```
root@slax:/var/log# ps -x | grep syslog

1847 ? Ss 0:00 /usr/sbin/syslogd
```

Use kill -9 PID to kill the syslogd process:

```
kill -9 1847
```

Start a new syslogd process with the –r option:

```
/usr/sbin/syslogd -r
```

6. Edit the /etc/hosts file on the firewall and add an entry for a host called logserver with the IP address of the SLAX machine:

```
logserver     192.168.1.1
```

7. Edit the /etc/syslog.conf file and change the logging entry for auth, authpriv to log to the remote logserver:

```
auth,authpriv.*    @logserver
```

8. Execute a kill -1 on the syslogd process on the firewall:

```
# ps -x | grep syslogd

29721 root 816 S /sbin/syslogd -m 240

# kill -1 29721
```

9. Logout and login to the firewall and see if the entry is written to /var/log/secure file on the SLAX host.

9

Case Study

ResTech University is having a hard time managing log files. The university currently has a Cisco router that attaches its network to the Internet and a LEAF firewall installed in each of its eight residence hall buildings. It has a mail server and a Web server on the network also. The system and network administrators currently spend at least one hour each day logging into each of these servers and checking the log files.

Develop a detailed plan to help ResTech centralize its log files. Indicate what specific changes and configuration changes would be necessary on each system to achieve this centralization and what software would be necessary. Provide a detailed summary of how this will change the administrators' daily task of reviewing the log files.

Appendix | A

Generating CD and Diskette Bootable Media

Generating Operating Systems Images

All of the images for CDs on the book Web site are ISO-9660 standard images. All of the floppy images are in ".IMZ" format as well as the .BIN format. The IMZ format is predominantly supported by the package WinImage, but can be converted to other formats.

You should know a few relevant facts about the ISO-9660 format. First, the ISO format is an image of a 9660 file system. There is wide operating system support for ISOs, as files with the .iso extension are called. The ISO concept is that any operating system should be able to read and write the ISO-9660 file system.

There are extensions to ISO that go beyond a few ISO limitations. Since ISOs are, in theory, operating system neutral, there is a problem allowing permissions like NTFS™ or Unix™ to be propagated. To get around this, the Rock Ridge extension allows preservation of Unix™ permissions and longer ASCII names. Microsoft's Joliet extension allows Unicode names. (The LEAF firewalls support the Joliet extension.) The El Torito extension allows the CDs to be bootable. The first version of the El Torito standard was a joint effort between Phoenix Technologies and IBM in 1995. Virtually all computers manufactured since that time have supported the El Torito standard in the PC BIOS.

Downloading the SLAX CD Images

The SLAX images must be downloaded to a computer with the following two features:

- A CD-R or CD-R/W CDROM drive

- CD burning software

A CD-R drive is a CD-Recordable drive, which allows you to actually write the CD media called a CD/R. A CD-R/W drive is a CD-Re-Writable drive. This type of drive uses a different type of CD media that can be rewritten many times. These drives can also write a CD/R.

There are many popular CD-burning software packages. Some computers may come with this software as a complement to the operating system distribution. When Windows XP first débuted, there was a concern about copyright infringement. Windows XP alone does not have CD-burning software available from the Programs menu, but when a CD/R is inserted into the drive, a menu will pop up with some options for burning the CD.

CD burning software often has direct capabilities for generating music or data CDs. Data CDs are not the same as bootable image CDs. Data CDs are used simply for the transfer of files. Often, CD-burning software has a "backup" menu, which will allow you to record an image to the CD.

There are several options upon bootup that are available with SLAX. Once the SLAX CD is inserted into the drive and rebooted, a **very brief** opportunity exists when this prompt appears:

```
boot: linux
```

If you do nothing at this point, this prompt will shortly proceed with the boot process and the mode that SLAX will produce is "client" mode. No services, such as telnet or DNS, will be available. If you immediately begin to type when you see this prompt, the boot process will wait until you have entered one or more options. One such option is:

```
boot: linux server
```

Typing this prompt causes several services to be offered by the machine. Another option is:

```
boot: linux copy2ram
```

SLAX normally requires the CD to stay in the drive, and as programs are needed, they are pulled from the CD. With the copy2ram option, the CD will not be locked into the drive, and you may eject it at any time. However, the entire SLAX CD will be loaded into memory, requiring at least 256 Mbytes of RAM. These above options may be used in combination with each other, for example:

```
boot: linux server copy2ram
```

You will be instructed to use other options from several chapters in the book, for example the "load=" option. This option can be appended to the boot prompt as well

Finally, we have spoken extensively about Windows-related issues. You need not use a Windows machine to perform the burning process. See the next section on firewall images for information about using Linux systems to burn CDs.

Burning the CD

Once you have ensured the above requirements are met, download the image from the book Web site to the computer. Navigate your CD-burning software to select the image and burn the CD. If you have Windows XP, and are using a separate CD-burning package, you will still get the pop-up dialog box about using the built-in Windows XP capability. Simply cancel this dialog box and proceed with your own CD-burning package.

Generating Firewall Images

CDROM Images The firewall images for CDs on the book Web site are also ISOs. The same procedure for SLAX applies to these images. You will need a computer with the same features, but it need not be a Windows computer. Let's use the example of a Linux system. With minimal installation of Linux, most systems will have the following commands:

- mount
- dd

With these two commands you can download any image from the book Web site and burn a CD. Simply download your image and issue the command at a Linux prompt:

```
dd if=<image file name of>=/dev/cdrom
```

Some Linux systems may have a SCSI CDROM drive, or a DVD drive that can burn CDs. In these cases you may need to use commands like:

```
dd if=<image file name> of=/dev/dvd
dd if=<image file name> of=/dev/scdo
```

Substitute the actual image file name, including the full path if you are not in the same directory as the image, for the text **<image file name>** in the above commands.

If you wish, you may verify the media you just burned. To do this, issue the following commands (before or after you burn the CD):

```
md5sum <image file name> > md5sum-file.txt
md5sum /dev/cdrom < md5sum-cdrom.txt
diff md5sum-file.txt md5sum-cdrom.txt
```

Alternatively, you can use the loop-back mount method on the original image:

```
mount /dev/cdrom
mount -t iso9660 <image file name> /mnt/isotest -o loop
diff -r /dev/cdrom /mnt/isotext
```

In addition, some Linux systems may also have the commands:

- cdrecord
- mkisofs

The cdrecord command can be used to burn the image to CD:

```
cdrecord -v dev=3,0,0 <image file name>
```

Finally, you can make an ISO image out of any collection of files using the mkisofs command. This is useful if you have a Linux system, perhaps without GUI tools that allow you to add and delete files from an ISO. In the course of your work, you will need to update packages. When you have finalized several packages, it is more reliable to put them back into the CD image. To do this, you will have to have previously extracted the files from the original image or CD. One way to do this is to transfer the original image into a directory using the command:

```
mkisofs -RJ -o /<burndir>/ <image file name>
```

where **<burndir>** is a directory of your choice (hint: use `mkdir` **<burndir>**). The –R and –J parameters are optional, but implement the Rock Ridge and Joliet extensions.

Then, let us suppose that the method you are using is CD-ROM boot with a standard MS-DOS 1.44-Mbyte "helper" floppy. Once you have several packages finalized for your environment, copy the packages into **<burndir>** by the commands:

```
mount -t msdos /dev/fd0 /mnt
cp <package1> <burndir>
cp ....
```

Then, using a new CD/R media (or a CDR/W), issue the commands:

```
mkisofs -RJ -o <image file name2> /<burndir>/
dd if=<image file name2> of=/dev/cdrom
```

Note that we suggest preserving you original image until you can verify that the new one works, by using a different image name, **<image file name2>**.

Floppy Diskette Images To create a floppy diskette from an image, we first visit the situation where you have a Linux or other Unix operating system available. Most of the time this will be for a floppy boot system, so the format will be 1.68 Mbyte. Issue the commands:

```
fdformat /dev/fd0u1680
dd if=<image file name> of=/dev/fd0u1680
```

As you learned in Chapter 5, the dd command above is a method of creating a 1.68-Mbyte floppy diskette. Occasionally some machines may have low-quality floppy drives that will not boot from a floppy at that density. To get around this, you must have a CD-ROM from which you can read packages, since the only option may be to boot from a 1.44-Mbyte floppy. It turns out the basic contents of the boot diskette image for LEAF firewalls will fit on a 1.44-Mbyte floppy (barely). If this is your situation, issue the commands:

```
fdformat /dev/fd0
dd if=<image file name> of=/dev/fd0
```

This will create a boot floppy at 1.44 Mbytes and you will need to adjust the syslinux.cfg kernel boot line to read packages from the CD-ROM. (Leaf.cfg should still fit on the boot floppy.)

Creating a Crossover Cable

The most common Ethernet cable is the unshielded twisted pair (UTP) with RJ45 connectors on each end. The opposite of a crossover cable is a regular or straight-though cable. In straight-through cables, as the name implies, each wire is on the same pin on either end's connector. To make a crossover cable, you will need:

- Crimpers for RJ45 connectors
- RJ45 connectors
- Wire strippers or cutters
- Ethernet cabling (bulk roll)

RJ45 connectors have eight gold pins, or fingers, exposed. An RJ45 connector is by convention a male connector, while a switch or Ethernet NIC will have the female connector. The purpose of a crossover cable is to swap the Transmit (Tx) and Receive (Rx) pins at one end of the cable.

The following figure illustrates the pin arrangement and the crossover function. The "crossed-over" end is on the right side of Figure A.1. In a straight-through cable, the top two pins would be two Tx lines. Note that the pin numbers begin at the bottom of the connector on the left, but begin at the top on the right. Essentially, by following the colors of the cable pairs, Tx, which is orange/orange-white twisted pair, is pins 1 and 2 on the left. It is routed to pins 3 and 6, counting from the top of the connector on the right. The Rx twisted pair is similarly swapped from its normal position.

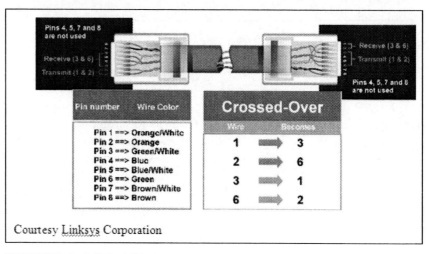

Courtesy Linksys Corporation

FIGURE A.1 RJ45 Pin-outs.

The crossover cable has several purposes:

■ Allowing two Ethernet NICs to be used back-to-back without a switch

■ Allowing two switches to be used back-to-back

The latter purpose has become unnecessary for most new ethernet switches, but occasionally old switches or broadcast hubs require crossover cables between their regular ports. The exception to this is a port on a switch marked "uplink." Then, no crossover cable is necessary.

If you look closely at the RJ45 connector, you will see that each gold pin has a sharp triangular "knife" that the crimper tool presses through the wire insulation to make a contact with the wire. Cut them off evenly so that the wires will extend completely under these triangular edges. You will not need to actually strip the wires.

Finally, realize that the purpose of twisted pairs of wires is to reduce interference. You must untwist the wires and flatten them to fit into the rectangular slot of the RJ45 connector leading to the gold pins. The recommendation is to untwist no more than one-half inch of each pair.

Appendix B

Laboratory Setup and Hardware Requirements

One of the goals of this book is to use low-cost, easily available hardware to create a small network and to help you understand and learn about firewalls and VPNs. A combination of one, two, or three computers is necessary to complete the exercises and projects in the book. In the full firewall configuration, one computer will serve as the firewall, and two computers will serve as internal and external systems on each side of the firewall. This appendix will provide details to prepare your hardware for the exercises and projects.

FYI: No hard drive needed

SLAX Linux and the Bering Firewall do not require that any information be stored on the hard drive. The computer doesn't need to have a hard drive installed. Therefore, you can use an existing computer for the exercises and projects and, immediately after you complete the exercise, reboot the computer and use it for its intended purpose. In this scenario it is important to reconnect any network cables appropriately.

SLAX

SLAX (**http://slax.linux-live.org**), created by Tomas Matejicek, is one of several Linux Live distributions providing a bootable CD running Linux directly from the CD without the need for installation on a hard drive. This provides a full Linux installation you can carry with you and use on almost any computer in a matter of seconds. In this book, SLAX provides the ability to use several UNIX tools and utilities without the need of installing the Linux operating system on a computer. Because SLAX runs entirely from the CD-ROM, you can use it on almost any computer without fear of damaging an existing operating system installation or needing administrator access to the machine.

The system requirements for SLAX are very minimal. If you are trying to use SLAX with minimal hardware, the main consideration is for the machine to have the ability to boot directly from the CD-ROM. The BIOS chip on older 486 and Pentium based systems may not provide the ability to boot directly from the CD-ROM.

SLAX Requirements

- BIOS – CD Boot-Enabled
- 128-MB Memory
- 486DX 66MHz or faster PC
- CD-ROM Drive
- Ethernet Network Adapter
- PS/2 or USB Keyboard and mouse
- VGA Video Card & Monitor
- NO HARD DRIVE IS REQUIRED

Booting the Computer

After determining your hardware meets the minimum requirements, you are ready to start. Create a bootable CD-ROM from the ISO image on the book's Web site. See Appendix A if you are unsure of how to write the SLAX ISO image to the CD-ROM. Once you have created the CD, you are ready to insert the CD into the computer and begin using SLAX. You should test to ensure you can boot SLAX on a computer with the CD before attempting to start the lab exercises. SLAX startup steps:

1. Create a bootable SLAX CD-ROM (See Appendix A).
2. Turn on the computer.

Welcome to YOUR Live CD. Hit Enter to continue booting or press F1 for help...
boot:

FIGURE B.1 SLAX boot screen.

3. Place the CD-ROM in the drive on the computer.

4. Reset the computer so it will boot from the CD.

If the SLAX boot screen (Figure B.1) does not appear after a few seconds, the boot order on your computer's BIOS may need to be changed. Most computers have a BIOS setting that determines the order in which devices are checked to locate a bootable operating system. The system must be configured to check the CD-ROM before it checks the hard drive. If this is not the case, you will need to enter the BIOS configuration (Del, F2, or the appropriate BIOS setup key sequence when your computer starts) and change the boot order.

When the initial SLAX boot screen appears, you have about two seconds to enter the boot parameters at the boot: prompt. If you do not press a key, SLAX will begin to boot normally. Pressing F1 at the boot: prompt will allow you to view a list of boot options, as shown in Table B.1.

After the SLAX boot completes, you are presented with the login prompt. The login to use for the SLAX system is:

```
slax login: root
Password:   toor
```

TABLE B.1 SLAX boot options

Boot Command	Description
boot: linux server	Boot SLAX into server mode. Server mode automatically starts DNS, sshd, SMTP, httpd and other server services.
boot: linux server copy2ram	Start in server mode and copy all module images to RAM so the CD-ROM isn't accessed. You must have enough free RAM to do this. Not recommended on machines with less than 256 MB.
boot: linux server load=internal	Start in server mode and configure system IP address for internal mode. Interfaces configured as follows: eth0 192.168.10.1 eth0:1 192.168.10.2 eth0:2 192.168.10.3
boot: linux server load=external	Start in server mode and configure system IP address for external mode. Interfaces configured as follows: eth0 192.168.1.1 eth0:1 192.168.1.2 eth0:2 192.168.1.3

Bering Firewall

The LEAF Bering (**http://leaf.sourceforge.net/bering**) firewall distribution is one of several Linux Embedded Appliance Firewall (LEAF) distributions. Bering uses the Linux 2.4.x kernel and iptables to provide firewall functionality. The Shorewall firewall is built into Bering and provides a basic interface for configuring the firewall features. Bering is intended to provide an embedded firewall with little overhead and is capable of running entirely from a floppy disk. A CD-ROM of Bering is available on the book Web site and this image will be used for exercises and projects in the book. The Bering firewall also has the ability to add plug-in modules including VPN support and proxy services. The VPN support is used in Chapter 8.

The system requirements for Bering are very minimal. The most important hardware components for the Bering firewall are the two Ethernet interface adapters, floppy drive, and a bootable CD-ROM. The BIOS chip on older 486 and Pentium-based systems may not provide the ability to boot directly from the CD-ROM.

Bering Firewall Minimum System Requirements

- 486DX 66MHz or faster PC
- BIOS—CD Boot Enabled
- 32 MB RAM
- 3.5-inch Floppy to save system changes
- Bootable CD-ROM
- 2 Supported Ethernet Network Adapters
- PS/2 Keyboard
- NO HARD DRIVE IS REQUIRED

Booting the Computer

After determining that your hardware meets the minimum requirements, you are ready to start. Create a bootable CD-ROM from the ISO image on the book's web site. See Appendix A if you are unsure of how to write the Bering ISO image to the CD-ROM. Once you have created the CD, you are ready to insert the CD into the computer and begin using and configuring the Bering firewall.

1. Create a bootable Bering CD-ROM (See Appendix A).
2. Turn on the computer.
3. Place the CD-ROM in the drive on the computer.
4. Reset the computer so it will boot from the inserted CD.

If the Bering boot screen (Figure A.2) does not appear after a few seconds, the boot order on your computer may need to be changed. Most computers have a BIOS setting that determines the order devices are checked to locate a bootable operating system. The system must be configured to check the CD-ROM before it checks the hard drive. If this is not the case, you will need to enter the BIOS configuration (Del, F2, or some the appropriate BIOS setup key sequence when your computer starts) and change the boot order.

After the Bering boot completes, you are presented with the login prompt. The login to use for the Bering firewall is as follows:

```
firewall login:   root
Password:   Rootr00t
```

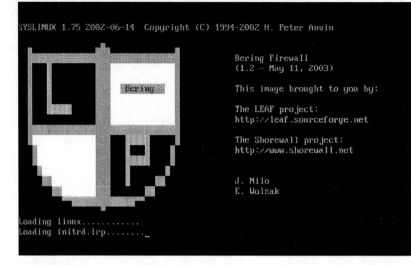

FIGURE B.2 Bering boot screen.

Bering Ethernet Adapters

One of the first challenges to address before beginning to configure and use the Bering firewall is making sure that your Ethernet adapters are recognized properly. The Bering firewall supports a variety of Ethernet adapters. It is important for you to know what adapter is installed in your computer before trying to configure the adapters. The default image available on the book Web site has the 3Com driver 3c59x.o installed. If you are using the 3Com adapter, you should not need to do anything more.

If your Ethernet adapter is not recognized by default, the appropriate driver or *.o file for your card must be installed in the /lib/modules directory and you must edit the /etc/modules file to be sure the line corresponding to your Ethernet adapter is uncommented. Chapter 5 provides additional information on this configuration. The following are the primary steps necessary for this configuration (Olszewski 2002):

- Copy the proper driver *.o file and any support files such as eepro100.o and pci-scan.o to the /lib/modules directory.

- Add the appropriate module name/driver to the /etc/modules file. Note that lines that begin with a # are comments and are ignored by the system at boot.

- Use the lrcfg program to backup the modules and etc packages.

- Reboot the firewall.

TABLE B.2 Drivers and Ethernet adapters.

/lib/modules Driver	Description
3c59x.o	3Com Ethernet Adapters 3c5xx and 3c9xx
eepro100.o	On-board Intel EtherExpress Prot100 adapters
Natsemi	National Semiconductor DP83810 PCI Adapters
ne.o	NE1000/NE2000 ISA Adapters
ne2k-pci.o	NE2000 PCI Adapters
tulip.o	DECchip Tulip dc21x4x PCI adapters.

Note: pci-scan.o must be loaded before PCI modules. 8390.o must be loaded before ne.o and ne2k-pci.o.

Additional details on configuring the network adapter can be found at **http://sourceforge.net/docman/display_doc.php?docid=1418&group_id=13751**

Connecting the Equipment

Throughout the book, a variety of configurations are used in exercises and projects to create a networking environment. Each configuration requires a slightly different cabling and lab setup. The following diagrams and notes are intended to assist you in setting up each of these environments.

Back-to-Back Configuration

The back-to-back configuration provides two computers connected via a single crossover cable. This provides a completely isolated network and is used for projects in Chapter 1 and Chapter 2. The configuration may also be useful for the Chapter 3 and Chapter 4 projects with Nmap and Nessus scanning to ensure the scanning is confined to a restricted environment. Because this is an isolated network with no DHCP server, the IP addresses on both computers must be configured manually. SLAX provides an environment with all of the necessary components for this exercise. Two SLAX CDs will be required, one CD in each computer. You will need to boot the two systems using the server boot option for SLAX.

```
boot: linux server
```

Once the systems are booted and you login with the root user and the password toor, you will need to configure the Ethernet interfaces. To do this

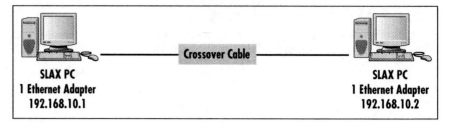

FIGURE B.3 Back-to-back configuration.

using ifconfig, execute the following command on the appropriate system as indicated by Figure B.3.

```
ifconfig eth0 192.168.10.1 netmask 255.255.255.0 broad-
cast 192.168.10.255
ifconfig eth0 192.168.10.2 netmask 255.255.255.0 broad-
cast 192.168.10.255
```

Once the configuration has been completed you should use the ifconfig command on each machine to insure the interfaces are configured properly.

Isolated Network with Firewall, Internal and External Machines

Chapter 5 provides an initial setup of a firewall with an external and an internal machine attached to the firewall. This setup can be completed with three computers and two crossover cables. Figure B.4 demonstrates the components of this configuration. This configuration is detailed at great length in Chapter 5.

FIGURE B.4 Isolated network configuration.

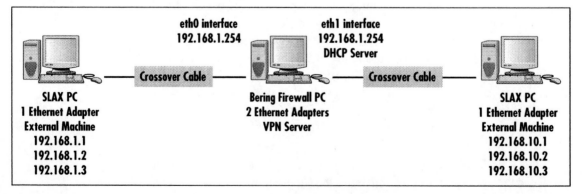

Firewall and Internal Network Connected to the Internet

Once everything has been tested and is working properly using the isolated network configuration above, the firewall can be connected to the Internet as shown in Figure B.5. Most ISPs or local networks will use DHCP to provide an address to the external interface (eth0) of the firewall. If the eth0 interface should obtain a DHCP address from an external DHCP server, the /etc/network/interfaces file on the Bering firewall will need to be modified to allow the interface to receive an IP address via dhcp.

```
auto eth0
iface eth0 inet dhcp
```

Remember to use lrcfg to back up the etc module before rebooting.

Caution
DHCP Warning

It is extremely important to ensure that eth0 is the interface connected to the Internet and that DHCP is not running on this interface. Other users on the external network may have problems if eth1 is connected to the Internet and the DHCP server is running on this port.

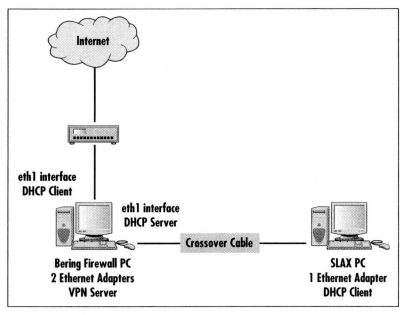

FIGURE B.5 Internet connected firewall and VPN

Appendix  C

TCP and UDP Port List

Well-Known Ports (0–1023)

The Internet Assigned Numbers Authority (IANA) is responsible for assigning numbers for the well-known ports. These ports are 0–1023 and can only be used by processes with privileged or root access on most systems. A current list of well-known ports can be found at **www.iana.org/assignments/port-numbers**. Table C.1 provides a list of some assigned well-known ports. The Protocol column in the table is populated for the most commonly used services. Both the TCP and UDP port numbers are registered for most services although many do not use both TCP and UDP.

TABLE C.1 Well-known ports for TCP services.

Port	Protocol	Service	Description
7	TCP & UDP	echo	Echo (RFC 792)
9	TCP & UDP	discard	Discard
11		systat	Active Users
17	TCP	qotd	Quote of the Day
20	TCP	ftp-data	File Transfer [Default Data] (RFC 959)
21	TCP	ftp	File Transfer [Control] (RFC 959)
22	TCP	Ssh	SSH Remote Login Protocol (SSH RFC)
23	TCP	telnet	Telnet (RFC 854)
25	TCP	smtp	Simple Mail Transfer (RFC 821, 822)
37	TCP & UDP	time	Time
43	TCP	nickname	Who Is
49	TCP & UDP	tacacs	Login Host Protocol (TACACS)
53	UDP & TCP	domain	Domain Name Server (RFC 1034,1035)

CONTINUED ON NEXT PAGE

Port	Protocol	Service	Description
63		whois++	whois++
65		tacacs-ds	TACACS-Database Service
66		sql*net	Oracle SQL*NET
67	UDP	bootps	Bootstrap Protocol Server
68	UDP	bootpc	Bootstrap Protocol Client (RFC 2131)
69	UDP	tftp	Trivial File Transfer
70	TCP	gopher	Gopher (RFC 1436)
79	TCP	finger	Finger (RFC 1288)
80	TCP	http	World Wide Web HTTP (RFC 1945,2068)
88	TCP	kerberos	Kerberos (RFC 1510)
92		npp	Network Printing Protocol
110	TCP	pop3	Post Office Protocol - Version 3 (RFC 1081, 1082)
111	TCP & UDP	sunrpc	SUN Remote Procedure Call (RFC 1057)
113	TCP	ident	Authentication Service (RFC 931)
115		sftp	Simple File Transfer Protocol (RFC 913)
119	TCP	nntp	Network News Transfer Protocol (RFC 977)
123		ntp	Network Time Protocol (RFC 1119,1305)
135	TCP & UDP	epmap	DCE endpoint resolution – Microsoft RPC locator
136		profile	PROFILE Naming System
137	TCP & UDP	netbios-ns	Microsoft NETBIOS Name Service (RFC 1001)
138	TCP & UDP	netbios-dgm	Microsoft NETBIOS Datagram Service (RFC 1001)
139	TCP & UDP	netbios-ssn	Microsoft NETBIOS Session Service (RFC 1001, 1002)
143	TCP	imap	Internet Message Access Protocol (RFC 2060)
160	UDP	sgmp-traps	SGMP-TRAPS
161	UDP	snmp	SNMP (RFC 1157)
162		snmptrap	SNMPTRAP
177		xdmcp	X Display Manager Control Protocol
179	TCP	bgp	Border Gateway Protocol
194	tcp	irc	Internet Relay Chat Protocol
201		at-rtmp	AppleTalk Routing Maintenance
202		at-nbp	AppleTalk Name Binding
203		at-3	AppleTalk Unused
204		at-echo	AppleTalk Echo

CONTINUED ON NEXT PAGE

Port	Protocol	Service	Description
205		at-5	AppleTalk Unused
206		at-zis	AppleTalk Zone Information
213		ipx	IPX
215		softpc	Insignia Solutions
220		imap3	Interactive Mail Access Protocol v3
264	TCP	bgmp	Border Gateway multicast Protocol
387	UDP	aurp	Appletalk Update-Based Routing Pro.
389	TCP	ldap	Lightweight Directory Access Protocol (RFC 1777,1778)
396		netware-ip	Novell Netware over IP
407		timbuktu	Timbuktu
443	TCP	https	http protocol over TLS/SSL
445	TCP & UDP	microsoft-ds	Microsoft-DS Active Directory
458		appleqtc	apple quick time
464	TCP & UDP	kpasswd	kpasswd
500	UDP	isakmp	isakmp
512		exec	remote process execution;
513	TCP	login	remote login Rlogin
514	UDP	syslog	cmd - syslog
515	TCP	lpr	printer spooler (RFC 1179)
517		talk	like tenex link, but across
518		ntalk	
519		utime	unixtime
520	UDP	router-rip	Routing Information Protocol (RIP-1 and RIP-2)
521		ripng	ripng
525		timed	timeserver
529		irc-serv	IRC-SERV
543		klogin	
544		kshell	krcmd
545		appleqtcsrvr	appleqtcsrvr
546	UDP	dhcpv6-client	DHCPv6 Client
547	UDP	dhcpv6-server	DHCPv6 Server
554	TCP & UDP	rtsp	Real Time Stream Control Protocol (RFC 2326)
563		nntps	nntp protocol over TLS/SSL (was snntp)

CONTINUED ON NEXT PAGE

Port	Protocol	Service	Description
565		whoami	whoami
631		ipp	Internet Printing Protocol (RFC 2910)
636	TCP	ldaps	ldap protocol over TLS/SSL (RFC 2246)
647		dhcp-failover	DHCP Failover
660		mac-srvr-admin	MacOS Server Admin
674		acap	ACAP
689		nmap	NMAP
744		flexlm	Flexible License Manager
749		kerberos-adm	kerberos administration
762		quotad	
774		rpasswd	
847		dhcp-failover2	dhcp-failover 2
860		iscsi	iSCSI
873		rsync	rsync
989		ftps-data	ftp protocol, data, over TLS/SSL
990		ftps	ftp protocol, control, over TLS/SSL
992		telnets	telnet protocol over TLS/SSL
993	TCP	imaps	imap4 protocol over TLS/SSL
994		ircs	irc protocol over TLS/SSL
995	TCP	pop3s	pop3 protocol over TLS/SSL (was spop3)

Appendix D

ICMP Types

TABLE D.1 ICMP type codes and descriptions.

Type	Protocol	Type	Protocol
0	Echo Reply	18	Address Mask Reply
3	Destination Unreachable	30	Traceroute
4	Source Quench	31	Datagram Conversion Error
5	Redirect		
6	Alternate Host Address	32	Mobile Host Redirect
8	Echo Request	33	IPv6 Where-Are-You
9	Router Advertisement	34	IPv6 I-Am-Here
10	Router Solicitation	35	Mobile Registration Request
11	Time Exceeded		
12	Parameter Problem	36	Mobile Registration Reply
13	Timestamp Request	37	Domain Name Request
14	Timestamp Reply	38	Domain Name Reply
15	Information Request	39	SKIP
16	Information Reply	40	Photuris
17	Address Mask Request		

Appendix | E

IP Protocol Transport Numbers

The 8-bit Protocol field in the IP version 4 header indicates the transport protocol. ICMP (1), TCP (6), and UDP (17) are the three most common protocols. The Next Header field in the IP version 6 header indicates the protocol number. Table E.1 provides a list of the assigned Internet protocol numbers. A current list of protocol numbers can be found at the IANA Web site (**www.iana.org/assignments/protocol-numbers**).

TABLE E.1 IP Protocol numbers.

#	Protocol	Description
0	HOPOPT	IPv6 Hoop-by-Hop Option
1	ICMP	Internet Control Message Protocol
2	IGMP	Internet Group Management Protocol
3	GGP	Gateway to Gateway Protocol
4	IP	IP in IP Encapsulation
5	ST	Internet Stream Protocol
6	TCP	Transmission Control Protocol
7	CBT	Core Based Trees
8	EGP	Exterior Gateway Protocol
9	IGRP	Interior Gateway Routing Protocol
10	BBN-RCC-MON	BBN RCC Monitoring
11	NVP	Network Voice Protocol
12	PUP	PUP

CONTINUED ON NEXT PAGE

#	Protocol	Description
13	ARGUS	ARGUS
14	EMCON	EMCON
15	XNET	Cross Net Debugger
16	CHAOS	Chaos
17	UDP	User Datagram Protocol
18	MUX	Transport Multiplexing Protocol
19	DCN-MEAS	DCN Measurement Subsystem
20	HMP	Host Monitoring Protocol
21	PRM	Packet Radio Measurement
22	XNS-IDP	XEROX NS IDP
23	TRUNK-1	Trunk-1
24	TRUNK-2	Trunk-2
25	LEAF-1	Leaf-1
26	LEAF-2	Leaf-2
27	RDP	Reliable Data Protocol
28	IRTP	Internet Reliable Transaction Protocol
29	ISO-TP4	ISO Transport Protocol Class 4
30	NETBLT	Network Block Transfer
31	MFE-NSP	MFE Network Services Protocol
32	MERIT-INP	MERIT Internodal Protocol
33	SEP	Sequential Exchange Protocol
34	3PC	Third Party Connect Protocol
35	IDPR	Inter-Domain Policy Routing Protocol
36	XTP	XTP
37	DDP	Datagram Delivery Protocol
38	IDPR	Inter-Domain Policy Routing Protocol
39	TP++	TP++ Transport Protocol
40	IL	IL Transport Protocol
41	IPv6	Ipv6
42	SDRP	Source Demand Routing Protocol
43	IPv6-Route	Routing Header for IPv6
44	IPv6-Frag	Fragment Header for IPv6
45	IDRP	Inter-Domain Routing Protocol

CONTINUED ON NEXT PAGE

#	Protocol	Description
46	RSVP	Reservation Protocol
47	GRE	Generic Routing Encapsulation
48	MHRP	Mobile Host Routing Protocol
49	BNA	BNA
50	ESP	Encapsulation Security Payload
51	AH	Authentication Header
52	I-NLSP	Integrated Net Layer Security
53	SWIPE	IP with Encryption
54	NARP	NBMA Address Resolution Protocol
55	MOBILE	Minimal Encapsulation Protocol
56	TLSP	Transport Layer Security Protocol
57	SKIP	Simple Key management for Internet Protocol
58	IPv6-ICMP	Internet Control Message Protocol for Ipv6
59	IPv6-NoNxt	No Next Header for IPv6
60	IPv6-Opts	Destination Options for IPv6
61		Any host internal protocol
62	CFTP	CFTP
63		Anly local network
64	SAT-EXPAK	SATNET and Backroom EXPAK
65	KRYPTOLAN	Kryptolan
66	RVD	MIT Remote Virtual Disk Protocol
67	IPPC	Internet Pluribus Packet Core
68		Any Distributed File System
69	SAT-MON	SATNET Monitoring
70	VISA	VISA Protocol
71	IPCV	Internet Packet Core Utility
72	CPNX	Computer Protocol Network Executive
73	WSN	Wang Span Network
74	WSN	Wang Span Network
75	PVP	Packet Video Protocol
76	BR-SAT-M	ON Backroom SATNET Monitoring
77	SUN-ND	SUN ND PROTOCOL-Temporary
78	WB-MON	WIDEBAND Monitoring

CONTINUED ON NEXT PAGE

#	Protocol	Description
79	WB-EXPAK	WIDEBAND EXPAK
80	ISO-IP	ISO Internet Protocol
81	VMTP	Versatile Message Transaction Protocol
82	SECURE-V	MTP SECURE-VMTP
83	VINES	VINES
84	TTP	TTP
85	NSFNET-I	GP NSFNET-IGP
86	DGP	Dissimilar Gateway Protocol
87	TCF	TCF
88	EIGRP	EIGRP
89	OSPF	Open Shortest Path First Protocol
90	Sprite-R	PC Sprite RPC Protocol
91	LARP	Locus Address Resolution Protocol
92	MTP	Multicast Transport Protocol
93	AX.25	
94	IPIP	IP-within-IP Encapsulation Prot
95	MICP	Mobile Internetworking Control
96	SCC-SP	Semaphore Communications Sec. P
97	ETHERIP	Ethernet-within-IP Encapsulatio
98	ENCAP	Encapsulation Header [R
99		any private encryption scheme
100	GMTP	GMTP
101	IFMP	Ipsilon Flow Management Protocol
102	PNNI	PNNI over IP
103	PIM	Protocol Independent Multicast
104	ARIS	ARIS
105	SCPS	SCPS
106	QNX	QNX
107	A/N	Active Networks
108	IPPCP	IP Payload Compression Protocol
109	SNP	Sitara Networks Protocol
110	Compaq-Peer	Compaq Peer Protocol
111	IPX-in-IP	IPX in IP

CONTINUED ON NEXT PAGE

#	Protocol	Description
112	VRRP	Virtual Router Redundancy Protocol
113	PGM	Pragmatic General Multicast
114		Any 0-hop protocol
115	L2TP	Level 2 Tunneling Protocol
116	DDX	D-II Data Exchange (DDX)
117	IATP	Interactive Agent Transfer Protoco
118	STP	Schedule Transfer Protocol
119	SRP	SpectraLink Radio Protocol
120	UTI	UTI
121	SMP	Simple Message Protocol
122	SM	SM
123	PTP	Performance Transparency Protocol
124	ISIS	ISIS over IPv4
125	FIRE	
126	CRTP	Combat Radio Transport Protocol
127	CRUDP	Combat Radio User Datagram
128	SSCOPMCE	
129	IPLT	
130	SPS	Secure Packet Shield
131	PIPE	Private IP Encapsulation within IP
132	SCTP	Stream Control Transmission Protocol
133	FC	Fiber Channel
134	RSVP-E2E	
135		Mobility Header
136	UDP-Lite	Lightweight User Datagram Protocol
137	MPLS-in-IP	

Glossary

A

Access Control Lists (ACLs) A list maintained on a router interface that inspects the IP packet header information to determine whether a packet is permitted or denied.

action iptables or ACL designator determining whether to accept, reject or deny a packet.

Application Service Provider (ASP) A company that provides dedicated and virtual hosting services to other companies and organizations.

Address Resolution Protocol (ARP) A protocol that associates IP addresses with hardware addresses (e.g., Ethernet MAC addresses), maintaining those associations in an ARP cache on each machine.

authentication The process of verifying the identity of a person or an application.

Authentication Header (AH) A security protocol providing data authentication and anti-replay services.

Authentication Protocol One of many protocols used to provide user authentication, including but not limited to PAP and CHAP.

B

Bering firewall, version 1.2 A LEAF based firewall distribution using the Linux 2.4.x kernel and relying on Shorewall for extended firewall facilities and configuration.

blacklisting A list of hosts or IP addresses that are not allowed to enter the network.

boot loader A program located on the master boot record of the hard disk that is the first program to execute when a computer is turned on and tells the system how to load the OS kernel.

bootable image A single file containing software or programs that can be copied to a CD, floppy or other media and containing everything necessary to boot the computer to a running operating system.

broadcast address An address used to send a message to all interfaces on the network. A broadcast address is a MAC address of all ones.

C

certificate authority (CA) An entity or organization responsible for issuing digital certificates for individuals and vouching for the authenticity of those certificates.

chain A series of security statements such as a list of IPTABLES commands.

Challenge Handshake Authentication Protocol (CHAP) A method of periodic, random "challenges" to re-authenticate the user during the communication session

Christmas Tree attack An attack where a TCP packet is sent with all TCP header flags set to one in an attempt to cause a system crash.

CIDR See Classless Inter Domain Routing.

ciphertext Text that has been encrypted.

Classless Inter-Domain Routing (CIDR) A definition of subnets based on the number of binary bits they have in common. A class B subnet is a 16 bit subnet. A class C subnet is a

24 bit subnet. CIDR allows routers to group routes together to reduce the quantity of routing information carried by the core routers.

cleartext   Text that is unencrypted, or sent "in the clear" through an unsecured channel

congestion control   The ability of TCP to determine the available network bandwidth and compute the amount of packets that can safely be injected into the network. Algorithms including slow start, congestion avoidance, fast retransmit, and fast recovery are available for TCP congestion control.

content-aware firewall   A firewall that inspects the contents of a packet for suspicious material. A content aware firewall can determine if a packet bound for port 80 is a valid http request before sending it to the web server.

cron daemon   A server daemon used to automatically execute a program at a given time on an hourly, daily, weekly, or monthly basis.

crontab   A configuration file used by the cron daemon to determine when and what programs to execute.

crossover cables   A cable with the send and receive wires crossed, often used when connecting computer back-to-back without a hub or switch.

cyber-forensics   The science of establishing factual evidence about a break-in to a computer.

D

dedicated hosting   A service where an external company provides dedicated servers and all support and maintenance for those servers to a company.

Defense in Depth   A layered approach to network security providing multiple levels of protection.

Demilitarized Zone (DMZ)   A buffer zone between two networks containing servers or resources that must be available to the Internet with a different level of security than other internal systems.

Denial of Service (DOS) attack   An attack where a large volume of network requests are generated, thereby degrading performance on the attacked server to the point where it is difficult or impossible to use.

Destination NAT (DNAT)   A form of NAT allowing the destination IP address and optionally the destination port to be changed or rewritten.

DHCP   See Dynamic Host Configuration Protocol

digital certificate   A method of establishing trust between two individuals or organizations. Sometimes vouched for by Certificate Authorities.

digital signatures   A method of determining the true sender of a document by using hash codes.

Digital Signature Algorithm (DSA)   A public key algorithm used to generate a digital signature for the authentication of electronic documents.

DNAT   See Destination NAT.

DNS reverse zone   A DNS zone that maps IP addresses to names.

Dynamic Host Configuration Protocol (DHCP)   A service for dynamically allocating IP address to hosts on a network.

Dynamic NAT   The process by which the firewall masquerades as internal servers and rewrites the address information in the packet header as necessary. Also known as Network Port Address Translation and/or Masquerading.

E

e-commerce   Electronic commerce. Buying and selling of goods over the Internet.

Electromagnetic Interference (EMI)   Interference by electromagnetic signals increasing the error rates on network cabling.

Encapsulation Security Payload (ESP)   A security protocol providing data confidentiality service in IP. ESP provides authentication service, connectionless data integrity, anti-replay service and limited traffic flow confidentiality.

Ephemeral ports   According to standards, a port in the range of 49152–65535 that is dynamically allocated by the client as the client port for a TCP or UDP communication.

Established connections   A TCP connection that both systems have acknowledged the SYN or setup of the connection.

Ethernet MAC address   A 6 byte (48 bit) number typically expressed as 12 hexadecimal digits, and used to uniquely identify a NIC. EX: a1:b2:c3:d4:e5:f6

Extranet   A specialized network or set of services tailored to allow external businesses to securely complete online transactions with a company.

F

filter table   A table used for filtering of packets and the place where the action is taken to drop or accept a packet based on content and iptables rules.

firewall configuration files   Files that control the operations of the firewall, including syslinux.cfg, leaf.cfg, policy, and rules.

first-matching rule   The first rule that matches a packet will have the action for that rule applied.

four way handshake   The teardown of a previously established TCP connection.

Fraggle attack   An attack that inundates a site with UDP packets, inducing echo requests and replies.

full backup   A backup of all files or modules on a system.

G

Generic Routing Encapsulation (GRE)   An IP protocol type used to provide secure transmission of data between a remote PC and the corporate Intranet.

Gnu-zip utility (gzip)   A free GNU based compression utility that normally produces files with a gz extension or tgz when combined with the tar utility.

H

H.323   An International Telecommunication Union (ITU) standard protocol for providing video and audio communications between systems on a network.

Hash codes   Methods to take a file of arbitrary length and produce a fixed length digest that is unique to the file.

Health Insurance Portability and Accountability Act of 1996 (HIPAA)   A set of standards and regulations for the transmission, storage, access, and usage of patient records and information.

I

ICMP   see Internet Control Message Protocol

IEEE 802 LAN standards (802.1, 802.2, 802.3)   A suite of networking standards developed by the IEEE for local area and metropolitan area networks including Ethernet, Token Ring, Wireless, bridging and virtual bridged LANs.

IEEE 802.11i   A network security standard defining three methods of data protection, including CCMP, WRAP and TKIP, as an improvement and more secure solution than WEP.

IM—Instant Messaging   A real time chat between two individuals over the Internet, traditionally using text messages.

initialization vector (IV)   The 24 bit portion of the RC4 key in a WEP connection.

Institute for Electrical and Electronics Engineers (IEEE)   A professional organization that guides the development of standards for networks and communications.

integrity   Any of a number of methods to ensure that data received is identical to that sent.

Interior Gateway Routing Protocol (IGRP)   A routing protocol developed by Cisco to address the issues associated with routing in large, heterogeneous networks.

internal hosting An instance where a company maintains its own DNS, web, mail and other servers internally.

Internet Assigned Numbers Authority (IANA) The organization responsible for assigning the TCP and UDP Well Known Ports in use on the Internet and the assignment of IP address and domain names to the InterNIC and other organizations.

Internet Control Message Protocol (ICMP) An IP network layer that reports errors and provides other information relevant to IP packet processing and network routing. Documented by RFC 792.

Internet Key Exchange (IKE) The key management protocol used by IPSEC using public and private keys to sign packets and unlock encryption algorithms. Uses UDP port 500.

Internet Security Association and Key Management Protocol (ISAKMP) An authentication system for the secure management of keys using authentication and security associations to establish a secure and private connection.

intrusion detection A technology that detects intrusions to host computers or networks and optionally takes corrective action.

Intrusion detection tools Tools that analyze network traffic and error logs looking for unauthorized attempts to access resources on the network.

IP address A 32-bit binary number, normally written in dotted-decimal form, that indicates the unique address for a computer on the network. Ex: 192.168.1.12

IP header Control addressing and routing information located at the front of an IP packet. Similar to the address information on an envelope.

IP Packet Filtering The use of a router or other network device to inspect the IP header of incoming and outgoing packets and determine whether or not to allow the traffic to pass.

IP protocol (IP) The protocol that defines how information is transferred between computers on the Internet.

IP Security (IPSec) A technology developed by the IETF that provides data confidentiality, data integrity and data authentication between hosts. Composed of IKE (UDP port 500) and ESP and AH protocols.

IP-in-IP A type of VPN that does not provide encryption or authentication and serves as an alternative to NAT.

K

key fingerprints A checksum of the host key that can be used to verify the key without distributing the public key in an insecure way

keyed hash A one-way hash function where a key is shared between the sender and recipient of the message.

L

LAN See Local area network

Layer 2 Tunneling Protocol (L2TP) A protocol independent tunneling protocol intended to support network layers like IPX because of its ability to work with many data link protocols.

leaf-router-configuration (lrcfg) The LEAF configuration program used to edit files, configure settings, and back up modules for the leaf firewall.

Linux Embedded Appliance Firewalls (LEAF) A small customizable Linux firewall appliance for use in embedded network environments.

Linux kernel The core of the Linux operating system that loads into memory first and provides all essential services required by other parts of the operating system.

Linux Router Project (LRP) A small Linux distribution intended to fit on a 1.68MB floppy and simplify the construction of routers, access servers, and network appliances. This project provided the basis for LEAF.

local area network (LAN) A network composed of computers connected in close geographic proximity to one another such as a building or group of buildings with high speed connections to each other.

M

MAC Address Filtering The use of a switch or router to inspect the hardware or MAC address of a packet to determine whether or not to allow the traffic to pass.

mangle table A table used to change flags in the TCP header for fields such as TOS or TTL fields.

martian addresses Host or network address where the routing information is ignored. This usually occurs when a system is configured with an invalid address.

martian next-hops An error message generated because the routing information is invalid and therefore the next hop is invalid.

Masquerade The ability for the firewall to appear as several different internal systems and the header of any traffic to those systems rewritten by the firewall. External users will assume the firewall is the mail, web and DNS server although they are actually separate servers on the internal subnet.

Mean Time To Failure (MTTF) An estimate of the mean or average time until the first failure.

Mean Time To Restore (MTTR) An estimate of the mean or average time to recover from a network failure.

Media Access Control (MAC) Address A 6 byte (48 bit) number typically expressed as 12 hexadecimal digits, and used to uniquely identify a NIC.

Message Authentication Code (MAC) key A key that is used to generate a keyed hash.

Message Digest 5 (MD5) A one way hashing algorithm used to verify data integrity through the creation of a 128-bit message from input data.

Microsoft Point-to-Point Compression (MPPC) Proprietary compression algorithm used by Microsoft to enhance VPN performance.

Microsoft Point-to-Point Encryption (MPPE) Proprietary Microsoft point to point encryption protocol.

Multicast address An address that is used to send a message to a specified group of interfaces on the network.

Multi-Protocol Label Switching (MPLS) A method of forwarding IP traffic using labels that instruct the routers and switches where to forward the packets to.

N

nat table Changes the IP address and or the port number of the encapsulated TCP or UDP segment.

NetFilter/iptables A framework inside of the Linux kernel enabling packet filtering, network address translation, port translation and packet mangling.

Network Access Server (NAS) Also known as RAS,device or server that ISPís use to allow customers to connect to the Internet. It includes connections to both phone lines from the phone company and a local network.

Network Interface Card (NIC) The adapter card installed inside of the computer that provides the physical interface to the network.

network interface numbering A numbering scheme used to define the network adapters installed in a host. Example: eth0, eth1, eth2.

Network Port Address Translation (NPAT) The process by which the firewall masquerades as internal servers and rewrites the address information in the packet header as necessary. Also known as dynamic NAT.

Network Time Protocol (NTP) Commonly-used Internet time protocol for synchronizing of time on computers and network devices

NIC driver module The module or object file that contains the necessary driver details for the operating system to detect and access the network adapter.

nonrepudiation the property that establishes whether the sender was authenticated as having originated the communication, preventing the sender from claiming that a different individual or entity originated the content

O

Oakley key exchange A hybrid Diffie-Hellman key exchange used with ISAKMP and Perfect Forward Security.

Open Shortest Path First (OSPF) An interior gateway routing protocol designed to provide least-cost routing, multipath routing and load balancing.

P

P2P See Peer to Peer.

package destinations The media where the Bering packages are located.

package path The variable in the syslinux.cfg that indicates what device (CDROM or floppy) where the packages are located.

Packet filtering See IP Packet Filtering

partial backup A backup that consists of only configuration files or files that have changed since a given date.

Password Authentication Protocol (PAP) An encrypted password and user ID are sent over a communication link.

Peer to Peer (P2P) A method of sharing files among computers often coordinated by a database server. Applications such as Napster, Gnutella, and Kazza are examples of p2p applications used to share music files.

Perfect Forward Secrecy (PFS) A cryptography method with a derived shared secret value. If one key is compromised, subsequent keys remain secure because they are not derived from the previous key.

permanent storage volumes An internal storage volume that cannot be removed from the computer. IE: A hard drive.

ping A command line tool that utilizes the echo-request (ICMP Type 8 Code 0) and echo-reply (ICTMP Type 0 Code 0) to provide a tool for testing network connectivity.

Point-to-Point Protocol (PPP) A method for establishing connections over a modem or serial link.

Point-to-Point Tunneling Protocol (PPTP) A tunneling protocol used in Microsoft VPN implementations.

policy A default policy or rule that is applied if a packet does not meet any of the criteria specified by the rules.

port address translation (PAT) The process by which the firewall masquerades as internal servers and rewrites the address and port information in the packet header as necessary.

port forwarding See destination NAT.

port-agile Programs that search for other open ports to establish connections if their standard port is blocked.

PPTP Access Concentrator (PAC) A device attached to several PSTN or ISDN phone lines capable of accepting PPTP connections.

PPTP Network Server (PNS) A device that handles the server side of the PPTP protocol.

Preshared Secret Key (PSK) An authentication key where the two parties agree on a shared secret key.

Promiscuous mode   A mode that tells a network interface adapter to listen to all traffic on the network regardless of the destination's network interface.

Protocol layering   The technique of dividing a large computer programming task into smaller, manageable bodies code.

protocol suite   A suite of network standards that together dictate how information is transferred between systems on the network. IP, TCP, UDP, and ICMP together make up the TCP/IP Protocol Suite.

proxy   A server that sits between the client and the server and acts as an intermediate server to ensure security and control.

Public Key Infrastructure (PKI)   A public key, known to anyone, and a private key held in secret by a single individual.

Public Switched Data Network (PSDN)   A data communications network based on packet switching that is commonly used in public telephone networks.

R

registered ports   Ports 1024–49151 used by registered services. Some operating systems also use this range of ports as ephemeral ports.

re-keying   Renegotiation of security keys.

related connections   Connections that are related to an existing established connection, such as the data and control connections used with an ftp connection.

reliable boot mechanism   The need to copy files to some media other than a floppy to provide a more reliable backup of modified files.

removable storage volume   An external storage volume that can be removed from the computer. E.g., a floppy, a USB jump drive, or a zip drive.

replay attack   Capturing a set of critical data such as authentication information and replaying this

information to gain access to a computer system such as a database server

restart sequence   A sequence used to reboot the computer. Normally performed via the shutdown or reboot command or CTRL-ALT-DEL.

Reverse DNS Lookup   Using a known IP address to determine the fully qualified name of a host.

reverse proxy   A reverse proxy serves the server, by offering load-balancing and geographic distribution of content as well as security services.

RFC 1918   Request for Comments document 1918, which describes the address allocations for private internets.

road warrior   A traveling executive or technical individual who often needs to access the internal network from a public insecure Internet connection.

Ron Rivest, Adi Shamir and Len Adleman (RSA)   The most commonly used encryption and authentication algorithm invented by Ron Rivest, Adi Shamir and Len Adleman.

root CA   The top level certificate authority that signs other certificates. Usually the root CA has a self-signed certificate containing its own public key.

route filtering   The process of deciding what routes to prefer, and applies to firewalls and routers equally.

rules   Exceptions to policies that are matched against packet, frame and segment header contents that are evaluated prior to policies.

S

Secure sockets layer (SSL)   A protocol that transmits data over the Internet in an encrypted form, commonly used by e-commerce sites, secure HTTP (HTTPS) and Virtual Private Network technology.

Security Association (SA)   The channel negotiated by IKE and used by ESP between each pair of trusted machines.

server hardening   A technique to assess what services should be running on a server and turn off any unnecessary services.

Shielded Twisted Pair (STP)   A copper telephone wire with a shielded outer covering. Typically this is only used only in environments with interference problems.

Shoreline Firewall   A high-level tool for easing the task of configuring Netfilter. Configuration files are read to create the appropriate iptables entries. Also known as Shorewall.

sliding window flow control   The ability of TCP sender to use the speed with which the receiver is sending back acknowledgements and slow down transmissions as needed before the network or receiving host becomes congested.

smurf attack   An attack that inundates a site with ICMP echo-requests and the resulting echo-replies—simulating a rapid sequence of commands like the popular ping utility.

Social Engineering   A means of obtaining passwords, or enough information to guess passwords, by asking for favors from system administrators, etc.

Stateful Packet Inspection   Stateful inspection looks not only at the header contents but analyzes the payload data to determine if it is indeed valid and relates the return traffic from the session.

Stateless   A firewall that only looks at the connection setup and does not maintain state information about established or related packets.

straight-through cables   A cable where the wiring is the same on both sides. This type of cable is used to connect a computer to a hub or router.

SYN flood attack   An attack where a rapid sequence of SYN packets are sent, without responding to the return SYN from the opposite end.

syslog daemon (syslogd)   A server daemon for the logging of events and information on kernel and system utilities

T

Tape-Archive-Retrieval (tar)   A Unix utility that combines several files or directories into a single file with the .tar extension.

tar   See Tape-Archive-Retrieval

Target   iptables designator providing information as to whether to accept, drop, queue or return a packet. Additionally, a user defined chain may serve as a target.

TCP   See Transmission Control Protocol

TCP:ACK   TCP Flag indicating that the packet includes an acknowledgement.

TCP:FIN   TCP Flag indicating the sender has no more data to send.

TCP:PSH   TCP Flag indicating an upper level protocol or application needs data immediately and all of the queued data should be sent.

TCP:RST   TCP Flag indicating the connection should be reset.

TCP:SYN   TCP Flag indicating the hosts need to synchronize sequence numbers.

TCP:URG   TCP Flag indicating the urgent pointer field includes significant information.

Three way handshake   The initialization or setup of a TCP connection where hosts initialize sequence numbers and establish a reliable channel for the TCP session.

traceroute   A utility that traces the path a packet takes from the local system to a remote host showing the hops along the way and the amount of time required to reach each hop using ICMP TTL's.

Transmission Control Protocol (TCP)   A connection oriented protocol utilizing the TCP/IP stack to provide reliable full duplex communication between hosts.

Transport Layer Security (TLS) A security layer to provide privacy in communications over the Internet and replace SSL.

trojan horses An application that runs on a computer and is either hidden from the user or performs some unknown harmful action in the background.

U

UDP See User Datagram Protocol.

ulogd An alternative logging mechanism in iptables-based firewalls allowing logging of packets to plaintext files and databases

unicast address The individual hardware addresses configured by the vendor on each NIC at the time of manufacturer.

Unicast Reverse-Path forwarding A check on the source IP address of a packet performed at the upstream end of a connection.

Universal Time (UTC) Formerly referred to as GMT (Greenwich Mean Time), the time zone at zero degrees longitude.

Unshielded Twisted Pair (UTP) The most common telephone wiring that uses pairs that are twisted around each other to reduce crosstalk.

US Secure Hash Algorithm 1 (SHA1) A cryptographic message digest algorithm developed by NIST and NSA for use with Diguatle Signature Standards.

User Datagram Protocol (UDP) A connectionless transport layer in the TCP/IP protocol suite that does not provide reliability or error correction, usually used for query and response.

V

Variable Length Subnet Masks (VLSM) A technique established by RFC 1519 (see CIDR)

allows a single subnet to have more than one mask length to conserve IP address space.

virtual hosting An external web server hosting service that allows an external company to host web, mail and DNS services, eliminating the need for a company to purchase and maintain its own server.

Virtual Private Network (VPN) A network that is established using encryption and authorization to securely transmit data over a public network

viruses Self-replicating systems that require signatures to detect.

W

WAN See Wide Area Network.

Well known ports The standard port numbers for services such has SMTP, HTTP, FTP, using ports between 1 and 1023.

Wide area network (WAN) A network composed of computers in different geographic areas connected via connections from telephone carriers and using protocols such as Frame Relay, SMDS, ATM and others.

WiFi Protected Access 2 (WPA2) The second generation of WPA security based on 802.11i.

Wired Equivalent Privacy (WEP) A security protocol defined in the 802.11b for use with wireless networks. WEP encrypts data before transmitting it to the receiver.

worms Self-replicating systems that require signatures to detect.

Z

zones Specific areas of the network that help define groups of computers or address ranges. Net and local are two zones specified by default in the shorewall firewall, with Net specifying all external computers and local specifying all internal computers.

References

Note: RFCs are available online at **http://rfc.net/rfc-index.html** or **www. faqs.org/rfcs/**

Publications of the IIIE Computer Society are available online at: **http:// standards.ieee.org/getieee802/portfolio.html**

Chapter 1

Deering, S. August 1989. Host extensions for IP multicasting. RFC 1112.

Fuller, V., T. Li, J. Yu, and K. Varadhan. June 1992. Supernetting: an address assignment and aggregation strategy. RFC 1338.

Fuller, V., T. Li, J. Yu, and K. Varadhan. September 1993. Classless inter-domain routing (CIDR): an address assignment and aggregation strategy. RFC 1519.

IEEE Computer Society. May 2003. IEEE 802.1Q: IEEE Standards for Local and Metropolitan Area Networks. Virtual Bridged Local Area Networks.

IEEE Computer Society. 1998. IEEE 802.2: IEEE standard for information technology. Telecommunications and information exchange between systems. Local and metropolitan area networks. Specific requirements Part 2: Logical link control.

IEEE Computer Society. March 2002. IEEE 802.3: IEEE standard for information technology. Telecommunications and information exchange between systems. Local and metropolitan area networks. Specific requirements Part 3: Carrier sense multiple access with collision detection (CSMA/CD) access method and physical layer specifications.

Information Sciences Institute. September 1981. Internet protocol. RFC 0791.

Malkin, G. November 1998. "RIP Version 2," RFC 2453

Meyer, D. July 1998. Administratively scoped IP multicast. RFC 2365.

Mogul, J.C. and J. Postel. August 1985. Internet standard subnetting procedure. RFC 0950.

Nichols, K., S. Blake, F. Baker, and D. Black. December 1998. Definition of the differentiated services field (DS Field). RFC 2474.

Postel, J. September 1981. Service mappings. RFC 0795.

Rekhter, Y. and T. Li., Eds. September 1993. An Architecture for IP Address Allocation with CIDR. RFC 1518

Reynolds, J. and J. Postel. April 1985. Assigned numbers. RFC 0943.

Reynolds, J. and J. Postel. October 1994. Assigned Numbers. RFC 1700.

Robertson, R. 2003. CIS/FBI computer crime and security survey. **http://www.security.fsu.edu/docs/FBI2003.pdf**

SANS. 2005. What is ID? **http://www.sans.org/resources/idfaq/what_is_id.php**

Stevens, W. Richard. 1993. *TCP/IP Illustrated: The Protocols.* Boston, MA: Addison-Wesley. (Note: This book is also available online at **http://www.thinkingsecure.com/docs/TCPIP-Illustrated-1/**)

Chapter 2

Postel, J. September 1981. Internet control message protocol. RFC 792.

Postel, J. September 1981. Transmission control protocol. RFC 793.

Chapter 3

Cisco Systems. September 14, 2004. Using network based application recognition and access control lists for blocking the Code Red Worm. Document ID 27842. **http://www.cisco.com/warp/public/63/nbar_acl_codered.shtml**

Granger, S. December 8, 2003. Home user security: Personal firewalls. *Security Focus.* **http://www.securityfocus.com/infocus/1750**

Miles, T. July 26, 2004. Applied principles of Defense in Depth: a parent's perspective. *SANS, GIAC Security Essentials Certification.* **http://www.sans.org/rr/papers/index.php?id=1458&rss=Y**

Northcutt, Stephen, Lenny Zeltser, Scott Winters, Karen Frederick, and Ronald W. Ritchey. 2003. *Inside Network Perimeter Security: The Definitive Guide to Firewalls, VPNs, Routers, and Intrusion Detection Systems.* Indianapolis, IN: New Riders.

Wack, J., K. Cutler, and J. Pole. January 2002. Guidelines on firewalls and firewall policy, The National Institute of Standards and Technology. *Publication 800-41.* **http://csrc.nist.gov/publications/nistpubs/800-41/sp800-41.pdf**

Chapter 4

Albitz, Paul and Cricket Liu. 2001. *DNS and BIND, 4th Ed.* Sebastopol, CA: O'Reilly.

Baker, F. June 1995. Requirements for IP version 4 routers. RFC 1812.

Barrett, D. J., R. E. Silverman, and R. G. Byrnes. 2003. *Linux Security Cookbook.* Sebastopol, CA: O'Reilly.

Bellovin, S. M. 1989. Security problems in the TCP/IP protocol suite. *Computer Communications Review.* April, 32-48.

Bernstein, D. J. 2004. DNSCache and TinyDNS web page. **http://cr.yp.to/**

Cisco. April 2000. Unicast reverse path forwarding commands. **http://www.cisco.com/univercd/cc/td/doc/product/software/ios121/121cgcr/secur_r/srprt5/srdrpf.pdf.**

Cisco. September 2004. Characterizing and tracing packet floods using Cisco routers. **http://www.cisco.com/warp/public/707/22.html**. Document ID 13609.

Cisco Systems. December 2002. Reverse proxy caching. *Cisco ACNS software caching configuration guide, Chapter 7.* **http://www.cisco.com/univercd/cc/td/doc/product/webscale/uce/acns42/cnfg42/rproxy.pdf**.

Cisco Systems. 2003. Strategies to protect against distributed Denial of Service (DDoS) attacks. **http://www.cisco.com/warp/public/707/newsflash.pdf**.

Eastep, T. 2005. RFC 1918 file for Shorewall version 1.4. **www.shorewall.net/1.4/index.htm**, click on Errata.

Ford-Hutchison, Paul. August 2004. FTP/TLS friendly firewalls. Work in progress. **draft-fordh-ftp-ssl-firewall-05.txt**

Ferguson, P. and D. Senie. January 1998. Defeating denial of service attacks which employ IP source address spoofing. RFC 2267.

Greene, B. R., C. L. Morrow, and B. W. Gemberling. October 2001. ISP security—real world techniques remote triggered black hole filtering and backscatter traceback. **http://www.nanog.org/mtg-0110/greene.html**.

Holden, Greg. 2004. *Guide To Firewalls and Networks Security: Intrusion Detection and VPNs*. Boston, MA: Thomson.

Kay, Trevor. 2003. *Mike Meyers' Certification Passport: Security.* New York, NY: McGraw-Hill.

Kopparapu, Chandra. 2002. *Load Balancing Servers, Firewalls and Caches.* Hoboken, NJ: Wiley.

Lockwood, J. W., C. Neely, C. Zuver, J. Moscola, S. Dharmapurikar, and D. Lim. 2004. An extensible, system-on-programmable-chip, content-aware

Internet firewall. *Inventigo Corp.* **http://www.inventigo.com/products.html**.

Loeb, L. January 2001. On the lookout for D-sniff: Part 1. **http://www-106.ibm.com/developerworks/library/s-sniff.html**.

Lonvick, C. Ed. December 2004. SSH protocol architecture. Work in progress. **draft-ietf-ssecsh-architecture-20.txt**.

The Meta Group. June 2004. The evolution of network security: From DMZ designs to devices. Meta Part# 200084-001.

Northcutt, Stephen, Lenny Zeltser, Scott Winters, Karen Frederick, and Ronald W. Ritchey. 2003. *Inside Network Perimeter Security: The Definitive Guide to Firewalls, VPNs, Routers, and Intrusion Detection Systems.* Indianapolis, IN: New Riders.

Norton, Duane. April 2004. An Ettercap primer. **www.giac.org/practical/GSEC/Duane_Norton_GSEC.pdf**.

Nottingham, M. July 2000. On defining a role for demand "driven surrogate origin servers, *5th Annual Web Caching Conference.* **http://www.iwcw.org/2000/Proceedings/S4/S4-3.pdf**.

Rekhter, Y., B. Moskowitz, D. Karrenberg, G. J. de Groot, and E. Lear. February 1996. Address allocation for private Internets. RFC 1918.

Securiteam. July 2002. SSH protocol vulnerability (MITM). **http://www.securiteam.com/securitynews/5BP0M157PG.html**.

Shimomura, T. January 1995. How Mitnick hacked Tsutomu Shimomura with an IP sequence attack. **http://www.nwo.net/security/texts/shimomur.txt**.

Sorensen, S. 2004. Summary of Attacks and Attack Detection Methods. **http://www.juniper.net/solutions/literature/white_papers/wp_attack_summary.pdf**.

Stekolshchik, R. 2005. Traceroute protocols. **http://cities.lk.net/trproto.html/**.

Stevens, W. Richard. 1993. *TCP/IP Illustrated: The Protocols.* Boston, MA: Addison-Wesley. (Note: This book is also available online at **http://www.thinkingsecure.com/docs/TCPIP-Illustrated-1/**)

Tanase, M. March 2003. IP spoofing: an introduction. **http://www.securityfocus.com/infocus/1674**.

Chapter 5

Crispin, M. December 1996. Internet message access protocol—version 4rev1. RFC 2060.

Myers, J. and M. Rose. November 1994. Post Office Protocol—Version 3. RFC 1725.

Nilo, J. and E. Wolzak. May 2003. The Bering installation guide. **http://leaf.sourceforge.net/doc/guide/binstall.html**.

Nilo, J., Ed. May 2003. The Bering user's guide. **http://leaf.sourceforge. net/doc/guide/busers.html**.

Postel, J. B. August 1982. Simple mail transfer protocol. RFC 821.

Chapter 6

Convery, S. June 2004. General design considerations for secure networks. *Cisco Press.* **http://www.ciscopress.com/articles/article.asp?p=174313 &seqNum=4**.

Greeff, E. April 2003. Firewall + firewall policy = Improved security, MIS corporate defense solutions. **www.net-security.org/article.php?id=440**.

Wack, J., K. Cutler, and J. Pole. January 2002. Guidelines on firewalls and firewall policy. *National Institute of Standards and Technology.* Special Publication 800-41: 33-43. **http://csrc.nist.gov/publications/nistpubs/ 800-41/sp800-41.pdf**.

Chapter 7

Berghel, H. 2004. Wireless infidelity I: War driving. *Communications of the ACM.* September, 21-26.

Dornan, A. 2002. Roadblocks for war drivers: Stop WiFi from making private networks public. *Network Magazine,* December, 30-33.

Rekhter, Y., B. Moskowitz, D. Karrenberg, G. J. de Groot, and E. Lear. February 1996. Address allocation for private Internets. RFC 1918.

Sorensen, S. 2004. Securing wireless LANs. **http://www.juniper.net/ solutions/literature/white_papers/wp_wirelesslan.pdf.**

Chapter 8

Atreya, M. 2005. Digital signatures and digital envelopes. Online white paper. **http://www.rsasecurity.com/content_library.asp**.

Berghel, H. and J. Uecker. 2004. Wireless infidelity II: Airjacking. *Communications of the ACM,* December, 15-20.

Cam-Winget, N., T. Moore, D. Stanley, and J. Walker. December 4-5 2002. IEEE 802.11i Overview. *NIST 802.11 Wireless LAN Security Workshop, Falls Church VA.* **http://csrc.nist.gov/wireless/S10_802.11i%20 Overview-jw1.pdf**.

Conry-Murray, A. 2003. SSL VPNs: Remote access for the masses. *Network Magazine.* October.

Dierks, T., and C. Allen. January 1999. The TLS protocol version 1.0. RFC 2246.

Eastlake, D. and P. Jones. September 2001. US secure hash algorithm 1 (SHA1). RFC 3174.

FR Doc 03-3877, Federal Register: February 20, 2003 (Volume 68, Number 34) Rules and Regulations, **wais.access.gpo.gov DOCID:fr20fe03-4**.

Freier, A. O., P. Karlton, and P. C. Kocher. 1996. The SSL protocol. Version 3.0 <draft-freier-ssl-version3-02.txt>. Work in progress. **http://wp. netscape.com/eng/ssl3/draft302.txt**.

Gutmann, P. September 2003. Linux's answer to MS-PPTP. **http://www.cs. auckland.ac.nz/~pgut001/pubs/linux_vpn.txt**.

Harkins, D., and D. Carrel. November 1998. The Internet key exchange (IKE). RFC 2409.

Hickman, K. E. B. 1995. The SSL protocol. Version 2 specification. **http://wp.netscape.com/eng/security/SSL_2.html**.

Higgins, K. J., 2004. Reconstructing the VPN. *Network Computing,* August.

Kaufman, C., R. Perlman and M. Speciner. 2002. *Network Security—Private Communication in a Public World 2nd Ed.* Upper Saddle River, NJ: Prentice-Hall.

Khanvilkar, S. and A. Khokhar. 2004. Virtual private networks: An overview with performance evaluation. *IEEE Communications Magazine,* October, 146–154.

Khare, R. and S. Lawrence. May 2000. Upgrading to TLS within HTTP/1.1. RFC 2817.

Krawczyk, H. 2003. SIGMA: The 'SIGn-and-Mac' approach to authenticated diffie-hellman and its use in the IKE protocols. *Proceedings of CRYPTO '03.*

Levi, A. 2003. How secure is web browsing? *Communications of the ACM,* July.

Madson, C., and R. Glenn, November 1998. The use of HMAC-MD5-96 within ESP and AH. RFC 2403.

Maughan, D., M. Schertler, M. Schneider and J. Turner. November 1998. Internet security association and key management protocol (ISAKMP). RFC 2408.

Microsoft. November 2004. L2TP/IPSec NAT-T update for Windows XP and Windows 2000. **http://support.microsoft.com/default.aspx?scid= kb%3Ben-us%3B818043**.

Orman, H. November 1998. The Oakley key determination protocol. RFC 2412.

Pall, G. and G. Zorn. March 2001. Microsoft point-to-point encryption (MPPE) protocol. RFC 3078.

Pepelnjak, I. and J. Guichard. 2000. MPLS and VPN Architectures. Cisco Press.

Rescorla, E. May 2000. HTTP over TLS. RFC 2818.

Rissler, R. VPN decision guide. **http://www.juniper.net/solutions/ literature/white_papers/350037.pdf**.

Rivest, R. April 1992. The MD5 message-digest algorithm. RFC 1321.

Telechoice. September 2002. IPSec VPNs—ready for prime time. **http:// www.juniper.net/solutions/literature/white_papers/wp_vpnprime. pdf**.

Trivedi, K. S. 1982. *Probability & Statistics with Reliability, Queuing, and Computer Science Applications.* Upper Saddle River, NJ: Prentice Hall.

Yonan, J. 2004. The user-space VPN and OpenVPN. Linux Fest Northwest. **http://OpenVPN.sourceforge.net/**.

Zorn, G. March 2001. Deriving keys for use with Microsoft Point-to-Point Encryption (MPPE). RFC 3079.

Chapter 9

Bartz, M. 2001. Netfilter log format. **http://logi.cc/linux/netfileter-log-format.php3**.

Eastep, T. 2004. Shorewall logging. **http://shorewall.sourceforge.net/ shorewall_logging.html**.

Welte, H. 2004. ulogd 1.02 Userspace packet logging for netfilter. *Gnumonks.org projects.* **http://gnumonks.org/projects/ulogd**.

Appendix B

Olszewski, R., and L. Avants. 2002. How do I make LEAF see my Ethernet cards? *SourceForge.net.* **http://sourceforge.net/docman/display_doc. php?docid=1418&group_id=13751**.

Index